FLUID JURISDICTIONS

FLUID
JURISDICTIONS

Colonial Law and Arabs
in Southeast Asia

NURFADZILAH YAHAYA

CORNELL UNIVERSITY PRESS
Ithaca and London

First published 2020 by Cornell University Press

Library of Congress Cataloging-in-Publication Data

Names: Yahaya, Nurfadzilah, 1980– author.
Title: Fluid jurisdictions : colonial law and Arabs in
    Southeast Asia / Nurfadzilah Yahaya.
Description: Ithaca [New York] : Cornell University Press,
    2020. | Includes bibliographical references and index.
Identifiers: LCCN 2020000459 (print) | LCCN 2020000460
    (ebook) | ISBN 9781501750878 (cloth) |
    ISBN 9781501750885 (epub) | ISBN 9781501750892 (pdf)
Subjects: LCSH: Arabs—Legal status, laws, etc.—Straits
    Settlements. | Arabs—Legal status, laws, etc.—
    Indonesia | Imperialism—Social aspects—Southeast
    Asia—History. | Great Britain—Colonies—Asia—Race
    relations—History. | Netherlands—Colonies—Asia—
    Race relations—History.
Classification: LCC KNC145.A55 Y34 2020 (print) |
    LCC KNC145.A55 (ebook) | DDC 349.59509/03—dc23
LC record available at https://lccn.loc.gov/2020000459
LC ebook record available at https://lccn.loc.gov/2020000460

For my parents, Yahaya Abdul Kadir and Sharifah Azizah Almahdali

Contents

ACKNOWLEDGMENTS

In the course of researching and writing my book, I was supported by many individuals to whom I am truly grateful. At Princeton University, Michael Laffan, Linda Colley, and Muhammad Qasim Zaman helped early on to shape the direction the book would eventually take. I am also indebted to Bhavani Raman and Susan Naquin. Kim Lane Scheppele provided me with space to workshop each chapter in the Program in Law and Public Affairs. I count myself immensely fortunate that I could benefit from Dirk Hartog's tutelage and support when he led the Hurst Summer Institute in Legal History at the University of Wisconsin-Madison in June 2013.

Over the years, I have been buoyed by support from Alex Bevilacqua, Edna Bonhomme, Jim Bonk, Parween Ebrahim, Catherine Evans, Kathi Ivanyi, Hannah Weiss Muller, Margaret Ng, Helen Pfeifer, Suzanne Podhurst, Intisar Rabb, Kalyani Ramnath, Padraic Scanlan, Wayne Soon, and Michael Woldemariam. Megan Brankley Abbas patiently read drafts of my early chapters and gave comments. Hailing from the other end of the Indian Ocean, Sarah Jappie added more perspective, humor, and a counterbalance to my life in Princeton. Rohit De, Rotem Geva, Radha Kumar, and I formed a writing group that helped keep me on schedule and provided great feedback. Above all, I am indebted to Rohit De and Alden Young for making my time at Princeton a wonderful one. Words cannot describe how they enriched my life many times over both intellectually and socially.

At Washington University in St. Louis, Liz Borgwardt, Lori Watt, Nancy Reynolds, and Nancy Berg generously provided mentorship and made St. Louis seem like another home for me. I would also like to thank Anika Walke and Timothy Parsons for their comments on my drafts. Catherine Kelly provided support and friendship across our small hallway. Our conversations and writing sessions cheered me up considerably. Outside of Washington University, the presence of Jeff Redding and Charlotte Walker-Said were like rays of sunshine, and I count myself truly lucky to have so many legal scholars wherever I moved to.

The late Benedict Anderson pushed me to make bolder arguments, and I will never forget his advice. In Leiden, Nico Kaptein and Kees van Dijk provided me with advice. I am especially grateful to Lisbeth Ouwehand and her British shorthair, Oolong, for their support and friendship and for making my visits to the Netherlands constantly joyful. I thank Jeff Petersen at the Cornell Library and Annabel Teh Gallop at the British Library, as well as Jaap Anten and Lam Ngo at the KITLV in Leiden. I am thankful to the excellent editors at Cornell University Press, namely Emily Andrew, Alexis Siemon, Karen Hwa, and Julia Cook.

I was fortunate to be invited to present parts of the book in various places. The Hurst seminar at University of Wisconsin-Madison was particularly illuminating, and I thank all of the participants, especially Mitra Sharafi, Laurie Wood, and Natalie Zemon Davis. At various conferences and workshops I benefitted hugely from generous feedback on chapter drafts by Kamran Ali, Jerusa Ali, Stuart Banner, Debjani Bhattacharyya, Ritu Birla, Beshara Doumani, Michael Gilsenan, Iza Hussin, Martha Jones, Mahmood Kooria, Sumit Mandal, Renisa Mawani, Ronit Ricci, Charlie Peevers, Sanne Ravensbergen, Julia Stephens, Eric Tagliacozzo, and Barbara Welke.

I am grateful to Engseng Ho, who continued to advise me on the book at various stages of revision. I am touched by his constant generosity. I am also very thankful to Mitra Sharafi, who gave me her time and knowledge. She is a model intellectual whom I hope to emulate.

At the National University of Singapore, I am grateful to Maitrii Aung-Thwin, Chan Cheow Thia, Jack Chia, Ian Chong, Michael Feener, Loh Shi Lin, Tan Li-Jen, and Wang Jinping for their support. Cheah Wui Ling has encouraged me from the beginning, which made my homecoming that much sweeter. I also thank my colleagues at the Asia Research Institute in the Religion and Globalization Cluster, especially Giuseppe Bolotta, Amelia Fauzia, and Catherine Scheer. Kenneth Dean is a wonderful mentor and has provided much gentle guidance in terms of framing and context, and for that I am thankful to him.

I would also like to thank Claudine Ang, Will Hanley, Amali Ibrahim, Nadia Dahak Ibrahim, Jack Jin Gary Lee, Mark Fathi Massoud, Naderah Mansour, Nada Moumtaz, Nahed Samour, and Hanisah Abdullah Sani. Khalidal Huda Sukhaimi and Nurul Asyikin constantly provided support from the other side of the globe, and their love and care bolstered me from afar.

I thank my brother, Yazid, for all his love and support, which never wavered across huge distances—I could not ask for a better sibling. I am immensely grateful to my parents, Yahaya Abdul Kadir and Sharifah Azizah Syed Ismail Almahdali, who taught me everything I know, who gave me strength, and who have sacrificed so much for my brother and me. I dedicate this book to them.

Note on Transliteration and Translation

I have followed the *International Journal of Middle East Studies (IJMES)* transliteration system for Arabic and Jawi scripts except when sources in romanized Malay, Indonesian, French, English, and Dutch indicate otherwise. Spellings of names are particularly inconsistent. Wherever possible, I use the most common iteration of a person's name across all sources—for example, Syed instead of Sayyid. Translations are mine unless otherwise indicated.

FLUID JURISDICTIONS

Introduction

Establishing Legal Domains

On March 15, 1599, a ship named *Geldria* landed at a place called Oertatan somewhere among the Banda islands in the Moluccas, the famed Spice Islands, located in the eastern part of present-day Indonesia. Lured by nutmeg and mace that grew only on these islands, the ship had left Texel in North Holland ten months earlier. The ship, the second Dutch foray to the East Indies, carried two hundred sailors, soldiers, and merchants and was manned by the Dutch captain Jacob van Heemskerk.[1] The first person that he, like any visitor to a port in the region, met in Oertatan was the *shahbandar* (harbormaster) of the island, who came aboard the *Geldria* to enter into long, drawn-out negotiations with Van Heemskerk in Portuguese.[2] Heads of villages had less power than both the *shahbandar* and the Arab merchants in the area, the Dutch noticed.[3] Four or five Arab men then approached the ship and were greeted with Van Heemskerk's complaints that the *shahbandar* had wanted him to pay an exorbitant amount for mace. Van Heemskerk decided to negotiate with "the oldest and richest of the Arabs" instead. At a time when the price of mace was not yet fixed according to the price of silver, these Arab merchants determined the cost of this precious commodity, available only in the Spice Islands. The Arabs told Van Heemskerk that the local Bandanese had been stoked by the Javanese on the islands to attack him and his crew, but this was later dismissed as rumor. Most tellingly, in recounting his first meeting with these Arabs aboard his ship,

1

Van Heemskerk noted their "Oriental cunning" (*Oostersche geslepenheid*) and believed they approached him because they were motivated by "blatant covetousness."[4] Suspicion, innuendo, and intrigue would continue to hound the relationship between European colonial elite and the Arabs.

The meeting on board *Geldria* demonstrates how Arabs actively positioned themselves as intermediaries between the Bandanese and the Dutch and proved to be powerful merchants able to influence power structures on the islands. This image became so ingrained in the Dutch imagination that eighty years later, when Maurits van Happel, a lieutenant under the governor-general of Java, Cornelis van Speelman, attempted to win the hearts and minds of locals in the archipelago in the 1680s, he chose to masquerade as an Arab middleman.[5]

In 1602, three years after Van Heemskerk's expedition, another ship sailed from Texel under the authority of the newly sealed charter endorsing the sovereign rights of the Vereenigde Oostindische Compagnie (VOC; Dutch East India Company) and its first fleet.[6] The VOC wanted to quickly set up a monopoly by cutting out other traders—the Javanese, the Gujeratis, Malays, the Arabs, and the Portuguese—but they could not immediately do so due to the need to honor advance payments from these same traders, a situation that further underscores the threat they posed to European traders. By 1621, the Banda islands were controlled by the VOC and their populations had been killed or enslaved under Dutch planters.[7]

The place known as Oertatan does not exist on any map because it was either a Portuguese or Dutch corruption of the Malay term *orang datang*, which means "newcomer" or "new arrival" in Malay and Indonesian. In other words, Oertatan was a flexible category that included all foreigners— Arab, European, and otherwise—who had settled on the island. It is not hard to imagine numerous Oertatans throughout the vast archipelago. However, the arrival of the Dutch heralded a transformation of the idea of sovereignty in the region. Over the next two centuries, the egalitarian multicultural promise of Oertatan was cut short by violent manifestations of imperialist ambitions.[8] The historian Lisa Ford writes that empire changed sovereignty because it altered people's relationship with space.[9] Imperialism created the conditions for the redefinition of sovereignty through the legal subordination of people in defined territorial units such that over time, territorial jurisdiction became a necessary handmaiden to sovereignty. Under this new form of sovereignty, new power structures emerged.

This book flips the more common historical perspective that European imperialism led to new patterns of legal pluralism across empires that spawned possibilities for interpolity contact and trade, acting as catalysts for the emergence of global legal regimes. It demonstrates how British and Dutch territorial jurisdictions expressed very specific relationships between territory, authority, and forms of law, and it simultaneously puts into stark relief the preponderance of diasporic Arab merchants generating their own jurisdictions across the Indian Ocean in tandem with those of the European colonists. Not only were these Arabs attuned to legal pluralism being the operative condition of law, they were also acutely aware of jurisdictional ordering and the concentration of power across time and space. Because they were very much aware of how fluid jurisdictions could be over time and space. they committed to creating their own legal domains across the Indian Ocean even as the world shifted quickly around them from the mid-nineteenth century onward.[10] This book proposes a spatial repositioning of the Indian Ocean from the perspective of Southeast Asia outward toward Ḥaḍramawt, a region located in present-day Yemen from which most Arabs in Southeast Asia originated (20 to 30 percent of the Ḥaḍramī population lived abroad by the 1930s).[11] Members of the Ḥaḍramī diaspora attempted to bring their own legislation with them, inscribing territorial lines across the Indian Ocean through law. The result was not so much a jurisdictional domain crisscrossed by multiple sovereignties as a surge toward colonial jurisdictions in Southeast Asia. Diasporic Arabs oriented themselves by visualizing something known as shari'a or Islamic law, consisting of a core of ideas and a loose collection of norms sometimes slightly off their sightline but close enough to always be visible. Shari'a would be the lodestar that would guide their way over the next century. In both British and Dutch colonial jurisdictions in Southeast Asia, shari'a law became a symbol of Arab identity.

The twist to the stock colonial narrative is that a significant driving force behind the expansion of colonial jurisdiction in Southeast Asia during the late nineteenth and early twentieth centuries came from colonial subjects themselves. Rather than circumventing colonial legal institutions and systems, members of the Arab diaspora based in Southeast Asia used colonial channels to try to shape the jurisdictional world of the Indian Ocean in their image at a time when there was no single dominant legal jurisdiction across the ocean. Their collective decision to rely heavily on colonial bureaucracies and institutions in various ways introduced the legitimacy that colonial legal regimes otherwise lacked. By doing so, they extended, deepened, and exploited these patterns of legal pluralism in order to enforce their own global legal regimes entwined with colonial jurisdictions.

The Netherlands Indies

The VOC's "returning fleet" system gradually changed to a more permanent VOC presence in the region under a governor-general with the center of administration established at Batavia on the island of Java in 1619. Dutch dominance in Southeast Asia came on the tail of Portuguese decline, which culminated in the Dutch conquest of Portuguese in 1641. Over the course of the seventeenth century, the VOC perpetrated massacres of local populations and waged wars with other European traders as they consolidated their position to become a major commercial, military, and political entity in the archipelago. They managed to stave off competition in order to establish a monopoly over the spice trade by introducing exploitative violent policies in the Moluccas, including Banda, as well as parts of Java, Sumatra, Sulawesi, and Malacca. From 1720 onward, the VOC steadily declined and was dissolved on December 31, 1799, after which the Dutch government took over control of VOC territories. Thereafter, different parts of Indonesia experienced colonialism at different scales, with Aceh being colonized in the 1870s while Bali fell under Dutch rule only in 1906. By contrast, Java and Maluku were colonies for nearly 350 years.

Though based in Batavia, Dutch colonial rule remained highly decentralized over the seventeen-thousand-island archipelago, with different degrees of colonial rule. From 1830 onward, the island of Java was increasingly drawn into the powerful extractive grid of the cultivation system officially

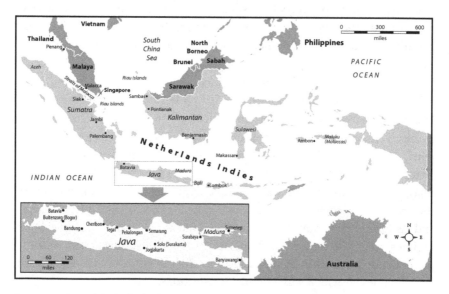

FIGURE 1. Map of the Netherlands Indies.

known as *Cultuurstelsel* and more accurately represented by the Indonesian term *tanam paksa* (forced cultivation), whereby peasants were forced to grow tropical agricultural products, such as coffee, rice, sugar, indigo, tobacco, tea, pepper, cinnamon, and other products, to cater to the European market, with all profits going to the Dutch government treasury.[12] Up to 60 percent of the Javanese population became planters for the Dutch colonial government supervised by Dutch inspectors (*binnenlands bestuur*).[13] Cultuurstelsel effectively transformed the agricultural landscape of Java permanently as subsistence farmers became commodity producers whose labor toward profit-making for the Netherlands was made compulsory.

The policy entrenched new property regimes in the colony. In introducing the policy in 1839, Governor-General Johannes van den Bosch claimed to be inspired by William I, who instituted similar measures in parts of the Netherlands Indies, but he actually owed a debt to his British predecessor in Java, Thomas Stamford Raffles, lieutenant-governor of Java from 1811 to 1815, who introduced an official land settlement system from Madras, India, known as *ryotwari*, to Java during the British interregnum in 1813.[14] The *ryotwari* system assumed that Indian sovereigns were absolute proprietors, and the government made a compact with cultivators as occupants.[15] By extension, European colonial powers owned all the land in the colony, which meant that peasants had to pay them rent. Not surprisingly, the Dutch preserved this view when they returned to rule Java in 1815, a step that was smoothly done since Raffles ruled with the help of Dutch colonial government officials. Crucially, according to Raffles' scheme, farmers had to pay land tax to the colonial government either in the form of produce or money if they were not able to meet requirements.[16] The policy of Cultuurstelsel was a form of tax since more land was set aside for compulsory labor— sometimes up to 100 percent in certain parts of Java.[17] Cultuurstelsel transformed the Indies into a highly profitable colony but came at a high cost for Javanese subjects, leading to poverty among farmers and severe famines in Cirebon in 1844, in Tegal and Semarang in 1850, and in Central Java in 1851.[18] The policy encroached extensively upon Javanese land ownership because while these cash crops meant for the European market were supposed to be planted in land classified as uncultivated land (*woeste gronden*), Dutch colonial government deliberately misunderstood Javanese property regimes or claimed they had not discovered local customary laws in order to pave the way for the colonial scheme to take root in Java.[19] The painful effects of Cultuurstelsel, described in unflinching detail in the famous novel *Max Havelaar* by Eduard Douwes Dekker (written under the pen name "Multatuli"), led to widespread criticism back in the Netherlands.[20] Colonial guilt was displaced onto a group designated "Foreign Orientals," deemed to be exploiters of the labor of the Javanese "Natives." Jan Jacob Rochussen, governor-general of the Netherlands Indies, opined in an 1850 letter to his colleague that "the European makes the law, but is unfair when dividing the burdens. Too many burdens fall on the native, too few on himself and on the Chinese and the Arab." Rochussen thus equated the colonial government with Foreign Orientals, who supposedly benefitted from the Natives' toil under the Cultuurstelsel policy. This view led Dutch colonialists to officially adopt protectionist policies on behalf of the Natives against Foreign Orientals. In colonial courts, they deployed new Natives' ownership (*eigendomsrecht*) and property rights (*bezitsrecht*) against Foreign Orientals. Cultuurstelsel was avowedly declared a failure by 1870, leading to what is known as the Liberal Period in the Netherlands Indies, which in turn gave way to the Ethical Period in 1901. However, the laws implemented during Cultuurstelsel, a period of severe oppression, proved sticky. Well into the twentieth century, high-profile feuds between scholars at Leiden University, headed by Cornelis van Vollenhoven, and at Utrecht University, led by Nolst Trenite, dwelt on how significant the village power of disposal over unused lands was.[21] Vollenhoven believed that the village had more significant power of disposal over such land than Trenite believed, but the latter's policies not surprisingly gained more sympathy among Dutch administrators who wanted more access to land.

It is within this context of punitive policies and mounting colonial guilt that the Arab population suddenly found itself suffering from a perceived lack of rootedness as they were categorized as Foreign Orientals despite having settled in Southeast Asia for several generations. For a long time prior to the 1850s, their lives in the colony was accepted by Dutch authorities as a historical outcome of transregional trade, and legal differentiation, if any, was framed as a concession rather than an imposition. Indeed, from the early seventeenth century onward, the VOC allowed local populations to abide by their own laws with minimal interference, although VOC authorities did appoint heads of various communities. By 1760, civil law in VOC courts was extended to both Natives and Foreign Orientals only in areas of commercial interest, namely port cities and coastal areas where the VOC was based. In 1848, nearly half a century after the Dutch government officially took over from the VOC as political rulers of the Netherlands Indies, colonial authorities began to take a firmer hard in the legal lives of subjects as a range of new codes was introduced, including a civil code, a code of commerce, and a code of criminal procedure. The relationship between the Dutch and Foreign Orientals was historically contingent on several factors. During the seventeenth and eighteenth centuries, the VOC perceived that Arab and

FIGURE 2.   Tram car with passengers in Batavia. Lithograph after an original watercolor by J. C. Rappard (1881–89). Collection Nationaal Museum van Wereldculturen, the Netherlands, coll. no. TM-3728–770.

Chinese merchants amassed much capital in the Indonesian islands but the VOC chose not to interfere in the trade between Natives and these other traders who later came to be classified as Foreign Orientals because, despite their trade monopoly, they relied heavily on these merchants to trade from port to port and with the hinterland in the interior. Not only that, some Arab and Chinese merchants were also moneylenders to the ailing VOC from the mid-sixteenth century onward.[22] Even after the Dutch government took over governance from the VOC in 1800, Foreign Orientals remained prominent in commerce in Semarang, Batavia, and Surabaya in Java. They were active in what the Dutch termed *binnenlandsche handel*, akin to "country trade" within the region, especially with the British entrepot of Singapore, further afield with British India, and across the Indian Ocean to Mauritius.[23] Arab merchant-rulers continued to be key participants in the well-established trade between west coast of Borneo (Pontianak), in Sumba beyond east Java, Banjarmasin on the island of Sulawesi, and Palembang throughout the colonial period.[24]

Because these Foreign Orientals could not be easily expelled from the colony by Dutch authorities, exclusion would have to be done by other means, such as through legislation. In law, their identity as colonial subjects hinged upon their level of assimilation—not within the archipelago over several centuries historically, but within the colony as determined by Dutch authorities in the nineteenth century. Centuries of interaction and intermarriage fell away within this framework to be replaced by notions of nativism and indigeneity subordinated to colonial profits. Metrics of classification, which I describe in chapter 3, remained vague since no rubric was ever produced. This is because it was not actually ethnicity that determined the status of the Foreign Oriental but Dutch economic pragmatism and colonial political interests, which were constantly fluctuating.[25]

The first regulation in 1818 casting the Arabs, Chinese, and other "Orientals" as separate communities in the Netherlands Indies was vague, referring to them as "Moors, Arabs and other foreigners, non-Europeans, established and living in one of the sites of the Dutch East Indies."[26] Subsequent regulations in 1827, 1830, and 1836 further sharpened the contours of their identities as separate from Natives and Europeans.[27] Dutch racial ideologies became normative through law when in 1854, the Dutch government implemented a dual legal system for subject populations that was formalized in the landmark Article 109 of the Government Regulation (Regeeringsreglement):

> The provisions of this Regulation and of all other general regulations involving Europeans and Natives are applicable, where the contrary has not been determined, applicable to them with similar people. Grouped with Europeans are all assimilated Christians and all persons mentioned in the next sentence. Along with Natives are assimilated Arabs, Moors, Chinese and all those Mohammedan or heathen.[28]

It was promulgated, and subsequently led to a differentiation of laws in 1855 for Foreign Orientals, a category that included Chinese, Indian, Arab, and Japanese inhabitants who became subject to the same laws as Europeans under private and commercial law but subject to the same laws as "Natives" under public law.[29] The Arabs' dual legal status simultaneously situated them apart from the bulk of Muslim subject populations due to their ethnicity but within local Muslim societies due to their religious faith. In terms of personal law, Arabs were grouped with other native Muslims who were not only subjected to Islamic law but also to local laws known as *adat*. although it was never determined what local adat should be applied to Arabs across the Netherlands Indies.[30]

In a way, the category of "Foreign Orientals" emerged as form of quasi-sovereignty, albeit under colonial rule. The differentiation of colonial populations into three sections—Natives, Foreign Orientals, and Europeans—gave rise to *quasi internationaal privaatrecht* where each legal system meant for each group was attributed fictional territorial jurisdiction.[31] The phenomenon fits what Lauren Benton describes as the "emerging model" of an international legal community composed of polities recognized as "civilized" by the societies already considered "members of the international community" during the nineteenth century.[32] The fact that international law, glossed as *intergentiel recht,* was invoked in cases involving Natives, Foreign Orientals, and/or Europeans from 1887 onward meant that a conflict of laws was inherent in every case involving parties in different colonial categories.[33] This system is incongruous since international law could only be applied between nations; it certainly did not reach within states because that would violate a state's sovereignty.[34] Moreover, the application of international law assumes that there are identifiable "nations" within the colony. On a superficial level, it flattered the Dutch colonial government to conceive of the population of the Netherlands Indies as a territorially compact people rather than the sprawling and stratified colony that it was.[35] An optimistic teleology would be that this so-called international system was the harbinger of its future implementation.[36] It is easy therefore to imagine how some of the Arab elite were inspired to achieve actual quasi-sovereignty, a term that refers to the status of subpolities within empire-states that were said to retain some measure of authority over their internal legal affairs while holding only limited capacity to form international relations.[37] While extraterritorial arrangements found in Japan, China, and the Ottoman Empire in the nineteenth and twentieth centuries are well documented, aspirations by subject populations in colonies for the status of exemption from the law of the land have not been investigated, though Lisa Ford points out how Aboriginal populations in New South Wales were exempted from settler law for a time in an anomalous arrangement.[38] As I examine in chapter 4, the attempt by the Arab elite in the Netherlands Indies to appeal to Ottoman protection as subjects potentially led to a paradigm of diplomacy in the colony that inadvertently allowed some colonial subjects more latitude than the Dutch colonialists intended for them, since they certainly did not possess equal status.

British Straits Settlements

Colonial legal authorities projected the foundations of their jurisdictions further back in time and across larger territories—through retrospective declarations predicated on a mixture of certain values and norms of behavior on one hand; and through treaties, charters of justice, binding judgments in case law, and legal ordinances that formed milestones in law and became irrevocable in the colonies on the other. In other words, colonial legal history is an "invented" legal tradition, in the words of Eric Hobsbawm, and therefore rife with epochal fallacies that were weaponized against indigenous populations.[39] Building on the work of David Harvey, Franz von Benda-Beckmann and Keebet von Benda-Beckmann argue that legal spaces coexist with other spaces at different paces depending on the kind of legal system that constitutes the space, for each legal (sub) system has characteristic ways in which spaces are being "timed."[40]

Both the Netherlands Indies and the British Straits Settlements experienced this, although the scale of population and geography was vastly different. As a colony, the Straits Settlements on Penang, Malacca, and Singapore were unusual in that they were noncontiguous with one another, connected by the sea, in the form of the narrow channel known as the Straits of Malacca, which they all abut. The Straits Settlements was largely urban and of course much smaller in size than the Netherlands Indies. As port cities primarily, they quickly grew in scale and complexity from the second half of the nineteenth century onward. Although the economy of the Straits Settlements was varied, trade was the raison d'etre of these port cities. As a result, the British colonial government consistently tried their best to retain capital held by any wealthy merchant, including colonial subjects. A city, Paul Boyer writes, was no mere chance accumulation of free-floating human atoms but rather a cohesive interconnected social organism that deserved—indeed demanded—the dedicated loyalty of all its constituent parts.[41] British authorities in the Straits Settlements recognized that the loyalty of the Straits Settlements' constituents, especially colonial subjects who formed the bulk of the population, was key to the success of the colony. This is partly why epochal fallacies were more patently instrumental in the legal administration of the British Straits Settlements than in the Netherlands Indies because they were deployed with more energy and enthusiasm with a clear aim—to make the trading settlements as profitable as possible.

The Straits Settlements had uncertain legal origins that had to be smoothed out to convey the impression of stability and continuity. Toward the end of the eighteenth century, British traders—privateers and East India Company men alike—thought it necessary to counter Dutch dominance in the Straits of Malacca. In 1786, the king of Kedah on the Malay Peninsula ceded the island of Penang to Captain Francis Light, a former privateer turned East India Company trader.[42] Consequently, the English captain hoisted British colors in the name of King George III and renamed it Prince of Wales Island.[43] In 1787, Light appointed leaders among the various races who came to live in Penang "to be their captain, to settle their disputes, and to superintend their conduct."[44] Thereafter, the port city attracted residents from nearby regions, especially merchants who traded mainly in opium, tin, pepper, betel nut, and textiles. In 1824, the Anglo-Dutch Treaty was signed in London, dividing the archipelago into two spheres of influence between the two European powers. Malacca was handed over to English East India Company (EIC) according to the terms of the treaty. Singapore, already an EIC settlement since 1819, formally joined the Straits Settlements in 1826. The Second Charter of Justice in 1826 formally introduced English Law as the basic law in the Straits Settlements and relegated local laws—whether Chinese, Hindu, or Islamic—to the realm of family law. The Straits Settlements was under the government of Fort William of Bengal, under East India Company rule until 1858 when the company was abolished.

Moshe Yegar claims that Indian and Arab elites were able to gain leadership positions in the Straits Settlements due to the absence of hereditary nobility and religious offices prior to colonization.[45] The fact that the British government painstakingly tried to construct the argument that the three Straits Settlements had no established indigenous authority prior to Francis Light's arrival suggests that they did not necessarily believe that forms of local authority were absent in the Straits Settlements. In May 1858, the colony was retrospectively declared "uninhabited" by Chief Justice Benson Maxwell in the landmark case of *Regina v. Willans*, effectively stripping earlier layers of jurisdiction.[46] The case involved a magistrate named William Willans Willans who had earlier presided over a case involving a South Asian male indentured laborer named Chivatean who broke his contract in November 1857 by fleeing his estate in Province Wellesley, to whom he still owed a debt.[47] Maxwell ruled that Willans was right to invoke the rules and principles of English common law, specifically Act 4, Geo. IV., c. 34, which protected a workman from being put into prison more than once for not fulfilling his contract.

Penang was not exactly unowned land—better known as "terra nullius," which became legal doctrine in Australia—but it was as good as empty, Maxwell implied.[48] By emptying out the Straits Settlements of actual inhabitants through legal rhetoric, he employed an extreme move by any measure, especially absurd since one of the Straits Settlements was Malacca, a populous port city whose spectacular rise in the fifteenth century before declining under Portuguese rule in 1511 was well documented. He did so in order to get around the general principle of English jurisprudence that local custom, when not opposed to English law, has all the force of a statute. The legal precedent set by Penang was important for the whole of the British Straits Settlements because it was the first such settlement. It could not have been a coincidence that Maxwell declared complete British jurisdiction in the Straits Settlements in anticipation of the dissolution of the East India Company later that year. Following the Government of India Act of 1858 that was promulgated in August and commenced in November, the company was dissolved and therefore lost all its administrative powers, and the Straits Settlements were taken over by the India Office to be administered by agents in Calcutta. Maxwell could not abide by the possibility that the laws of the last sovereign prior to EIC settlement might take priority over the privilege of what he later deemed to be the actual "inhabitants"—that is, the settlers who more recently arrived at the end of the nineteenth century.

The second landmark case of *Fatimah & Others v. Logan* in September 1871 compelled the Straits Settlements Supreme Court to firmly determine the status of Islamic law in the colony. The issue for the court was what law must be applied to determine the validity of a Muslim's will. During court proceedings, lawyers for the defendant denied that Islamic law existed in Penang before the publication of the first Charter of Justice.[49] On the other side, the attorney-general argued that prior to the Charter of 1807, Islamic law was not only in force in Penang, but in fact the Charter of 1807 made no alteration in the law in this respect. Penang was a part of the territories of the Rajah of Kedah, a "Mahomedan Prince," prior to being an EIC settlement, which meant that "Mahomedan law" could continue to be applied in Penang until altered by "competent authority." Judge William Hackett ruled out this possibility based on the already established idea that the island was "uninhabited" in 1786. He went further to cast Francis Light as far more than a garrison commander—in fact, as someone with executive powers in Penang with the right to administer law throughout the colony.

Claims of a legal "blank slate" had to have a historical basis, so both Maxwell and Hackett harked back to the Charter of 1807, which mentioned that Penang was "uninhabited," for the first time enabling the clear application of the law of England.[50] Both Hackett and Maxwell rested their claims on one empirical assertion—that although there were supposedly "four Malay families encamped upon it" when Francis Light arrived in 1786, these families were supposedly "wandering" and "itinerant fishermen," which implied that they did not have a fixed abode or institution, living their lives out at sea rather than on land. Following this view, they did not qualify as "inhabitants."[51] Maxwell and Hackett referred to Penang as "a desert island" and "an uncultivated island."[52] Through these two landmark cases, the colony was thus unbound from actual history, disavowing knowledge of precolonial settlement and indigeneity to allow colonial authorities to get on with the business of establishing territorial sovereignty on a clean slate without complication.

In other words, the process by which British legislators and judges displaced local populations was a procedural and administrative triumph rather than an intellectual process. In contrast to the uninhabited status of the Straits Settlements, colonial law-making in the Netherlands Indies was buoyed by indigenous claim-making constructed by the Dutch colonial government, who asserted colonial sovereignty in the language of protection of Natives against non-Native and non-Dutch individuals. This was a powerful move by the Dutch with the potential of garnering support from subject populations on the grounds of legitimacy. While British legislators erased the presence of indigenous populations in the Straits Settlements, Dutch authorities underscored Natives' incapacity to guarantee protection for themselves from certain elements in society. The category of "Natives" was restricted to indigenous Javanese, their laws and customs determined by colonial legal authorities with little input from subject populations.[53] This generalization of Javanese identity as "Native" might make Dutch indigenous claim-making seem sloppy, but this formulation was actually convenient for the Dutch since all other groups were rendered potential interlopers and usurpers even if they were indigenous to other nearby locations outside of the Dutch political and economic stronghold of Java in the Netherlands Indies.

In light of such nativist understandings of law in the Dutch colony, Arabs were collectively seen as a less "legitimate" presence in the Netherlands Indies than in the Straits Settlements. Dutch recognition of Native rights became an instrument of dispossession of the rights of Foreign Orientals. Arab efforts to dominate law were tempered by the Dutch view that the customary laws of Indonesians (adat) should not be supplanted by Arab conceptions of law presumed to be restricted to conservative interpretations of Islamic law with little or no place for local adat. While the British bypassed the religious elite in passing legal rulings on religious matters, the Dutch preserved local elites within a more formal legal structure in the form of the *priesterraden* (priest councils) after the issue of Staatsblad 1882 no. 152 that came into force on August 1, 1882.[54] The *priesterraden*'s judgments were subjected to approval by the secular *landraad*, the higher civil courts within the colonial legal structure.

By contrast, the foreignness of Arabs did not disadvantage them in the Straits Settlements. Immediately after Straits Settlements became a Crown colony in 1867, governed by the Colonial Office instead of the India Office, the Arab diaspora must have been aware that their status too was in transition as their social and financial capital intersected with the new colonial regime in novel ways. Coincidentally, the opening of the Suez Canal two years later led to an uptick in immigration across the Indian Ocean to Southeast Asia. As the Arab population became wealthier, they became more invested in their lives in the colonies. The closing decades of the nineteenth century therefore formed a pivotal moment, with British permanence in the colony arriving in the form of its reconstitution as a Crown colony, accompanied by the expectation that administrative practices would be similar to those of other Crown colonies. The commensurability of the rule of law across the empire was as attractive as the lure of a legal blank slate. Although an imperial legal architecture was already established, with the Privy Council in London at the apex, for a few decades at least in the relatively young colony the Arabs noticed that nothing was technically defined as yet, which meant there was room for negotiation. This mixture of standardization, a clean legal slate, and flexibility was a huge draw for the Arab diaspora.

Table 1   Arab population in the British Straits Settlements

YEAR	SINGAPORE	PENANG	MALACCA	STRAITS SETTLEMENTS
1824	15			
1825	10			
1826	17			
1827	18			
1828	17			
1829	32		36	
1830	28			
1832	64		94	
1833	96	142	94	332
1834	66		36	
1835			32	
1836	41		72	
1871	465	354	303	1,122
1881	836	574	220	1,630
1891	806	567	95	1,468
1901	888	544	45	1,477
1911	1,237	702	135	2,074
1921	1,282	520	56	1,858
1931	1,939	605	88	2,632
1947	2,591	202	272	3,065

Sources: T. J. Newbold, *Political and Statistical Account of the British Settlements in the Straits of Malacca, Volume 1* (London: John Murray, 1839); John Frederick Adolphus McNair, *Miscellaneous Numerical Returns [and] Straits Settlements Population [for the Year] 1871* (Singapore: n.p, 1871); E. M. Merewether, *Report on the Census of the Straits Settlements, Taken on the 5th April 1891* (Singapore: Government Printing Office, 1892); J. R. Innes, *Report on the Census of the Straits Settlements Taken on the 1st March 1901* (Singapore: Government Printing Office, 1901); C. A. Vlieland, *British Malaya: A Report on the 1931 Census and on Certain Problems of Vital Statistics* (London: Crown Agents of the Colonies, 1932).

Writing

Private wealth, Brinkley Messick writes, requires a variety of basic written instruments in the form of wills, deeds, and leases, which in turn generate conflicts carried out in other evaluative documents such as court judgments.[55] One of the most commonly used legal devices was the power of attorney, which is the focus of chapter 2. Although they were not supposed to, these documents ended up resembling title deeds, the basis of a property-ownership system that was not yet in place but highly welcome by colonial governments. The power of attorney is hardly the only legal document that transcended long distances. In his book *A Sea of Debt*, Fahad Bishara writes of the legal instrument known as the *waraqa*, the contract of debt made between Arabs or Africans with Indian lenders, which had been circulating in the Indian Ocean for centuries. Originally the *waraqa*, as a short attestation of a loan secured by land for a specific duration, was prepared by a scribe.[56] It too was remarkably durable, functioning as a debtor's deed, a land deed, and a mortgage, and formed the basis for accessing credit across several generations. It was recognized by merchants and legal authorities throughout the region, transcending religious faiths, territorial jurisdictions, and legal systems. Like the *waraqa*, powers of attorney were generational and future-oriented. Unlike the *waraqa*, the language and legal accoutrements such as seals and stamps inscribed in the powers of attorney demonstrate that they were principally meant to be ratified and stored in colonial legal repositories from their inception. In other words, although these powers of attorney ended up having multiple audiences across several generations, they were primarily playing to colonial legal authorities and were therefore purposefully constructed to ensure compliance with colonial law.

As multiple attachments continued to be avidly developed due to family connections and property ownership, the Arab community formed what James Clifford would call a "geniza world," the lowercase letters implying a general characteristic rather than the historical Geniza archive in Cairo.[57] Ilana Feldman and Cornelia Vismann claim that files provide a basis for law as a repository of forms of authoritarian and administrative acts that assume concrete shape, giving it direction and directive while fortifying its power.[58] The Arab diaspora went one step further in producing paper; they tasked the colonial governments with managing their affairs. They were counting on the very fact that paperwork extended state's authority while also holding them accountable to citizens.[59] On the one hand, the corpus of powers of attorney went against the colonial assumption of the supposed contrast between "metropolitan literacy and native orality," in the words of Lydia Liu.[60]

But this framework masks the colonial preoccupation with writing in the first place. Building on Vismann's view, Renisa Mawani rightly points out that law both justifies and obscures the violence of the rod through the violence of legal writing.[61] My book demonstrates how the Arab elite's actions strengthened the potent, troubling link between writing and power, specifically the power of archived documents in government repositories cast in officially recognized colonial languages—English, Dutch, Malay, or Indonesian—and in durable legalese, a specialized language not accessible to all.[62] Writing became an obsession, a compulsion, and likely a burden for the Arab diaspora as they generated these powers of attorney, creating an archive, a repository of hope in the form of transfer of duties and endless circuitry. In her book on the role that Indian scribes in Madras played in the formation of the early colonial state in south India, Bhavani Raman writes that continuous writing became the idealized solution to the problem of managing trust and reliability across distance.[63] The colonial government pushed the idea that writing could ensure political accountability and possibly even limit the abuse of power by making actions transparent and legible.[64] However, Raman warns that this "papereality" makes invisible the artifice of writing and points out that legibility and storage should not be treated as self-evident but rather warrant scrutiny, since the phenomenon of writing created new modes of attestation, documentation, and evidence that rendered most precolonial practices obsolete while privileging others, such as chronologically organized records on paper. The textual habitus engendered by the practice of writing constituted a world in the making by generating jurisdictions.

My book is a departure from the usual narratives of illicit activities in the shadowy maritime spaces away from colonial surveillance, found for instance in the excellent works of Eric Tagliacozzo and Johan Mathew.[65] For the most part, the Arab Ḥaḍramī elite anxiously wanted to be seen by colonial authorities. Rather than hide away to control the margins, these Arabs sought to make themselves highly legible to colonial governments. If, as James Scott argues, states become powerful because they simplify complex social facts into a set of categories that are legible, then those who pushed to make themselves legible helped to buttress the state.[66] The Arab elite's zeal for legitimacy strongly hinted at a constant fear of being rendered illicit by colonial regimes from the mid-nineteenth century onward.[67] A heavy reliance on colonial state bureaucracy was definitely a way to gain trust from colonial governments who appreciated the transparency within their jurisdiction. Members of the Arab diaspora continually tried to prove their utility and legitimacy to colonial authorities, culminating in 1915, in the wake of the Sepoy Mutiny in Singapore, in an alliance of Muslims loyal to the king of England with the British, which I examine in chapter 5. At the same time, we can also interpret these constant attempts at transparency and alliance by colonial subjects as painful symptoms of the deeply unequal relationship under colonial rule.

Diasporas and the Indian Ocean

The mobility of the members of the Arab diaspora who settled in Southeast Asia was a cosmopolitan, Indian Ocean phenomenon entangled in and transcending British and Dutch colonial worlds. Arab identities were complex partly because they had settled in the archipelago centuries before the advent of European colonization. Since the seventh century, Arab and Persian merchants and sailors had travelled across the Indian Ocean to the Malay Archipelago on their way to China.[68] Although ports in the Malay Archipelago, collectively referred to as *zabaj*, started out as transit points for Arab traders, they became ports of settlement after 879 when foreign vessels in the port of Canton, including Arab vessels, were expelled following the massacre of foreign merchants in the port.[69] Arab shipping in Southeast Asia started to increase as a result.[70] By this time, port emporia in the archipelago situated at the intersection of two trading circuits—the Indian Ocean and the South China Sea—were already crucial meeting places for merchants, emissaries, and representatives hailing from various places stretching from Arabia to China. Arab trade in the region flourished till the ascension of the Ming dynasty, when once again Muslim inhabitants, including Arabs, were massacred, forcing survivors to retreat south from China to the Malay Archipelago, which possessed a more favorable climate, not least due to recent conversions to Islam of several merchant-rulers.[71] The circulation of Arab traders in Southeast Asia survived the Ming dynasty's withdrawal of a powerful Chinese fleet from the Indian Ocean in 1435 and the subsequent rise of Portuguese maritime power, which lasted until the end of the sixteenth century.[72]

Southeast Asia—especially island Southeast Asia—is a region that was conducive to new influences and historically did not prioritize nativist narratives.[73] In particular, the port cities of Southeast Asia were shaped to an unusual extent by mobility, and according to Amitav Ghosh, "to be different in a world of differences is irrevocably to belong."[74] The Arab communities in the Indian Ocean were diverse, and Ulrike Freitag's and Linda Boxberger's sweeping histories show that most settled in places throughout the Indian Ocean absorbed into local societies while others stood out within their host societies, retaining their Arab identity to instrumentalize it in different ways and gain political and social privileges.[75]

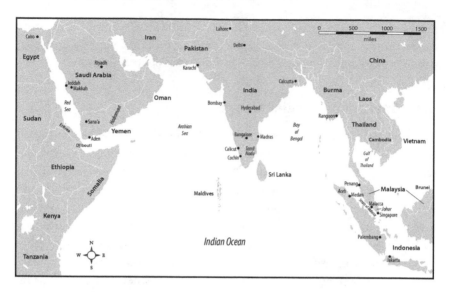

FIGURE 3.   Map of the Indian Ocean.

Sumit Mandal and Engseng Ho prefer to cast Arab identities in Southeast Asia as hybrid or creole to be more historically accurate.[76] Diasporic Arabs relished being mobile, having ports of call with their kin ready to provide support, but realistically speaking, emergent visions of diasporic modernity must have arisen at the expense of other modes of identification across space and time and of more local, improvised forms of community.[77] While analytical categories of "hybrid" and "creole" add nuance to the study of the diaspora, they blur racial boundaries—in fact, there were plenty of Arabs who solely identified as Arabs according to patrilineal descent. In the Indian Ocean, the category of Arab is remarkably durable. The term "Arab," similar to the term "Chinese," encapsulates the fluid condition of being Arab in the world.[78] While Southeast Asia formed the confluence of different regions, historically the colonial period formed a break from earlier periods in presenting populations with new opportunities to centralize control. This aspect of colonialism is particularly attractive to diasporas.

Mandal and Ho also tend to directly link Arabs to Ḥaḍramawt, even though most Ḥaḍramīs settled in South Asia—mostly in Surat, Hyderabad, and Malabar—before coming to Southeast Asia, especially those who arrived before the rise of the steamship, which facilitated direct travel.[79] Hence, there was no direct line from Ḥaḍramawt to the Netherlands Indies. Several Arab clans, such as the Algadri clan, were already mixed (Indian and Arab) before reaching the Netherlands Indies, thereby further undermining what Mandal calls "the fiction of racial coherence."[80] It was only in the second half of the nineteenth century that migrants were able to bypass South Asia and travel directly to Southeast Asia, where they often settled in various places within a single lifetime.[81] From the 1870s onward, ethnographic accounts of Arabs in the Netherlands Indies started to wane in the official government reports (*verslagen, bijlagen*), almanacs, and gazettes (*staatsbladen*). However, they continued to be mentioned in Dutch academic journals focusing on the Indies such as *De Indische Gids*, which were meant for Dutch colonial policymakers. Increasingly, the Arabs became a community who had to be understood and studied in order to be managed and control. While discourse on Foreign Orientals became overwhelmingly negative without differentiation, the parallel track of academic investigations yielded more nuance and ambiguity about the foreign status of Arabs, which caused the legal status of the Arabs to remain the haziest within the already imprecise category of Foreign Orientals.[82] Time and time again, Dutch legal practitioners would return to the root of the Arabs' legal ambiguity—the dual identity of Arabs that straddled both local and foreign worlds in the Netherlands Indies.[83] While the first generation of Arab migrants might have been Arab, subsequent generations were usually of mixed descent. Yet colonial scholar-bureaucrats labeled them unproblematically as "Arabs," though from 1889 onward there were scattered references to their mixed ethnicity.[84] Even then, only one census in Kroë in South Sumatra officially classified them accurately as "Arabieren (Peranakans)" to indicate mixed descent, and in colonial correspondence some bureaucrats referred to them more precisely as "Indo-Arabieren" or "Maleisch-Arabieren," a distinction that full-blooded Arabs tended to emphasize as a mark of status while vying for leadership positions in Arab associations in the colony right up till the 1940s.[85] Similarly, an encyclopedia for the Indies published in 1905 referred to them as *mesties* (mestizos).[86] Yet another Dutch official referred to them derogatorily as *bastard-Arabieren* to indicate their mixed descent, though *halfbloed* was used more often.[87] Although Dutch colonial bureaucrats largely acknowledged that most Arabs in the Netherlands Indies were of mixed descent, born to Arab fathers and Native mothers, they officially based ethnic identities solely according to patrilineal descent.[88]

In most histories of Southeast Asia and the Indian Ocean, the sea connects rather than separates.[89] Sana Aiyar specifically demonstrates how Kenya and India were connected in the minds of members of the Indian diaspora in Kenya.[90] The valence of their connections to India shifted over time as they became increasingly moored in certain places along the littoral. Following Sunil Amrith's suggestive insights, I argue that diasporic consciousness emerged out of absence from the original homeland, as "a consciousness of immobilization" rather than mobility.[91] Not surprisingly, absence shapes the Ḥaḍramī diasporic experience to a large extent.[92] Due to the extent of emigration from the late nineteenth century onward, in terms of material wealth and dispersal of family histories, the center and periphery became flipped such that the point of origin (Ḥaḍramawt) looked more like the periphery in the story of the diaspora. Ho highlights how they were intent on maintaining "resolute localism" in specific places by investing their resources along the Indian Ocean as they widened their orbit of obligations across the Indian Ocean.[93] More members of the Arab diaspora in Southeast Asia too chose to remain in particular locations in Southeast Asia, and as they did so, they cultivated yet firmer connections through the use of law in the form of powers of attorney, wills, bureaucratic records, and remittances.

Renisa Mawani highlights how oceanic histories as productive sites of encounter yield new historical perspectives on world history as they draw attention to circulations, interconnections, and overlaps across time and space and between colonial and imperial worlds.[94] In response to earlier historians who highlight the unity of the Indian Ocean rather than its diversity, Sugata Bose points out that the Indian Ocean is an interregional arena that lies somewhere between the generalities of a "world system" and the specificities of particular regions.[95] There are claims that it had become a "British lake" by the nineteenth century, formerly a "Muslim sea," but these labels conceal from view that the ocean remained a variegated landscape jurisdictionally at all times.[96] Fortunately, recent histories of the Indian Ocean provide many vantage points that highlight nuanced stories in specific contexts. Along with Bishara and Mathew, the historians Pedro Machado and Scott Reese have considerably expanded our view of trade in the western Indian Ocean between South Asia and Africa.[97] Collectively, they demonstrate how trade and religious networks overlapped considerably and how increasingly from the nineteenth century onward, European imperialists became more influential to different degrees depending on the location. Generally South Asia was more governed by British regulations, marked by a heavier presence of British capital, merchants, and government than the Red Sea region and East Africa, where older forms of networks remained dominant for longer.

It is easy to romanticize the ocean and its attendant phenomena of diaspora, cosmopolitanism, and mobility, especially when they are artificially unmoored from the institutions of power and class domination. It is worth exploring whether members of the Arab diaspora were truly cosmopolitan, a mainstay of writing about diasporas.[98] Through legal differentiation, colonialism heightened visibility of race and class, thus further widening rifts among people.

Legal Pluralism in Indonesia

Colonial law in the Netherlands Indies, more so than in the British Straits Settlements, was conspicuously marked by legal pluralism.[99] Laws applied to Muslim colonial subjects in the *priesterraden* was predicated on adat, "traditions, customs and customary laws" that were "something halfway between social consensus and moral style."[100] While Indonesians conceive of adat as loose set of rules, practices of social life, feelings, a sense of propriety, and a somewhat thinner sense of tradition and custom, Dutch colonial conceptions of adat were not as nuanced because Dutch authorities extrapolated rules from expressions and proverbs that once had been public starting-points for complex legal and political processes.[101] These rules, collectively known as *adatrecht*, experienced a great revival in the early twentieth century due to the efforts of Cornelis van Vollenhoven professor of adat law at the University of Leiden. Although there are more than three hundred forms of adat, Vollenhoven identified nineteen circles of adat throughout the Netherlands Indies.[102] Until the end of the colonial period, adat law that was in force in the colony was in the forms conceived by Vollenhoven and his followers.[103] While debates between Vollenhoven and Trenite on how much adat should play a role in the lives of subjects vis-à-vis Dutch civil law regarding property rights and state ownership generally did not have much impact on legal administration in the Netherlands Indies, the bifurcation of adat and Islamic law did.[104] In the *priesterraden*, a mixture of both adat and Islamic law was applied.[105] Increasingly, Islamic law was pitted against adat, often glossed as customary law although Indonesian Muslims did not necessarily separate the two sets of laws in this manner.[106] It was impossible to bifurcate adat and Islamic law in practice because there was great variation in the relationship between the two throughout the colony.[107]

The critical work of legal historian Lauren Benton traces how empires instituted legal pluralism, leading to ambiguous jurisdictions that proved fruitful for several parties.[108] New colonial societies allowed the Arab diaspora to enter a different bracket of social status at the other end of the Indian Ocean in Southeast Asia. Arabs in the Netherlands Indies and the British Straits Settlements had no qualms about undermining the authority of local indigenous populations vis-à-vis European colonial authorities whenever it suited them. On one level, it is anachronistic to ascribe terms such as "legal pluralism" that modern legal scholars use, but the Arab elite's sophisticated methods and tactics coincide with the myriad complex understandings of the phenomenon. A legal system, according to Sally Merry, is pluralistic in the juristic sense when the sovereign commands different bodies of law for different groups varying by ethnicity, religion, nationality, or geography and when the parallel legal regimes are all dependent on the state legal system.[109] Scholars apply the versatile concept to historical settings where law emanates from a multiplicity of normative legal orders.[110]

One channel that was consistently open to colonial subjects in almost all empires was that of petitions. In 1875, the Muslim elite in Singapore, most of whom were identified as Arab by the colonial government, requested more British involvement in appointment of qadis, hence undermining the authority of local Muslim communities over their own qadis throughout the Straits Settlements. They complained that the local qadis were granting divorces to their wives by proxy in their absence. In 1890 and 1905, Arabs of Batavia and Surabaya petitioned the Dutch colonial government to form an Arab court separate from other Muslims in the Dutch colony. Petitions could also enable diverse kinds of mobile subjects to insert themselves into networks of social and political power.[111] These petitions, along with the alliance of Sayyid Uthmān bin Yaḥyā with powerful colonial officials such as Christiaan Snouck Hurgronje, cemented the view of the Arab elite at the top.[112] Tellingly, petitions by Arab colonial subjects featured in chapters 1 and 4 were motivated by marital problems. Petitioners specifically complained that their wives were granted divorces by proxy through local qadis. In her book *Divorcing Traditions,* Katherine Lemons examines divorce proceedings to demonstrate that marriage is as much a space of exchange and of jockeying for resources as it is the domain of care, intimacy, and affection.[113] She contends that because the jurisdiction of Islamic legal forums falls within the purview of religious authority granted by the colonial legal system, the separation of family, home, and religion from politics and exchange does not precede adjudication, but rather is one of its key outcomes. This compartmentalization has two consequences, the first being that kinship became central to secular governance. It is not only or even primarily the secular state that carries out the labor of separating these spheres, but rather the religious legal institutions that hitherto operate beyond its purview.[114] By appealing to colonial governments to step in to adjudicate their marital lives, the Arab diasporic elite in Southeast Asia further compartmentalized family, home, and religion from politics and exchange within the realm that is Islamic law. By doing so, they further ossified this realm as separate from other realms. Simultaneously, by opting to peddle their influence in Islamic law under colonial rule, specifically through marital disputes, the

Arab diaspora extended colonial control of their lives and those of fellow Muslims.

The acute fear of estrangement and disintegration compelled them to rely on law to maintain control of their financial assets and property through powers of attorney. It also led some members of the Arab elite in the colony to lean on colonial bureaucracy to rein in local qadis from granting divorces to their wives by proxy and ratifying the wives' marriages to other men afterwards. What the Arab petitioners were objecting to was the frequency of a particular form of dissolution of marriage known as *faskh*, which takes place at the insistence of the wife or her relatives on the grounds that the husband has abandoned the wife physically and financially. *Faskh* requires a third-party such as a qadi to effectuate it. A *faskh* divorce is a type of Islamic divorce that is distinguished from *khula* divorce because it does not require that the husband consent to the divorce or even require that he be present.[115] This practice has long standing throughout the Islamic world, where women across all social strata have sought qadis' courts seeking to dissolve their marriage, to claim debts, and to protect their property, with their success in court being contingent on being able to produce evidence satisfactory for the qadi.[116] Therefore, the Arabs' criticism of local qadis went against standard Islamic legal practice. Because they could not question the legal capacity of women, which was entrenched in Islamic doctrines, they curtailed it by calling on British government bureaucracy to take a firmer hand in reining in the practices of the qadis.[117]

The petitioners recognized that the qadi was powerful within his own community because his purview was actually very wide, ranging from being an arbitrator in marital and other family disputes and monitoring care of orphans and the poor to acting as a guardian in marriages for women with no male relatives.[118] To qualify for this position, a qadi had to be knowledgeable with the local customs and way of life in the community in which he served. Unlike colonial judges, qadis had to be familiar with and be willing to investigate relationships between the disputants wherever possible, to prevent the collapse of relationships and preserve amicable relations in the community. Considering the qadis' social position and authority within their communities, it was a challenge for anyone to undercut their authority among Muslims. The Arab elite therefore had to appeal to colonial governments whose authority superseded that of the qadis under colonial rule to impose a regulatory regime.

Their petition led directly to the promulgation of the Mohamedan Marriage Ordinance of 1880, which subsequently resulted in the appointment of a non-Muslim British Registrar to oversee the conduct and records of all qadis. In this way, despite being a small minority, the Arab elite shaped the administration of Islamic law in the colony. The Mohamedan Marriage Ordinance later led to the expansion of colonial and Arab authority through the establishment of the Mohamedan Endowments Board in 1905. More immediately, however, this empowered British judges to rule in cases involving Islamic law without considering the opinions of local religious experts, whose influence in court dropped off after 1880.[119] Because the British colonial government would not have interfered in Muslim affairs otherwise, it could be said that the Arab elite accelerated and deepened colonial involvement in religious affairs in the British Straits Settlements.

While colonial legal systems did not introduce legal pluralism in Southeast Asia, which was already very diverse, they certainly intensified legal pluralism. It is fair to say that although the Arabs of course never used the concept themselves, legal pluralism was the central organizing concept of their actions. Legal pluralism was so ubiquitous that there was no special term for it historically because everyone engaged with it. It was a habitus not an abstraction, Frederick Cooper and Jane Burbank contend.[120] Likewise, Sally Merry points out that legal pluralism was neither a theory of law nor an explanation of how it functions but rather a description of what law is like.[121] As a heuristic aid in the study of legal history, legal pluralism certainly provides an invaluable guide for scholars to think about law in its multiple instantiations and intersections and to pay attention to alternative understandings and practices of law.

Within the system of legal pluralism, the Arab elite played a pernicious role in extending an intrusive form of colonial law called personal law (sometimes known as personal status law), a term that refers to the law that is applied to a person rather than a territory. In most places, such as in British India, where the system had been introduced in 1772 by Governor-General William Hastings of Bengal, the laws applied were religious laws in the realm of family law, concerning marriage, divorce, adoption, inheritance, and guardianship of minors.[122] Muslim subjects in Southeast Asia were extremely diverse in terms of ethnicity, geographical origin, and class and therefore hardly unified even when grouped under the same category of "Muslims." The question became who was allowed to determine what was "Islamic law." Because it was a category preserved by colonial governments, personal law became an arena for competition among Muslim subjects for supremacy in the realm of cultural defense.[123] Familial strife motivated the Arab elite to deploy complicated legal maneuvers associated with legal pluralism as the domain of action became scrambled under colonial rule. They quickly recognized that it was not enough to exist within legal pluralism; one had to be recognized by the state as part of what is more precisely known as "norma-tive legal pluralism."[124]

In the realm of personal law, the Arabs in the Straits Settlements engaged in "lawfare," defined by John Comaroff as the "effort to conquer and control indigenous peoples by the coercive use of legal means."[125] In contrast to Co-maroff's specific conception, Arab elite perpetrated lawfare on their fellow colonial subjects through colonial legal channels, beginning with the move to undermine the power of qadis, granting more power to British admin-istrators and judges who tended to issue judicial decisions that conformed to the worldview of the Arab elite and the law with which they were most familiar. In both British and Dutch colonies, the Arab elite aggressively par-ticipated in the phenomenon known as "forum shopping," which refers to the attempt to push one's case into a jurisdiction promising an optimal result when there is ambiguity over the controlling jurisdiction.[126] By choosing to participate in colonial legal systems, they wielded "forum shopping" as a weapon against their spouses and local communities who empowered them and as a shield to protect their own financial and real estate investments. They converged toward colonial jurisdictions because they realized they could count on colonial rulers to invalidate other laws in the colonies. Their actions effectively tied law to institutional norm enforcement as they aligned themselves with sovereign rulers of the colony. Their sequence of actions embodied what Robert Cover describes as the jurispathic role of judges—a coercive dimension of law that erases other laws—suggesting that "because of the violence they command, judges characteristically do not create law, but kill it."[127] Jurispathic state law is destructive, unlike jurisgenerative poli-tics, which is a strategic bargaining among the parties according to Seyla Ben-habib.[128] In Southeast Asia, the Arab diaspora went one step further—it was not enough to eradicate established legal authorities and with that the form of laws they implemented; it was equally important to safeguard the space it used to occupy. The Arab elite preserved the contour around the forms left by the colonial state's act of hollowing out local indigenous authority in the colonies. The Arab elite neither created additional room nor inserted themselves as intermediaries between the British and other Muslim subjects. Neither did the British make room for yet more diverse authorities, so the Arab elite could not hope to exceed the colonial form anyway.

Once formed, the colonial creation that was religious law became a bul-wark against subsequent colonial interference. To illustrate this, I adapt the persuasive metaphor provided by Hussein Agrama in his study of religious authority in Egypt after the revolution of 2011 where he compares the Egyp-tian Fatwa Council to "a bubble within a bubble, produced by the secular but no longer of it, bouncing around within its confines yet otherwise largely in-different to it."[129] The bubble could expand at the risk of popping, or shrink, thus concentrating competition for supremacy in a small sphere. Once cre-ated, this religious bubble remains impervious to future intervention, at least in theory. Colonial governments preserved the aspects that they deemed re-ligious by constantly determining what aspect of religion was enforceable in colonial courts. Over time, the Arab elite slowly lost their grip over colo-nial officials, who administered Islamic law with minimal input from subject populations. Hence, they had to contend with colonial imposition of Anglo-Mohamedan law over their lives, as detailed in chapter 1. They likely did not foresee this, only later learning of it as an outcome of their litigiousness—and capitalizing on it for material gain, as I demonstrate in chapter 6.[130]

The contributions of the Arab elite to the shape of Islamic law in the Straits Settlements would play out through litigation because the results of their legal cases eventually became legal precedents. This fits Brinkley Messick's idea that "shari'a" without the definitive article meant simply litigation—conducting a lawsuit before a judge.[131] Their litigiousness echoes that of another distinct group that traversed the Indian Ocean, namely the Parsis, who formed the focus of Mitra Sharafi's book.[132] While the Parsi co-lonial subjects successfully entered into the infrastructure of colonial law, the Arabs in Southeast Asia compelled the colonial government to control their domestic lives and corral their financial resources while they themselves chose to stay out of the legal infrastructure, apart from being disputants in court.

Why did members of the Arab diaspora gravitate toward colonial ju-risdictions and why did they choose not to assert their own legal system over the region—or, at the very least, assert their own laws? They likely felt handicapped by their relative newness to the region. They appreciated that notions of indigeneity are predicated on continual habitation so they would have been sidelined had the colonies not started out as blank legal slates. Over generations, they invested in Southeast Asia, becoming pragmatists and developing a partiality for entrenched interests that led them to cling to authority to safeguard their property and their relationships with their families. Did they acknowledge that their choices formed a set compromises of values and freedom for the sake of their property and businesses? As a diaspora, what the Arab elite feared was estrangement from their families and property. In fact, all their actions and decisions—powers of attorney, bureaucratizing their marital arrangements, taking the helm of Muslim leadership—were aimed at staving off the disintegration of their families, property, and power.

Their attempts at world-making encompassed both the point of origin and the destination alike without prioritizing either, blurring the line between home and point of origin. As Julie Chu demonstrates in her book *Cosmologies of Credit: Transnational Mobility and the Politics of Destination in China*, one cannot assume that one's identity and experiences are only whole and well when rooted in a territorial homeland.[133] Like Chu's work, this book cuts at sedentary analytic bias. Furthermore, people experience multiple scale-making projects that complement and contradict each other—in this case, the Arab diaspora in Southeast Asia can be viewed as part of the Muslim world, Southeast Asia, the Indian Ocean milieu, colonial subject populations, merchants, the Arab community, Ḥaḍramīs, and elite Arabs with illustrious lineages that reached back to the Prophet.

Considering the high cost of siding with European colonialists, decisions to do so have to be explained. It is possible that the Arab elite compartmentalized subjectivity into the three aspects identified by Yoav Di-Capua as freedom, authenticity, and sovereignty.[134] Attaining all three meant owning the capacity for self-determination, Di-Capua argues. By abiding by colonial rules, the mobile elite members of the Arab diaspora sacrificed sovereignty to attain freedom and authenticity in their efforts to recondition their lives to suit their new wealthy lifestyles across the Indian Ocean. As this book shows, the challenge for historians is that notions of freedom, authenticity, and sovereignty are constantly changing across time. Hence only through historical narratives can their stories be told in their full complexity.

Decisions to abide by colonial norms were likely a matter of expedience. Janet Abu-Lughod states that what mobile merchants value above all else is freedom from oppressive restrictions and taxes and the ability to store their wealth safely and to switch their capital at will from one trading circuit to another.[135] The institution of the religious endowment known as waqf, which I examine in chapter 6, embodied both this anxiety and the resulting strategy to mitigate it. Waqfs enabled members of the Arab diaspora to preserve their families' prosperity and social capital in the British Straits Settlements, where Arab investment was very high and where such endowments were not banned, unlike in the Netherlands Indies. Cases involving waqfs eventually presented the supreme challenge to colonial separation of economic and religious spheres of life.

At the same time, because they were primarily merchants, the Arab elite might have found it inconvenient to also govern another sphere in addition to their commercial activities. Courts, Marc Galanter writes, are sites of administrative processing, record-keeping, ceremonial changes of status, settlement negotiations, mediation, arbitration, and warfare (the threatening, overpowering and disabling of opponents), as well as of adjudication.[136] Perhaps the Arabs stretched themselves too thin across the Indian Ocean, having to manage their family lives and commercial affairs, and therefore found it easier to simply use available legal infrastructure provided by colonial governments as hopeful litigants flocked to what they perceived to be the jurisdiction of least resistance and an anticipated future based on well-developed colonial legal infrastructure.[137] They could have been drawn to the universalism of imperial legal system that transcends boundaries, especially after, as Jennifer Pitts points out, the dominant register of European legal doctrine had begun to shift from the religious to the civilizational during the nineteenth century.[138] More specifically, the Arab elite were attempting to generalize their own conceptions of Islamic law to be representative of the universal anyway and therefore felt an affinity with the more universal conception of Islamic law within British colonialism. Juxtaposed against the ethnic category "Malay," the religious category of "Muslim" appeared more inclusive. Historically, although Muslims conceived of themselves as belonging in principle to a global community known as the *umma*, they still identified with more localized communities who recognized their own religious experts and appointed their own authorities. This attempt by a small section of a community to generalize a broader conception of religious authority was not unique to the Arab diaspora in Southeast Asia. In another setting within the British Empire, elite-caste Hindu norms were extended to a variety of non-elite communities in British India as part of the personal status law system in the 1860s and 1870s, as Rachel Sturman has shown.[139] Elke Stockreiter demonstrates that the Arab elite in Zanzibar used ethnicity as a criteria for determining a person's degree of Islamization.[140] In Southeast Asia, the Arab elite instrumentalized their ethnicity to signal their level of Islamic knowledge vis-à-vis local Muslims to colonial authorities, although in reality access to specialized knowledge of legal practice was as varied among Arab Muslims as it was among Southeast Asian Muslims. Nonetheless, a universal perspective of Islam privileged Arabs as the most knowledgeable community because they hailed from Arabia, a place considered to be the authentic core of the Islamic world.

Another reason why the Arab elite chose to yoke their lives to colonial legal systems could be their belief in a flatter hierarchy even under colonial rule. This might be construed as naiveté or wishful thinking, but the truth is, colonialism presented new ecologies that created opportunities. Scholars tend not to note this possibility because colonial subjects, including the Arab elite in Southeast Asia, failed to eventually achieve parity. The actions of the Arab diaspora suggested that they did not perceive themselves as subordinate to colonial governments in Southeast Asia even when they did not openly resist against them. Throughout the colonial period, there was dissonance between actual colonial policies and Arab aspirations for power in Southeast Asia, as if they were creating a world of their own through new legalities. One of the reasons for this phenomenon is that colonial law reinforced its hold on subjects by dangling before them the possibility of individual relief through rule-of-law proceduralism.[141] The colonial legal system may have created small spaces for the exercise of agency but it reinforced its hold on colonized social life by strengthening its legitimacy, eliciting the participation of players, and blurring the view of the system's larger biases.[142] Although colonial litigants may have felt that they were acting strategically in making "forum shopping" arguments, they were merely seduced by the mechanism of the legal lottery—the promise that they might win this time even if they probably would not in the long run. The problem for the Muslim elite who relied heavily on law to effect change in their favor in the Netherlands Indies and the British Straits Settlements was that further modification of laws became a difficult maneuver once colonial powers had defined and encased shari'a in their own procedural law and political power.[143] Scholars are only now beginning to understand the impact of this phenomenon. The judicialization of religion led to cycles of legalization, reification, contestation, and yet more jurisgenesis that goes well beyond the court of law to encompass broader sociolegal worlds.[144]

Islamic Law

This book ties in with recent works on Islamic law under colonial rule that highlight how development of Islamic law became warped and stunted as it became a powerful political symbol and a battleground for cultural ideas throughout the world.[145] In both the Straits Settlements and the Netherlands Indies, Islamic law constituted a part of the official legal system through the personal law system, which enabled some Muslim subjects to instrumentalize it for more power in the colony. Since colonialism is a form of structured dispossession, the uncomfortable truth is that Arabs in the Netherlands Indies and the British Straits Settlements contributed to the displacement of indigenous jurisdiction.

Personal status law usually meant "family law," but neither of these terms were ever circumscribed. More crucially, both Muslim subjects and colonial governments purposefully underscored the correctness of "Islamic law" in particular ways after it became the designated battleground for Muslims. With hindsight, we note that Muslim subjects also contributed to the reduction of Islamic law to a set of rules, punishments, and procedures according to colonial conceptions. Generally, in the realm of Islamic law, European colonial prejudice accorded primacy to text over interpretive practice, a drastic change from Islamic legal practice. Pure textual authority ran counter to the Islamic legal tradition where the authority of the legal interpreter (judge) and the legal interpretation did not yield a system of codes and precedents that oriented future legal decisions.[146] Islamic law was essentially divorced from jurisprudence (*fiqh*) and the science of this jurisprudence (*usul al-fiqh*)[147] Competition for interpretations of Islamic law abound among colonial subjects and colonial officials who claimed to be experts—the extremely prolific Dutch Orientalist scholar Christiaan Snouck Hurgronje being a prime example of this.[148]

The bulk of discussions during colonial legal proceedings focused more on the boundaries of personal law jurisdiction and the "correct" form of Islamic law rather than actual legal content. What constituted Islamic law, "religious law," or "Arab law," colonial legislators asked? Indeed, studies on Islamic law under colonial rule reveal how idiosyncratic colonial understandings of Islamic law were, and that "Islamic law," adat, and "customary law" were constituted anew during this period. There was no prior conception of adat or Islamic law in the Netherlands Indies and British Straits Settlements before colonial authorities embarked on a mission to "discover" them—on their own, for the sake of efficient legal administration; because they were forced to adjudicate competing interpretations; or due to requests for the bureaucratization of Islamic law. Hence it is not that colonial authorities gave the normative force of law to specific legal systems beforehand; rather, colonial officials attempted to appropriate the specific norms of freshly discovered Islamic law and adat to its own institutions.[149] Both Dutch and British authorities were ready to listen to local Muslim subjects and record their opinions, but not necessarily in order to carry them out.

The term "shari'a," often glossed as Islamic law, actually contains much more than law, and its most comprehensive definition represents the divine delineation of the life of submission.[150] Shahab Ahmed has pointed out that while scholars of Islamic studies concur that the term "Islam" does not express a coherent object of meaning, the term "Islamic law" is more often regarded as authentically Islamic, as if it is the core of Islam, a phenomenon associated with normative understandings of law and enforceability.[151]

This totalizing "legal supremacist" conceptualization of Islam as *law*, whereby the "essence" of Islam is a phenomenon of prescription and proscription, induces, indeed *constrains* us to think of Muslims as subjects who are defined and constituted by and in a cult of regulation, restriction and control . . . historically, Muslims have constructed normative meaning for Islam in terms that allowed them to live by and/or with norms other than and at odds with those put forward by legal discourse.[152]

Some scholars such as Iza Hussin and Sarah Eltantawi find it useful to conceptually separate "the political life of Islamic law" and "political shari'a" from "idealized Shari'a," which is thought to be divinely inspired.[153] Since the term "Islamic law" evidently had traction among colonial officials and Muslim subjects during the colonial period, I attend to the performative work the phrase did beyond its functionality as an analytical category. Certainly, both colonial subjects and colonial legal administrators trafficked in the fiction of the category of Islamic law—Muslim colonial subjects, more so than others, became especially tethered to religious laws during the colonial period. It is important for scholars to distinguish between, on the one hand, making judgments about Islamic legal practices and, on the other, building an open-ended inquiry into the decision-making processes of Muslims. Their actions of the Arab elite truly reflected the capaciousness of the term "Islamic law" even as they went against established Islamic legal norms.

Most remarkably, they used the new colonial category of "Islamic law" to deftly commandeer the terrain of legal pluralism with different levels of success in the Netherlands Indies and the British Straits Settlements. They did so partly in the interests of representing Muslims in a new world characterized by colonialism. Mainly, however, they aimed to create a whole new world for themselves. In the end, the copious amounts of documents created by the Arab diaspora formed contingent writings that portrayed more situated histories of Islamic law rather than transforming Islamic legal practices in their vision. The Arab diaspora in Southeast Asia successfully contributed to creating an "archive" but did not continue to dominate the "library," according to the schema described in Brinkley Messick's *Shari'a Scripts*. The "library" and the "archive" indicate the separate yet interdependent textual realms that occupy different discursive modalities within an overarching juridical culture, encompassing the book and the document respectively.[154] In the Netherlands Indies, Dutch bureaucratic-scholars enthusiastically built their own library based primarily on context-free, atemporal Orientalist scholarship and, to a limited extent, empirical general observations in Southeast Asia and the rest of the Islamic world, while adat scholars marginalized the role of Islamic law associated with the Arab diaspora. Although the Arab elite initially dominated the implementation of Islamic law in the Straits

Settlements, their efforts eventually led to the cession of interpretive power
to British judges who derived their verdicts from their own libraries stocked
with Anglo-Mohamedan literature—with unpredictable results for Muslim
subjects. The archive of documentary sources created by the Arab diaspora
in Southeast Asia was formidable, brimming with specific detail—names,
various currencies, precise locations, exact property values—but was by nature, transient. It turns out that during the late colonial period, members of
the Arab diaspora in Southeast Asia were no longer the "authors" of Islamic
law and merely the "writers."[155]

CHAPTER 1

The Lure of Bureaucracy

British Administration of Islamic Law
in the Straits Settlements

The Arab elite in Southeast Asia played an out-sized role in the development of Islamic law in the British Straits Settlements (Penang, Malacca, and Singapore) and, to a smaller extent, the Netherlands Indies. Colonial jurisdictions permeated the colonies incrementally over time not simply by statute or decree but gradually through the steady accretion of litigation and petitions—legal formulas that conform to specific legal formats propelled by colonial subjects to a significant extent. In both colonies, the Arab elite compelled colonial jurisdictions to be applied to more areas of life, and wider sections of colonial population than before. Considering that the ratio of Arabs to "Malays and other Natives of the Archipelago" in the official Straits Settlements censuses was about 7 to 100,000 toward the end of the nineteenth century, their impact was disproportionate.[1] Even in Singapore, which held the largest Arab population in the Straits Settlements, the local Muslim population, glossed as "Malay," outnumbered them with a ratio of 3:500. British involvement in Muslim affairs in the Straits Settlements was done at the behest of Arab mercantile elites in the colony who continually tugged at the hem of colonial governments, asking them to take charge of Muslim lives and thus displacing more indigenous forms of authority even further in the process. By insisting on the "correct" interpretation of laws, the Arab elite shifted the trajectory of legal administration in the colonies. They persuaded British and Dutch colonial governments to facilitate change in their favor, to centralize legal infrastructure to stave off future dialogue, and to let them fill the role of religious arbitrator in the colonies. Their choice to continually appeal to colonial authorities suggests that they were granted a social sense of citizenship rights due to their class although they must have been aware of the impossibility of full enfranchisement under colonial rule.

The Arab diaspora had yet to possess much authority in the Straits Settlements in 1875. They were not yet elite and still adrift, without a clear-cut hierarchy in the colony, eight years after British India had relinquished control over the colony, to be replaced by direct Crown rule. They were, in other words, not the natural candidates for leadership of the Muslim community at this time. By choosing to ally with the colonial government, they momentarily dissociated their struggle in the realm of family law—a question of jurisdiction—from the larger situation of political subjugation associated with sovereignty. The realm of jurisdiction is often filled with multiple and competing understandings of the foundations of law as well as the limits of legal control, as Renisa Mawani points out, differentiating it from sovereignty, which by contrast implies a coherence, infallibility, and uniformity of thought, coalescing in a state or polity.[2] In voluntarily gravitating toward colonial authority, the Arab diaspora reinforced the coherence of the sovereign and its distinction from the field of jurisdiction, which they left open as a site of contestation.

Essentially, the Arab elite tried to inaugurate a new legal and bureaucratic regime by taking advantage of the liminal moment of legal and political ambiguity immediately after 1867, when the Straits Settlements became a Crown colony ruled directly by England, hence becoming part of a much larger entity from a bureaucratic perspective, administered by the Colonial Office rather than the India Office. The Arab elite channeled their efforts toward the centralization of legal administration, steadfastly aligning themselves with colonial state structures in the process, their aims being fortuitously congruent for the time being. The petition of the Arab elite to colonial authorities requesting colonial administration of Islamic law exposed the fault lines of colonial/subject dynamics by bringing to the fore troubling questions of racial prejudice, chauvinism, and class disparity. However tempting it is to frame their usage of petitions as a narrative of empowerment for colonial subjects, to do so would obscure the fundamental injustice driving it.[3] The Arab elite eventually deprived others of a voice through their temerity in asserting their own because their base was not broad and unified. They advocated for themselves, not even for their entire ethnic community, and certainly not for the Muslim community.

At some point between his arrival in 1821 from Palembang and his death in November 1852 in Singapore, the Arab philanthropist and merchant Syed Omar Ali Aljunied presented British authorities with his own "plan of surveillance" over "mosques and priests" by floating vague insinuations of corruption and improper application of Islamic law. However, the British government did not take up his proposal due to lack of personnel.[4] Over several decades, the Arab elite would continue to be unimpressed with local qadis' conduct and frequently complained to British authorities. These grievances struck a chord with frustrated British legal administrators, who were already reluctantly handling cases involving Islamic law when they were brought to higher courts because they could not be settled by qadis.[5] In 1875, 143 Muslims, most of whom were identified as Arabs by the British government, submitted a memorial or a petition requesting that the government record Muslim marriages and divorces in the Crown colony and officially appoint qadis. They complained that that the existing mode of recording Muslim marriages and divorces had produced incomplete entries in qadis' books without the full names and addresses of spouses and witnesses. Qadis who solemnized Muslim marriages relied solely on oral testimony of persons involved, which made it extremely difficult to prove the validity of marriages, legitimacy of progeny, and property titles. The memorialists unfairly cast this practice as incompetence when in fact, historically, oral testimony was not only adequate, it was actually preferred in Islamic courts.[6] Another grievance that could not be easily defended was the qadis' tendency to ratify marital unions that were contrary to Islamic law, such as marriages without the permission of a woman's guardian—her *walī*—a stipulation required under Shafi'i law specifically. The memorialists claimed it was also common for qadis to declare a marriage invalid for a woman who was "tired of her husband"—the flippancy of the wording suggesting disdain toward fickle wives more than the qadis' conduct. Outnumbered by the rest of the Muslim population, the male Arab elite in the Straits Settlements feared that a qadi might favor his own ethnic community over another, thus putting the mobile Arab migrants without influential footing in the colony at a disadvantage against their wives, who were mostly local women. In acquiescence to their female kin, qadis often willingly forged an entry for divorce into the register of marriages for "a good fee," the Arab elite claimed.[7] In other words, the memorialists claimed that the qadis were granting many divorces to women too easily.

At the time, there were numerous qadis throughout the Straits Settlements, since each ethnic community elected its own qadi.[8] The qadis were not only immensely diverse but also mostly indigenous to the region, the Arabs realized to their discomfort. Each appointment was announced in the public press, which mentioned that several Javanese, Malay, Arab, and Indian qadis would sometimes operate in the same town or village without defined territorial jurisdiction because they exercised authority over any Muslim who voluntarily recognized them, even though they had originally been appointed by their own communities loosely defined by ethnicity and location.[9] A qadi in the Straits Settlements would make sure to carry a letter-patent from "the chief lights of the Mohamedan religion in the town of settlement to which he belongs"—although, memorialists claimed, these letter-patents could be acquired for a sum of money, a practice that led to a certain arbitrariness in appointments.[10] The exercise of power by several qadis within each settlement was construed as a problem by the memorialists, who believed that this might lead to highly disorganized records, or no records at all. For the sake of bureaucratic efficiency, the memorialists requested that the governor of the Straits Settlements appoint only one qadi in each settlement, to be answerable to the Mahomedan registrar, a government-appointed British official who could be a non-Muslim under the supervision of the British registrar-general.[11] By doing so they conceived of each settlement as an undifferentiated entity in keeping with their universal conception of Islamic law. They strongly recommended that no marriage or divorce should be recognized except those solemnized by qadis licensed by the government. The registrar should create a centralized depository by recording the names of individual qadis and spouses as well as marriage settlements consisting of promises in consideration of marriages involving money and property.[12]

The memorial reached the Legislative Council, where the views of the Arab elite were represented by two British men, F. C. Bishop and Thomas Shelford, who spoke on their behalf by providing two examples of common grievances that could be alleviated by the introduction of a compulsory system of marriage registration.[13] The first example was that of a hypothetical pregnant Muslim woman who was entitled to redress from her husband according to Islamic law. Shelford and Bishop reasoned that if she was unable to prove her marriage in the colony due to the lack of a system of marriage registration in the colony, she risked being in great hardship. The second example doubtlessly struck at the core of Arab anxiety throughout Southeast Asia: a Muslim man found himself divorced from his wife as the result of a bribe (from the wife or her family) to the qadis.[14] The children of polygamous unions also ran the risk of being considered illegitimate in the courts of law, Shelford and Bishop warned. The actual experiences by women and children were coldly serviced to further the agenda of displacing Muslim legal authorities.

Nonetheless, in 1875, British authorities were reluctant to take on the mantle of administration of Islamic law, steadfastly holding on to the policy of noninterference in religious affairs that dated back to the aftermath of the Sepoy Rebellion, also known as the First Indian War of Independence (1857–58), when Queen Victoria took control of India from the East India Company and guaranteed religious toleration to all Indian subjects.[15] Issues that were designated "religious" were deemed outside of colonial intervention by British authorities in the Straits Settlements, although scholars of British Empire have shown how colonial authorities claimed to avoid interfering in religious affairs while actually transforming religious laws in significant ways.[16] In British India, colonial administrative policies led to a shift from Islamic law's "substantial rationality" to a more "formal rationality" implemented by colonial authorities, although this played out in myriad ways in practice.[17]

In Malaya and the Straits Settlements, authorities generally acknowledged that religious practice was diverse and possessed very distinct localized forms and coloring, as was evident in the numerous colonial digests and loose collections of local laws known as *undang-undang* which included both Islamic law and local customary laws known as adat.[18] They were also aware of the tension that emerged among Muslims in the region since the early nineteenth century between proponents of adat, and returning Haj pilgrims and religious scholars.[19] Through the nineteenth century, adat and Islamic law were increasingly bifurcated into two distinct spheres by both British and Dutch colonialists. Legal codes were avidly collected by British Orientalist William Marsden, as well as by East India Company employees such as Thomas Stamford Raffles and William Farquhar, from Sumatra, Java, Borneo, Singapore, and the Malay Peninsula during the early nineteenth century.[20] Richard O. Winstedt and Richard J. Wilkinson continued these efforts a century later.[21] The legal codes were not implemented in the Straits Settlements, though these colonial collections remained of scholarly interest as ethnographic studies that could illuminate British understanding of local societies.[22]

Judge Benjamin Malkin had stressed in 1835 that although English law was the default law in the Straits Settlements, the established law in the colony gave unlimited freedom of disposal of property by will to "any man who wishes his property to devolve according to the Mahomedan, Chinese, or other law," in which case he "has only to make his Will to that effect, and the Court will be bound to ascertain that law and apply it for him."[23] The default application of English law in the colony had advantages for Muslim testators as it granted more testamentary freedom than a strict application of

Islamic law would allow.[24] For example, testators could, if they wished, pass on the whole of their property in the form of a waqf, and not just a third of it, as prescribed by Islamic law.[25] It was not until January 1, 1924, that property was devolved according to Islamic law by default should a Muslim die intestate, and even then he or she could still devolve his or her property contrary to Islamic law and in accordance with English law.[26] In other words, the default administration of Islamic law allowed Muslim testators more liberty in disposing their property than traditional Islamic law would allow. Through two landmark cases in 1858 and 1871 that enshrined the label of "uninhabited," Islamic law was written out as the legal basis for the Straits Settlements once and for all—with only two exceptions, both in Malacca, whose "uninhabited" status was harder to prove since it once lent its name to a civilization and, unlike Singapore and Pinang, lay primarily on the peninsula, which was certainly recognized as inhabited by British authorities.[27] The first exception to this was the law governing *harta syarikat* or *harta sepencarian*, which refers to the property acquired jointly by the couple during marriage, a law that was actually applied throughout the Straits Settlements.[28] This law of joint marital property allowed a wife to claim a portion of the property gained during the course of a marriage, including that earned by the husband.

The second exception was the Malacca Customary Land Laws, formalized in 1886. Since the Portuguese and Dutch colonial powers retained Malay laws (customary adat and Islamic) in Malacca prior to formal British occupation in 1824, British colonial legal officials decided to recognize these laws as well. Malacca customary land automatically descended on the death of the holder to the holder's heirs according to Islamic law, regardless of stipulations in the holder's will.[29] Again, this particular exception was an acknowledgement of earlier European imperial sovereignties in the region rather than recognition of local Malay rights. For that reason, the law was initially restricted to Malacca, where the Portuguese and Dutch rule held sway from 1511 to 1641 and from 1641 to 1824 respectively. Legal and historical continuity were a privilege for European rulers only.

Within this framework, the subsequent Mohamedan Marriage Ordinance of 1880 that emerged from the petition was simply the last in a series of systematic erasures that further lent credence to the uninhabited status of the colony. The memorialists exploited the shaky legal foundations of the Straits Settlements by endowing British authorities with an opportunity to further deepen colonial jurisdiction at the expense of competing legalities associated with indigenous cultures in the region. With this invitation from Muslim subjects themselves, British legal authorities confidently shrugged off the weight of centuries of adat that permeated Southeast Asia. By contrast, in the Netherlands Indies, Dutch legal administrators entrenched the idea that the islands were saturated with ancient customs and traditions as they held off from enacting more substantive transformations beyond the procedural, even when requested by Muslim subjects.

Yet three years after the memorial was submitted to the British government, there was still no sign of a registry, although information had been procured by the Legislative Council from governments in Ceylon, Madras, Calcutta, and Bombay on the administration of Islamic law in these places.[30] In February 1878, ongoing discontentment with local qadis' conduct in the Crown colony came to a head in a high-profile case that was brought to the Supreme Court in Singapore.[31] A qadi had solemnized a marriage between an Arab woman and a non-Arab man in Singapore without the consent of the bride's guardian (walī), who was her paternal uncle. The young woman, Fatimah, had shrewdly chosen to marry her Indian husband, Ismail, during her uncle's absence. Upon his return, her uncle Shaik Omar bin Salaf challenged the validity of the marriage in British colonial court in the case of *Salmah and Fatimah, Infants, by Their Next Friend Shaik Omar v. Soolong* (henceforth *Salmah and Fatimah v. Soolong*) for two reasons. First of all, he claimed he had not consented to the marriage, such approval being incumbent in instances where the bride had never previously been married, according to Shafi'i law. Secondly, he argued that the marriage was unequal. The only equal marriage for Fatimah would be to another Arab. He stressed that this prerequisite was especially important since she was a descendant of the Prophet, a Sayyid.[32] Chief Justice Sir Thomas Sidgreaves dismissed the second point and latched on to the first by stating that if it was indeed true that Fatimah did not obtain her rightful guardian's approval in her marriage, the marriage was null.[33]

An Arab mufti (expert in Islamic law) named Syed Mohamed bin Shaik bin Sahil, from the neighboring state of Johore on the southern tip of the Malay Peninsula, was consulted by Sidgreaves.[34] After admitting that he was thoroughly conversant with the Mohamedan Law of Marriage, having been educated in the "Mohamedan Law of Hydermaut" in Arabia, the mufti stated that Fatimah, who followed the Shafi'i *madhhab* (one of the four main Sunni schools of law), required the consent of her guardian, who was her paternal uncle, for her marriage to be valid since she had never been married before.[35] If her guardian was away in another country such that it would take "twenty-four hours journey" by foot or forty-five miles by sea, a qadi "appointed as such by the Government of the country" should stand in as a woman's walī or guardian. Since the mufti only recognized government-appointed qadis, there were effectively no qadis in the Straits Settlements in February 1878 in his eyes. Hence, he believed, according to proper procedure, that Fatimah had no choice but to wait for her guardian to return, and the mufti chided her publicly in court for arranging her own marriage independent of her uncle's approval. He told the court that indeed Fatimah needed her guardian's consent in order to marry according to the stipulations of the Shafi'i legal school. Yet, to avoid this stipulation, she had converted to the Hanafi *madhhab*, which meant that her marriage could be validated by a qadi without the consent of her guardian. The mufti did not relent in the face of this new development in Fatimah's life, and clarified that a Shafi'i woman could indeed switch to another sect after attaining puberty, but she still had to ensure that the marriage was "koofoo" (*kafā'a*) or sufficient with a partner who was her equal. He emphasized that according to the laws of both the Hanafi and Shafi'i *madhhabs*, Indians, whom he referred to as "Klings," and Malays were not equal to the Arabs, and therefore Fatimah's marriage to Ismail was null and void.

In response to the mufti's testimony, Sidgreaves boldly set himself up to be a rival "mufti" by citing no less than three legal manuals that had been produced in British India, namely William Hay Macnaghten's *Principles of Hindu and Mohammadan Law*, John Baillie's *A Digest of Mohummudan Law*, and Shama Churun Sircar's *The Muhammadan Law*.[36] He dismissed the Arab mufti's notion of equality of marriage, since he did not see this as a concern "amongst Muslims outside of Arabia," without explanation, and instead referred to a case in Bombay High Court Reports in 1864.[37] He stated:

> The Hanifites hold that a girl who arrives at puberty, without having been married by her father or guardian, is then legally emancipated from all guardianship, and can select a husband without reference to his wishes. The Shafites, on the other hand, hold that a virgin, whether before or after puberty, cannot give herself in marriage without the consent of her father. The effect of a lawful change from the sect of Shafi to that of Hanifa, would be to emancipate the girl, who had arrived at puberty, from the control of her father, and to enable her to marry without consulting his wishes or obtaining his consent.[38]

He ended his judgment with the following words:

> Now the words used here "legally emancipated from all guardianship" and "can select a husband without reference to his wishes" are very strong, and, it appears to me, that I should be acting in direct contravention of this decision, if I held that, on the ground of inequality, this girl Fatimah was still subject to her guardian, and that she could not select a husband without reference to his wishes.[39]

The judge dismissed the mufti's ruling and ruled that Fatimah's marriage to Ismail was indeed valid.

Prior to *Salmah and Fatimah v. Soolong*, attempts to import Anglo-Mohamedan Law encountered limitations in the Straits Settlements. It was only in 1871 that Judge William Hackett implied that a "great many cases decided in India were cited by [a British lawyer in Singapore] but these cases are no authority here; as they were decided on the Mahomedan law which is not in force here."[40] Hence, it was remarkable that Sidgreaves now referred to several texts in that tradition a mere seven years later. He likely felt empowered by the memorial submitted by Muslim colonial subjects in 1875 requesting a heavier colonial hand in cases involving Islamic law and believed he had access to a century of British colonial experience in administering Islamic law. During the late eighteenth century, the process of streamlining Islamic law was hastened by codification that had already been systematically conducted under the aegis of modernization and centralization in British India.[41] British legal administrators in the Straits Settlements derived strength and confidence from a new hybrid mixture known as Anglo-Mahomedan Law, comprising both Islamic law and English law, created by their predecessors in India. This new set of laws had been compiled in a corpus of legal codes, commentaries, translations, and judicial precedents that their predecessors had accumulated since the late eighteenth century in South Asia. The process of codification of Islamic law in the British Empire occurred in two phases, the first beginning in the late eighteenth century under the auspices of the East India Company, followed by a second phase from the 1860s onward directly overseen by the metropolitan state.[42] The Charter of George II in 1753 had already granted Hindu and Muslim subjects exemption from company courts, allowing them to have recourse to their own religious laws.[43] In 1772, Governor Warren Hastings introduced the Adalat system, a watershed moment in the legal history of British India.[44] Subsequently, matters of inheritance, marriage, caste, and other religious institutions fell under the purview of religious laws, since Hastings believed that certain beliefs should be respected instead of being kept under the control of English common law, of which he thought subject populations were wholly ignorant.[45] The Adalat system made it compulsory for local Muslim and Hindu religious experts to function as juriconsults (legal experts) to assist English officers in both criminal courts and civil courts—known as the Mofussil Diwani Adalat—in Bengal, Bihar, and Orissa.[46] In this way, the Hastings regulations subtly introduced a new legal fulcrum—English legal authority—around which Hindu and Muslim religious laws pivoted.[47]

The last four decades of the nineteenth century also witnessed the prolific production of legal textbooks, digests, and jurisprudential works that led to further consolidation and refinement of legal ideology in the early twentieth century.[48] Pure textual authority ran counter to the Islamic legal tradition, where the authority of the legal interpreter (judge) and the legal interpretation did not yield a system of codes and precedents that oriented future legal decisions.[49] By contrast, the traditional method of Islamic jurisprudence involved extensive references to the Qur'an, hadiths, and legal opinions of Muslim jurists and scholars, which were often diverse and contradictory. In other words, the precolonial Islamic legal milieu was characterized by a multiplicity of systems with no fixed authoritative body of law, no set of binding precedents, and no single legitimate way of applying or changing them. In the process of colonial codification and translation, traditional religious literature, which was filled with rich jurisprudential ruminations and conflicting legal opinions, was reduced to collections of binding legal precedents. Colonial legal literature removed complications and subtleties in certain areas of law that were regarded by colonial authorities as extraneous or even cumbersome. Translators admitted that translations were done precisely to clarify ambiguities in the text and to choose the "correct" opinion among contradictory ones.[50] Inconsistencies in Islamic legal texts were not regarded as a mark of rich diversity but as signs that Muslim religious elite were either ignorant of the subject matter or "carried the law in their heads" anyway, which precluded proper legal codes in writing.[51] Codified laws in India and translated legal texts collectively known as Anglo-Mohamedan Law supposedly applied to all Muslim subjects regardless of their historical and cultural background.[52]

Hanafi laws prevailed throughout the empire wherever Hanafi-based Anglo-Mohamedan laws were exported, even in Southeast Asia, where Shafi'i adherents predominated. Even as late as 1940, Faiz Tyabji's list of recommended books for courtroom use by English legal practitioners contained thirteen titles on the Hanafi *madhhab* specifically, but only five on Shafi'i *madhhab*.[53] The Shafi'is received relatively little attention in colonial literature on the whole, since there were fewer adherents to the *madhhab* within British India. R. K. Wilson's five-hundred-page digest of Anglo-Muhammadan laws only dedicated thirty-two pages to Shafi'i law.[54] Indian laws were inherited in whole as the bases of authority because Hanafi and Shafi'i *madhhabs* were perceived to share many similarities. Thus, in the eyes of British legal administrators, there was no need to devise a whole other legal code based on Shafi'i laws.[55]

Although the weight of Anglo-Mohamedan Law formed the basis of Islamic law in the Straits Settlements, to a great extent, Islamic law was devised in situ, in courtrooms, where litigation provided occasions for dialogue between the colonizers and colonized.[56] E. C. Howard's translation of the definitive Shafi'i legal text, *Minhāj al-ṭālibīn,* in 1914 was one of the few attempts by a British official based in the Malay world to produce a work on Islamic law.[57] Shafi'i legal doctrine was discovered on a case-by-case basis by colonial legal practitioners, like in the case of *Salmah and Fatimah v. Soolong* in 1878. Over time, legal precedents established a binding legal corpus in the English common law tradition. From the perspective of legislation, British colonial authorities' universal conception of Islamic law prevailed. Local customary laws that were not deemed part of Islamic law were not recognized in legislation, with only two exceptions—the Malacca Customary Land Law and laws of joint marital property. In British India, legal codification had already undermined the Islamic classical tradition. Codification of the shari'a had enabled authorities to neatly sidestep the plurality of legal opinions held by Muslim scholars and, eventually, ignore the spectrum of legal interpretations on a single issue. Despite an awareness of key differences between the schools of law, especially with regard to family law (such as the need for guardians' permission for marriages), British legal authorities did not create a separate legal code anywhere else in the empire. Arab subjects in the Straits Settlements too yearned for the universality of Islamic law, but of another kind. Anglo-Mohamedan law, based on Hanafi law and English common law, was not what they had in mind, but this was what they obtained.

The case of *Salmah and Fatimah v. Soolong* in 1878 was the most significant case concerning Islamic law that immediately preceded the passing of the Mahomedan Marriage Ordinance of 1880. The courtroom proceedings boosted British confidence in the Straits Settlements and made them more receptive to the idea of direct intervention in Islamic law in the colony; it also bolstered the Arabs' view of the inadequacy of the qadis as religious authorities, their possible corruption, and unfair alliances between the qadis and some women based in the colony, such as Fatimah, who was allowed to marry a non-Arab by a qadi. The case revealed that the authority of the British judges clearly superseded that of muftis who might be called as an expert witness in British courts but in effect had neither real power nor influence. Sidgreaves in particular appeared rankled by the mufti's opinions because they contradicted his own interpretations of Hanafi law. *Salmah and Fatimah v. Soolong* also affected the colonial legal administration's view of Islamic law in the colony. Court proceedings in the case of *Salmah and Fatimah v. Soolong* brought to light the copious amount of materials on Islamic law already at hand, albeit mostly pertaining to Hanafi law, inherited from British India. Ironically, because Salmah had converted to the Hanafi school of law, *Salmah and Fatimah v. Soolong* turned out to be an exceptional opportunity for a British judge in the Straits Settlements, since most Muslims in the region actually belonged to the Shafi'i school of law.[58] Subsequent attempts by judges to impose Anglo-Mohamedan law in the colony met with limitations.

Finally, in 1880, an ordinance to "provide for the registration of Marriages and Divorces among Mahomedans" was passed. The ordinance not only provided for the appointment of qadis but also defined the modifications of "the Laws of Property to be recognized in the case of Mahomedan Marriages." More specifically, the ordinance had three parts—the first part providing for the registration of marriages and divorces so as to facilitate proof in court, the second for the recognition of qadis appointed by the Muslim public, and the third to deal with the rights of widows and children of Muslims who died intestate.[59] It came into operation on December 1, 1882, two years after its promulgation. More commonly referred to as the Mahomedan Marriage Bill, it restricted the purview of the qadi to matters of marriage and divorce only.

The Mohamedan Marriage Ordinance was an enormous commitment for the British colonial government to undertake because these practices were unprecedented in the British Empire. Being ahead of British India in this respect caused anxiety, a sign of imperial hierarchy. There was no ready template to implement, no colonial model to emulate. The writer of the legislative report nervously noted that

> under these circumstances, clearly the only course open for our Legislature is to await the passage of this law, in order that we may profit by the wider experience of India, and reap the benefit of the legal talent that will be brought to bear upon the Bill before it becomes law. We should thus be afforded some fixed data for the preparation of a similar law for this Colony, instead of groping in the dark, as we shall otherwise be compelled to do.[60]

Although Arab elites had invoked their prerogative as British imperial subjects to firm up colonial jurisdictions over their lives and the lives of their fellow Muslims through state bureaucracy, the British government dreaded being an anomaly vis-à-vis India, and this fear held them back from forging more radical changes that would deepen colonial structures. Imperial territories were interconnected and interdependent, but they were organized vertically as well.[61] The attorney-general of the Straits Settlements, Thomas Braddell, confessed to the India Office in London that he was deeply uncomfortable with the proposed ordinance, which he considered to be of "a very special character" because it required British officials to recognize qadis.[62] Qadis in British India were not even appointed by "the Indian Government with all its experience, and it would therefore be unsafe as the result could not be known."[63]

The Legislative Council worried that

in addition to a numerous native population from various parts of India and Arabia, we have the Malay element, in which each clan adheres to its own customs; and in case of intermarriages among these clans, which are not infrequent, intricate questions arise, and failing an amicable settlement of the differences between husband and wife and their relatives, the disputants appeal to our courts of law for a final adjustment,—only to find however, that the law can render them no assistance.[64]

Braddell stressed that the Mahomedan Marriage Ordinance was not compulsory because "the lower classes of Muslims" would not find it easy to register their marriages, in contrast to "the higher classes of Arabs" who happened to be the main class of memorialists clamoring for compulsory laws.[65] Unlike in the Netherlands Indies, class, rather than race, was the defining factor that divided Muslim society. While the Arab elite in parts of Java also complained about being unfairly separated from their wives by local qadis through divorce, their requests to establish separate jurisdictions for themselves and their families were not acceded to by Dutch authorities because their spouses were mostly classified as Natives. In the Straits Settlements and Malaya, inter-ethnic marriages were common too, and at the turn of the twentieth century, Frank Swettenham observed, "In all the Malay States these so-called Arab families are to be found, sprung originally from a wandering Seyyid, who, either recently or remotely, had visited Malaya and taken a wife from the rest of the people."[66] The difference was that Muslim subject populations were officially classified as whole without ethnic differentiation in the Straits Settlements. Reservations revolving around class within Muslim subject population led the Legislative Council to stop short of officially appointing qadis, preferring instead to only recognize existing qadis as a precaution. Because the 143 memorialists were in the minority as members of the upper classes (their status as ethnic minorities was acknowledged but downplayed), their demands were not entirely met. They had to be contented with the fact that the Mahomedan Marriage Ordinance would simply place qadis squarely within colonial bureaucracy—officially as "deputy Registrars of Muslim marriages," in effect as colonial civil servants who kept records in either Malay or English.[67]

The council held on to the view that bureaucracy over religious affairs would not be accessible to lower classes, thus acknowledging the potential alienating powers of bureaucracy for the majority of colonial subjects.

Primarily, Braddell and the rest of the Legislative Council were reluctant to accede to the memorialists' demands in 1875 to prevent upper-class subjects from gaining an advantage over the rest of the colonial population. There was another reason for their hesitation—it was certainly not because of lack of expertise or fear of unrest, since they already interpreted Islamic law in some capacity in certain cases in the colony, at times undercutting local Muslim authority in the process. Rather, their skittishness about interfering in Muslim religious affairs stemmed more from nervousness in overstepping British Indian colonial policy. Less than a decade after being divorced administratively from Calcutta, what British legislative authorities in the Straits Settlements feared was going down a path that had not been trodden before in British India, which still had a hold over the minds of administrators in the Straits Settlements.

General caution regarding Muslim affairs pervaded the entire British Empire, where officials often warned each other not to overstep although boundaries were constantly being tested. In 1911, a Muslim reader who identified as "a Mohamedan" reiterated this point when he stated that: "The Mohamedans, as you know, Sir, have a great dislike of outside interference in their religious affairs. This is quite natural. They allow you to legislate in other directions, but touch their religion and you tamper with their most sensitive feeling."[68]

It was only in 1936 that the governor of the Straits Settlements appointed a qadi in each settlement of Penang, Malacca, and Singapore, with limited jurisdiction, as his decisions were subjected to the registrar under the governor's supreme authority.[69] From this perspective, the British appointment of qadis in 1880 might seem like a minor tweak to an ongoing historical practice at the time, but this request in itself went against the authority of Muslim communities who entrusted themselves to pick the most suitable person among them for this important role. The memorial in 1875 that resulted in the Mohamedan Marriage Ordinance granted colonial authorities yet more license to assert singular voices on religious issues, hence undermining the multiple voices by muftis and qadis even more through the entry of the corpus of Anglo-Mohamedan legal codes and literature. We glimpsed how Sidgreaves dismissed the Johor mufti's thoughtful opinion in the case of *Salmah and Fatimah v. Soolong* because he had access to this corpus. From 1882 onwards, muftis and qadis were no longer consulted in Straits Settlements courts as their opinions became irrelevant. Thereafter, armed with statutes, legal codes, and local precedents, colonial judges usurped the authority of qadis and muftis as they ratified marriages and divorces and presided over more cases involving Islamic law. Historically, opinions of qadis and muftis were not binding and were continually open to challenge. Neither were they enforceable without the state's authority in most settings. According to the colonial legal hierarchy, the opinions of British judges were final and could not be challenged further because their legal decisions were legally binding in the English common law tradition.

The Case of Fatimah bin Obudh bin Salleh bin Abdad

By appealing to colonial administrators to chip away at the authority of local Muslim legal judges because they were granting women too many divorces, Arab elites stripped marriage to its barest structure—an arrangement of power. Their actions cut deep at the religious sphere, which was already restricted to family law in the colony. Family law was the last sliver of freedom enjoyed by colonial subjects; it was this that the memorialists were so eager to yield to colonial authorities. The principal motivation for their actions was the management of property and kin. Property was the defining quality that determined the outcome of family law, and there was an undertow of bias against women inheriting both money and power. Since women do inherit and control their own property according to Islamic law, Arab women in mercantile families had to explicitly appoint someone if they wished to delegate the administration of their property. They signed documents and gave testimonies in courtrooms, much to the discomfort of judges unaccustomed to women handling their own affairs. Because women rarely spoke in open court, more weight tended to be ascribed to them when they did. There was a certain kind of power that their words yielded, and litigants, judges, and lawyers were not indifferent to it. Yet they remained nervous about women's wide latitude for action, especially if they boldly went against the wishes of their legal guardians. Women's liberty was seen as corrosion of virtue. In 1924, the complicated case of Fatimah Abdad, which took place over three separate trials, crystalized these attitudes. Her story, which she told herself in open court, was a tale of financial resources and property being forcibly withheld.

Fatimah bin Obudh bin Salleh bin Abdad was the widow of the wealthy Shaikh Abdullah bin Sayeed bin Marie of Batavia, who died just short of seventy years old on March 10, 1920.[70] On March 16, 1922, letters of administration of Shaikh Abdullah's estate and effects in Singapore were granted to Fatimah and his second widow, Shaikha binte Jaafar bin Omar bin Abdul Aziz, by the Supreme Court of the Straits Settlements of Singapore.[71] Shortly afterwards, Fatimah followed her father, who had become her guardian following her husband's death, to Cheribon, another city in Java.[72] While there she supposedly granted her father a power of attorney. Consequently, her father managed all her affairs with regard to her deceased husband's estate and brought her various documents to sign.[73] Sometime in 1922 or 1923, Fatimah returned to Singapore with the intention of remarrying and was shocked to discover a deed in the Registry of Deeds purporting to be a gift from her to her father of her share in the property of her deceased husband. A contract of sale was also produced in court that supposedly proved that she had transferred her share of the estate of her deceased husband to her father. Fatimah claimed that she did not understand the contents of the contract of sale when it was shown to her, although she did sign it.[74] She denied she had received the amount of money from her father, an amount that was "grossly inadequate anyway."[75] Her father, the defendant, however claimed that she was in fact fully cognizant of the contents of the document when she signed it. He also claimed that the 30,000 guilders had been paid to her in the form of jewelry and property in Arabia, which included a date farm.

In December 1924, Fatimah sued her father, Shaikh Obudh bin Salleh bin Abdad, for making her sign a document that, unbeknownst to her, was a contract of sale to him for 30,000 guilders (in interest) out of the estate of her late husband.[76] Counsel claimed that Shaikh Obud had effectively bought this land from her, not knowing its exact value. Shaikh Obud then took a considerable share in the property and put the rest in trust for twenty-one years for her and her brothers without taking a cent for his own benefit. Intent on projecting an image of a dutiful father, Shaikh Obudh vehemently stated in court that his daughter was the one who had offered to sell her share of the estate to him.[77]

After hearing of her husband's death, Fatimah's cousin Shaik Esah bin Omar bin Abdad arrived from Arabia with the intention of marrying her in Batavia. Fatimah accepted his proposal and stated in court that she intended to go to Arabia with him after selling her estates in Singapore and Batavia. However, moments before her marriage, a member of the Arab community pointed out that because her prospective husband was the foster-child of her deceased husband, the marriage could not occur since he was within the prohibited degrees of consanguinity or affinity with the bride.[78] Consequently, Fatimah decided not to marry Shaik Esah, nor to sell her estates in Singapore and Batavia. Instead, she married another man, identified only as a Sayyid, a descendant of the Prophet, causing "very considerable offence" to her family at the end of 1923.[79] Shaik Obudh certainly did not approve of his daughter's marriage to the latter and admitted that if the marriage had been proposed through him, he "could have seen the man and satisfied himself," but since she had been previously married she did not need his consent.

Successive judges in colonial courts had trouble dealing with Fatimah's agency even as she offered her lucid testimony right there in court. Her lawyer claimed that in the Supreme Court, "everybody knew how cognizant of business matters was the average Arab woman"—a claim that went unchallenged by opposing counsel and in public press.[80] True enough, Fatimah had entered into a partnership with her husband's other wife, Shaikha Jaffar bin Omar bin Abdul Aziz, who had two daughters with him and a grandson.[81] Together with Shaikha Jaffar and her progeny, Fatimah had transferred power of attorney to two men, Abdullah bin Salman bin Marie and his son Soliman bin Abdullah bin Salman bin Marie, in 1920.[82] In July 1922, she bought back her deceased husband's property at auctions worth a total of $10,900 in Singapore dollars.[83]

Despite handling her own business, she did not escape being subjected to condescending remarks by British lawyers and judges. Throughout the trial, the judge presiding over the case, Chief Justice Walter Shaw, displayed a strong protective impulse toward Fatimah. He repeatedly implied that Shaikh Esah, the former prospective groom, had come all the way from Arabia in order to marry her because he heard that she was a wealthy widow, especially since he had been eager to marry her even without seeing her, although this was actually common practice. Nonetheless, Shaikh Esah and Fatimah's father, Shaikh Obudh, refuted the judge's insinuation that the marriage was motivated by money. Chief Justice Shaw then moved on to cast doubt on the documentary evidence presented to him because he did not believe they represented Fatimah's wishes. He stated that it was obvious that the contract of sale, for example, could not be allowed to stand as it was executed by Fatimah without her having independent advice at all, causing her to assign all her rights in a very valuable estate to her father in consideration of the payment of the sum of 30,000 guilders. Moreover, further enquiries showed that no such sum had ever been paid to Fatimah. In fact, Fatimah stated that he had only given her 25 cents a day for expenses. In addition, he also believed that Shaikh Obudh had only a vague and doubtful right in the date plantation in Arabia since he could not prove possession for the last thirty years and Fatimah had never seen the date plantation after all. The chief justice's suspicions of the defendant were exacerbated by the fact Shaikh Obudh had mortgaged Fatimah's estate for a sum of $10,000, which had been lent to him. In other words, Fatimah's credit was already being pledged for the return of this money. Being far from convinced by the defendant's argument that he wished to protect his daughter, and harboring deep sympathy for Fatimah, Chief Justice Walter Shaw predictably ruled in her favor.[84]

Although the case against her father was won by Fatimah, the outcome was actually decided upon by the very little she could provide. Despite being the one who initiated legal action against her father, in court, Fatimah responded "I do not know" or "I don't remember" to several of the counsel's questions. As a result, even Chief Justice Walter Shaw agreed that what she actually remembered was worth very little.[85] The counsel for the defendant also faulted her for being very inconsistent in her testimonies.[86] Accordingly, press reports placed little emphasis on what she said and chose to describe her physical appearance and mannerisms in court in vivid dramatic detail with roman à clef minutiae.[87] One report stated that she was dressed in "picturesque native costume" and kept her face closely veiled. Another described her as "a striking figure" who had exchanged her brilliant red head scarf (*tudung kepala*) for one of a "striking Tartan creation which would have turned many a Scot green with envy." In the third trial in September 1926, she entered the court of the second police magistrate, "veiled from the top of her head to her slippered feet." Her father demanded that she should uncover so that he could be sure that she was her daughter, and not some other woman. Whenever she was in the witness box, she had to be persuaded with difficulty to remove her face veil.[88] After much persuasion from the counsel for the prosecution and from the bench, she "peeped out shyly from under her silken cover."[89] She also claimed could not hire a white male lawyer without her father being present, leading to her ignorance of the contents of the paper she signed, which in turn allowed her father to look after her business.

In contrast to Chief Justice Walter Shaw, Acting Chief Justice P. J. Sproule, in the second trial in October 1925, was less convinced about the amount of protection Fatimah needed against her father, her current husband, and, possibly, future husbands. In arguing his case, the defendant's lawyer, Page, highlighted his client's obligation as a father to a Muslim woman who had been twice divorced and once widowed. The lawyer crudely painted a bleak portrait when he said, "She might pass through the hands of a dozen husbands in a dozen years, and it might be that there was an intention here to protect this lady's property from a future husband." This implied that marriage was considered the only context in which Fatimah, a woman with income, could work out her destiny. Stevens, Fatimah's lawyer, argued that the onus was upon her father to establish that there was not undue influence exercised in causing the plaintiff to make the deed of a gift to her father.[90] According to him, it was for a parent to prove that parental influence did not taint the gift.[91] Page however argued that the presumption of undue influence was an English rule applicable only to English people. "These people were not English, nor was a daughter who had already been three times married in a position to require protection." This implied that surviving three husbands formed an adequate education for a woman toward achieving self-sufficiency. So was Fatimah a helpless woman in need of protection, or an independent worldly woman who could manage her own affairs and transfer authority on her own wisdom? Page clarified his stand:

> She was capable of knowing her own mind, at any rate, but under Mohamedan Law the property of a wife passes to her husband, although it passes back on divorce. She is in an entirely different position to the ordinary married English girl.

Judge Sproule was unconvinced and rebutted:

> Surely a Mohamedan woman has her property separate from her husband. Mohamed decreed that a thousand years before the Married Women's Property Act.

Page remained undaunted:

> In the case of an English girl it would be an unnatural and unexpected thing for her to hand over her property to anybody. In the case of a Mohamedan woman, unaccustomed to collecting rents in a different country [she was resident in Java] it was perfectly natural for her to hand over her property to male relatives to be administered.

In 1926, at the conclusion of the third trial, the second police magistrate forced Shaik Obudh to sign a bond of good behavior for a year, a lenient punishment on account of the "bitter fate" that he had already endured during trial. He also urged Shaik Obudh to leave his daughter alone since she appeared to be quite capable of looking after herself. The trial ended and we hear no more of Fatimah's adventures in court, until May 1939 when it was briefly mentioned that she sued another Arab man named Syed Mohamed bin Aidross Albahar.[92] Because the cases garnered much public interest, we are able to see how legal courts empowered male family members who asserted their authority in their roles as male guardians. Fatimah's emotional life within and outside her marriage was strictly regulated by her father and other male relatives. Although all parties involved in the case concurred that she was an independent businesswoman legally able to contract her own affairs, her identity was used against her to imply that she was not capable or not acting as a free agent. The historian Julia Stephens highlights how women in purdah were disadvantaged in secular courts in India, which marginalized Indian women's position within financial markets by overdetermining their isolation and applying it to their economic affairs as well.[93] It did not help that Fatimah's father harnessed state anxiety about Muslim women to his advantage. Poor business choices were common, but somehow she was simultaneously held to higher standards and deemed preternaturally vulnerable without actual evidence of her failures. Her marriage choices, past and future, were also cast as suspect. Alternatingly helpless and empowered, Fatimah provided great titillating fodder for the public press, who stuck closely to stock representations of women: she sued her father—how emotional; she made poor decisions—how predictable.

Cases like Fatimah's involving wealthy Arabs garnered a lot of attention in Singapore and Malaya because of the amount of property at stake, which heightened courtroom drama. In 1921, a case involving the prominent Alsagoff family in Singapore caused an uproar among Muslim subjects. Justice Fiennes Cecil Arthur Barrett-Lennard offended Muslim subjects by directly criticizing Islamic law regarding marriage and divorce.[94] The case that triggered Barrett-Lennard's censure revolved around the pronouncement of *talaq*, which, the lawyer H. D. Mundell helpfully informed him in court, need not be conveyed to the wife by the husband for the divorce to be valid.[95] Pronouncement of talaq, the unilateral declaration of divorce by men, was jealously guarded by male Muslim colonial subjects because it formed the narrow bastion of autonomy they had over the household that still remained under the purview of Islamic law. Not only did the trial attract a lot of attention in court but a partial transcript of the highlights of the trial was reproduced in the newspaper *The Straits Times*.[96] It revealed an antagonistic line of questioning aimed at castigating Islamic law, which went as follows:

> At one stage during Mr. Mundell's exposition of the Mohamedan law regarding divorce Mr. Justice Barrett-Lennard observed it seems monstrous when no intimation of the divorce is conveyed to the unfortunate wife, and the child is brought up believing the man to be his father under the law as well as in fact, heir perhaps to a great estate and then suddenly to learn he is illegitimate.

> MUNDELL: It does seem wrong indeed but it is the law my lord [in response to Barrett-Lennard's incredulity]
> JUSTICE BARRETT-LENNARD: Monstrous law at that.

> Arguing on the pronounce of the talak Mr. Mundell said divorce took effect from the pronouncement of the talak, or the date of writing, and the fact of non-communication to the wife did not in any way alter it.

> CHIEF JUSTICE: No particular time in which notice to the wife should be given.

Mr. Mundell reiterated that divorce took effect from the pronouncement and the effect of the non-communication did not affect the divorce
but the question of maintenance. He quoted authorities in support of
his arguments, and then went on to cite a case in which the husband
gave notice to his wife and she avoided him.

> CHIEF JUSTICE: That is just what the other side say.
>
> JUSTICE BRANCH: I take it that if the talak is not pronounced in the
> presence of the woman you must pronounce it in the presence
> of some recognized official.

Mr. Mundell submitted it was not essential.

> JUSTICE BARRETT-LENNARD: Should not the communication be
> made in the presence of witnesses, who would come forward
> and say "we heard the words spoken."
>
> CHIEF JUSTICE: If he said talak in the bath-room even if nobody was
> there, the fact that he told witnesses afterwards that he had tal-
> aked, would make the divorce absolute. The statement by a hus-
> band that he had talaked his wife was proof that he had done so.

Barrett-Lennard's criticism of Islamic law rankled Muslim subjects and
led to public protest in Singapore and the rest of Malaya. Colonial authorities were generally concerned about Muslim marriage, which was "so unlike
the indissoluble contract as known among Christians [that the Muslim man]
can dissolve the contract by divorcing his wife."[97] Although his criticism was
hardly new and even echoed that of Thomas Braddell in 1889, the problem
was that he did it in open court in a very high-profile case attended by hundreds of spectators.[98] More important, the Mohamedan Advisory Board that
had been formed in 1915 had accrued clout in the colony, its members being
the elite Muslim merchants of the day associated with the Alsagoff family
whose family life was being laid out bare in the courtroom. Newly arrived in
the colony, Barrett-Lennard was caught unawares by the collective leverage
of the Muslim community.[99] Widespread Muslim resentment led Laurence
Guillemard to write a letter to Winston Churchill, who was then secretary
of state for the colonies, to remove him as judge in Singapore, underlining
previous indiscretions as well against the Muslim community in the Straits
Settlements prior to 1921.[100] He warned,

> While the educated portion of the Mohamedan community will re-
> alise that such conduct as is the subject of this protest cannot possibly
> obtain the approval of His Majesty, the more ignorant sections of the
> Community are prone to attribute to the words of officers holding

high positions an importance and a sanction which they may not merit. The dangers that may arise from such conduct at the present time are too obvious to need elaboration.[101]

Eventually, Barrett-Lennard was privately censured by Guillemard, and he in turn angrily accused Guillemard, who retorted, "It does not make for public security or good Government when a Judge by the frequency and tone of this stricture, conveys the impression to the Oriental races inhabiting this Colony that they are living under unjust laws or under conditions which a decent Government would not tolerate."[102] It would be unwise, Guillemard had explained in his letter to Churchill, to "under-rate the mischief which may be worked and the unrest which may be fomented in a mixed community of sensitive and excitable Orientals."[103] Barrett-Lennard remained unrepentant and wrote to Guillemard that "When the judgments are delivered, Your Excellency will doubtless not only know what the Prophet himself wrote, but also the malediction ascribed to him by the Creator."[104] His retort, along with Sproule's glib comment about the Prophet's decree a thousand years before the Married Women's Property Act, suggest a sense of ownership over Islamic law by the 1920s, though not without strong overtones of derision.

As in the Netherlands Indies, the main seed of discontent among Arab subjects was marriage, and the momentum for transformation was fueled by cases involving women in Arab households. Anxiety about their domestic lives suffused the actions of the Arab elite so much so that they were willing to supplant the authority of local qadis who had formed pillars of support for their families based in the region. By weaponizing moral outrage against qadis, memorialists ultimately persuaded British authorities to bureaucratize qadi records, monitor their actions, and ratify their appointments. The Arab elite was directly implicated in the erasure of indigenous autonomy and, subsequently, authority. They might not have known it at the time, but the Mohamedan Marriage Ordinance of 1880 marked the crest of the wave of changes initiated by Muslim subjects.[105] Thereafter, Arab litigants managed to change law over several decades in a limited fashion only by establishing legal precedent in the English common law tradition. They did not manage to do so in a purposeful manner but simply because they formed the majority of litigants in colonial cases involving Islamic law.[106] Just like in Victorian England where privacy was fading between a legal system that insisted upon transparency and a burgeoning and relentless press in the nineteenth century, we see this phenomenon developing in the Straits Settlements too as both law reports and the public press doggedly provided details of cases on family strife.[107]

Qadis' view of viable marriages between two Muslims did not gel with Arabs' extreme view of *kafā'a* (sufficiency in marriage), based entirely on notions of race and descent and preoccupied with ensuring female descendants only marry male descendants of the Prophet, although economic class was a major factor.[108] In the words of a former mufti of Singapore, "[Marrying a fellow Arab] was more just to ensure that the daughter will be well taken care of and her status is preserved."[109] A fatwa from a raad agama (religious court) in the Netherlands Indies state that such marriages between a non-descendant and a descendant were permissible although reprehensible (*makrūh*).[110]

The Arab elite did not consider their alliance with the British colonial government stigmatizing. At first glance, one might assume that they were cleverly associating with the strongest players in the colony who possessed political power—legal enforcement could only be guaranteed by the British after all. On a deeper level, this alliance allowed them to circumvent the authority of indigenous and local forms of power that had taken root in the colony over centuries. As much as the Arab elite courted the new source of political power provided by British colonial rule, they avoided having to rely on more established and legitimate forms of power that has been in the region for far longer. By appealing to colonial authorities, they effectively displaced local leadership.

Court cases reveal that Muslim women faced challenges in staving off paternalistic attitudes from lawyers and judges who doubted their legal capacity to act on their own, uncomfortable as they were with the reality that Islamic law accorded women possibly more freedom than English common law in some cases. British legal authorities shared the concerns of their colleagues across the empire on the question of talaq, which they believed greatly disadvantaged women, but they also displayed a tendency to fold daughters' and divorcés' lives back into those of their families, even when it was unnecessary in both Islamic law and English common law. Perhaps they saw this as a fulfillment of their roles as custodians of women's lives, which had superseded that of the qadis in the British Straits Settlements, as requested by some Muslim subjects in 1875.

The Mohamedan Marriage Ordinance granted what members of the Arab diaspora craved—accountability. While qadis in the Straits Settlements already kept registers, which were readily produced in courts, the Ordinance ensured that proper steps were taken to preserve documents and keep records in prescribed standard format in either English or Malay. Every month, each qadi had to appear before the registrar in order to deposit copies of all entries made in his register and index verified on oath.[111] However, even in 1922, forty years after the promulgation of the Mohamedan Marriage Ordinance, bureaucratization remained an aspiration, failing one of the court's frequent clients in a case involving the Alsagoff clan. The judge explained how the registrar was inadequate:

> I have felt considerable doubt what if any weight should be given to exhibit 8 which is a certified copy of what purports to be if an angry divorce by Syed Mohammed of his wife Asia effected on January 1 1896, or 16 Rajab 1313. The copy, and the original in the book of the registrar of Mohammedan Marriages which was made up from returns rendered monthly by the Mohammedan Registrar under the repealed Ordinance no. 5 of 1880 seems to be irregular in that the witnesses to the divorce and the witness identifying the husband do not appear to have signed. The original register kept by the Mohammedan Registrar cannot be found and all the persons who are said to have been present are dead. The date appears to be uncertain for the calendar gives the 16 Rejab 1313 to be January 2 1896 and not January 1. The date of Syed Mohammed's departure was agreed by the parties at the trial as being December 31 1895. The date however does not appear to be correct as the evidence seems to show that he left on 15th Rejab 1313 which the calendar shows was in fact January 1 1896. Altogether I think it would be best to place no reliance on the document.[112]

Despite the judge's acknowledgement of the limitations of paper records, he still relied on government bureaucratic record at the expense of verbal testimonies in court, a development cemented by the passing of the Mohamedan Marriage Ordinance. Paper became paramount.

CHAPTER 2

Surat Kuasa

Powers of Attorney across the Indian Ocean

Paper was a powerful conduit for the spread of jurisdictions in the late colonial period, compelling different authorities to recognize and heed the words of colonial subjects. In no other country was the instrument known as *surat kuasa* (lit: letter of power) used this often, a Dutch reporter of the colonial newspaper *De Sumatra Post* lamented in 1903.[1] *Surat kuasa* was the Malay and Indonesian term for power of attorney, probate, and letters of administration.[2] The power of attorney, also known as *volmacht* in Dutch, was such a popular device in the Dutch colony that when the sultan of Mukallā in Ḥaḍramawt kidnapped an Arab man originally from Surabaya in July 1932, he forced him to set up a power of attorney as ransom instead asking for cash.[3] The sultan specifically instructed the imprisoned man, Said Muhammad bin Omar Ba-Agil, to coerce his brother Syed Mochsen bin Omar Ba-Agil to give him (the sultan) power of attorney, which would allow him to benefit from the sale of real estate in Surabaya. He stood to gain fifty thousand rupees from the sale. At first, Said Muhammad refused to accede to the sultan's wishes, but the prospect of four years of imprisonment in Mukallā and the threat of being killed by the Sultan's skilled swordfighter quickly changed his mind. He pleaded to his brother Syed Mochsen to construct a power of attorney in the name of the sultan so that he and his son who was also kidnapped would be free from imprisonment. However, upon gaining freedom from the sultan, Said Muhammad refused to compensate his brother for the ransom paid for his freedom. Betrayed, his brother angrily went to the Dutch colonial court of justice (Raad van Justitie) in Surabaya to institute a civil claim against his brother. To Syed Mochsen's astonishment, the court was willing to rule in Said Muhammad's favor, if he could prove that he was indeed under imminent threat of death in Mukallā and that during his imprisonment he had warned Syed Mochsen not to open documents from Mukallā that were not from him. This warning, the court stated, would be taken as proof that Said Muhammad had looked out for his brother's welfare to prevent him from being further disadvantaged. The court also strongly encouraged Syed Mochsen to not open any correspondence from Mukallā—including from his brother, who stayed on in Mukallā—from then onward as a precaution. In this instance, the Dutch colonial court attempted to cut off links between Mukallā and Surabaya by simply pretending they did not exist. The court was after all conveniently powerless to enforce legal action across the Indian Ocean. In this dramatic case involving the uppermost echelons of Ḥaḍramī society, we glimpse the limitations of powers of attorney in that they could be blatantly snubbed—simply and absurdly by disavowal of connections.

Yet the device was commonly utilized among members of the Arab diaspora, whose frequent usage of the power of attorney caused it to become durable in multiple jurisdictions. Time lag remained an issue to be remedied by powers of attorney, which served as a corrective to lapses by errant or careless trustees. Upon his mother's death, Shaikh Omar Bayasout of Inat in Ḥaḍramawt appointed Syed Omar bin Mohamed Alsagoff to handle her property and inserted a clause urging him to try and recover her property, which suggests that some of it had already been lost by the time the power of attorney was prepared.[4] Each power of attorney produced in Ḥaḍramawt became legally binding in both British and Dutch colonies in Southeast Asia, and its specific terms and demands could not be cast aside easily, as the Ba-Agil ransom case demonstrates. No matter the outcome, it was impossible for a court of law to be indifferent to a power of attorney because it compelled action by law. As this case of ransom demonstrates, only in legal courts could they be repudiated, and even there with great difficulty. Moreover, universally the power of attorney was a commonplace legal tool that granted users greater latitude for action transcending vast distances and was therefore similar to other contracts which transferred power from one person to another. After all, genuine problems in the realm of commerce constantly demanded expedient solutions. *Wakala* contracts in which an agent (*wakil*) establishes contractual relations between a principal and a third party have been widely used for centuries in the Islamic world.[5] Likewise, Ḥaḍramī merchants were experienced at using contracts to appoint agents in their stead, since they held property across the Indian Ocean.

Standardization

The wealthy Arab elite harnessed colonial legal resources in the form of powers of attorney infused with new British and Dutch legal idioms to manage their wealth across the Indian Ocean, but they still operated within a familiar procedural framework. Although powers of attorney were inscribed with the authority of colonial governments without necessarily accepting their legitimacy over other areas, they were potent precisely because they had the power to generate and subsequently firm up jurisdictions. Signatories were bound to abide by the conventions of European colonial law, enabling its thrust into their lives and their property even further. Whether the Arab diaspora intended it or not, the wide proliferation of powers of attorney likely contributed to the material infrastructure of colonial governments and perpetuated norms that eventually led to the expansion of colonial jurisdictions over time. On one level, each power of attorney oriented toward colonies in Southeast Asia was a document that essentially recognized and confirmed mercantile and kinship ties across the Indian Ocean. The normal operation of bureaucracies lies precisely in depoliticizing structural conflict, as Akhil Gupta highlights.[6] To some extent, a power of attorney conveyed this semblance of neutrality because procedural rules shielded from view structural inequalities that ran through bureaucracy. On the other hand, metatext in the form of qadis' seals in Ḥaḍramawt or Mecca and stamps in British and Dutch colonial courts betray the constant need for validity for these documents to be effective in the first place.[7] This metatext infused these documents with power since they functioned as emblems of law and legal institutions. Not all forms of metatext were equal in weight and effect since they had different functions and symbolized the power of diverse authorities that varied by location. Each element of the metatext was pegged to a legal requirement that users imagined were requirements of the colonial legal institutions that were supposed to ratify these documents. Consequently, metatext produced by colonial courts confirmed their legitimacy in the colonies as well as in Ḥaḍramawt. Collectively, these legal accoutrements not only formed a common language across multiple jurisdictions that guaranteed validity in many diverse settings; they also provided graphic reminders of a drive toward standardization that was partially dictated by legal systems that were able to enforce the terms of the contracts on both sides of the Indian Ocean. Because there were no regulations on what made a power of attorney legally sound, the users themselves were the main drivers of standardization.

While powers of attorney were not translated in the Netherlands Indies unless challenged in court, in the British Straits Settlements each power of attorney had to be translated into English before entering probate. In the early twentieth century, some were translated from Arabic to English directly by an Albanian broker and commission agent with a British passport named Hussein Abdeen Effendi, a colorful, highly opinionated man who grew resentful of his clients, the wealthy Arabs whose documents he rendered into English. Most Arabic powers of attorney, however, were translated first into the Malay language in Jawi (Malay in Arabic script) by an Arab man named Shaikh Awad bin Saidan, and subsequently by one of three professional translators—N. M. Hashim, Haji Abdullah bin Omar, Alexander Phipps, or Ismail—from Malay into English.[8] All translators above had been recognized by the Supreme Court as reliable and had their own declaration appended to each power of attorney and translation. Without exception, each translator stated: "I made this solemn declaration conscientiously believing the same to be true and by virtue of the Provisions of The Statutory Declaration Act 1835." While Hussein Abdeen Effendi and Shaikh Awad bin Saidan did their translation work in their own private offices, the other translators were based in the Supreme Court of the Straits Settlements, which suggested that they were directly employed by British colonial court. Arabic translators were not needed often enough to warrant full-time employment by the courts of the Straits Settlements, which is rather surprising considering that numerous powers of attorney poured in from Ḥaḍramawt. In the Straits Settlements, translators practiced economy of language because their primary aim was to make powers of attorney more legible in colonial jurisdictions. Lengthy prayers that opened and closed powers of attorney produced in Arabia were eliminated in subsequent Malay and English translations. References to shari'a were consistently translated as "Mohamedan law," a term that Muslims found offensive but that was commonly used throughout the British Empire to refer to Islamic law, so the choice of this translation likely spoke to legibility in a colonial setting. Similarly, the word *nazar* or "will" that appeared in some original Arabic versions was translated as power of attorney because, in effect, that was its function in the colony.

As an object that lies at the junction of colonial law and subjects' rights, the power of attorney is a very distinct expression of legality. Despite conforming to colonial requirements, a power of attorney still forms a unique historical source produced by the willing hand of the colonial subjects or people outside colonial jurisdictions voluntarily linking themselves to colonial jurisdictions. Power of attorney in colonial settings was a powerful proclamation of an individual's agency in the face of European colonialism, even while extending its hold over their lives. Whether written in the first or third person, each document was a personal declaration of intent that colonial authorities had to not only acknowledge but also heed. Each document was unalterable, to be obeyed, and insisted on the sanction of the accreditation of colonial legal institutions. Remarkably, despite the distinctly different thresholds of legal authenticity involved, legal authorities in both the Straits Settlements and the Netherlands Indies readily notarized these documents produced by Muslims in Arabia and Southeast Asia and generally did not doubt their authenticity until they were contested by interested parties. The popularity of the legal device is a testament to the high level of standardization of commercial law, particularly in contract law, that existed in the Indian Ocean by the second half of the nineteenth century, albeit now dictated by European colonial legal criteria. The uniformity in language and format of these powers of attorney revealed that merchants based in Ḥaḍramawt carefully acquired transnational knowledge of property and commercial laws in the Straits Settlements and the Netherlands Indies. Their litigiousness in family and commercial matters, by no means separate, directly acquainted them with colonial laws over the decades.

How was such specialized legal knowledge transmitted? Male youth sent back to Ḥaḍramawt—a common practice—could have been the conduits for information.[9] Of course, these documents were mostly produced with the help of legal professionals, lawyers who were sensitive to particular administrative norms, ideals, and grammars while anticipating future judicial requirements if these documents were ever disputed. Solicitors at the Singapore law firms Drew and Napier, Rodyk and Davidson, and Sisson and Delay were popular among Arab merchants in the Straits Settlements. Furthermore, most powers of attorney were created by Ḥaḍramī merchants in Southeast Asia who travelled back to Ḥaḍramawt in their old age. It is likely that they imparted their knowledge and expertise to brethren in their homeland.

Each power of attorney typifies the modern government document produced in the twentieth century, which Hull describes as "an unusual sort of artifact because signs of its history are continuously and deliberately inscribed upon the artifact itself, a peculiarity that gives it an event-like quality."[10] Several witnesses were involved in each event that was the production of a power of attorney. Each power of attorney drew many individuals into the mesh of colonial legal jurisdiction, because each document was signed by one to three male witnesses, and even more if it was produced by a woman. Upon renewal, a different set of witnesses was called, further expanding the web of legal knowledge, compliance, and obligations to each other and to

government institutions. By the 1920s, it was common practice for wealthy
Arabs to write a will in Arabic, then hire a local lawyer and write it again in
English. The same expectation had already applied to powers of attorney.
As a result, several lawyers and translators were involved in the construction
of each document, including witnesses' declarations. In Ḥaḍramawt, each
power of attorney produced was witnessed and authorized by a qadi of the
region, who placed his seal on the document thus validating it.[11] In Dutch
courts, this seal determined the *volmacht*'s authenticity from the outset without question, affirmed in a case in January 1920 in Surabaya.[12] If disputed
in colonial courts, the seal sufficed as validation for the entire document
without question. One qadi in particular, Shaik Ali bin Salim bin Omar Ar-
fan Baraja of Tarīm, witnessed the highest number of powers of attorney
prepared by Ḥaḍramīs for their representatives in the Singapore and Java.
He had a relatively more practical seal, clear and sparse in design. Qadis in
Ḥaḍramawt tended to have clear, uncomplicated seals with legible script in
both Arabic lettering and Roman alphabet, which suggests that they dealt
with European authorities often enough to warrant such stamps. Much attention was placed on the examination of these seals because they enabled
European colonial authorities to confidently recognize the document as a
legal document already ratified by their legal counterparts across the Indian
Ocean. In one power of attorney, the words *khadamushara bebalad Saiyun*
around the seal were translated into Dutch in court as "servant of the law
of Siwoen," signifying that the Qadi's seal authenticated the power of attorney and allowed Dutch courts to recognize the terms of the document
as binding. Each qadi's seal was different. The qadi of Shibām for example
had, in Roman script, *Hakim el Shariah fi Shebam*, which refers to the "Judge
of the law in Shibām," on the outer ring of his seal as a sort of compromise
between Arabic and European languages. The most elaborate seal belonged
to the Grand Qadi of Mecca. Painstakingly crafted in beautiful calligraphic
script in bold black ink, it occupied about 7.5 centimeters in height—up to
about a third of the page of the document. The intricate detail was a huge
contrast to the more modest seals utilized by Ḥaḍramī qadis. The seal was a
testament to the wealth of Mecca, a site of pilgrimage for all Muslims from
all over the world.

Uses of Powers of Attorney

Produced for diverse reasons, powers of attorney were versatile and revocable. There were three common kinds of powers of attorney. The first kind
dealt with disbursing inheritance shares according to Islamic law. Islamic laws

of inheritance operate on a fixed share-based system outlined in the Qur'an without recognizing the concept of heir apparent or living heir. After the payment of outstanding debts, funeral expenses, and the costs of obtaining probate and letters of administration, the net estate of the deceased is immediately disbursed according to fixed precise mathematical formulae known as *faraid*. Algebraic formulae were devised according to predetermined quotas in order to define how much money each surviving heir got. These formulae had been devised by *ulama'* who extrapolated from lines in the Qur'an what each heir should get. Following this view of divine disbursement, the appointment of heirs (including the rule of primogeniture) is a controversial point in Islamic law. Since every rightful heir has to be accounted for, the fixity of Islamic laws of inheritance contributed to the proliferation of powers of attorney. Based on the same logic, acts of repudiation of rightful heirs with the intention of disinheriting them were also not allowed. Islamic laws of inheritance were meant to safeguard the interests and welfare of blood relations upon the death of the deceased. That being said, the making of a testamentary will is recognized in Islamic law up to a maximum of one-third of the whole estate, and the wills sometimes had powers of attorney attached to them.

While several powers of attorney were created in anticipation of death, others were created in preparation for the testator's departure for their homeland in Arabia. Many were created by a trustee or an heir upon the death of someone who held property in Southeast Asia but died intestate, or by a trustee or an heir who realized that a will did not account for all living relatives either deliberately or accidentally. These powers of attorney tended to have a corrective element in that they attempted to include those overlooked in the original disbursement of inheritance shares. This was common partly because no one, not even the testator, could be adequately apprised of the identities of eligible heirs within far-flung diasporic families. One can easily imagine how new heirs often sprung out of the woodwork across the Indian Ocean. Powers of attorney were granted to make sure that both Qur'anic and appointed heirs would receive their proper allocated shares of property held in Southeast Asia according to Islamic law. In a power of attorney created in August 1919, a woman who was left out of a will was reinserted as an heir by her other relatives upon the death of her father, but in the same document, she transferred her power to a male relative who was also an heir.[13]

The second kind of power of attorney was granted by Arabs in Ḥaḍramawt to fellow Arabs, usually their relatives or business partners, specifically to manage their business and property in Southeast Asia. Most of these powers of attorney were granted to the Arabs based in Java and the British Straits

Settlement of Singapore, where the Dutch colonial official and Orientalist scholar L. W. C. van den Berg (1845–1927) estimated the value of Arab investment in real estate was worth 4 million guilders in 1885, a quarter of the estimated combined value of Arab-owned real estate in Malaya and the Straits Settlements as well as the Netherlands Indies.[14] The Alkaff clan, said to be the wealthiest Ḥaḍramī clan in Singapore, produced thirty-eight powers of attorney between 1906 and 1922. The Alsagoff clan, whose lawsuits concerning their vast family religious endowments were regular features of legal life in Singapore, produced eleven powers of attorney within the same time period.[15] By 1931, Arab landowners were the largest group of owners of house property in Singapore together with the Jewish population, despite constituting only 0.34 percent of the population.[16] In 1936, they were the richest group in terms of ownership of assets per head.[17] From 1942 to 1945, under Japanese Occupation, 10 percent of land deeds registered with the Syonan government was by Arab landowners. In so much as they were linked with land deeds, the abundance of powers of attorney provided a way for property to be accounted for in the colony. The huge amounts of powers of attorney generated by diasporic Muslims echoed that of the Torrens system, a new property regime based on land title by registration that was devised by Robert Richard Torrens in southern Australia and spread to other parts of the British Empire. Because deterritorialization of indigenous peoples was vital to its introduction, one could argue that powers of attorney contributed to their displacement in the Straits Settlements.[18] Members of the Arab diaspora in Southeast Asia shared Torrens's obsession with ownership and recordkeeping, which led them to appreciate the importance of the instrumentality of registration and entering into probate. Though not introduced

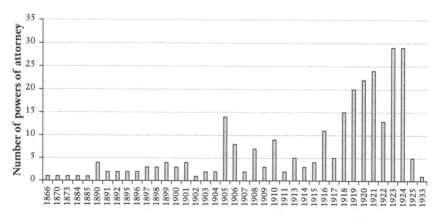

FIGURE 4. Powers of attorney by year stored in the Supreme Court of the Straits Settlements.

to the colony until 1960, the Torrens system of title by registration was favored by Chief Justice William Maxwell, who wrote a report on it in 1883. The legal climate was rife for more accountability, according to him.[19] The powers of attorney essentially functioned as proto-titles.

Illegal Occupations

The third kind of power of attorney was legally controversial and found only in the Netherlands Indies, where colonial subjects classified as "Foreign Orientals," including Arabs, were restricted from owning certain kinds of property, such as agrarian land, which were reserved for colonial subjects classified as Natives by Dutch authorities. According to Ordinance No. 179 in the *Staatsblad* 1875, the land legally designated for Natives could not be transferred to Foreign Orientals and other non-Natives, which meant that all agreements that led to such alienation were either directly or indirectly void. Powers of attorney provided a useful loophole because transfer of power itself from one party to another was regarded as perfectly legitimate by Dutch authorities. The opening decades of the twentieth century saw Dutch legal authorities attempting to curb land ownership by Foreign Orientals even more. To different degrees throughout the colony, Foreign Orientals were denied *oesaharechten*, a Dutch-Malay portmanteau legal term that referred to the right to cultivate land and profit from it, depending on their location in the colony. Because *oesaharechten* was associated with conjugal property, the legal move artificially cleaved social relationships between Foreign Orientals and Natives at their very core. Outright sale was forbidden but also irreversible so these transactions were heavily scrutinized. One way Foreign Orientals could circumvent this prohibition was through powers of attorney granted by those classified as Natives who held land-owning privileges granted by Dutch colonial authorities. Henceforth, Dutch authorities perceived this widespread practice as "illegal occupations" (*onwettige occupaties*) by Foreign Orientals.[20] As an unnamed Dutch reporter suggested in 1903, Dutch legal authorities were aggrieved at subjects' general savviness in utilizing powers of attorney to their advantage. Although Dutch authorities identified Chinese and Arab Foreign Orientals as abusers of powers of attorney in this manner, they believed that the Arabs, more so than the Chinese, often transferred powers of attorney to their "Native" wives to manage their property, in order to escape the taxation and land ownership restrictions that were applied to Foreign Orientals.[21] Likewise, their wives could also easily transfer powers of attorney to their husbands when needed. Powers of attorney allowed Foreign Orientals to obfuscate their actions more easily, causing anxiety among colonial officials interested in accountability, surveillance, and policing. Sometimes, parties named in powers of attorney had never even met the person who actually had the legal right to act, and the person who had the right to act often did not meet the party to whom he was signing over his rights. Only when legal action was initiated would the details be released to all parties.[22] In this way, it was easy for Arab Foreign Orientals to "hide" their property from the eyes of Dutch authorities, who continually suspected they were being hoodwinked. A juridical response in 1931 imagined the worst: "For Arab heirs, it is certainly easier to conceal the greatness of the inheritance than for a European. Rich Arabs potentially possessed real estate, houses, plots, which one cannot imagine."[23]

In the eyes of the Dutch colonial government at the beginning of the twentieth century, the whole colony seemed to have been held hostage by a paper regime consisting of powers of attorney devised by colonial subjects whose rights to own property in the colony were limited by law. Arab machinations were framed in the colonial press as deliberate attempts to exploit Natives, whom Dutch authorities were supposedly trying to protect. Dutch colonial newspapers were littered with stories of unfortunate Natives who fell prey to wily Arab creditors, handing over their property due to their inability to decipher legalese or ascertain what was their debt equivalent in terms of property. Dutch authorities observed that this practice was especially rampant at the start of every year, when colonial subjects planned their finances. One typical newspaper report in 1933 tells the story of an illiterate Native named Salam who unwittingly submitted his signature for the payment of a debt, which later proved to be a proxy (*volmacht*). Salam was shocked to discover that he no longer held the property mentioned in the *volmacht*.[24] He claimed that had been deceived into putting up his house property as payment in an arrangement with his Arab creditor. In such cases, criminal prosecution could be tricky. True to form, because the Netherlands Indies lay under a surfeit of jurisdictions, landed property was also governed by adat laws that further made it difficult for Dutch authorities to reverse transactions that involved Natives' property. Adatrecht, formed the substrate of the law of the colony, floating just above the firm strata of colonial jurisdiction that encompassed the entire Dutch archipelago, affecting all kinds of transactions involving Natives. For example, in 1922, when a Native acquired a piece of land from a European, a specific adatrecht clause was applied to the transaction, making it a unique property known as a "hibat wasijat" where the gift became revocable only upon the death of the original owner—the European— after which the beneficiary—the Native—had first rights to acquire it for good.[25] According to adatrecht, one could not ask for dissolution of a mutual agreement (*wederzijdse overeenkomst*).[26] Once a property transaction had gone through, any structure built on it, for example a house or a barn, was considered separate from the land it stood on according to adatrecht, which meant that full restitution of land to original owner was impossible.[27]

In an effort to prevent Foreign Orientals from becoming owners of such land, the author of Salam's tale of woe reiterated that once a Native person renounced his rights to a piece of property, it automatically became *landsdomein* (lit.: country domain), which was essentially state land. The author hardly had to resort to "sophisticated reasoning," as he himself admitted, because the basis of colonialism was that there was only one sovereign ruler over the territory, however imperfect that sovereignty was. Such legal disentanglements were hardly necessary since under colonial rule, the land held by those classified Natives was not even originally theirs to give, sell or transfer ownership of. There were always exceptions but any kind of transfer—including sale and land transfer through power of attorney—had to be approved by the Dutch Resident, although without a proper registry of land deeds and a convoluted system, he was often unable to monitor most transactions within his jurisdiction.[28]

Rules regarding transfer of property powers of attorney changed over time. For example, from 1904 onward, lower-income Europeans who previously shared many restrictions with Foreign Orientals in the Netherlands Indies could legally acquire and own property normally reserved for Natives. Not surprisingly, these kinds of exceptions created loopholes for Foreign Orientals to own property as well. The only uncontroversial legal transfer from Natives to Foreign Orientals and Europeans was by will and testament or by inheritance laws prescribed in specific detail in the Qur'an, although the Dutch government resented this as well.

Since power could be easily transferred and revoked via slips of paper across long distances—and in some instances even under duress, as in the case of ransom by power of attorney by the Sultan of Mukallā—a system based on powers of attorney could be precarious. It was challenging for all parties and legal authorities to keep up with how power slipped in and out of people's hands. This predicament was more prevalent in the Netherlands Indies than in the British Straits Settlements, where powers of attorney had to enter into probate in the Supreme Court of the Straits Settlements in order to be valid. In this way, British colonial authorities ensured their access to information regarding property holdings. Dutch and British authorities were also dealing with different scales in terms of size of colony and population. While British authorities dealt with three noncontiguous port cities, the vast proportion of property was held on the small island of Singapore. However, the Netherlands Indies was a huge archipelago, which made it difficult for the Dutch to keep track of property holdings. Dutch authorities became more frustrated than British authorities. An article in 1883 ruefully stated, "We do not have to analyze the consequences of the transaction, . . . do not have to analyze for the reader, who is only familiar with Indies situations. It is difficult, for the simple reason that residents and assistants are 'residents,' not gods of their region or division, not being omniscient."[29] Due to their inability to effectively monitor and police transfers of legal power across the vast archipelago, Dutch authorities resented the popularity of the device among colonial subjects. By contrast, British authorities in the Straits Settlements readily recognized the utility of powers of attorney in monitoring and controlling the property holdings of colonial subjects. Moreover, the problem of illegal occupations that plagued the Netherlands Indies was not an issue for British authorities, who did not curb property rights among colonial subjects in the Straits Settlements based on ethnicity.

The Problem of Multiple Jurisdictions

The specter of forgery continually hovered over all powers of attorney, and each case in court recalled this fear. On March 23, 1919, an Arab woman Sharifah Alwiyah Alsagoff from Say'un in Ḥaḍramawt transferred a power of attorney to Shaikh Salah bin Ahmad Basherawan, a merchant based in the town of Surabaya in Java.[30] In the same document, written in Arabic, she simultaneously revoked powers that had been earlier granted to her brother, Sayyid Alwi bin Shaikh Alsagoff, a merchant in Palembang in the neighboring island of Sumatra. Five months later, however, her brother alleged that Shaikh Salah bin Ahmad Basherawan, who had been granted the power of attorney, had collected rents illegally from his sister's plots of land in Surabaya. She had endowed her attorney the power to do the following in her name: "To regulate, administer all my houses and yards, commodities . . . to recover and receive, including rent and any other monies occurring from the receipt of rents and leases owed to me." The court deemed Sharifah Alwiyah Alsagoff's orders too vague since she did not take into account possible permutations that could reasonably emerge in the future. Since uncertainty in wording could potentially lead to a broader scope of power than intended, it was all the more important to ascertain who her appointed attorney was. To challenge the legal applicability of this latest document, her brother, the plaintiff, Sayyid Alwi Alsagoff produced another document dated four years earlier, on December 11, 1915, that showed that his sister had granted him the power of attorney to settle her affairs in Java in her name, instead of

Shaikh Salah Basherawan. The Arabic translator, Sech Hasan bin Abdulla Bobsaid, who was also the head of the Arab community, was summoned by the court to certify the details of the power of attorney. His purview as head included religious and business affairs.[31] He confidently told the court that the document was written in the same hand as the power of attorney produced in 1919.[32] The only difference was that the document in 1915 did not have her mark in the form of a cross or an "x" on it.[33] The names of two witnesses who were distant blood relatives of Sharifah Alwiyah were also different.[34] Bobsaid pointedly stated to the court that Sharifah Alwiyah could not have produced the power of attorney by herself, since "[it] is generally known that a woman cannot write Arabic," a statement which was of course untrue. His testimony, however, led the court to decide the 1915 document was most likely a forgery.

At this point, the Raad van Justitie of Surabaya unexpectedly pursued a different line of inquiry. The court declared that it was presumptuous to simply apply Dutch laws of deeds and contracts to foreign *volmachten*. The court decided that laws applied in the land of origin of parties involved, in this case Say'un in Ḥaḍramawt, should also be considered. The court was willing to embark on a journey of discovery of foreign laws with the possibility of enacting them in the colony because Arab Foreign Orientals were regarded as aliens in the colony. This decision came close to the tradition of English common law, which was premised on artificial discovery by British judges of long-standing common practice throughout Britain and Empire. In this rare instance, Dutch authorities were ready to project law regarding powers of attorney as practiced in Say'un in Ḥaḍramawt to Arabs residing in the Dutch colony and to accommodate this law within the framework of legal pluralism. To their disappointment, however, they discovered that the laws of Say'un, which were based on Islamic law, had little to say about procedure regarding written contracts and proxies, since oral testimony and contracts were valued more highly as evidence. They further discovered to their dismay that in several Muslim countries, qadis gave almost no weight to written evidence at all.

The momentum for discovery had been set, though, and the Raad van Justitie was not yet ready to give up, so they consulted the Dutch official in charge of Arabic and Islamic affairs, Christiaan Snouck Hurgronje, who helpfully pointed out that "the development of law and society, independently of Islamic law," had, fortuitously, granted more weight to written evidence in recent years, even in Muslim-majority countries.[35] He pointed out that even the Arab advisor to the Dutch government, Sayyid 'Uthmān bin Yaḥyā, who wrote the reference book on Islamic law for qadis in the

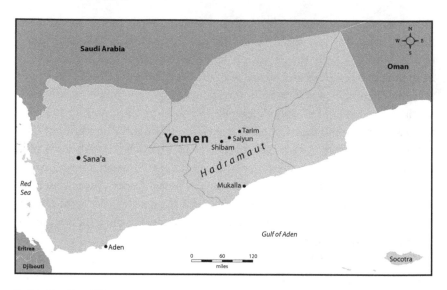

FIGURE 5.   Map of Yemen.

Netherlands Indies, conceded that according to the legal practicalities of the day, more weight could be attached to written documents than to oral testimony. Moreover, the Raad van Justitie learnt from L. W. C. van den Berg that Muslim marriages had always been based on a written contract between two parties. Finally, by 1919, within Ḥaḍramawt itself, the use of power of attorney was already common, with property rights being transferred through notarized deeds. Hence, to the court's relief, paper definitely had traction in Ḥaḍramawt, and powers of attorney were valid on both ends of the Indian Ocean. This also suggests that by the early twentieth century, the balance had swung in favor of writing-based forms of legal authenticity.

Here we see the powerful figure of the Arabic translator Bobsaid, a person propelled to a position of authority as an expert in Islam, though he was far from it, and called upon to judge the veracity of a power of attorney written in another language steeped in legal idiom relatively unknown to European colonial authorities. His unwarranted power recalls that of the notary, a stock figure in the picaresque narratives that flourished in Golden Age Spain and America as a legal writer par excellence with the opportunities to broker his own profits and gain leverage.[36] Likewise, in this case, Bobsaid was able to manipulate the Dutch colonial lack of understanding about the weight of Muslim women's authority and redirect power and wealth into the hands of certain male relatives, thus potentially causing all the other witnesses and people present to be partisans cooperating in a possible fraud.

Considering that powers of attorney were already being used so often in the neighboring Straits Settlements and within the Netherlands Indies itself, it might seem surprising that in 1919 the Raad van Justitie of Surabaya suddenly concerned itself about the possible validity of powers of attorney among Arabs. Though the Raad von Justitie did not explicitly admit as much, it could be argued that these doubts arose as a direct consequence of Bobsaid's testimony that Arab women could not read and write Arabic. If what Bobsaid said was true, what did this mean for the powers of attorney created by women already circulating in the Netherlands Indies? The dystopian image of a crumbling legal world built on paper was too much for the court to bear, so it swiftly displaced its anxiety onto the problem of personal jurisdictions, necessitating an attempt at discovery of laws. It might appear ludicrous that this effort should be undertaken seriously as late as 1919, three centuries after Dutch rule was established in Java, but the phenomenon also coincided with the Dutch courts' keenness to underscore the legal fiction that Arabs were foreigners in the colony, a recent legal development that gained traction from the latter half of the nineteenth century onward.

British and Dutch colonial authorities shared the opinion that the territorial fixity of jurisdiction applied to powers of attorney. In matters concerning documents and contracts, Islamic law was not to be generalized in the scrutiny of legal documents. Instead, it was the "law" of Arabia, Ḥaḍramawt, or Say'un that took hold as we have seen. Just like their Dutch counterparts, British authorities too struggled to ascertain what the law of Ḥaḍramawt was. In the case of a disputed will in 1908, an expert witness was consulted in colonial court, claiming he "knew a little law."[37] Counsel explained that this was modesty on his part since he did not want to be considered a boaster, but out of caution they called upon another recognized "expert" in this case, a qadi, "licensed by Government." This qadi's words carried more weight in court, which tells us the about the hierarchy of religious experts in colonial courts, which favored those appointed by the government. The qadi confirmed that

> so long as the witnesses said that they hear what the testator stated, that will would be valid. They must sign the will. It was not necessary to make people sign, but if the will is to go to court the witnesses must sign. The same rule applies to the testator. The will produced purports to be signed by the testator, by two witnesses, and the scribe. The witnesses were present and the will says so.

For their part, Arabs in British jurisdictions conceived of themselves and operated as Muslim actors rather than "Arab actors" from a specific locale,

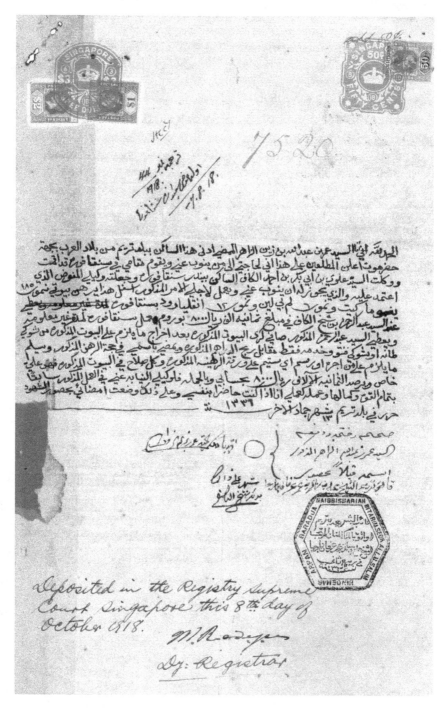

FIGURE 6. Power of attorney of Syed Omar bin Abdullah bin Zain Alzahir granted to Syed Alwi bin Abubakar bin Ahmed Alkaf, August 7, 1918. Koh Seow Chuan collection, National Library, Singapore, reference no. 040000080.

unlike in the Netherlands Indies. Judges as well often recognized them as such, since wills were deemed to be valid according to "Islamic law" instead of the laws of Ḥaḍramawt. But powers of attorney produced in Singapore did not consistently abide by Islamic law in format either. For example, not all powers of attorney produced by women were witnessed by three males, a requirement according to Islamic law.[38] Such discrepancies indicate that laws and jurisdictions concerning powers of attorney were not fully ascertained. Unlike personal law, which was governed by religious laws in both colonies, the realm of powers of attorney was one area of colonial law that was not overdetermined.[39]

The case of Sharifah Alwiyah Alsagoff's *volmacht* embodied typical problems such as multiple jurisdictions, the admissibility of written documents as valid evidence in Islamic law, the uncertainty surrounding the weight of women's authority in Muslim jurisdictions, translation problems, and the presence of multiple versions of the same document competing for legal recognition in several jurisdictions simultaneously. Even in the friendlier Straits Settlements, the legal validity of documents produced in foreign jurisdictions that had been accepted into probate in the colony ran the perennial risk of being challenged in the future. A British judge declared in 1908, "It is a question of foreign law and has to be proved every time, a question of fact which can only be accepted for the particular case."[40] Still, the situation was far more complicated in the Netherlands Indies, where Dutch judges opted for a less convenient and practical route when they conceived of Arabs as people who had their own separate jurisdictions, effectively situating Arabs residing within the Netherlands Indies outside of the colony legally. They imposed on themselves the added burden of discovering foreign laws that they had the right to repudiate anyway. Whatever the outcome, whenever *volmachten* devised by Arabs appeared in Dutch civil courts, Dutch legal authorities potentially had to not only mull over different sets of laws (civil law and Islamic law) but also ascertain their legal jurisdiction over these Arabs in the first place to determine what laws should be applied in the end.

In a case in 1927, the *landraad* decided not to interfere in a case involving two children of an Arab mother domiciled in Batavia, although the two representatives of the children's three legal guardians was living in Saiyun in Ḥaḍramawt.[41] Cases involving Arab minors were often transnational, resulting in different jurisdictions for minors and guardians.[42] In the 1927 case, the two male children became co-owners of a piece of real estate upon the death of their mother, Sharifah Alwiah binti Achmad Alsagoff. Being minors, they were officially represented by their guardian, Said Oemar bin Mochdar Alhabshi, who informed the court that the two male minors wanted to mortgage their shares since they did not possess enough cash to buy their shares. Fortunately for them, the other co-owners of the piece of property too wished to mortgage their shares. According to fixed laws of inheritance, the price of each of the minors' shares (28/372 shares) was calculated to be worth 20,322.58 guilders in real estate. The Batavia *landraad* decided to frame this petition as a request made by *vreemdelingen*, a specific term reserved for "foreigners" who were not local residents of the Netherlands Indies, unlike *Vreemde Oosterlingen,* who were at least recognized as colonial subjects residing in the Netherlands Indies.[43] Having firmly situated the parties involved outside of Java, in Arabia specifically, the Batavia *landraad,* just like the Raad van Justitie in Surabaya in 1919, set itself the task of determining the laws of Arabia, which they also ascertained to be Islamic law. Foreign Orientals were usually subjected to Dutch civil law in the matter of property management of minors. Subsequently, the Batavia *landraad* declared itself unauthorized to hear the contents of Said Oemar's petition since it could not administer Islamic law, which was the purview of the *priesterraden,* a lower court. Therefore, the case remained unresolved. In this way, *volmachten* produced by Arabs were potentially of limited use in the Netherlands Indies since Dutch legal structures were extremely pluralistic, unpredictable, and, most crucially, sought to exclude migrant populations from fully participating in legal sites open to Europeans and Natives.

Powers of attorney were not without problems in British territories either because attorneys could be substituted quite easily by testators who retained the right of nomination without having to inform legal authorities. After all, it is not clear whether probate was even necessary before any legal action concerned with the power of attorney was initiated, but more often than not it was because the court could not keep up with procedure of probate, especially because powers of attorney tended to be produced in tandem with wills. Distance remained a liability for British legal authorities, who remained acutely aware that a writ or letter from Southeast Asia would first have to reach Aden and then journey another several weeks through the desert by camel.[44] Because a writ can only be served personally, when a defendant lived abroad, trading and managing property through an attorney, the writ could not be served on the attorney. An article in 1938 alerted British government to this loophole: "They lie practically outside the law [through their attorney] enjoying the full benefit of it, they can sue but practically cannot be sued as no process server would come out of Hadhamaut alive."[45] The incapacity of law enforcement to transcend jurisdictions demonstrates the limits of the regime based on *surat kuasa.* English common law was also unclear on whether attorneys were able to sue in their own name on behalf of those whom they represented. For example, in 1933 Shaikha Fatimah, an Arab widow, found that she could not sue through her attorneys because they did not have any personal interest in her estate.[46]

In light of all this uncertainty, it is poignant how Arab testators trusted not only that European colonial legal authorities would ratify the terms—possibly even to the extent of recognizing foreign jurisdictions—but that they would also do so for generations after the testators' own demise. Powers of attorney formed repositories of colonial subjects' confidence in colonial legal regimes. For these Arabs, law was hardly an abstract, vague sense of compliance to a jurisdiction; the meticulous fine-grained details in their powers of attorney tell us not only of their strong attachment to the future fulfillment of their plans but also of long-term plans to remain in Southeast Asia under colonial rule. Family cohesion and ties to one's original homeland were retained by what historian Ghislaine Lydon calls the "paper economy of faith."[47] In her trenchant historical study of the inhabitants of the Sahara desert, she observes that for "both Jews and Muslims, their literacy enhanced network externality, allowing for complex accounting, information flows, and accountability or legal transparency to solve the commitment problem and enforce earthly sanctions."[48] Obviously, powers of attorney permitted far-flung family partnerships to act promptly in a world where slow communication could be detrimental to striking a good bargain.[49] Ḥaḍramī merchants with holdings in Southeast Asia relied on the colonial ability to enforce laws. In other words, their "paper economy of faith" rested not so much on their mutual trust in God united by a common religious faith as it did on the colonial states' authority to endow legitimacy to powers of attorney. Ḥaḍramīs tended to belong to the same clans due to repeated endogamous marriages within a familial-centered construction of social and economic milieus. The sense of *asabiyya* or "group feeling" that held members of the Ḥaḍramī diaspora together did not arise naturally but rather rested on painstakingly constructed extended patriarchal clan networks. However, effective performance could not be sufficiently regulated via dense social networks of interaction consisting of members of tightly knit communities based on kinship.[50] Even kinship could not be equated with trust, although trust might be primarily channeled through kinship alliances.[51]

Powers of Attorney by Women

Property regimes and income strategies of transregional Ḥaḍramī families reveal how capital was concentrated and distributed mostly through men. There were signs that women were pressured to give up their claims to managing property. About 101 out of more than 350 powers of attorney devised by Arabs in the holdings of the Supreme Court of Singapore were produced by women. Taken as a whole, the corpus of powers of attorney demonstrates that inheritances that rightfully came down to daughters and widows according to fixed principles of Islamic laws of inheritance rapidly fell under the control and management of male relatives and former business partners of their fathers or husband, especially when the properties were scattered over several locations. For example, in 1906, a widow identified in her own power of attorney simply as Moonah, an indication perhaps as to her insignificance moving forward, found herself saddled with her deceased husband's extensive property in Singapore, Batavia, Surabaya, Bengal, Aden, Mukallā, and Muscat upon his death. Through a power of attorney, she transferred power to manage these properties to her husband's son.[52] Perhaps some women considered themselves unqualified to handle complicated transactions that required high level of business acumen. Whatever the case, it seemed that these powers of attorney tended to create agnatically structured economic lineages since they purposefully placed property management firmly in the hands of male heirs and relatives when women inherited property or when power was placed in their hands by a will.

The question remains as to who could ascertain that the women in the powers of attorney stored in the Straits Settlements Supreme Court were indeed directing their representatives who were merely dutifully acting on their behalf. After all, only a cross was needed beside the woman's name for legal repositories to accept the document as sound.[53] It was not uncommon to see a power of attorney written by a woman's husband, father, or brother granting more powers to himself.[54] In addition, women hardly ever referred to themselves in the first person, unlike men, who referred themselves as such about 20 percent of the time.

Considering how common powers of attorney made by women were, it is perhaps too easy to argue that the sheer number of powers of attorney created by women meant that they were subsequently disempowered or incapacitated such that they were constantly compelled to transfer power to others in the Dutch colony. This argument is troubling and misses half the picture. It also reinforces the notion that Muslim women were eager to relinquish their authority because they preferred to divest themselves of power. We must attend to what powers of attorney actually enabled women to do. Powers of attorney were used to manage specific property holdings in particular places. Appointment of attorneys was definitely a form of agency. Once power was given up, women often monitored the actions of their

FIGURE 7. Power of attorney by Sheriffa Alooyeah binte Ali bin Abdulrahman bin Abu Bakar Al-mashor within a cross as the testator's mark, May 10, 1906. Koh Seow Chuan collection, National Library, Singapore, reference no. 040000172.

attorneys and did not hesitate to go to court to change attorneys once trust was broken.

In a way, powers of attorney actually granted women immensely more scope for action than otherwise. Due to fixed laws of inheritance in the Qur'an, women were, for the most part, stuck with the luck of a single draw with regards to the location of property they inherited. Due to the same laws, they could not easily divest themselves of their inheritance either, and some were unprepared to manage it. By creating power of attorneys, they were able to grant and revoke authority and identify responsible attorneys as time went by. For these reasons, it was less risky for women without business acumen to appoint a relative, friend, or business partner to take charge of their property than to go at it alone. In 1908, for instance, two recently manumitted Javanese women not surprisingly transferred power to their brother to handle the administration of their father's estate, which they had inherited.[55]

The benefit of a transferring power of attorney as opposed to the appointment of an executor is derived from its easy revocability. A case in 1936 proved this argument. On April 1, 1931, a warrant was issued for Syed Mohamed bin Abdulkadir Alhabshee, who had been appointed the executor of his father's will. Between 1930 and 1931, he was entrusted with money representing the converted share belonging to his sister, Sharifah Salimah binte Abdul Kadir bin Ali Alhabshee, in the rents and corpus of the estate of their dead father. As directed, he invested his siblings' respective shares and received rents, but turned to his own use $1,632.96 that belonged to Salima and her two brothers, out of a total of $13,260.91. His father's widow (his stepmother and the mother of Salimah and her two brothers) noticed that something was wrong and took action by granting power of attorney to one Syed Abdullah, a member of the firm Alkaff and Co., who started proceedings in court asking for an account of all monies. Since Syed Mohamed bin Abdulkadir Alhabshee was explicitly named the executor of his father's will, there was no way for his stepmother or his siblings to revoke power from him. The scope of the power of attorney was specifically to look into the financial dealings of Alhabshee. He was dramatically extradited to Singapore from the remote island of Flores in the Netherlands East Indies four years later. On the morning of January 20, 1936, Alhabshee appeared before Judge Arthur à Beckett Terell in the case of *Rex v. Syed Mohamed bin Abdulkadir Alhabshee* and was charged with criminal breach of trust in the amount of $1,322.97.[56] He was subsequently jailed for three years for his offence.

An appointed representative could obtain extensive control over the grantor's entire property holdings with a stroke of the pen. In 1908, a woman named Sharifah Fatimah binti Omar bin Ahmed bin Omar Al-Shattri gave over her rights to manage not only all her existing property but also her future potential holdings that she might gain to her father:

> This power of attorney is granted to her father to hold, take, accept, and manage all her belongings, inherited from her mother, Salha binti Syed Awad bin Omar al Shattri, in Singapore, Hydermaut, and other places. The above shall include all property goods and chattels now and hereafter belonging to her either inherited by her as an heir, given to her as a gift, left by her by will or by vow or otherwise either moveable or immoveable in Singapore, Java, Hydermaut, and other places to hold, accept, manage, take possession of the same. . . . when he shall consider it beneficial to her and to do all that is required by the Muhammadan law and usages such as the giving of zakat or other religious donations. His acts are her acts and his instructions are her instructions in all matters and things necessary to be done according to the custom in Singapore, Hydermaut, Java, and other places. The above Sharifah Fatimah legally and lawfully according to the Muhammadan law makes this power of attorney in favor of her father.[57]

Due to the extensive scope of these powers of attorney, one sometimes senses that women were signing their entire fortunes away. This alarming prospect is not true. In 1917, two sisters, Sheriffa Mahani Binte Ahmad Bin Abdulrahman Alsagoff and Sheriffa Rogayah Binte Ahmad Bin Abdulrahman Alsagoff, contracted their own lawyers from the British law firm Drew and Napier to draw up a power of attorney in Singapore.[58] In it, Sharifah Mahani Alsagoff and her sister signed over the management of their fortunes, including future fortunes, to their nephew. But they remained wealthy. Sharifah Mahani created a rich endowment in her will on March 13, 1925.[59] When she died without issue nearly two years later in January, the details of her trust kicked in as follows:

1. Madrasah El-Nathah El-Elmeyah, Ḥaḍramawt (income from 245 Jalan Besar)
2. $100 on the death anniversary for prayers
3. $60 for reading Qur'an on *wakif*'s grave
4. $20 for purchase of *zamzam* water to be distributed to the poor
5. $50 for the purchase of bread to be distributed to the poor in Mecca[60]

British judges displayed anxiety and discomfort when presented with cases involving Muslim women in general, as we saw in chapter 1. Women's authority was weighed less according to Islamic law. British judges readily understood this, puzzled as to why these Muslim women inherited property in the first place. Women's economic activity was suspect in British courts as judges were unable to believe that Muslim women were subject to more progressive laws than their English counterparts, including those in British India, who only gained the right to marital property during the late nineteenth century, as Julia Stephens has shown.[61] For them, seclusion was presumptively equated with an inability to act as fully independent economic agents. The incapacity of Muslim women was something that judges willingly presumed, and isolation was imposed on Muslim women in various ways, as in a case in 1924 when the Supreme Court of the Straits Settlements suddenly wanted to appoint other persons in place of a Muslim woman when the other party in a case against her was a male.[62] No such law existed in the colony, however. On the one hand, this one-off stipulation could have been a concession according to British colonial understandings of Islamic law in their desire to accommodate colonial subjects, but on the other hand, it could also mean that a Muslim woman was assumed to be unable to hold her own during legal proceedings.

Paper suffused the Indian Ocean. As the creators of these powers of attorney conformed to particular bureaucratic procedures and formats, they articulated jurisdictions at both ends of the Indian Ocean. The letters of power propelled jurisdictions in territories already replete with layered, competing, and sometimes unacknowledged jurisdictions. Each power of attorney commanded attention in legal settings and asserted the jurisdiction of its place of creation elsewhere. More often than not, the colonial courts in Southeast Asia eventually declared extraterritorial jurisdictions null and void in colonial legal courts. But for a little while, a foreign jurisdiction took hold of the colonial court, forcing legal practitioners to acknowledge and consider the contours and boundaries of its potential force field.

Powers of attorney did not simply allow testators to leap across the ocean; they also enabled temporal leaps. They long outlasted the lifetimes of their testators by projecting meaning into the future and knitting past and future together. Detailed instructions in the powers of attorney took for granted that property holdings would long remain in the hands of the family. Certainly, time moved more rapidly in the crowded bustling cities of Southeast Asia than in Ḥaḍramawt, and long distances allowed some attorneys to be incompetent and corrupt for longer than they should have. Undoubtedly however, the numerous powers of attorney granted by Arabs in Ḥaḍramawt to their kin in Southeast Asia expanded their capacity for action by transcending jurisdictional and territorial boundaries and diffusing their responsibility considerably across the Indian Ocean. But the enforcement of these terms depended on the perpetuation of colonial jurisdictions invested by these powers of attorney. Paradoxically, each power of attorney acknowledges one's encumbrances across long distances only to cede one's authority momentarily or permanently. These powers of attorney carried the weight of obligations of Arabs toward each other over several generations and resolutely embedded these obligations in several locations. While the Arab diaspora aimed to surmount distance and blend jurisdictions, colonial regimes were built on evidence of rights to possession superior to whatever other contenders could muster in their bid to assert rights to possession, as Dutch colonial claims of illegal occupations by Arabs in the Netherlands Indies chronically demonstrated.[63] The goal was exclusion, which is the subject of the next two chapters.

CHAPTER 3

Resident Aliens

Exclusions of Arabs in the Netherlands Indies

A short story written in 1941 by a Dutch writer tells of a young Javanese man named Karto, the gullible oldest son of the village head (*penghoeloe*), who met "an old Arabian, wrapped in a white cloak, wearing a clean and tall turban around his head. He looked impressive, with his big, dark eyes, his bent nose, his beard which was already white."[1]

The accompanying illustration depicted the old Arab man as a mysterious figure with his face partially covered. Most strikingly, he had the talons of a vulture on one foot, and his shadow on the ground appeared to be that of a bird of prey. Karto was, however, blind to this, distracted by rumors that his money was being swiftly devalued because Dutch guilders were going to be replaced by a new currency.[2] He feared his wife's rancor at his unwise investment. The Arab man conveniently promised to recoup Karto's money, but not before persuading the panicked Karto to part with even more of his money. Karto was relieved and wanted to hug his savior, but he knew this to be against the *adat* (customary law), so instead, he said to him: "Allow me to touch the hem of your robe, holy man. You have been in Mecca for some time." Karto then "nodded down to the Arabian, and took his garment in his hands. Then he got up, walked quickly to the back and returned ten minutes later with his thirty-six guilders."[3] Citing the story of Karto, a Dutch legal scholar lamented in 1891 that whatever an Arab did and said was perceived as good and would be followed by the Natives.[4] Karto was eventually saved

FIGURE 8.   Illustration of the Arab man whom Karto met. Louis de Bourbon, "De Slechte Guldens," in *Twaalf Maal Azië* (Amsterdam: Boek-en Courantmaatschappij, 1941), 22. KB | National Library.

from being completely swindled by the Arab by his father, who proudly said to him "I'm a good connoisseur of money. I know it better than the Chinese or Arabs."[5] The depiction of the Arab man as a vulture suggests that Arabs in the Dutch Indies were opportunistic scavengers always ready to

pounce on the spoils of Natives' misfortunes and prey on their presumed
naiveté. As Dutch jurisdictions hardened, the identities of the Arabs became
more rooted in prejudice. In popular fiction and public press, their piety was
portrayed as deeply hypocritical, a cloak worn to signal respect among Natives. According to one Dutch colonial official, "one Arab was equal to two
Chinese in the minds of Natives."[6] Several Dutch officials especially rankled
at the sight of Southeast Asian subservience to Arab descendants of the
Prophet.[7] A typical Dutch account in 1895 described how Arabs supposedly
rose to prominence over the centuries in Borneo through nefarious means,
beginning as the archetypal fortune seekers (*fortuinzoekers*):

> Most of them are poor when they leave their native land, and must be
> supported on their arrival by the never-failing help of their compatri-
> ots; but through thrift and consultation, often accompanied by scams,
> they often acquire considerable wealth. Great is the reverence the na-
> tives of the islands have for those strangers who inform them of the
> knowledge of the holy language of the Qur'an and of the laws.[8]

Drawing upon these prejudices, Dutch legal authorities intensely cultivated
the exclusion of Arabs from the bulk of the Native population from the mid-
nineteenth century onward.

The proportion of Arab Foreign Orientals was small compared to the rest
of the population, at 5 to 7 percent depending on the location within the
archipelago.[9] By 1900, the legal category of Foreign Orientals included Malays, Bugis (Boegineezen), Madurese, Makassareese, Coastal Peoples (Kust-
volkens), South Indians (Klingaleezen), North Indians (Bengaleezen), Jews,
Persians, and Japanese, as well as Arabs, throughout the Netherlands Indies.[10]
Only the Javanese never ran the risk of being classified as Foreign Orientals. Among the Foreign Orientals, the Chinese consistently constituted the
highest number throughout the Netherlands Indies, with the exception of
Palembang and West Borneo, where the Arabs formed the majority.[11] The
population almost doubled from the 1860s to 1880 after the opening of the
Suez Canal, better census-taking methods, or more likely, both.[12] It is possible that this sudden spike might have alarmed Dutch colonial officials, who
thereafter overestimated Arab political and economic influence in the Netherlands Indies, exacerbating their fears of pan-Islamism.[13]

Foreign Orientals were divided into nations, which meant that laws that
pertained to them sometimes verged on mimicking international law, as the
next chapter will demonstrate. The "heads" of each nation were most often
known as *kaptein*, often locally rendered as *kapitan* in major cities and in some
instances given other military ranks such as *luitenant* or *majoor*, although

Table 2 Number of Arabs in the Netherlands-Indies

YEAR	NUMBER
1860	8,909
1880	16,025
1885	17,250
1890	21,640
1895	24,410
1900	27,399
1905	29,588
1920	44,902
1930	71,335

Source: *Deel VII: Chineezen en Andere Vreemde Oosterlingen in Nederlandsch-Indie* (Batavia: Departement van Economische Zaken, 1935), 46.

most were simply called *wijkmeester* (quarter-master) or, more commonly, *hoofd* (head).[14] Each head was under direct orders from the Resident and Assistant Resident in each town[15] They were appointed by their own communities subject to the approval of the colonial government, although they did not receive a salary from the government. They tended to be prominent wealthy merchants and community leaders, as indicated by auction advertisements, which often listed their holdings and property. For example, the rich *kapitan* Arab of Moluccas had fifty cutters to his name, a collection of pearls, and two houses in the European style in Banda and Ambon.[16] Appointed heads had to maintain public order in their designated districts and present the complaints of their constituents to Dutch authorities.[17] They were responsible for recording births, deaths, migration trajectories, and trade routes, which they had to submit to the government each year, although the Dutch Resident of Java and Madura Fokko Fokkens reported in 1904 that they were often unable to track the movements of their constituents.[18]

After all, Arabs in the Netherlands Indies were scattered over a huge geographical expanse across several thousand islands in the colony, making it impossible for their movement to be tracked. In contrast to their counterparts in the Straits Settlements, their influence was limited by local political rulers with long dynasties, especially in Java. Unevenly distributed throughout the archipelago, they were mostly found in the cities of Batavia, Surabaya, Gresik, Cirebon, Tegal, Pekalongan, Samarang, Sumenep, Bangil, Banyuwangi, Toeban, Palembang, Siak, Riau, Pontianak, and Banjarmasin.[19] During the course of the nineteenth century, port cities such as Batavia and Surabaya arose due to new colonial infrastructure and capital investments, while older cities such as Gresik and Aceh declined.[20] By and large, Arabs in

Java were concentrated in areas with a strong Dutch presence. In 1873, Herman Otto van den Linden, a lawyer based in Batavia, observed that Foreign Orientals were parties in half of civil court cases in some cities.[21]

Land Grab under *Cultuurstelsel*

Colonial land grab was accompanied by colonial narratives geared toward the protection of Native rights. Natives were not always deemed to be a protected class, and the discernible shift occurred during the period of *Cultuurstelsel* between 1830 and 1836, when the lack of economic progress in the Netherlands Indies became linked to Natives' well-being and productivity, and the enemy of the colony's progress became the Foreign Orientals. Article 74 of the government regulations (*regeeringsreglement*) of 1830 stated that "the lands of the island of Java, which are still owned by the government, shall, insofar as they are cultivated by the Javanese, be permanently leased to the native people."[22] In 1836, Article 62 of the government regulations explicitly cemented the view with an added element of "protection": "The lands on the island of Java . . . will be preserved for the sake of the Javanese such that they will be let to the native population continually."[23] Note that in both articles the land was removed from Javanese hands by the Dutch, then "leased" or "let" back to them. Even older colonial policies like the preservation of the Javanese regencies were suddenly recast by Dutch officials to be protective of Javanese against Foreign Orientals. Of all the oppressive policies Foreign Orientals were subjected to, the most impactful was the *vervreemdingsverbod* or land alienation law, which was intended to protect the rights of Natives, specifically the Native cultivators of agrarian land.[24] While Europeans and Natives could settle and acquire land freely in interior of Java, Foreign Orientals could not do so by law.[25] In places such as Tjimanoek in West Java, Foreign Orientals had to prove that they had been there for more than three generations in order to own land. The land alienation law was a source of grievance that cut deep into the social fabric of Indies communities who had resided there for decades or even centuries to be robbed of the opportunity to own and acquire land. The Agrarian Law of 1870 prohibited the sale or permanent transfer of land from Natives to Europeans and Foreign Orientals. Furthermore, Ordinance no. 179 in the *Staatsblad* 1875 expressly prohibited the alienation of land held by non-Native population groups.[26] Restrictions were already placed on ownership of agricultural land by Foreign Orientals in 1839 and renewed in 1857 but did not seem to have much of an impact, since in 1849, the amount of private land owned by Arabs and Chinese was far higher proportionally than the amount owned by the Native population, but not higher than that owned by Europeans.[27] Even in 1892, the Arab share was 6 percent behind the Chinese (at 46 percent) and the Europeans (at 48 percent), which meant that the Arab population, at only one-fifteenth the size of the Chinese population, still owned a disproportionate amount of property.[28] Dutch authorities were irritated to observe that Arabs still owned conspicuous amounts of agricultural land, including rice plantations in in Batavia, Madura, and Surabaya, and that they, along with the Chinese, owned 280 of 345 private estates in Java by the early twentieth century.[29] How was this possible? Some of the land was given to Arabs by the Dutch before restrictions were enforced.[30] Furthermore, as the historian Cornelis van Vollenhoven famously claimed, every word of the land alienation law was a struggle, and several issues remained unresolved till the end of the colonial period.[31] Land was often confiscated by Arab creditors from their Native clients, who had put up their property as collateral. This phenomenon, discussed in chapter 2, was deemed "illegal occupation." Some of the land was acquired through the recouping of debts and by transfer of land through powers of attorney, also demonstrated in chapter 2. Beginning in 1913, Foreign Orientals could apply to be granted property and be accorded the same opportunities as Europeans, especially outside of Java—only eighteen Europeans and two Arabs applied from New Guinea and Palembang. The low number of applications suggests that restrictions were already being flouted before.[32]

The Pass and Quarter System

Territorial jurisdictions did not map onto persons neatly within the Netherlands Indies. While Arabs, Chinese, and Japanese were automatically foreign everywhere in the region, other groups became Foreign Orientals when they left their place of origin, which was determined by the Dutch colonial government. Except for the Javanese, every ethnic community ran the risk of being foreign within the Netherlands Indies. Leaving one's place of origin, however arbitrarily identified by Dutch authorities, was deemed a transgressive act. The Makassareese, the Javanese, the Malays, and the Bugis were cast as different "nations" throughout the Netherlands Indies, associated with specific geographical locations with hard boundaries rooted in the ideal that "nations" should be sealed off from each other. In his study of the Kai islands at the edge of the Banda Sea, Dutch colonial official Baron van Hoevell opined that the Chinese, Arabs, and Makassarese exploited the Natives on these islands simply by entering into economic relations with them.[33] According to this schema, whenever one ventured out to other places within the archipelago, one was contravening laws of trade in the Netherlands Indies because economic profit could only be sought at the place of origin of the community.

From 1819 to 1863, both Natives and Foreign Orientals had to obtain passes from the government to travel over land and sea. After 1863, Natives no longer had to do so, but Foreign Orientals still had to. Bit by bit, the system was dismantled during the 1910s. Passes were so hard to obtain during this period that a black market emerged in Singapore. Article 1 of *Staatsblad* 1872 No. 40 required that each European, Chinese, and Arab resident in the Netherlands Indies apply for an admission pass (*toelatingskaart*) within three days of arrival.[34] European residents violated this ban more than Foreign Orientals but were granted more leeway than the latter. Foreign Orientals had to reside in designated quarters throughout the Netherlands Indies. Although they could trade freely in the *pasar* or market, they had to be granted the right of residence (*recht van verblijf*) by the governor-general through the Ministry of Colonies.[35] Surveillance of Foreign Orientals was thickest in Batavia, where their arrival was overseen by the *waterschout* inspector, a government official of maritime affairs tasked with keeping censuses, which necessitated an investigation into the identities of newcomers to determine whether they could be granted admission to the colony. In Surabaya, a newcomer's papers would be sent to the local police for inspection before admission to the city. In Semarang, their respective heads were entrusted with this task. Fokkens, Dutch Resident of Java and Madura, observed that they were treated like prisoners while waiting for admission to the colony.[36] Foreign Orientals had to prove they had sufficient funds before being granted admission. While the Chinese were often employed prior to arrival, the Arabs often had enough money upon arrival to sustain themselves for a while. Additionally, Arabs, unlike the Chinese, were more likely to be prevented from resuming their lives in the Dutch colony after extended periods of time away through the interchangeability of the terms *vreemde oosterlingen* (Foreign Orientals) and *vreemdelingen* (foreigners).[37]

The Pass and Quarter (*wijkenstelsel* and *passenstelsel*) system introduced in the 1860s was regularly contravened by all sections of society up until 1915, when it was officially abolished.[38] Restrictions were arbitrarily enforced although generally the Arab populations remained the most scrutinized.[39] Outside of areas with relatively high numbers of Foreign Orientals, admission practices were more lax, enabling them to disembark from vessels, undetected. Some Foreign Orientals were officially notified afterwards to submit themselves to investigation, but orders were given in Malay, a language that was not understood by every Foreign Oriental, especially newcomers. In

Table 3 Number of Arabs admitted to the Netherlands
Indies with their families (1900–1933)

TIME PERIOD	NUMBER
1900–1903	1,367
1904–7	1,958
1908–11	1,793
1912–15	2,186
1916–19	910
1920–23	2,200
1924–27	2,377
1928–31	2,882

Source: *Deel VII: Chineezen en Andere Vreemde Oosterlingen in Nederlandsch- Indie*
(Batavia: Departement van Economische Zaken, 1935), 46.

most cases, they would be granted admission if they could produce deeds
of residence, which could be procured easily in places such as Singapore,
where they often stopped after travelling from China and Arabia. Almost all
new arrivals came to the Netherlands Indies through Singapore from across
the Indian Ocean, such that the Dutch Consulate in Singapore was tasked
with investigating their papers but was not always able to determine their
authenticity. Outside of Java, residential policies were not even enforced
especially in coastal areas where a significant number of inhabitants were
already recognized to be of mixed descent (such as Palembang).[40] Even residential quarters were determined by historical settlement and were therefore not precisely established. Hendrikus Colijn, a military official, observed
that "where they form numerous groups, the government designated their
distinct districts to be inhabited, some fifty in the entire colony."[41] On the
west coast of Borneo, Arabs were too dominant to be restricted to particular
districts.[42] Within Java, specifically in Surabaya and Jogjakarta, Foreign Orientals of all ethnicities were sometimes grouped together.[43] Since most Foreign Orientals were Chinese, it was possible for them reside in Chinese-only
districts. In Pekalongan, they lived in four allocated exclusive districts beside
the Natives' residential areas. Although the Arabs were the second largest
group of Foreign Orientals in Pekalongan, they often did not even manage
to fill one district and sometimes lived with other non-Chinese Foreign Orientals.[44] In Semarang, while the Chinese lived in one camp, the Arabs resided
in the Malay camp (*Maleische* camp) with South Indians (*Klingaleezen*). This
pattern was repeated throughout the Netherlands Indies.[45]

In this way, the extent of the separation of Arabs from other Foreign Orientals and Natives was not as deep as for the Chinese. The lives of Arabs were

more entangled with those of other residents in the Netherlands Indies, especially with Muslim Natives and other Muslim Foreign Orientals such as the Malays, Buginese, Makasareese, and South Asians. Regardless, estrangement did intensify. In October 1918, a case that appeared in the *landraad* of Batavia revolved around the guardianship of a four-year-old girl.[46] The Arab plaintiff, Sayyid Moehamad Ashmoeni, requested that his daughter be placed under his care, but Moehsina, his former wife and the girl's mother, who was classified as Native, refused.[47] He asked that the *landraad* order his former wife to hand over his daughter to him, capitalizing on the idea that he—and, by extension, his daughter according to patrilineal descent—fell under a different jurisdiction than his former wife. The court reasoned that guardianship (defined in the report as *wilayah*) was different from nursing (defined as *hadhanah*).[48] According to Islamic law, if the child was still being nursed, she would be under the care of her mother, but since she was no longer being nursed, the court ordered that she be returned to her father. Regardless, the Supreme Court was careful to only judge on matters of jurisdiction and not on the finer details of religious laws, which they did not dispute because these lay outside of their purview. In this instance, we see a case of literal separation of families.

While Chinese Foreign Orientals consistently lived as a distinct separate group, Arabs and other South Asians were at times lumped together such that they shared a *hoofd*, as in Northern Bali.[49] More often than not, the *hoofd der Arabieren* was also the leader of other Foreign Orientals in the Netherlands Indies, such as the South and North Indian Muslims, Malays, and the Bugis.[50] In 1892, Said Alim bin Miran bin Hamid al Gadrie was the *hoofd* of the Arabs and all other Foreign Orientals except the Chinese in Pasoeroean in East Java, in charge of their mercantile and religious affairs.[51] In 1902, Sech Omar bin Joeseof Manggoes was in charge of the Arabs and all other Foreign Orientals except the Chinese, Moors, and Bengalis in the city of Batavia and its suburbs.[52] Actual segregation of colonial subjects was likely overstated in the colonial record. Throughout the colony, intermarriages traversed both ethnic lines and town borders, especially in coastal cities.[53] Some wealthy Arabs could afford to marry more than one wife, and their wives often lived in several places separately with their progeny.[54] This meant that the Arab men also likely lived in all these places at various points in their lives, hence blurring the borders of segregated living. The official marital domicile determined by the husband's ethnic classification was often fictional, observed L. W. C. van den Berg, and often there would be several individuals unaccounted for in any place of domicile.

Considering the severe legal restrictions on residency, it should hardly come as a surprise that Foreign Orientals sometimes tried to pass as Natives in order to be more physically mobile. One method, as we have seen in chapter 2, was through marriage with Native women. Therefore marriages became a fraught issue for Dutch colonial authorities, who were concerned with how the institution could serve as a possible conduit for the transformation of ethnic classifications for other racial groups as well.[55] Muslim subjects in the Netherlands Indies might have believed they had contracted ordinary Muslim marriages, but in the eyes of the colonial legal authorities they had entered mixed marriages (*gemengde huwelijken*), which caused jurisdictional complications to occur for all spouses. Since Foreign Orientals were equivalent to Europeans in public law, they were not exempted from a law known as Article 64 of Rules of Civil Procedure (Het Reglement op de Burgerlijke Rechtsvordering) that required all contracts, including marriages, be recorded on paper.[56] Physical records were crucial in tracking down mobile populations under surveillance. By contrast, marriages among Natives did not need to be recorded for them to be recognized as valid by Dutch colonial state authorities. By this law, the Native wives of Foreign Orientals too were sometimes subjected to laws to which they would not otherwise have been subjected until they challenged this in court. Upon marriage, a Native woman followed her husband in private law but publicly, in the eyes of the state, she remained a Native according to a legal decision in 1908.[57] Chinese and Arab *kapitans* in Surabaya restricted the wives of Chinese and Arab Foreign Orientals from contracting on their own accord, something which other women in the colony retained the right to do. They cited Article 64, as well as mixture of religious regulations, laws, and institutions. Because there were no restrictions on women contracting business relations according to Islamic law, this seems to be an example of how colonial subjects tried to establish new religious norms under European colonial rule.[58] In 1912, the Supreme Court in Batavia investigated whether Katidjah binti Abdullah, a Javanese widow, could continue conducting her late Arab husband's business as specified in his will even after her remarriage to another man without her late Arab husband's permission.[59] In 1934, another Javanese woman, keen on avoiding being judged according to civil law, directly pleaded with G. F. Pijper, then advisor for Native and Arab affairs, not to be considered an Arab simply because she was married to one.[60] Such cases demonstrate how women linked to Foreign Oriental husbands got caught up in jurisdictional complications that could potentially stifle their abilities to act freely.

Despite their frequent intermarriages with Natives, Dutch authorities insisted on viewing Arabs as strangers to the region and, above all, as self-serving merchants.[61] Herman Otto van den Linden, a lawyer in Batavia, recorded his observations of the Arabs: "One thing that distinguishes Arabs from others was that their religion made them resist being rooted in a particular place. As soon as the bag is full, he goes with his children to Arabia, and sometimes even when the bag was not sufficiently full, he would leave his family. His poor descendants who remain in the Netherlands Indies would mix with the native population."[62] The cynical quote implies that Dutch officials believed the Arabs were not invested in the colony—even to the extent of leaving their families in the Netherlands Indies. Marriage was contracted to gain access to more wealth—that of their native wives—to be channeled back to their true homeland in Arabia. A report in 1905 by the director of education, religious affairs, and industry denigrated the Foreign Oriental as a *wereldburger*, a term synonymous with "cosmopolitan," which in this context carried a negative connotation associated with rootlessness and disloyalty.[63] Yet the "simple, childlike, carefree Javanese," argued one Dutch official, was easily taken in by these Foreign Orientals.[64] "Usury, money and blood (through slavehold-ing)"—Dutch colonial literature relentlessly yoked Foreign Orientals in the Netherlands Indies to these three elements.[65] Indeed, this argument was made more forcefully during the early twentieth century than in the nine-teenth century.[66] Thereafter, the "backwardness" of the colony was directly connected to Foreign Orientals' supposed tactics. One Dutch official was convinced that abandoning residential quartering would immediately lead to the oppression and destruction of the Javanese by Foreign Orientals.[67] Dutch authorities had effectively displaced their anxiety and guilt onto the Foreign Orientals, who became convenient bogeymen who did not deserve to be in the Netherlands Indies. The title of one 1908 article on Arabs' exorbitant rates of interest encapsulates Dutch displacement of colonial guilt onto the Arabs—"Arabieren en de Kleine Man" (Arabs and the Little Man).[68] Due to practical and logistical limitations, colonial restrictive policies pertaining spe-cifically to Arabs were usually not enforced, but invective against the Arabs occurred too frequently to be ignored and it outlasted the pass-and-quarter system, which was officially abolished in 1915.[69] By then, Foreign Orientals' commercial profits had already suffered.

Commercial Rivals

This was of course a desired outcome of Dutch colonial policy. The long-standing cooperation between Natives and Foreign Orientals that began long before the arrival of the Dutch had already led to land and property acqui-sition by the latter group.[70] As the story of Karto at the beginning of the chapter demonstrates, the stock narrative in the Netherlands Indies was that Native heads (*penghoeloe*), usually being relatively well off, often borrowed money from Foreign Orientals and paid their debts in the form of houses and land, such that the latter became the largest owners of house property in 1900, gaining success especially in Batavia and West Java where they owned private land, surprising since they were not even allowed to rent property meant for Natives.[71] But this phenomenon was apparently so common that Foreign Orientals rarely requested land titles from the Dutch government.[72] Besides land ownership, the other form of collaboration among colonial subjects that rankled the Dutch elite consisted of partnerships in coffee plantations in Java. Many Chinese and Arab Foreign Orientals remained *opkoopers*, or forestallers, who exported coffee to markets in Batavia and Singapore, often by engaging in illegal deals (from the Dutch perspective) with Native heads of coffee plantations in Java by buying crops in advance at profitable prices, directly flouting the Dutch monopoly of determining prices.[73] The presence of these Arab and Chinese middlemen challenged the intended Dutch alienation of plantations that would facilitate better control and exclusively serve Dutch interests.[74] Trade in other commodities, such as bird's nests, birds of paradise, pearls, rice, wax, yarn, gold, and diamonds, was still dominated by Arabs in Sulawesi, Timor, Aru, Moluccas, and the Javanese interior, despite a range of restrictions imposed on Foreign Orientals in all these places.[75] Other forms of trade were tolerated and not directly challenged—trade in stallions (*hengsten*) was also dominated by the Arabs well into the twentieth century, especially out of Sumba, with auctions held in Batavia and Surabaya, and batik and linen were exclusively under the control of the Chinese and Arabs in Indonesia.[76]

Dutch authorities were particularly concerned about the dominance of Foreign Orientals in the maritime shipping industry, which was not surprising since the sector was financially lucrative and facilitated movement, two benefits that were supposed to be denied to Foreign Orientals.[77] Foreign Orientals had to pay higher taxes on shipping in the region even before the mid-nineteenth century. Since the 1820s, ships owned by Foreign Orientals going to Formosa (Taiwan) or the Coromandel had to pay 25 reals. In addition, cargo and slaves brought by "Moors" (a category that included Arabs and Indian Muslims in this instance) were targeted to be seized by Dutch aldermen.[78] Opinions shifted from year to year as to which group—Moors, Chinese, or Arabs—was more dangerous to Dutch interests—and, supposedly, to Natives' interests as well. The number of vehicle and maritime passes (*zeebrieven*) granted to these Foreign Orientals was determined by constantly shifting policies. Arabs and Chinese were more successful than the Dutch in the shipping business because Dutch-owned ships faced restrictions in having to hire Christian pilots who had to be properly trained at specified maritime schools in Amsterdam at higher costs.[79] Furthermore, Arab-owned ships were mostly barques (vessels with three or more square masts and the mizzen rigged fore-and-aft), which required a smaller crew than full-rigged ships. Foreign Orientals were also closely linked with the slave trade in the region, which the Dutch were trying to eradicate.[80] The people of Madiun in east Java were said to be "wholly owned" by Foreign Orientals. An ordinance to end slavery was issued on July 1, 1863, though of course the practice continued in various forms throughout the archipelago.[81] Even as late as 1896, Arabs reportedly owned slaves in Celebes.[82] Most of the slaves being trafficked fell under the category of Natives. Among Dutch colonial officials, the link between the Foreign Orientals and the slave trade further fueled their protective policies toward Natives, who should, the Dutch argued, be protected from being exploited by Foreign Orientals. Lurid details published by both the Dutch and British press of the cruel treatment of slaves by Sayyid Abdullah bin Abdoerahim Alkadrie Djelani, agent to the king of Lombok, were in part responsible for the enduring image of the Arab slaveholder.[83]

At first, Foreign Orientals were lumped together, collectively considered "vampires" and "a plague upon the Natives."[84] Toward the end of the nineteenth century, Arab Foreign Orientals were increasingly differentiated from the Chinese. Gradually there became more champions for increased rights for the Chinese among the Dutch legal elite, but almost no one urged the government to ease up restrictions for the Arabs.[85] By this time, Foreign Orientals petitioned the government separately both from the Natives and from each other because they were treated differently by the Dutch colonial government.[86] For example, in January 1903, those classified as Arabs, Bengalis, and Moors in Batavia petitioned the Dutch colonial government for more residence permits on the same level as the Chinese, who had already been granted these residence permits.[87] More Chinese knew the Dutch language than Arabs, one article wrote, implying that they were more progressive and advanced as a people.[88] The fact that non-Chinese Foreign Orientals came from different points of origin came to be increasingly underscored too by Dutch authorities as an argument against granting them privileges on par with Chinese Foreign Orientals.[89]

In 1889, the Dutch sinologist J. J. M. de Groot argued that since trade in the Dutch Indies could not survive without Foreign Orientals, the Chinese (rather than the more "dangerous" Arabs) should continue to occupy the role of wholesaler in the region.[90] What made Chinese Foreign Orientals seem less insidious than Arab Foreign Orientals in the closing decades of the nineteenth century? In 1908, the minister of colonies, Alexander Idenburg, underscored that within the group of Foreign Orientals, Arabs should remain distinct from Chinese because they were highly influential among locals.[91] Although Arabs generally possessed less capital than the Chinese, Dutch authorities believed they had an upper hand in trade with Natives, with whom they shared a religious faith.[92] In other words, the Chinese, though a more formidable commercial rival to the Dutch by the early twentieth century, were considered the lesser evil due to their perceived limited kinship proximity with the majority of the population. In contrast to Dutch colonial policy toward the Chinese, which was at times sympathetic, Dutch colonial policy toward the Arabs was constantly rooted in fear. Dutch officials repeatedly observed that Arabs charged the highest interest rates among creditors and were excessively dogged in collecting what was due to them.[93] A Dutch newspaper labelled them "parasites on the Natives" because of the high interest rates that Arab creditors charged—much higher than what the Chinese charged.[94] Since usury is forbidden according to Islamic law, Muslim Arab moneylenders engaged in the practice under various other guises, which Dutch authorities took to be evidence of yet more deceit.[95] For example, Arabs were known to have sold goods at very high cost to those indebted to them—up to a 1,000 percent rate for a New Year's sarong in Lombok in 1908.[96] Another Dutch writer implied that Arabs were generally tougher than Chinese moneylenders when payments were short: "If the Native cannot afford to pay, then the Chinese is almost patient, he assumes the proposition: live and let live. But the Arab smacks the fist and makes the debtor ashamed of his neighbors."[97] The writer Edgar du Perron wrote about how the *kapitan* of the Arab community used to camp outside a woman's house to force her to pay her debt to him.[98] Dutch authorities assumed that the Arab moneylender, closer to the Natives culturally, would have a stronger hold on Natives and thus be able to win their trust, enabling them to shame the Natives more effectively into paying on time. An entry in the *Encyclopaedie van Nederlandsch-Indië* in 1905 stated that "with the exception of the occasional invitation for a spiritual man from Ḥaḍramawt to establish a mosque in one of the Arab settlements (in the Netherlands Indies) no Arab leaves his homeland with a purpose other than making fortune."[99] In the eyes of Dutch authorities, this sense of imminent departure from the Indies did not abate despite the fact that that Arabs, more so than the Chinese, rarely returned to their land of origin due to material interests in the Netherlands Indies and colonial travel restrictions. Moreover, most of their wealth was invested in stores, ships, lands, and other fixed assets, which were not easily transferred.

Marking Arab Difference

Generally, extant colonial records did not regard any colonial subjects highly; however, Dutch colonial sources were more cavalierly derogatory toward

Foreign Orientals, especially the Arabs and Chinese. Within the specific category of Foreign Orientals, the Arabs were singled out by the Dutch administration because they were influential among the bulk of the subject population in the Netherlands Indies. Even Dutch colonial literature—ranging from colonial bureaucrats' memoirs and Christian missionaries' reports to European adventurers' accounts—reveal an ingrained view of Arabs as foreign mercenary merchants with few social links to other residents of the Netherlands Indies.

The classification of Arab colonial subjects lay in contrast to that of another ethnic group known as Malays, who were likewise Muslim and racially mixed and were also classified as Foreign Orientals in the Netherlands Indies. Like Arabs, they too frequently intermarried with other Muslims wherever they traveled, blurring the lines between ethnic communities.[100] Yet Malays were jurisdictionally less problematic in Dutch courts than Arabs, who presented a jurisdictional puzzle for two reasons. Primarily, this was because their point of origin was not within the archipelago, unlike Malays, who were consistently identified with Sumatra's west coast (although they were scattered throughout the region).[101] Similarly, the Arabs of West Borneo (Pontianak and its environs) did not encounter this problem since their power base was rooted in the west coast of the island. These Arabs were exceptional in that they were classified as Natives. One missionary of the Order of Friars Capuchin familiar with the region pointed out that this was because the settlement of Pontianak was founded by the Arabs, who became rulers.[102] No restrictions were placed on them with regards to landholding.[103] More important, they did not have to pay taxes that were levied on other Foreign Orientals on the west coast of Borneo.[104] Likewise, the rulers of Bantam, Pelalawan, Siak, Cheribon, Ternate, Bantam, and Palembang were of Arab descent but classified as Natives since they were political sovereign rulers, albeit with limited powers under Dutch colonial rule.[105] Pontianak remained anomalous because the first Sultan of Pontianak had established himself there with the "advice and concurrence of the Dutch" and later he repaid them by helping them expand the VOC's reach in Borneo from 1786 onward.[106] As a mark of colonial privilege, their Arabness was subsequently downplayed by Dutch authorities, although it was observed that their dress still resembled that of the Arabs as late as 1912. They possessed the most social and symbolic capital since the first Arab monarch established his own dynasty, in contrast to other parts of the archipelago where Arabs married into local dynasties that then became Arab. This phenomenon pointed toward different rates of absorption of Arab lineages into local dynasties. In places where rulers were partly Arab, earlier monarchs had welcomed them,

probably because of their illustrious lineages, which usually stretched back
to the Prophet—but not all monarchs did so. Rulers in several parts of Java
and Madura regarded the Sayyid lineage as secondary to their own royal
lineage, for example in Bantam and Mataram.[107] Ordinary Arabs throughout
the Netherlands Indies, just like their more illustrious compatriots who married into royal families, made deliberate choices along a spectrum of possibilities not rooted in biological lineage—namely, to identify as

1. of pure Arab descent
2. of mixed descent but more prominently Arab,
3. of mixed descent but more prominently Native, and finally
4. Native.[108]

Some Arab migrants who arrived later to the region did not consider earlier,
assimilated migrants to be Arabs.[109]

Even as they experienced decades of economic and political repression,
Foreign Orientals continued to be perceived by the Dutch government as
successful and exploitative merchants in the Netherlands Indies from whom
Natives should be protected.[110] Economically, the Arabs were less powerful
than the Chinese, except in Pekalongan and Palembang.[111] Yet, they were
seen as rivals by the Dutch and sometimes deemed even more threatening
than the Chinese. Clearly, there were noneconomic reasons behind this perceived threat. Arabs' mobility was also associated with spreading dangerous
ideas about Islam to local Muslims. The State Budget Report for the year
1862 states, "The [Dutch authorities in the Indies] had mainly here in view
of the Arabs, who, it is believed, have freedom to access our possessions
than Indian archipelago. and there will freely, at least without any appre-
ciable superintendence, roam. They considered these Arabs, mostly fanatical
Mohammedans, as our natural enemies."[112] From the late 1880s until the
1920s, Dutch colonial officials became increasingly threatened by the Arabs' perceived political and religious influence over Javanese lives, especially
in light of collective Muslim resentment toward Dutch officials.[113] Dutch
scholar-bureaucrats wrote avidly on the issue—almost every issue of the
journal De Indische Gids in 1889 published at least one article that warned
of Arab religious influence over other colonial subjects. In 1908, there was
talk of relaxing restrictions for Foreign Orientals—except for Arabs, due to
the "risk of flooding of undesirable elements" within the specific context of
pan-Islamism.[114]

The lack of nuance persisted even though eight years earlier Van den
Berg had published an authoritative article entitled "Het Pan-Islamisme,"

which differentiated Arab migrants from Ḥaḍramawt who had settled in the Dutch colony from "Meccan fortune-seekers" who, he claimed, dressed as Arabs and spoke Arabic.[115] He emphasized that the links between Arabia and successive generations of Arabs in the Netherlands Indies had grown increasingly tenuous over time.[116] Still, Van den Berg was outnumbered by his colleagues who believed that because Arabs were believed to harbor pan-Islamic feelings, some should be expelled by the Dutch colonial government. Some Arabs from the Netherlands Indies tried to move to Singapore, but upon arrival in the British colonial port city they were not allowed to disembark, being perceived as impoverished. They were then ordered to return to the Netherlands Indies, which was no longer officially open to them, but in practice expelled Arabs could still easily embark and disembark within the Netherlands Indies undetected. Shipping companies such as Stoomvaart Maatschappij Nederland and Koninklijke Rotterdamsche Lloyd complained to the Dutch government about how common this practice was among Foreign Orientals.[117] Another favored destination was Jeddah, in modern-day Saudi Arabia, but even there they had to produce a pass (*geviseerden pas*) prior to obtaining an admission card from the Dutch consul in Jeddah.[118] Despite measures to restrict their movement, the specter of the mobile Arab continued to haunt the Dutch colonial administration.

Arabs remained visible in many ways, primarily through perceived wealth. Foreign Orientals' houses were purportedly larger, built from better, longer-lasting materials than those of the Natives, such as brick.[119] The Dutch painter Willem Witsen made an etching of one such house in Bogor (Buitenzorg) in 1921, clearly regarding it as remarkable curiosity while travelling through the Indies.[120] In Batavia, Arabs owned houses built in the European style, some of which were rented out to Europeans accustomed to such dwellings.[121] In Palembang, Arabs and Chinese built opulent houses made of precious woods such as *tembusu* wood, in contrast to Natives who built flimsier houses with bamboo instead.[122]

Another way Arabs stood out in the Netherlands Indies was through government-imposed dress codes, because centuries of mixing meant that many inhabitants were not easily identifiable otherwise. The novelist P. A. Daum offered a portrait of an Arab's potential ambiguity: "His European first name which also serves as his last name might make one think that he was a Christian, but nothing ever confirmed this notion. But that was all; he could just as well have been an Arab or Bengali."[123] The novelist and travel writer Maurits Wagenvoort noticed that while the Chinese were ubiquitous, and more obviously different, in early twentieth-century Batavia, one had to make an effort to "find the Arab" because they were less obvious[124] To make identification easier, all subjects were expressly prohibited from exhibiting or wearing in public attire anything other than that of the country to which they supposedly belonged.[125] Arabs were specifically required to dress as Arabs according Dutch officials' ideal conceptions. One official observed,

> All Arabs wear either a skirt [*foetah*] or trousers [*sirwal*], a long white shirt [*qamis*] that reached to the ankles and a top dress [*godairiah*], a buttoned long jacket [*djubba*], sometimes with a vest [*badan*] underneath. They wear sandals on their feet [*Na'al*], while their shaved head is covered with the turban, consisting of a rigid circular cap [*koefiah*] on which a piece of cloth [*Imamah*] is wound. They wear the '*Imamah* and *djubbah* only on special occasions; otherwise they cover their head with one linen *koefiah*, while wearing the *foetah* with *godairiah*. Distinguished Arabs who come into contact with Europeans often wear socks and shoes. Some Arabs born in the Dutch East Indies have adopted the modern Turkish costume.[126]

Descriptions of their dress and houses often point toward conspicuous wealth through luxurious materials and ornaments. In fictional literature, they were depicted with headgear, always with multiple layers of clothing, unlikely of course in tropical climates. A dapper Arab tailor in Fort de Kock (Bukit Tinggi) in West Sumatra was described by the writer Justus de Koek: "A very handsome, black-bearded Arabian came to me, neatly dressed with a finely crafted horse hair top [Acehnese hat]. The batik sarong, which he wore over his white waistcoat, suited him, his feet are in colored sandals and his golden jacket buttons proved to me he was very wealthy."[127] A fictional character in the work of the novelist P. A. Daum is described as a "great figure of an Arab, the colored turban a little crooked on the beautiful of jet-black curly hair rounded head; bright white flapped his long undercloth, between the opening of his ruffling garment of blue silk."[128] Disguise was common as both Arabs and Chinese constantly tried to pass off as Natives, and occasionally some Natives and Foreign Orientals attempted to pass off as Europeans by wearing shoes and tighter pants.[129] Passing was tolerated by the Dutch to some extent because even in the nineteenth century Foreign Orientals were still useful in plying the trade between the hinterland and the cities, especially in Java and Sumatra.[130] Ironically, their utility to the colonial government stemmed from their mobility, which was curtailed by new laws introduced from the second half of the nineteenth century onward. The State Budget Report in 1862, for example, even explicitly cautioned against enforcing harsh policies that limited Arab movement in the colony too much in case it led to bitterness among the Arabs, which could harm trade in the

region.[131] Being close to Native wholesalers meant that their lives were concentrated in port cities throughout the Netherlands Indies but they dealt
with the hinterland too as consummate intermediaries.[132]

The race-based legal system in the Netherlands Indies created much confusion because it was not actually race that determined the status of the Foreign Oriental but Dutch colonial political interests. What if convenience was
not the aim of Dutch legislation in the first place? What if legal certainty
was never the goal of Dutch colonial legislation? In fact, this uncertainty was
productive since it opened up opportunities for legal discretion for the Dutch
authorities in specific instances.[133] While the personal laws of other Foreign
Orientals such as Chinese and Japanese residents were elaborated upon in
detail in legislation, discussed extensively in colonial journals, even codified
and grounded in statute to some extent, there was strangely no attempt to
elaborate upon laws pertaining to Arabs beyond rules concerning travel restrictions and dress codes.[134] Government officials claimed that there was no
urgent need to do so since they were presumed to share laws with the native
Muslims after living among them for several generations, but the ambiguity
provided Dutch authorities opportunities to meet Arabs time and time again
to determine their lives on a more personal basis.[135] In other words, this was
likely a deliberate move. It signified simultaneous disavowal and recognition of the Dutch hold over colonial subjects in the era of late colonialism,
facilitated by the incongruousness of applying a version of international law
(*inter-gentiel recht*) on one's own colonial subjects during the late nineteenth
and early twentieth centuries. The ascription of nationality to Arab Foreign
Orientals held advantages for the Dutch regime, something that the system
in the British Straits Settlements, based ostensibly on religious classification
and, to some degree, financial wealth, lacked. One could become wealthier
over time or convert to another religion but one's language, culture, and
descent seemed harder to shed.[136] In this way the category of Foreign Orientals was guaranteed to remained fixed. Nonetheless, because the varied
population and geographical landscape of the Netherlands Indies resisted
the logic of a unified legal system, Arabs in the colony had good reason to
assume that they could continually negotiate their rights as colonial subjects
in particular locations.

CHAPTER 4

Legal Incompetence

Jurisdictional Complications in the Netherlands Indies

In response to a Dutch inspector's request for the removal of a coconut tree that had fallen onto his Dutch neighbor's property in Batavia, an Arab man defiantly replied in a mixture of Dutch and Malay, "Try, see if the assistant dares to take me on over this" ("Tjoba, als de assistent brani is om mij daarover op den rol te brengen").[1] This retort encapsulates Dutch colonial anxiety about potential acts of insubordination by Arab Foreign Orientals. Because the degree to which the Dutch had jurisdiction over Arab Foreign Orientals in the Netherlands Indies remained unresolved until the end of the colonial period, both the loyalty and subservience of Arabs were constantly called into question.

This chapter explores the jurisdictional problems that Arab populations experienced under Dutch colonial rule. The one thing that the Dutch feared above all else was not the slippage of Arab identity into the category of "Natives" but rather the possible equation of Arabs with themselves, Europeans. The possibility of fluid jurisdictions horrified Dutch authorities. As chapter 3 demonstrates, by the early twentieth century, the legal identities of colonial subjects determined both economic potential and political loyalty—if they were Natives, they were regarded as economically useful and loyal, already coerced into producing for the colony as part of *Cultuurstelsel*, and if they were Foreign Orientals, they were an intractable population who remained outside the cultivation scheme, which now made them a drain to the

Figure 9. Ohannes Kurkidjian, *The Arab Community in Front of a Gate Celebrating Queen Wilhelmina's Coronation in 1899*. Collection Nationaal Museum van Wereldculturen, The Netherlands, coll. no. TM-60003143.

economy on top of being commercial rivals. The Javanese, being classified as Natives, were the group of colonial subjects invested with colonial subject privileges, infantilized as they were in colonial discourse that sought to "protect" them against exploitative foreigners during and after the *Cultuurstelsel* period. Within this framework, Natives were transformed into "wards" of the government while Foreign Orientals were interlopers; their mobility only underscored their supposed flightiness and opportunism.

Because the category of "Europeans" (*Europeanen*) was jealously guarded and policed by the Dutch government, it might seem surprising that from 1899 onward, Japanese subjects living in the Netherlands Indies, normally classified as Foreign Orientals, were regarded as equal to Europeans, and some Chinese subjects too started to be regarded as such during the early twentieth century amid changing notions of power and race. But Arabs—and, for that matter, Indians (listed as *mooren* or *klingaleezen*)—would never be considered equal to Europeans at any point during the colonial period, although a few individual Arabs were at times classified as Europeans.[2] On the spectrum of civilization, the Dutch deemed them to be the least advanced and the most like the Natives over whom they ruled. It was not that Arabs based in the Netherlands Indies did not attempt to be classified as Europeans, who after all enjoyed more freedom of movement and property ownership than Foreign Orientals. Many Arab Foreign Orientals tried to claim a European status through identifying as part of the Ottoman Empire, since the heart of the empire—Istanbul—was in Europe. An Arab merchant from Baghdad residing in Batavia in 1871 attempted to claim equal status with Europeans just by referring to *Staatsblad* 1864 no. 179, which referenced a treaty between the Netherlands and Turkey, although both the Raad van Justitie in Batavia and the Supreme Court (*Hooggerechtshof*) were quick to ascertain that the merchant was mistaken.[3] In 1907, the identity of a man named Saleh Fagih presented a challenge to Dutch authorities—he was born in Mecca to parents who were Turks from Albania, with a grandfather who was Roman Catholic, though all his other members of the family were all Muslims. Dutch authorities did not know how to classify him.[4] Eventually he was classified as "Arab Turk" and momentarily grouped with the Foreign Orientals, his fellow litigants in the legal case. He appealed this ruling, and the Supreme Court subsequently declared him a European.[5] The case was then brought to the Raad van Justitie in Bandung rather than to the *landraad*, a lower court meant only for Natives and Foreign Orientals including Arabs. The Appellate Judicial Council (*Appellate Raad van Justitie*), of which there were six throughout the Netherlands Indies, was reserved for Europeans but also heard appeals from Natives and Foreign Orientals. The Supreme Court in Batavia, which had jurisdiction over the entire Netherlands Indies, formed the only tether to the seat of Dutch political authority for other courts. Their jurisdiction extended to all civil and commercial disputes within the European community, including criminal acts committed by Europeans. The headline of a report in 1934—"Arab or Native?"—on the case of guardianship over a boy who was half-Dutch, half-Arab in Meester Cornelis in Java encapsulates the absurdity of legal separations.[6] The boy's biological father had returned to Ḥaḍramawt. The case embodied the legal complexities wrought by a system predicated on difference, separation, and pluralism rather than the actual reality on the ground, which was that the boy had lived with his Arab guardian appointed by his father prior to the case.

Most Arabs in the Netherlands Indies were of course not from Baghdad or Turkey, in the Ottoman Empire proper, but from Ḥaḍramawt, where Ottoman hold was tenuous—although in 1872, the Ottoman Sultan did install a governor for the Ḥaḍramī coast.[7] Hence Dutch authorities believed that the claim of Ottoman subjecthood among Ḥaḍramīs was weak. This did not stop several Arabs in Batavia from claiming European status after pledging their allegiance to the Ottoman sultan in the 1880s, despite having never even lived in Ḥaḍramawt.[8] After all, the Ottoman consul in Singapore since 1864 had been an Arab of Ḥaḍramī descent named Abdullah Aljunied.[9] Some Arabs in the Netherlands Indies even produced "certificates" declaring European origin.

To complicate matters, although Dutch authorities in Batavia refused to recognize these claims of Ottoman subjecthood, they vested Ottoman authority in the 1880s with a legal hold over Arabs of Ḥaḍramī descent based in the Netherlands Indies, but only with regards to their property in Ḥaḍramawt. In this way, laws governing personal status was divorced from laws over property, a move that we see in many colonial arrangements. Thereafter, the Dutch government instituted that legal documents such as powers of attorney not only had to be approved by qadis in Ḥaḍramawt but also had to be ratified by the Ottoman consul in Batavia, Ghalib Bey.[10] Already robbed of his diplomatic status amid strained relations between Dutch and Ottoman authorities, the Ottoman consul now had to suffer the indignity of verifying the authenticity of seals and signatures on documents that originated in Ḥaḍramawt.[11] This requirement not surprisingly met with several complaints from members of the Arab community, who argued that it was ridiculous to expect the Ottoman consul to have knowledge of Ḥaḍramawt and the Netherlands Indies because neither Ḥaḍramawt or the Netherlands Indies was legally Ottoman territory. Rather absurdly, the Ottoman consul often had to consult the Arabs since he had no way of verifying anything by himself. Worse, there was a hefty fee for the Ottoman consul's legal services—between 40 and 50 guilders, an amount often worth more than the real estate property in question. Because the legal system in the Netherlands Indies was highly localized, documents deemed valid in Batavia were not automatically regarded as valid elsewhere in the colony, such as in the Orphan Chamber (*weeskamer*) of Surabaya.[12] This Kafkaesque jurisdictional situation led to inconsistency that could be exploited by colonial subjects to continually negotiate their status.

European status was highly desirable to Arabs, who were acutely aware of the inferior status that the classification of Foreign Orientals conferred on them. Legal parity in the courtroom remained, for the most part, only theoretical under any circumstance because the application of different laws to Foreign Orientals stemmed from a lack of trust that had to be mitigated by precautionary measures not applied to agreements with other populations. At first glance, attempts to reduce the unpredictability of the Dutch colonial legal administration in commercial lawsuits appear to be the least controversial aspect of legal differentiation, which intensified in the second half of the nineteenth century, because this was an area of law where the Dutch sought to establish legal certainty without erasing prior relationships and instead built on them. Since many Foreign Orientals were merchants, European merchant houses specifically requested that the Dutch government apply Dutch civil and commercial law to all their trading partners in the 1830s.[13] This request, which was ultimately successful, demonstrates how economic position was the primary determinant in legal parity in colonial courts in the Netherlands Indies, an exploitation colony where Native Indonesians were the primary producers and the Arabs, Chinese, and Indians were generalized as the economic middlemen.[14] Commercial efficiency demanded that transactions be subjected to common norms, and all colonial subjects who engaged in urban business transactions were conveniently presumed by a useful fiction to have acquiesced in the relevant rules of Dutch commercial law.[15] Dutch colonial officials thought it convenient to set standard laws in commercial matters.[16] Because an overwhelming number of legal cases involving Foreign Oriental and European litigants tended to revolve around settlement of debts, Dutch commercial laws were subsequently printed and widely distributed to Foreign Oriental communities.[17]

Trust was constantly an issue when it came to Foreign Orientals. According to Dutch colonial law, verbal agreements were deemed sufficient between Natives, but a material binder was required in order to enforce obligations with Indonesian "strangers"—Chinese, Arabs, and Europeans.[18] Their mercantile accounts books seemed to be scrutinized more often and legal agreements with them also tended to be more detailed, covering more eventualities.[19] But the real reason for the application of European commercial laws to Foreign Orientals was that Europeans could not be tried in local courts where Native Laws and Foreign Oriental laws were applied. Before 1848, when the new laws were introduced, Europeans were subjected to adat laws when litigants were Natives. Several notices in government gazettes in the 1840s and 1850s stated that Foreign Orientals should be subjected to European Law in commercial affairs. According to subsection 78(2) of the Regeeringsreglement in 1882, Foreign Orientals had to be subjected to laws normally reserved for Europeans in the Netherlands Indies in commercial cases involving Europeans.[20] While there was still uncertainty in legal disputes in civil courts regarding what laws governed cases involving both Foreign Orientals (Chinese and Arabs) and European litigants through end of the colonial period, increasingly over time these Foreign Orientals were subjected to European civil and commercial law even in commercial cases that did not involve Europeans.[21] Even so, despite the imposition of European laws on non-Europeans, Dutch authorities remained concerned about the differences in oath-taking in matters of commercial transaction, never fully convinced that the oath taken by Natives and Foreign Orientals was as significant as the Christian oath.[22]

Doubt concerning jurisdictions followed Foreign Orientals everywhere within the Dutch legal system. When cases involving Arabs were brought to higher civil courts such as the Raad van Justitie and the Supreme Court, their first task was to circumscribe jurisdiction for all litigants involved. Civil courts had mostly European judges, since local judges (mostly high-born Javanese) were not appointed to European jurisdictions.[23] Despite an aversion to administering religious and customary laws, legal authorities could not afford to be completely indifferent to these laws since some cases, especially inheritance cases that were brought to these civil courts, involved landed property that was subjected to Dutch civil law, which prohibited the perpetual alienation of land for private family purposes.[24] In 1882, the Raad van Justitie, which usually heard cases from litigants of all ethnic backgrounds, unexpectedly declared itself incompetent to hear the case brought by an Arab man named Said Mohamad bin Hoesin Alhabshi against the Dutch colonial government.[25] Hence the case was brought to the Supreme Court in March 1882. The case revolved around a piece of land in Central Java, the revenue of which was to go to the heirs of the deceased Said Aloei bin Sjech Aldjuffrie, who had died nearly seventy years earlier in 1815.[26] As far as the Supreme Court was concerned, the land had no legal owner between 1815 (when Java was under British colonial rule) and 1882 (when the case was brought to the Supreme Court).[27] The Supreme Court did not recognize that the land belonging testator Said Aloei bin Sjech Aldjuffrie devolved to anyone, although the case was brought to court precisely to ascertain its status in relation to his family.[28] The matter was classified under "civil affairs, not Islamic," although the description of the piece of land fit that of a family endowment known as waqf, an undoubtedly religious institution, held by the family of Said Aloei bin Sjech Aldjuffrie. While British authorities definitely considered alienation of land in their colonies to be legitimate up to a certain degree, Dutch colonial authorities considered it illegal since all uncultivated land was automatically granted to the Dutch government.[29] The report on the case is remarkably devoid of religious references, and rarely is the word waqf, or even "trust" or "endowment," used. This was a typical approach by a higher civil court toward religious laws. Instead, the report focused on the technicalities of sovereign law in the Netherlands Indies. Were laws applied in 1815, presumed to be mixture of Dutch civil law and English common law, relevant, the court asked? Since the government was, at the time of the lawsuit, none other than the Dutch colonial government, the piece of property should be squarely governed by Dutch colonial law. The law report stressed that Roman law, or Old Dutch law, would not have allowed Said Aloei's heirs to benefit from the land perpetually. It stated, "When the assignment was made, the land was by no means considered alienated as a fixed property to the Said, but expressly assigned for the permanent and honorable support, or such regulations and restrictions adopted by the government that he and his family were under."[30] The outcome is predictable as the status of the land was historicized in particular ways adhering to colonial timelines at the expense of local histories with deeper roots. Courts shrugged off their responsibilities, pushing cases up the hierarchy and sometimes off the hierarchy altogether. Judges debated inconsistencies of historical jurisdictions working backwards from their intended declarations and verdicts. The truth is that colonial jurisdictions were shallow, such that colonial fiat alone was insufficient to abolish accretion of jurisdictions. Just like the judges in the British Straits Settlements in 1858 and 1871, Dutch legal administrators too resorted to judicial interpretation rather than simple and outright abrogation. They had to reason through jurisdictional problems in specific legal cases instead of passing legislation, even at a time when colonial sovereignty was no longer in doubt during the nineteenth century.

Arab Petition

Colonial subjects, however, had no doubt about colonial sovereignty, and some strategically threw on a blanket of jurisdiction over their lives. In August 1890, sixty Arabs led by Said Abdullah bin Abu Bakar Alatas wrote a letter to the governor-general of the Netherlands Indies, Cornelis Hordijk, petitioning the colonial government to authorize the establishment of an Arab court (*Arab raad*) in each city within the Netherlands Indies with substantial Arab populations that would only cater to cases involving Arabs.[31] The petitioners complained that local existing *priesterraden* headed by Javanese qadis had wrongfully separated Arab husbands from their wives due to the incorrect application of Islamic law. This petition formed the latest complaint in a series of ongoing grievances that intensified from the 1880s into the early twentieth century. Arab residents protested the qadis' judgements by providing copies of these rulings to the advisor of Native and Arab affairs, Christiaan Snouck Hurgronje. This phenomenon picked up only then because as late as 1850, the priesterraden in Batavia declared they had no jurisdiction over Arabs, such that cases involving Arabs were always brought up to the Supreme Court even though they usually dealt with family matters and therefore involved Islamic law.[32] Strictly speaking, since Islamic law was already relegated to the local priesterraden staffed with Muslim judges, higher Dutch courts with non-Muslim legal authorities were prevented from administering Islamic law. Unhappy that they were called upon to administer laws they had little knowledge of, the Supreme Court gradually compelled the priesterraden to became the court for all Muslim subjects in the Dutch colony without ethnic differentiation. In 1881, Arabs in Surabaya declared that they no longer recognized justice meted out by priesterraden.[33] The Arabs believed that their desire for a more stringent adherence to Islamic law in the Netherlands Indies necessitated a separate court from the Natives. Through direct observation of the incompetence of the priesterraden and complaints from local Arabs, Snouck himself began to share the Arabs' concerns about the priesterraden.[34] In 1901, he sided with an Arab complainant when he vehemently concurred that the entire priesterraden in Surabaya should be discharged.[35] Snouck later wrote in 1904 to the governor-general of the Netherlands Indies that "the Arab has his own set of rules; although he has assimilated in local societies away from his native environment, his ancestry remains distinct and guarantees a certain priority among subject populations in the Netherlands Indies."[36] Certainly, the Arabs that he was well acquainted with prioritized their differences more than their similarities vis-à-vis Native Muslims, and by doing so ensured that their differences become central to their identities as colonial subjects.

The sixty Arab petitioners of Surabaya were particularly irritated by the tendency of the existing priesterraden to prioritize local customary laws over Islamic law. The petitioners pointed out that Islamic law was implemented more extensively in their land of origin, Ḥaḍramawt.[37] Why should they then be subjected to courts that administered a version of Islamic law, modified by adat in the Malay world, that had never been a part of their culture? Yet by submitting the petition, the sixty Arabs demonstrated that they recognized Dutch colonial authority as a binding force on legal judgments in the colony that made Dutch approval for any kind of legal forum essential. Outnumbered by Native Muslims, the Arabs could not count on affecting change within the local priesterraden themselves, such that Dutch colonial channels seemed a more effective avenue to enact any sort of transformation in the legal arena. This proved that these Arabs did not possess much clout within the priesterraden, despite believing themselves to be more knowledgeable about Islamic law than the local Muslim judges who administered their lives. After all, the term *priesters en hoofden* in Article 78 (2) of the Government Act (Regeeringsreglement) passed in 1882 referred to "priests and leaders" of Native communities and not of other minority Muslim communities.[38] As a result, Arabs came to be grouped together with other Muslim Natives in matters of personal law that involved family law. In addition to religious laws, all Muslim subjects were also subjected to so-called "laws of ancient origins," which usually referred to ancient customs of the land—that is, the laws of native Muslims according to their geographical location in the culturally diverse archipelago. The Arab communities were deeply unhappy because, since they did not subscribe to these highly localized customary laws, they constantly risked being subjected to laws that were not their own. Snouck recognized this and, speaking on behalf of his Arab allies and constituents to his Dutch colleagues, attempted to expand the notion of "laws of ancient origins" to include the laws that had been applied to Arab residents who had maintained their independence in matters of family law in varying degrees throughout the archipelago for several centuries prior to 1882. After all, there were already signs that Arab societies continued to lead somewhat separate lives from local Muslims under colonial rule. For one, Arab communities in cities with significant Arab populations such as Surabaya, Semarang, and Cirebon had their own marriage officers (the *huwelijksbeambten*) separate from the local marriage officers appointed by the Dutch colonial government (the *districtshuwelijksbeambten*).[39]

However, a completely separate jurisdiction for Arab residents in cases that involved family law was ultimately deemed too big a concession for the Dutch government to grant. Like his colleagues, Snouck was less concerned about his Arab friends' distress at what they perceived to be improper application of Islamic law than he was by the position of non-Arab women in marital unions with Arab men. Unlike ultraorthodox Jews in Mandate Palestine, who convinced British authorities that they deserved the right to establish their own independent courts since they led separate lives from other communities, Arab authorities did not succeed in making a case that their lives were truly separate from other Muslims in the region.[40] In fact, the problem with the sixty petitioners' request for separate jurisdictions was that not all litigants in cases involving Arabs' marriages were Arabs. Arab men in the archipelago married local women more often than Arab women, and 75 percent of the cases brought to priesterraden pertained to marriages between Arab men and their local wives.[41] Even Snouck was eventually unconvinced of the necessity of separate courts for Arabs and Muslim Natives. The frequency of interracial marital unions led him to question whether it would be fair to subject local women to Islamic law unmodified by the latter's local adat. Adat took precedence over Islamic law even among Muslim subjects in some parts of Indonesia because of its longevity.[42] Therefore, marital cases, he argued, should continue to be determined according to a mixture of adat and Islamic law by local judges in the priesterraden. In order to be fair to local women, he stipulated that only when all litigants involved were Arabs should courts consider implementing a separate set of laws. In response to another petition by eleven Arabs based in Batavia in 1905, Snouck stressed that it was unnecessary to appoint separate marriage officers for Arab marriages when current officers could very well ratify and register marriages for all Muslims, locals and Arabs alike.[43] He also considered it unnecessary for a separate council of three to be established in order to mediate marital disputes between Arab spouses, since this was already part of the duties of the priesterraden anyway.[44] Above all, he wanted to ensure that the priesterraden would not be declared incompetent in marital disputes involving mixed marriages between Arab men and local women. If anything, the priesterraden should be reined in, not given more latitude. Snouck claimed to Governor Cornelis Hordijk that Arab men notoriously entered into temporary unions with local women that lasted only several weeks or months. He argued that these impermanent marriages meant that these women already occupied legally precarious positions. Eventually, the priesterraden, despite its many imperfections, not only remained in control up until the end of the colonial period but also continued to administer the lives of Arabs. In January 1903, an article was published in the colonial newspaper *De Locomotief* that was very critical of Arab marriages with Native women in the cities of Gresik, Sitoebondo, and Bondowoso, where the proportion of Arabs was among the highest in Java—at 4.4 percent, 5.5 percent, and 7 percent respectively. The author of the article, identified simply as W.v.K, focused solely on "pure Arabs" (*totok-Arabieren*) who were newly arrived, thus portraying Arabs as temporary guests in the Indies who coldly abandoned their "widows" without a thought. Yet "a whiff of Arab holiness," the author lamented, continued to entice ignorant Native fathers to marry off their daughters to these Arab men.[45]

Because both Arabs and Muslim Natives had been mixing long before the Dutch arrived in the region in the early seventeenth century, colonial officials directly acquainted with Arabs in the colony such as Snouck observed that the distinction between Arabs and Natives in the colony was not as pronounced as they would like.[46] However, binaries were retained in legal classification, since Snouck's immediate successor, Bertram Johannes Otto Schrieke, maintained that the notion of "a native Sayyid" was a contradiction in 1920.[47] Fancying themselves scholar-bureaucrats, Snouck and Schrieke could not deny the history of communities they managed and controlled and so continually struggled with dichotomies they created and strove to uphold. Partly, this was because they were uncomfortable with advocating closer relations between Natives and Arabs in the colony, as much as they wanted to be realistic about social realities.[48] Tellingly, they did not argue for the dismantling of the colonial legal system that separated Arab Muslims from Natives. For his part, Snouck's response to the Arabs' petition allowed him to demonstrate to his Dutch colleagues his knowledge of the intricacies of Islamic law and his political acumen in choosing to espouse a policy of tolerance and vigilance concerning Arab communities.[49] Reluctant to give a hard "no" to the petitioners, he more or less put the matter aside. The matter of separate courts for Arabs remained unresolved and in 1925, a commission based in Batavia revisited the issue by specifically investigating whether Muslim Foreign Orientals should have their own court. In the end, the Dutch government decided not to establish separate jurisdictions for non-native Muslims.[50] As late as 1938, however, a case involving the Arab Belfas clan forced the *landraad* of Batavia to specifically consider Ḥaḍramī laws (not Islamic law) concerning marriages and guardianship.[51]

Lumping Arabs together with Native Muslims was likely a practical choice on the part of the Dutch legal authorities to avoid a legal morass involving marriages between Arab and Natives in the archipelago. On one hand, adat law proponents situated Arabs within the complicated colonial legal system divided into law circles. On the other hand, colonial officials who were better acquainted with Muslim affairs and Arab communities, such as L. W. C. van den Berg, Snouck, and G. F. Pijper, situated Arab subjects within the universal Muslim community and perceived them to be more inclined toward Islamic law untainted by local adat, which they often claimed was not always compatible with Islamic law.[52] For his part, Snouck was convinced that the vast majority of Muslims throughout the archipelago adhered to Islamic law that had been influenced by local adat, which remained resilient. This prospect made some colonial officials deeply anxious because the possibility of a competing universal appeal could potentially lead to anticolonial, pan-Islamic uprisings. This did not necessarily mean, however, that Van den Berg and Snouck were more secure and assured of Dutch colonial hold over local Muslim populations. As scholar-bureaucrats with an intellectual bent, they based their views of subject populations on Orientalist scholarship they had been acquainted with in Delft and Leiden and subsequent empirical observations in the colony, which led them to conclude that Islam as a spiritual faith undoubtedly influenced the lives of Indies Muslims, especially the Arabs, especially in personal law.[53]

Snouck's later successors as advisor for Native and Arab affairs, Douwe Adolf Rinkes and G. A. J. Hazeu, continued to question whether Arab residents of the Netherlands Indies should be subjected to civil law or Islamic law in courts.[54] This was done with an eye to deny colonial subjects opportunities for forum shopping, a great fear of Hazeu in particular. Due to profound legal uncertainty, an Arab could potentially shop from among the "labyrinth of unwritten adat laws" in which he believed.[55] A judge could easily be hood-winked into applying adat laws for which there was no written basis, since adat laws had only been codified in a fragmentary manner, Hazeu claimed, citing a case of a type by now familiar, between a Native village head (*hoofd-panghoeloe*) in Bandung and an Arab moneylender named Seche Abdul Rahman. He was alarmed by the crucial lack of consistency between government policy that underscored Arabs' "foreignness" and court decisions that showed remarkable variation. Both Hazeu and Rinkes acknowledged that the main inconsistency with the racial classification of Arabs derived from its sole emphasis on paternal descent through an infinite number of generations. Some Arabs of Palembang and Jambi in Sumatra were classified as Arabs even after seven generations during the early twentieth century, while others subsumed under the category of "Malays" were classified as Natives in Palembang but Foreign Orientals elsewhere.[56] For this reason, Hazeu argued that "assimilated Arabs" (*gelijkgestelde Arabieren*) should always be subjected to Islamic law, just like local Muslims, and never be subjected to the civil law that applied to other Foreign Orientals such as the Chinese and Japanese.[57] He compared the Arab population in the Netherlands Indies to Catholics in the Netherlands Indies, who were, after all, not subjected to ecclesiastical law being a recognized minority. He considered it equally absurd that a "pure" Arab (*onvervalschten Arabier*—literally, "unadulterated Arab") could be regarded as European by the Supreme Court in a case in 1908. On the whole, Hazeu held on to the opinion that although these Arabs would be more "native" than "foreign" after several generations, the fact that they frequently moved in and out of the colony made them a diasporic race. Hence mobility, rather than race, became a marker of Foreign Oriental identity.

Arab Influence on Islamic Law in the Netherlands Indies

Although the legal autonomy of Arabs was curtailed in the colony, Arab affairs—and one might even argue Muslim affairs in general—remained to some extent in Arab hands in the Netherlands Indies through the symbiotic relationships between colonial officials and the Arab elite. In November 1882, Van den Berg, based in Batavia, published the French translation of the *Minhāj al-Ṭālibīn*, an influential and important Shafii legal text.[58] The translation of Nawawi's *Minhāj* was not a purely Dutch endeavor, however, as Van den Berg was indebted to Moḥamad ibn Ḥasan Bābahīr, the head of the Arab community in Batavia, known for "his considerable faculties for judging" as a qadi and a member of the Orphan Chamber of Batavia. Originally from Say'un in Ḥaḍramawt, Bābahīr taught Van den Berg "contemporary Arabic morals and customs" in the late nineteenth century, especially in matters related to prayer and Haj pilgrimage, having embarked on the pilgrimage himself.[59] Van den Berg found it difficult to translate subtleties, double entendres, and ellipses from Arabic into a European language, especially in a subject as dense, nuanced, and complicated as religious practice, forcing him to rely on sometimes inaccurate Malay or Javanese translations already available in the Indies.[60] Bābahīr's expertise gave him the confidence to refer directly to the Arabic manuscript.[61] For his contributions to Dutch colonial knowledge, Bābahīr was named by the Netherlands Indies government as one of the outstanding (uitstekende) men of Ḥaḍramawt, alongside an Islamic scholar and religious teacher in Batavia, Sayyid 'Uthmān bin 'Abdallāh bin 'Aqil bin Yaḥyā al-'Alawī al-Ḥussaynī (1822–1913), who later became a mufti and Snouck's intellectual collaborator.[62]

This collaboration between Sayyid 'Uthmān and Snouck echoed and rivalled that between Van den Berg and Bābahīr.[63] Born in the town of Pekodjan in Batavia in 1822, Sayyid 'Uthmān was raised by his Egyptian maternal grandfather, Shaykh 'Abd Al-Raḥmān bin Aḥmad al-Miṣrī. Upon his grandfather's death in 1847, he travelled to Arabia to perform his pilgrimage. He later studied in Mecca with Sayyid Aḥmad Dahlān, a Shāfi'ī mufti.[64] After seven years in Mecca, he went to Ḥaḍramawt to study with several prominent teachers. He then returned to Mecca and continued his studies in Morocco, Tunisia, Algeria, Egypt, Syria, Palestine, and Istanbul. Sayyid 'Uthmān returned to Batavia in 1882 and became well-acquainted with Dutch residents there.[65] In 1881, Sayyid 'Uthmān wrote a widely read handbook on the main points of Islamic law in the Indies, Kitab al-Qawanin al-Shar'iyya li-Ahl al-Majalis al-Hukmiyya bi-Tahqiq al-Masd'il li-Yatamayyaza la-hum al-Haqq mi al-Batil (Book of administration of Islamic law). This handbook was revised, expanded, and reprinted in 1894. Originally written in Jawi for officials of the priesterraden, the book was translated into Dutch under the title De Gids voor Priesterraden in 1895. Because Islamic law in the Netherlands Indies was never codified by the Dutch colonial elite, Sayyid Uthmān's book provided a valuable resource for other qadis and Dutch colonial judges.[66] His lithographed atlas of Ḥaḍramawt, which could be taken as a nostalgic return to the region of his ancestors, won him considerable attention from Dutch officials.[67] By July 1888, Sayyid 'Uthmān had already formed a friendship with his most formidable ally in colonial bureaucracy, Snouck.[68] Referring to Sayyid 'Uthmān as an "ally of the government of the Netherlands-Indies," Snouck believed that he was a great scholar whose knowledge of Islamic theology and jurisprudence, Javanese customs, and the Malay language made him extremely valuable to the Dutch colonial elite.[69] Consequently, Snouck played a decisive role in appointing Sayyid 'Uthmān as the honorary advisor for Arabic affairs.[70] Although Sayyid 'Uthmān was not on the official government payroll, he was paid at least 100 guilders a month by Snouck to provide information on Islamic affairs.[71] Believing that his friend deserved more gratitude from the government than he received, Snouck claimed that Sayyid 'Uthmān was "worth much more than the liberal wine-drinking Javanese regents" to the Dutch colonial elite, who already faced the challenging task of governing millions of Muslims with great sensitivity and tact so as not to cause unnecessary discontentment.[72] Their friendship was so close that Snouck would not easily trust a Muslim religious authority who was unknown to Sayyid 'Uthmān.[73] Likewise, Snouck's denigration of adat, which he placed in direct opposition to Islamic law, could have also been influenced by Sayyid 'Uthmān's strong views on the issue. Like Sayyid 'Uthmān, Snouck consistently cast local subject populations as Muslims whose lives were primarily governed by Islamic principles instead of adat, which could sometimes be un-Islamic.[74] Sayyid 'Uthmān had a specific set of beliefs, mainly stemming from critical views of Sufi mysticism and what he perceived as a lack of religiosity among fellow Muslims and from an animosity toward adat such that he was said to tolerate non-Muslim rule more than adat.[75] Not surprisingly, his severe criticism of Sufi orders did not endear him to many Muslims in the Netherlands Indies, and to some extent his elite Arab identity was considered out of touch with local realities experienced by the bulk of the population.[76] Sayyid Uthmān hardly represented Arab opinions, and he therefore constantly faced opposition from fellow Arabs and other Muslims.[77] Most important, his close relationship with the Dutch contributed to local Muslims' antipathy toward Arabs during the early twentieth century.[78]

Although his beliefs were quite particular, Sayyid 'Uthmān was able to use his own proximity and special relationship with Snouck to influence the social and legal mores of Muslims in the Netherlands Indies, and more specifically, the social norms of Arabs living in the region. To some extent, his extensive oeuvre, written mostly in Malay and sometimes in Arabic, demonstrates that Sayyid 'Uthmān also worked outside of the colonial framework in order to police Muslim communities not only within the Netherlands Indies but also in the British Straits Settlements, thus offering us a vivid glimpse of Arabs that broke outside of strictly colonial legal structures. Yet it would be hard to deny that it was the collaborative underpinning of his relationship with Dutch colonial authorities that propelled Sayyid 'Uthmān to a position of authority. Indeed, Sayyid 'Uthmān deliberately drew upon colonial legitimacy to assert his influence over Muslim societies. He actively requested that Snouck appoint him as an advisor and mufti, explaining that he was the only expert consulted about *fiqh* matters in family law and inheritance law by Javanese and Malay judges and by European officials interested in Sufi *tariqas* (orders).[79] The fact that Sayyid ʿUthmān referred to his Islamic education to promote his unique capability in his request to Snouck indicates that the vast majority of the members of the priesterraden were not educated in *fiqh* at all, although a few prominent religious teachers were trained just as rigorously in Indonesia and part of the Middle East.[80] In 1898, Sayyid ʿUthmān wrote a prayer for the Dutch queen Wilhelmina on the occasion of her ascent to the throne as a sign of loyalty to the Dutch colonial power, thus sealing his role as a steadfast colonial ally.[81] His influence over other Muslims in the Netherlands Indies was probably limited, although he was a respected authority on Islam and theology.[82]

In order to bolster his importance in the eyes of the Dutch colonial elite, Snouck concentrated his efforts on discrediting Van den Berg and his Arab ally Bābahīr. Already he had questioned Van den Berg's knowledge of Arabic and Islam in a series of scathing book reviews, so he must have been jubilant when a more concrete opportunity presented itself in 1893 to specifically take Bābahīr to task. In April of that year, Sayyid ʿUthmān was called to the Supreme Court of the Netherlands Indies in Batavia to advise on an unusual case on guardianship.[83] Upon the recent death of his father, a man named Sayyid Abdullah bin Muḥammad bin Shihab was appointed guardian of his minor brothers and sisters, although their mother was still alive.[84] Sayyid ʿUthmān argued that that normally according to Shāfiʿī law in both the Netherlands Indies and Arabia, the children's mother would be the guardian of the children upon her husband's death. He disagreed with an earlier case heard in 1891 in the Orphan Chamber when another Arab man named Sayyid Ali bin Ahmad bin Shahab had been declared the guardian over his own minor brothers and sisters. Lo and behold, it turned out that case was decided upon the advice of the leader (*kapitan*) of the Arab community, Muḥammad ibn Ḥasan Bābahīr, who drew from principles stated in the Qur'an that he believed stated that the eldest son should be the guardian of his siblings after their father passed away.[85] However, the Qur'an did not touch upon the subject at hand at all, such that even Europeans in the Orphan Chamber expressed their surprise at Bābahīr's extrapolation although they accepted his legal advice anyway.

The case allowed Snouck an opportunity to eviscerate Bābahīr's claim to expertise on Islamic law. Through a series of insinuations, Snouck attempted to destroy Bābahīr's reputation as a reliable advisor to the Dutch colonial government on Muslim affairs in the colony. He unjustly dismissed Bābahīr as either ignorant or worse by floating the possibility that the latter had delivered his judgment out of malice. Quite alarmingly, Snouck readily admitted that he was even inclined to believe that Ḥasan Bābahīr had in fact been bribed to provide false rulings counter to Islamic law, though he was quick to add that these were simply rumors. Bābahīr's opinion fed into Snouck's argument that members of the priesterraden as well as government-appointed heads of Arab communities were often corrupt because they were not paid sufficiently by the Dutch colonial government if at all.[86] Always thorough in his judgment, Snouck held the European members of the Orphan Chamber responsible as well, in a way cementing his own authority on the subject of the appointment of a suitable Arab advisor to the Orphan Chamber on religious affairs. Five months later, in December 1893, Snouck again wrote a letter to the governor-general urging the government to investigate Bābahīr's rulings and his suitability as a member of the Orphan Chamber that ultimately led to his dismissal from the chamber altogether.[87]

Snouck and Van den Berg latched on to Arab allies because they were competing with each other and with other Dutch officials such as Ch. W. Margadant, Th. Juynboll, and J. G. Schot. The energetic flow of knowledge on Islam pulsed through Dutch colonial bureaucracy as these men published copiously in colonial journals on various issues ranging from history and criminal law to family law rituals to Sufi *tariqas* (orders). They eagerly engaged each other in intellectual conversations, which were not always cordial, especially in book reviews (known as *besprekingen*—literally, discussions) of books on Islam in the Netherlands Indies. These reviews, published in nearly every issue of every Dutch colonial journal, tended to be erudite, critical, and impassioned.[88] Particularly bitter debates occurred between Snouck and his peers, especially Van den Berg, who was actually more senior than Snouck within the ranks of colonial bureaucracy. In his critical review of Van den Berg's *De Beginselen Van Het Mohammedaansche Recht* (1878), Snouck accused Van den Berg of being lacking in legal expertise ("gebrek aan rechtskunde") and of being a quasi-practitioner ("quasi-beoefenaar") for making fundamental mistakes despite having specialized in Islamic law for more than a decade by then. Another scathing review of Van den Berg's translation of *Minhāj al-ṭālibīn* was published in the journal *De Indische Gids* in April 1883, where Snouck again gleefully pointed out Van den Berg's numerous errors.[89] Nonetheless, Van den Berg's work did not seem to suffer from Snouck's harsh criticism, probably because the latter was not level-headed. At one point, Snouck called a criticism directed at him "unthinking" and responded to it in a string of articles full of invectives in the journal *Javabode* in 1899, where he called one of his challengers an "incompetent lawyer."[90] With the same gusto, Snouck reviewed and discussed Sayyid 'Uthmān bin Yaḥyā's writings in colonial journals, thus granting them an even wider audience among colonial administrators.[91] By doing so, Snouck deftly instrumentalized Sayyid 'Uthmān to spread his own beliefs on the management of the colony, since he happened to share his interlocutor's opinions.

Kafā'a in Marriage

Separations take on many guises as some were fostered by colonial subjects themselves against fellow Muslims. The notion of separation held by the Arab elites in Southeast Asia was rooted specifically in anxiety over marriages between female descendants of the Prophet and male non-descendants. Sayyid 'Uthmān, like his counterparts in the Straits Settlements and like the Arab petitioners in Surabaya in 1890, was concerned about marriage, something he shared with his Dutch contemporaries.[92] He focused on the uncertain role of the priesterraden in the solemnization of marriages, keen as he was to conserve patriarchal authority within the family rather than cede it to government functionaries within the colonial institution. Much to his discomfort, Dutch colonial authorities recognized that the "Muslim priest," whether it be the qadi or *penghulu* (village head), could act as a *walī* (guardian) for a woman in any circumstance, contrary to the standard Islamic view that the qadi could act as a woman's *walī* instead of a male relative only in the case of the latter's absence or death.[93] His criticism did not chip away at the priesterraden's authority, however.

Within his own community of Arabs who were *sādah* (descendants of the Prophet), Sayyid 'Uthmān had more clout and was instrumental in further entrenching in the region the idea of equality in rank in marriages between daughters of *sādah* and other *sādah*, a notion shared by some Arabs in the British Straits Settlements as we saw in chapter 1. A famous case involving a marital union between a female descendant of the Prophet and a non-Sayyid of Singapore in 1905, which has already been examined in detail by Engseng Ho, revolved strictly around descent and ethnicity.[94] A controversial fatwa by Sayyid 'Uthmān was secured, declaring the marriage void although the marriage had been approved by the bride's *walī*.[95] Various legal opinions were sought by the family and Javanese religious authorities worldwide, including a fatwa that addressed this phenomenon in Southeast Asia by Muslim Syrian reformer Rashid Rida, which was printed in issues of Cairo's reformist publication *Al-Manār* that year arguing the opposite.[96] In 1912, the Sudanese-born Muslim reformer Ahmad Surkati was in Solo when he suspected that a Sharifah from the Al-Attas clan had become the mistress of a Chinese man.[97]

When he strongly suggested that she be married to a local Javanese man, presumably in order to protect her virtue, one of her family members exclaimed that such a union was haram (forbidden).[98] Like Rida, Ahmad Surkati too formally issued a fatwa that declared that such a marriage would be lawful, sparking a rift between the Sayyids and non-Sayyids within the Arab community.

This "extreme view" of kafā'a (sufficiency in marriage) based entirely on notions of race and descent seems to have uniquely arose in Southeast Asia as the Arab diaspora in the Straits Settlements and the Netherlands Indies became preoccupied with ensuring female descendants only marry male descendants.[99] In fact, in the Netherlands Indies, the only "law" that Dutch authorities potentially identified as Arabieren-recht was the law of kafā'a based on descent, although it was eventually not enforced, being peculiar to only some sections of the Arab community.[100]

Members of the Arab elite in the Netherlands Indies appealed to the colonial government's impulse to fragment colonial society in order to enforce their policy of separation from the rest of Muslim society in specific areas like marriage. They did not succeed because the identities of parties in marriages were not typically policed by colonial governments. Most Arabs wanted to be legally grouped with Native Muslims in recognition of actual relationships and evolution of identities that had occurred historically. In order to do so, they had to downplay differences highlighted by markers of Arab identity ascribed by the Dutch. In 1920, local Arabs in Riau decided to give up their titles of Sayyid or Sharīfa that indicated their descent from the Prophet Muhammad in order to qualify as Natives. Although several Dutch provincial administrators, including members of the Justice Department based in Batavia, were confused by the meaning of this gesture, they generally concurred that the cosmetic measure was deemed sufficient for the Arabs to change their legal status. The provenance of the decision to drop the titles remain a mystery. Because Dutch colonial laws did not mention titles as a marker of Arab identities at all, the Arabs' decision to drop their titles in order to prove that they were Natives is very curious. If the title of "Sayyid" was the only marker for their identity as "Arab," what about the non-Sayyid Arabs who were also classified as Foreign Orientals throughout the colony?

Not surprisingly, these Arabs retained their higher rank within local societies after dropping their titles.[101] In fact, the people of Riau considered Arabs to be of the same rank as the sultan of Riau, who was undoubtedly at the apex of their society. The Dutch controller highlighted that, just like the sultan of Riau, the Arabs were certainly not foreign, having lived there for several generations and having grown deep roots in the islands by intermarriage with local indigenous societies while preserving their Arab identities based on patrilineal descent.[102] In other words, their high rank in Riau society was predicated not just on the titles of Sayyid or Sharīfa but on actual biological descent as well as relationships cultivated with local communities over time.[103] Marriage practices in Riau support this view. Arabs remained Arabs even after they opted to drop their titles, primarily because Arab women still garnered a higher *mahr*, the compulsory payment that the bridegroom had to give the bride when the contract of marriage was made and that then became the property of the wife.[104] The *mahr* is a legal form, implicit in a marriage contract, but it is also part of a complex series of social exchanges within a network of kin and between households over time and it takes different forms across the world, usually in the form of cash, jewelry, or property because there are no exact standards for *mahr*.[105] The *mahr* for an Arab bride in Riau was 400 rial, equivalent to the *mahr* of a member of royalty, an indication of social rank and not foreign status. This amount was eight times more than the *mahr* for a local non-Arab, non-royal inhabitant.[106] A higher *mahr* and marriage restrictions did not point toward foreign status because local members of the Riau sultanate practiced similar traditions.[107] Just as Arab women in Riau were strongly discouraged from marrying local men unless they were part of the royal family, even when they shared the same legal category of Natives, female members of the royal family could not wed native commoners but were allowed to marry male Arabs who held the title of Sayyid even after they had dropped their titles officially.[108]

The development of colonial jurisdictions deliberately erased relationships that had formed over the years between different groups. One of the most problematic cases concerning the matter of legal jurisdiction involved royalty and Foreign Orientals. In 1919, the *landraad* had to decide whether an Arab defendant was to be subjected to either Native laws or European laws because the plaintiff was a member of the Javanese royalty.[109] To complicate matters further, the Javanese regents of Surakarta and Jogjakarta were classified as Europeans. Another case in 1925 heard in the Supreme Court superbly captured the jurisdictional complications in such a diverse colony.[110] A piece of land had been given to the Arab plaintiffs by the Javanese regent in Surakarta, already subjecting the property to indigenous legal concepts defined by Javanese rulers.[111] Hence, the piece of property, known as *soenansgrond* in the Indo-Dutch legal lexicon, not only fell outside of European colonial jurisdiction but was also exempted from the laws of Foreign Orientals, despite being owned by Arabs—for how could Native Javanese rulers gift "foreign" Arabs royal grounds? Colonial fantasy of separation persisted in law.

For mobile diasporic communities such as the Arabs who might have been accustomed to the universality of Islamic law, Dutch colonial legal configurations were understandably frustrating. In 1938, an exasperated judge wondered out loud what sort of "international private law" diasporic Arabs expected in the colonial courts of Batavia in cases involving family law. He asked, "Did they assume that the *landraad* would apply Islamic law to all Muslims no matter their nationality?"[112] Perhaps. After all, British colonial administrators attempted to implement Islamic law in the realm of personal law over the lives of Muslim subjects with as little variation as possible across the British Empire. In contrast to Arabs in the British Straits Settlements who could count on British commitment to administer Islamic law, however imperfect and incomplete, Dutch legal structures were not predictable at all.

For their part, Arabs in the Netherlands Indies were able to adopt a variety of legal strategies according to their circumstances. Their unstable legal identity in the colony allowed them to manipulate legal classifications at various junctures. In order to travel more freely abroad and within the colony during the late nineteenth and early twentieth centuries, some Arabs attempted to be categorized as Europeans by pledging allegiance to Ottoman rule via a protracted sense of loyalty toward their land of origin, Ḥaḍramawt. After 1920, it became possible for them to be classified as Natives by invoking previous judicial decisions to escape severe restrictions on land ownership. Members of the royalty in Pontianak seamlessly fell under the coveted category of Natives. In 1920, Arabs in Riau successfully became Natives by dropping their titles, although they were still perceived to be Arabs within local societies, to the confusion and frustration of Dutch colonial observers.

In the arena of legal pluralism, Arabs in the Netherlands Indies did not fare as well as their counterparts in the Straits Settlements, although the tactics of some of the Arab elite in the two regions were similar. In the arena of Islamic law, Arabs in Southeast Asia gained momentary supremacy as they capitalized on their heritage, propelling their ideas to a wider reach. Although requests for separate religious courts were continually turned down, Arabs' complicated mobile lives still created jurisdictional complications for Dutch courts. The fact that Arabs appealed to Dutch authorities to establish a separate court for them demonstrates how in a legal world where jurisdictions were determined by colonialists colonial subjects attempted to manufacture a legal space within colonial structures. They chose to carve out a space within the existing colonial legal system instead of departing from it, which meant that even their resistance to the colonialism was on colonial terms. When the Arab petitioners wanted to create separate jurisdictions for themselves under the colonial umbrella, they did so in dialogue with colonial authorities, forging tighter bonds with colonial administrators in the process. They adhered to the colonial mold so much that even their conception of the legal administration of religious laws in the Netherlands Indies relied on Dutch colonial authority. Then again, being a minority comprising an average of only 5 to 7 percent of the entire population of the Netherlands Indies, perhaps they had little choice but to appeal to the Dutch in order to counter legal rulings meted out by native Muslims who dominated the priesterraden. Ultimately, despite recognizing the inadequacies of the priesterraden in administering Islamic law, Dutch authorities were reluctant to grant Arabs more autonomy, for that meant granting them more control.

Alliances with the Dutch were sometimes forged more obviously, as in the case of Bābahīr, who aided Van den Berg in the production of a book on Ḥaḍramīs in the archipelago in 1866 and, more important, in the long-awaited translation of the Shafi'i text *Minhāj al-Ṭalibīn* in 1882. For his own part, Sayyid 'Uthmān shrewdly allied with Snouck in order to gain influence not just over Arab communities but over the entire Muslim community in the Netherlands Indies and beyond. On Sayyid 'Uthmān's behalf, Snouck viciously attacked both Van den Berg's and Bābahīr's authority on Islamic matters and actively propped him up his friend. Snouck's support certainly propelled Sayyid 'Uthmān to greater authority as a recognized expert in Islamic theology and jurisprudence. In turn, he granted Snouck credibility in the eyes of both the Dutch colonial elite as well as Muslim subjects. This symbiotic relationship thrived on the uncertainty of colonial legal structures and classifications in the Netherlands Indies, which were highly tentative and seemingly subject to negotiation, especially during the period of Ethical Policy (1901–42) when the Dutch government asserted their commitment to experimentation. By contrast, in the British Straits Settlements, legal configurations were more fixed since British legal authorities were already empowered by their experience in implementing Islamic law in British India. Hence alliances with local religious experts were unnecessary in court, and the relationships that developed between the Arab elite and British colonial officials had a markedly different complexion.

CHAPTER 5

Constructing the Index of Arabs

Colonial Imaginaries in Southeast Asia

In 1906, the British ambassador to the Court of the Sublime Porte of the Ottoman Empire wrote that the mufti of Java, identified as no one less than Sayyid Uthmān bin Yaḥyā himself, was collaborating with Sadik Bey, the Ottoman consul in Batavia, to spread news about the possibility of the Japanese adopting the Islamic faith.[1] Such propaganda, the ambassador claimed, was meant to spur Muslims in Southeast Asia to rally behind the cause of anticolonial pan-Islamism purportedly heralded by Japan, who was already recognized as a major Asian power in the region, having won the war against the Russians the year before.[2] Thereafter British authorities stepped up surveillance over Muslim communities in the region, especially Arabs. Unlike the Dutch, the British were uneasy about taking this step at first for fear of alienating substantial Arab investments in the Straits Settlements. Eager to retain their allies, British authorities in Southeast Asia therefore concurrently monitored and courted the Arab elite in the region as their relationship acquired a different complexion predicated on fear of Muslim revolt during the early twentieth century.

The "Arab Question"

From 1915 onward, the War Office in London began to view communities along the perimeter of the Indian Ocean primarily within the context of pan-Islamism, which we now know to be a creation of the British India Office in London.[3] In a memorandum to the British Viceroy of India, Mark Sykes of the War Office requested that British authorities focus their efforts around four issues, namely the Ottoman Caliphate, the Sherif of Mecca, Pan-Islamism, and Pan-Arabism.[4] Yet Southeast Asia would have remained outside of Sykes's surveillance framework had it not been for the fervent efforts of two officials based in Southeast Asia whose joint efforts extended their reach from their base in the Straits Settlements to the Netherlands Indies and Arabia. W. H. Lee-Warner was a British officer based in Singapore and Java during the war, and W. N. Dunn was the British consul-general in Batavia. In a lengthy 1919 memo titled "The Arab Question," Lee-Warner warned his colleagues throughout the empire, "We have seen the dangers to Singapore, Hydrebad, British India, Aden, Ḥaḍramawt and Egypt, if Java is permitted to become an insufficiently invigilated center of Asiatic Anti-British Moslem intrigue. The period from the early nineteenth century to the Second World War is accurately dubbed the "Age of Questions" by historian Holly Case.[5] A question comes into being, Case argues, where conditions beg expeditious redress, where something is wrong and badly needed fixing.[6] Even Christiaan Snouck Hurgronje referred to the "Arab Question" ("Arabierenquaestie" and the "Arabierenvraag") as he mulled over the relationship between the Ottomans and the Ḥaḍramis in 1909.[7] In the British colonial context however, the Arab Question were weaponized to further imperial expansion. Since British expansion into Ḥaḍramawt became more of a possibility from the 1910s onward, policies shifted more purposefully toward winning the hearts and minds of Arabs in the region in tandem with surveillance.[8] In order to garner more support from British authorities in wartime, Lee-Warner and Dunn astutely framed their surveillance efforts more broadly as part of the "Arab Question," which had three sides—the British territories (Straits Settlements and Malaya), the Netherlands Indies, and Arabia—hence universalizing the issue of local Arab discontentment in Southeast Asia.[9]

The gradual dissolution of the Ottoman Empire after the First World War contributed to the nationalization of the Arab diaspora in the British and Dutch colonial imagination. This phenomenon linked the diaspora to an Arab nation instead of the colonies in Southeast Asia where they had established themselves.[10] As much as the surveillance was focused on Southeast Asia, it was British interests in the Middle East in the wake of the demise of the major imperial power in the region (the Ottomans) that dictated the direction of surveillance policies. As part of British expansion into Arabia, several Arabs from Southeast Asia were employed by the British to spy on their communities in both Southeast Asia and Ḥaḍramawt. One of these Arabs,

Sayed Ali bin Abu Bakar Al Jifri, was paid an advance of 200 Straits dollars and another 100 upon his return to Singapore. His list of duties exemplified British concerns in 1916.[11]

> To find out all about the Jamiyah Al Haq.[12]
>   Of its progress, who are the heads of the Society, who is financing it
>   If the Society has any political project: how for it is inclined towards the Turks and the Germans and whether is in secret communication with them.
>   If the society is against any Gaiti and how is its attitude towards the Sultan of Makalla.
>   Any further news he can gather about the Society and its constitution and work.

Essentially, surveillance focused on leadership, financing sources of Arab organizations, their potential inclinations toward Turkey and Germany, and attitudes toward pro-British rulers in Ḥaḍramawt who attempted to exploit British surveillance for their own purposes. The sultan of Mukallā, for example, identified the Al-Irshad society as being anathema to them so they urged "our friend Brittania" to not just limit themselves to surveillance but also crack down on propaganda that was hostile to them. In a letter to W. H. Lee-Warner, the sultan of Mukallā wrote,

> We have therefore issued decisive orders applicable to everyone amenable to our orders to the effect that he should cut himself off from the Irshadia Society and its branches in compliance with the command of the Koran i.e. "Obey God and obey the apostle, and those among you invested with Authority." The Sultanate of Abdulla and the Resident of Aden have seconded us in the matter apropos. . . .[13]

The circular was printed, though all references to the "Resident of Aden" and to "my friend Britannia" were deleted by J. Crosby (the acting British consul general of Batavia), who wanted to maintain some distance lest one thought that the British authorities did the bidding of Ḥaḍramī sultans.[14]

Surveillance of Arab communities in Southeast Asia was further helped along by the establishment of the Arab Bureau in Cairo in 1916, which rendered the Arabs in the region more visible than other ethnic groups.[15] Barely three weeks after the armistice in November 1918, a memo was circulated from Southeast Asia to the Foreign Office via the Arab Bureau in Cairo, linking the region to the Middle East: "Some 300 years ago the Hadramis began to emigrate to Java and Sumatra with the sole idea of earning a livelihood. Among them were, and are, a certain number of the arm bearer class (i.e.

the non-Sayyids), whose lack of respect and arrogance now has culminated in endangering the position of all."[16] The memorandum went on to state, "In Java, the position is worse than in the Malay Peninsula, for the Dutch Government has adopted the principle of conferring power on the non-Syeds. The best example is that of Monggus, made by the Dutch Government the official Kapitein der Arabieren in Batavia. This man of the humblest origin can, and does, oppress—through his official position—not only non-syeds but Syeds." Lee-Warner also highlighted the role of the Arabs as influencers in Java in language reminiscent of long-standing Dutch colonial views of Arabs in their colony:

> In Java, the object was to poison the minds of the Moslem population (exceeding 35,000,000 against the British, as being persons who desired to do away entirely with the Caliphate—an entirely false deduction from the real origin of the trouble) and the Javanese like sheep, came to believe what any thinking person would at once dismiss as farcical on the face of it, that the English and the Syeds were in collusion against Islam.

Lee-Warner's numerous incendiary reports firmly pitted the Sayyids—deemed "Britain's warmest Islamic champions"—against the non-Sayyids—supposedly "backed by German gold."[17] In the face of actual reality, colonial correspondence and the resulting Index of Arabs perpetuated the strict dichotomies outlined in table 4.

Surveillance efforts highlighted how fluid Arab identities were—one could be a colonial collaborator and a subject of scrutiny concurrently, and British and Dutch colonial subjects were simultaneously spied upon by both governments across colonial boundaries. At a time when a high degree of mobility and a deep interest in world affairs were taken as an indication of suspicious behavior, both Arabs and Indian Muslims in British territory were monitored more than other communities due to their links outside of the region. Their diasporic ties in the world had always been linked to disruptive behavior in Southeast Asia. In August 1858, days after the end of the First Indian War

Table 4 Dichotomy of Arab loyalties

Pro-British	Anti-British
Sayyid	Non-Sayyid
Anti-German	Pro-German
Anti-Turkish	Pro-Turkish
Al-Alawi	Al-Irshad

of Independence (also known as the Sepoy Rebellion), European residents in Penang more than 2,000 kilometers away feared riot by Indian mutineer convicts specifically during the "festival of Muharram."[18] Mervyn L. Wynne, a senior police officer in Penang, traced the beginnings of several disruptions in the nineteenth century—such as the Klang War (1867-1974) in the Malay state of Selangor on the peninsula and rival gang skirmishes between the Red Flag and White Flag Societies in the Straits Settlement of Penang—to various Arab personalities.[19] In the early twentieth century, British colonial authorities consistently reported to the War Office that Arabs in Southeast Asia were generally more clued in to current events throughout the Islamic world than other Muslims. Arabs in Malaya and Singapore were observed to be particularly affected by two events, namely the execution of the journalist Abdul Hamid Al Zahrawi by the Ottoman government in May 1916 and the resignation of the Sheikh ul-Islam (the equivalent of the grand mufti of the Ottoman Empire), Ürgüplü Mustafa Hayri Efendi, after his authority was diminished under the Committee of Union and Progress (CUP) in Turkey that same year.[20] By contrast, Malays in Singapore and the Federated Malay States were perceived by British authorities as largely apathetic to the goings-on in Arabia and Turkey, and the Javanese as simply "bewildered."[21]

The First World War definitely formed a watershed moment in the history of British-Arab relations in Southeast Asia as strained wartime resources caused colonial officials to feel more vulnerable and isolated, leading them to cement their alliance with the Arab community. If the end of the nineteenth century was High Empire, the period of imperial rule from World War One onward could be termed "covert Empire," to borrow a term from Priya Satia.[22] A complete redefinition of British counterespionage networks occurred from 1914 to 1918, transforming the British intelligence system from a small, specialized system dedicated to the detection of German secret agents to a vast intelligence-gathering network, costing hundreds of thousands of pounds each year and collecting information on virtually anyone within their orbit suspected of being opposed to British government policy.[23] Covert surveillance policies in Southeast Asia intensified and gained more momentum as Britain fought against the Ottomans during the First World War. British authorities were worried about the potential chaos that might emerge with the breakup of the Ottoman Empire, which was thought to hold the allegiance of a significant proportion of the Muslim world, including those in Southeast Asia.[24] Arabs on both ends of the Indian Ocean tried to sway the direction of these policies to foster their own diverse agendas in Southeast Asia and the Middle East. What ultimately emerged in Southeast Asia were schemes based upon careful curation of information by various parties who positioned themselves as producers of authoritative knowledge amid the rapid shifts in global politics during the war. During the First World War, the British found themselves well positioned to be the main conduits of propaganda. Because the Ottoman Hijaz was under siege during the war, it was not easy for Sharīf Husayn of Mecca to spread his message—that he was the true leader the of the Islamic world—across the Islamic world in 1916, which would effectively undermine the already ailing authority of the Ottoman ruler hitherto considered to be the ruler of the Sunni world.[25] He found that the only way to communicate was with British assistance because although some telegraph lines were cut by warring factions, British submarine cables still dominated the world telegraph system. Translations of the proclamation were carefully curated by the British Foreign Office, the War Office, and the newly-formed War Propaganda Bureau in London so as not to incite unrest among Muslims.[26] This particular episode led Lee-Warner to claim that Islam was a world bound by "postal communications."[27] This view of the Islamic world as linked simply by means of communication ties in with Cemil Aydın's claim that the racialization of Islam occurred from the 1870s onward and that the persistence of the geopolitical idea of the Muslim world peaked during the First World War.[28]

The Sepoy Mutiny

Though Arabs in Southeast Asia were otherwise largely unaffected by the First World War, things took a turn in February 1915 when several Muslim Rajput soldiers from the Fifth Light Infantry stationed in Singapore rebelled after hearing rumors that they were to be sent to either Egypt or Galipoli to combat fellow Muslims under Ottoman rule who were fighting against the British.[29] Forty-five soldiers were sentenced to death by British authorities for rebelling, and the air was thick with tension between Muslim residents and the Europeans in colonial Singapore immediately afterwards.[30] Dubbed the Sepoy Mutiny, the event drove home the point that the British military officials and government bureaucrats felt that they were left alone to fend for themselves in the colonies, especially in times of war when resources were stretched thin in Europe.[31] To an extent, the fears of the British officials were allayed when just before four o'clock on Saturday, March 6, 1915, several Muslims—including Malays, Tamils, Malabaris, Javanese, and Arabs—marched along the Singapore River toward Victoria Memorial Hall, where the colonial secretary, R. J. Wilkinson, began his speech.[32] A resolution stating that "the Loyalty and Fealty of the Mohameddans of Singapore has in no whit altered from what it was before the War until the present" was passed and presented to the king of England via telegram on behalf of the entire Muslim community.[33] The resolution was signed by "O. Alsagoff, head of the Mohameddan Community."[34] In an accompanying report, the governor of the Straits Settlements, Arthur Young, revealed to the Colonial Office that Syed Omar Alsagoff and another prominent Arab, Syed Mohammed bin Agil, had approached him on their own accord on February 28, 1915, in order to express the feelings of the Arab community specifically toward the British Government and enquire how they could help.[35] While a secret agent who mixed with the crowd reported that he heard disloyal murmurings in the crowd, "he [did] not question the sincerity of the leading Moslems of Singapore."[36] Whisperings of discontentment were found only among Indians and lower classes of immigrant Arabs, but even these had been quieted after learning the "true action" of the British Government.[37] Although Muslims of all ethnicities listened to Wilkinson's speech at Victoria Memorial Hall, Arabs were singled out in subsequent newspaper reports and colonial correspondence.[38] Almost immediately after the mutiny, Omar Alsagoff propped himself up as the leader of the Muslim community and was granted the ear of the governor of the Straits Settlements. He not only placed his extensive house property at the disposal of the British government but also firmly aligned his interests against the Ottomans by ostentatiously congratulating Sharīf Husayn of Mecca, with whom he was acquainted, on his successful move toward independence from Turkish rule in May 1916.

How did Arabs rise so easily to be the voice of Muslim authority despite being a minority? The question is linked to the politics of representation in the colony where Muslims themselves placed a high premium on ethnic diversity. The 1914 public endowment deed (waqf) created by the sultan of Johore for Sultan Mosque, the largest mosque in Singapore, established in 1824, manifestly stated that two representatives from each of the respective racial communities who worshipped at the mosque—the Malays, Javanese, Arabs, Bugis, North Indian community, and South Indian community (Tamils)—were to be appointed as trustees.[39] The deed's overt acknowledgment of the mixed society residing in the area around the mosque did not reflect the racial proportion of Muslim communities in the area—there were certainly more Malays and Javanese compared to the Arabs. The endowment deed prioritized diversity but not proportion in underscoring representation in leadership of the mosque. This arrangement was echoed in the leadership of the entire colony, where a minority within the large Muslim community was able to dictate policy and influence colonial rulers.

True to form, the amount of money and moral support that that the wealthy Arabs in Singapore gave to Britain for their cause during the First

World War was tremendous and consistent. A week after the execution of the sepoys, several communities hastened to donate to the Prince of Wales War Relief Fund to support British efforts in the war.[40] Subscriptions were striated according to race, as indicated in figure 10.

The strong Arab hand at the helm of the Muslim community, announced in a public spectacle post-mutiny, could not be more different than the secretive leadership of the mutiny by a local Indian *pir* or holy man, a civilian named Nur Alam Shah associated with Kampong Java Mosque. In 1916, Dudley Ridout reported that he had quiet talks with "leading Arabs," including Omar Alsagoff, as part of "judicious probing of Mahometan feeling" in Malaya, Singapore, and the Netherlands Indies, suggesting that these Arabs were the most reliable informants regarding Muslim sentiments in the region.[41] Rattled by the mutiny, British authorities cautiously embraced their Arab allies, who had been useful economically but thus far not politically. Both Indian and Arab Muslims struggled to shake off the cloud of suspicion and would continue to renew their pledges of patriotism and loyalty to the British case every few months through lavish social functions, usually with Wilkinson as guest, until the end of 1916. Still, a wave of doubt lingered over all Muslim soldiers.

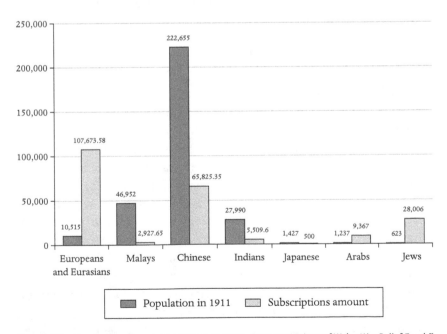

FIGURE 10.   Graph of wartime subscriptions in 1915. Sources: "Prince of Wales War Relief Fund," *SFPMA*, March 18, 1915, 10; J. E. Nathan, *The Census of British Malaya* (London: Waterlow and Sons Limited, 1922), 29, 92.

As they tried to make sense of Arab allegiances in the region, Lee-Warner and Dunn started out with the premise that Arabs in the British Straits Settlements were generally deemed pro-British while most Arabs in the Netherlands Indies were anti-British and pro-Turkish and therefore assumed to be constantly conspiring against the British, especially during the First World War. The population of Arabs was subjected to this strict binary classification. In actual fact, the relationship between so-called trustworthy Arabs and British authorities were not as clear-cut as it seemed, since the former had their own agenda for supporting the British against their rivals. Dunn and Lee-Warner, the two main creators of the index, were intensely suspicious of Arabs in the Netherlands Indies in general without much evidence to go upon. Their descriptions of anti-British Arabs were often hyperbolic and betray deep-seated mistrust that was not backed up by empirical evidence. No rubric was ever created to determine whether one was anti-British or not and to what degree. One of the men listed in the index, Saleh bin Abdat, was described by Lee-Warner as "extremely anti-British" and "thoroughly and permanently disloyal at heart," but Lee-Warner admitted in the same letter that Bin Abdat gave a hefty $2,000 donation to the Our Day Fund of the British Red Cross during the war.[42] Such instances were portrayed as anomalies by Dunn and Lee-Warner as their pro/anti-British dichotomy suffused their configuration of the region.

The Index of Arabs

From 1915 to 1920, several typed memos with the names and short biographies of various Arab individuals based in Southeast Asia suspected of harboring anti-British, pan-Islamic sentiments were continuously circulated by the Foreign Office in London, the War Office, and the British colonial governments throughout empire, although the memos originated from the British Consulate in Batavia, thus outside the British realm strictly speaking. The index listed the names of Arabs based in the Netherlands Indies who were thought to have been influenced by German and Ottoman (later, Turkish) propaganda during the First World War and its immediate aftermath. Sometimes the list was referred to as the Batavia List of Suspect Arabs, or the List of Dangerous Arabs in British colonial correspondence. Entries were continually added to the main list on slips of paper that were attached to the original document until 1920. Each entry lists the full name of the individual, his current age, place of birth, current location, occupation, and political allegiances with regard to Britain, Germany, Turkey, and the two Sultans of Ḥaḍramawt.[43] Some entries also include the individual's language capabilities, list of publications, and travel histories. A few entries cross-list the individual's coterie of friends and relations mentioned elsewhere in the index.

The Index of Arabs was repeatedly circulated among various agencies, including the British Straits Settlements government in Singapore and the British Consulate-General in Batavia as well as the Aden Protectorate. The most complete version of the index, dated September 27, 1919, was held by the India Office in London. It features the names of seven societies with predominantly Arab members and 240 individuals in alphabetical order. The listed societies are the Al Irshad Society, Djamiat Alwiyin wa-Ansarihim, Djamiat Geir, Mohamadiah Society, Oetoesan Islam, Swara Ra'jat, and Tentera Kandjeng Nabi Mohamad. Individuals labeled anti-British were often automatically denied a pass to enter Aden Protectorate.[44] It was the duty of the British Consulate-General in Batavia to inform the British authorities at Aden to deny entry of any Arab listed in the index. The aim of the British Consulate-General in Batavia in creating the index was two-pronged: to identify both pro-British Arabs who might be of service to colonial governments and anti-British Arabs who would then be denied access to the ports of Singapore, British India, and the Aden Protectorate.[45]

Out of 240 Arabs in the index, 78 were labelled anti-British, pro-German, and pro-Turkish, while 63 were labelled only anti-British. Five Arabs were listed as anti-British and pro-German, or anti-British and pro-Turkish. In all, 146 Arabs were listed as anti-British. These Arabs were described as "actively," "very actively," "extremely," "strongly," "very strongly," "frankly," 'fiercely," "notoriously," "openly," or "bitterly" anti-British and pro-Turkish. Having personal observable contact with Germans and Turks rendered one suspicious as well, though only forty-one were observed to have had direct contact. Seventy-two Arabs were not explicitly identified as having any kind of political allegiance.

Table 5   Classification of Arabs in the index

DESCRIPTION	FREQUENCY
Anti-British, pro-German, pro-Turkish	78
had personal contact with Germans	18
had personal contact with Turks	23
listed as only anti-British	63
anti-British, pro-German	4
anti-British, pro-Turkish	1
allegiance not identified at all	72

A typical entry on an individual in the Index of Arabs lists the Arab's birth-place, current location, age, and any dangerous association of which he was a member, followed by his political loyalties to identify where he was anti-British, pro-German, or pro-Turkish, which is usually the case in the index. The following is a typical entry:

Basalamah, Sjech Saeid bin Abdullah bin Saeid.
    Born Batavia. Address Parapattan, Batavia. Age 38. One of wealthy sup-
    porters of Al-Irshad. Anti-British activity. Pro-Turkish and pro-German.

In addition to this, details about the Arab's past movements might be pro-vided if known. Kinship links were sometimes referred to, usually with re-gard to other Arabs also listed in the index. Other details include academic qualifications and language proficiency. An example of a typical longer entry is below.

Ba-jenid. Sjech Ahmad bin Abdoelrahman.
    Born Buitenzorg. Age about 35. Address Djattinegara. Off Mr. Cor-
    nelis. (Batavia) Landowner. Educated in Turkey. Speaks a little Ara-
    bic, fluent Turkish and French. Turkish wife. A very close associate of
    Turkish Consul-General. Very actively pro-German and Pro-Turkish,
    and fiercely anti-British. Elder brother of Sjech Saeid bin Abdoelrah-
    man Ba Jenid.[46]

The movement of most Arabs under surveillance was usually charted from port to port as follows.

Java (Batavia, Sourabaya) ←→ Singapore ←→ India (Bombay, Madras) ←→ Aden (Mukallā)

At least three more separate short lists of Arabs supplemented the main index, although these mainly featured pro-British Arabs.[47]

Profiles of the Arabs

Most of the Arabs listed in the index were born in the late nineteenth cen-tury, and more than half were born in Ḥaḍramawt rather than in Southeast Asia. They mostly resided in cities on the island of Java. Certain clans fea-tured prominently in the list, such as the Annahdi, Bin Talib, and Bin Abdat families and the Alatas clans.[48]

One of the rubrics that was not explicitly reflected in the index was that of class, although British colonial officials and informants noted that the Sayy-ids generally tend to be of a higher class than the non-Sayyids.[49] Admittedly,

Table 6 Top five places where Arabs listed were born

PLACE OF BIRTH	FREQUENCY
Ḥaḍramawt	135
Batavia	22
Cheribon	15
Mecca	9
Pekalongan	7

Table 7 Top five places of residence in Java

PLACE OF RESIDENCE	FREQUENCY
Batavia	88
Pekalongan	46
Cheribon	25
Sourabaya	24
Tegal	20

Table 8 Top eleven clan names featured in the Index of Arabs

FAMILY/CLAN NAME	FREQUENCY
Annahdi	24
Bin-Talib	14
Alatas	12
Belfas	10
Ba-Isa	7
Albakeri	6
Bin-Abdat	6
Bin Rabba	6
Al Amoedi	5
Attamimi	5
Belwael	5

"a moneyed nucleus" within the anti-British faction was recognized as a threat, so thankfully for the British this was small in number.[50] Although Lee-Warner referred to the rivalry between pro- and anti-British Arabs as a series of "inter-class disputes," this was inaccurate because wealthy men such the Alatas clan also appeared in the Index of Arabs.[51] The Alatas clan patriarch was identified as follows:

Alatas. Syed Abdullah bin <Aloei>
Born Batavia. Age about 70. One of wealthiest Arabs in Batavia. Occupation house property. Educated in Java and Mecca. Been to

Ḥaḍramawt, Palestine, Turkey, Egypt, British India, Straits Settlements and Australia. Personal acquaintance with several Turkish ex-ministers. Egypt notables Established a school [illegible] Mu [illegible] children in 1912 which was closed entirely [illegible] Master of Arabic and Malay [illegible] languages [illegible] ly interested in Islamic propaganda [illegible] an intimate friend of Cr. S. Hurgronje with whom he studied Islamic teachings and laws in Mecca. Has four sons all educated in Egypt and Europe. P.T.O.

See under

ALATAS Syed Osman bin Abdullah.

Mohammad

Hachim

Ismail

Famous for his religious knowledge and modern ideas. Offered financial support to a Malay weekly "Pertimbangan" (anti-Ally) which was edited by Razoux Kuhr and which did not live long. Closely connected with Islamic propaganda in Preanger and in Central Java. Gave a donation of Fl. 1,000/—to the Tentera Kandjeng Nabi Mohammed. Heart and soul pro-Turkish.

Given to hyperbole, W. N. Dunn describes one Hachim Alatas as "most despotic in ideas and his hatred and contempt for all things British is beyond description."[52]

Arab Informants

Yet the Index of Arabs was not a purely British construction. To create the index, the British Consulate-General in Batavia had to rely on "pro-British" Arabs to spy on other Arabs already presumed to be "anti-British." This therefore formed a way for some members of the disgruntled Arab elite in the Netherlands Indies to possibly work against Dutch colonial oppression.

The platform of surveillance is powerful because it could help members of the Arab diaspora achieve legitimacy in an area of new legalities. By proving their loyalty, they again demonstrated that they were useful subjects. Nonetheless, reliance on Arabs created a precarious arrangement that blurred the line between spy and agent provocateur. In their correspondence with the Foreign, War, and Colonial Offices in London, both Dunn and Lee-Warner eagerly mentioned their Arab informants estate holdings in the region and across the Indian Ocean in order to prove the effectiveness of their surveillance policies, as if wealth aligned their interests with British colonial ones.[53]

Some Arab spies chose to keep a low profile, which seemed to make British officials more ambivalent about their level of capability and commitment to the cause. There was Syed Edroes Aldjoefri, a resident of Semarang, Java, who was perceived as weak but as a result "capable of being used as a tool." Another Arab named Shaikh Mohamed bin Salim Baraja was apparently already on the British payroll but was considered impulsive and impecunious. Mohamed bin Osman Al-Hashimi was also identified as an Arab who at one time did "useful propaganda work" for the British in return for pay. Nonetheless, like Aldjoefri and Baraja, his loyalty toward the British was regarded as unstable and erratic, and the Index of Arabs contained a warning that he was to be regarded as "a venal personage who is ready to sell his pen to whichever side will pay him most for it."[54] A year later, the acting British consul general of Batavia, J. Crosby, reported that Hashimi appeared to be "devoid of any fixed principles to be actuated mainly by considerations of personal gain."[55] In addition, the British stationed an Arab named Sheikh Hamid Bahaharis as a general servant in the house of two anti-British brothers named Syed Al-oei and Syed Achmad bin Zein Aldjoefri.[56] Yet another name is Sayed Omar bin Abdulla al Zam, who reported in March 1920 on the Arabs of Surabaya specifically that reconciliation between the two groups of Arabs, the Sayyids and the non-Sayyids, was impossible.[57]

During the First World War, British authorities leaned heavily on Bin Agil, a "leading pro-British Arab in the Malay peninsula and in the Netherlands East Indies" whom they regarded as a "trusted confidant on Muslims affairs."[58] A long-time resident in Singapore, having moved there in 1857 when he was fifteen, he was described as a well-known "savant" from Ḥaḍramawt.[59] Much mention was made about his wealth in reports.[60] He was acquainted with the governor of Yemen, Khedive ʿAbbās of Egypt, Sharīf Husayn of Mecca, and Egyptian reporters.[61] Lee-Warner noted that Bin Agil had great pull with the Imam Yaḥyā of Sana'a, who followed his advice in 1913 to stop Turkey from pitting Mecca against Sana'a and vice versa.[62] Since he was an informant, Bin Agil's behavior was also scrutinized. He was described positively as a frank, ordinarily dispassionate man with full command over his feelings, usually undemonstrative and shrinking from self-expression.[63] Such detailed correspondence served to bolster Bin Agil's image as a trustworthy British ally.[64]

Bin Agil was close to yet another prominent Arab named Syed Ali bin Ahmad bin-Shahab, who specifically requested that the former accompany him on a British-sponsored mission to Yemen to visit Imam Yaḥyā of Sana'a to in order to reach a clear agreement between the British and the Sayyids.[65] Lee-Warner pointed out that the cost of this mission to be undertaken by the two Arab informants would be low, as the "Arabs, even of the richest rank, travel(ed) in a far cheaper manner than Europeans." Lee-Warner went on to say that even if Bin Agil and Bin Shahab failed to convince Imam Yaḥyā to consent to an agreement between the British and the Sayyids, the whole mission would not be in vain as they would have "undoubtedly [obtained] valuable information gathered on the spot." He had full confidence in the two men, who were "extremely clever, quick of intellect, and well versed to gather information."[66] Lee-Warner hastened to inform the Colonial Office that the whole Yemen-Aden-Ḥaḍramawt issue had indeed "excited the chief interest of the Arabs of Malaya and Java." He emphasized that "although Aden is geographically the center for Southern Arabia, Singapore and Java are the brain centers of Ḥaḍramī . . . political activity and are intimately connected with the Lahej and Yemen . . . Ḥaḍramawt mainly."[67]

Of course, Lee-Warner and his colleagues at the British Consulate in Batavia did not simply take things at face value and instead carefully parsed information from his Arab informants and British professional agents, referred to in colonial correspondence only as Agents C and D. They discovered that the Arab informant Bin-Shahab often differed from British agents in asserting that certain people, including the Islamic modernist association Al-Irshad, were actively anti-British.[68] This hinted at a personal grievance Bin-Shahab had with the association. At some point, he discovered that it was possible to get British authorities to interfere in Ḥaḍramawt internal affairs in order to further the private interests of the Sayyid faction in Java. But like Bin-Agil, despite his manipulation of British backing in Southeast Asia to further his own agenda, Bin-Shahab was primarily valuable because of his links with the Middle East. Though born in Batavia, he frequently traveled to Ḥaḍramawt. He had also been to Egypt, Syria, Mecca, and Medina, and was listed in the index as a "general trader possessed with a perfect knowledge of geography of Ḥaḍramawt and character of every tribe inhabiting the country," and "first and most reliable and faithful link (of the British) in Java."[69]

Lee-Warner's overreliance on his Arab informants drew from his genuine sympathy with the plight of Arab residents of the Netherlands Indies, who, he believed, fled Arabia because of poverty only to be unjustly perceived by the Dutch as "financial vampires" who "bled the people."[70] In fact, he and Dunn believed that the Dutch advisor of Native affairs in the Netherlands East Indies, Dr. B. J. O. Schrieke, and his predecessor, G. A. J. Hazeu, were in cahoots with the Germans and the Turks. British and Dutch colonial authorities had different allies in the region. In 1881, when the shipping magnate Syed Mohamed Alsagoff's overtures to Javanese Arabs and Native leaders triggered an investigation by Frederik s'Jacob, the governor-general of the Netherlands Indies, into Alsagoff's assistance in supplying arms and ships in aid of anti-Dutch activities, British authorities were reluctant to investigate precisely because of Alsagoff's substantial cut in the haj shipping business, a major source of lucrative revenue for the British colonial government as well.[71]

Despite general mistrust of Dutch authorities, in creating the index, the British Consulate General in Batavia grudgingly accepted information acquired by their Dutch counterparts, especially after the Dutch promised to finance British sugar purchases in Java in 1920.[72] In the process, J. Crosby received confirmation through Agent D that his Arab sources were mostly tainted and one-sided,[73] Rather damningly, he discovered that the Al-Irshad Society was not in fact anti-British.[74] More level-headed than his predecessors, Crosby heeded Schrieke's warning that listening only to the Sayyids to gather information on the non-Sayyids (Sheikh party) with whom they were feuding was not the best way to gain a subjective view of Arab loyalty to the Britain and Turkey.[75] He painfully recognized that information that his predecessors gleaned on Arab support for Turkey was admittedly "almost invariably derived from Sayyid sources."

> I have some difficulty in believing that they may have so far abused their influence with us as to further their own peculiar cause by making us think that "anti-Sayed" necessarily implies being "anti-British" . . . In the first place, I am by no means sure that the radical elements represented by the Sheikh party will not ultimately win in their fight against the more reactionary tendencies typified by the Sayeds. Secondly, I cannot but think it regrettable that we should have incurred the suspicion of taking sides in what is primarily a religious quarrel among Mohammedans.[76]

The situation was likely worse since information had originated mainly from a single man – Sayyid Ali bin Shahab, whom Crosby realized was "a Sayyid first and foremost with the virtues, and also with the passions and prejudices, of his class."[77] Crosby admitted that because he was "a leading Arab of the Sayyid faction in Java," he most probably exaggerated the degree to which the society was actively behind the anti-British agitation in Java and Ḥaḍramawt.[78] On October 21, 1920, Crosby concluded his report by stating, "I pass on the information contained in the Notes with the reservation that it comes from Sayyid sources, and that I have had no opportunity of corroborating it."[79]

Even more damning to British policies was Schrieke's claim that the British Consulate in Batavia did not have the cooperation of the British government in London to become so involved in the quarrel between the Sayyids and the Sheikhs in Ḥaḍramawt and Southeast Asia.[80] The British

Consulate-General of Batavia sent copious amounts of information to various offices in London but rarely received any form of feedback. Although Earl Curzon, the secretary of state for foreign affairs, recognized that successful and accurate interpretation of messages required instant intercommunication between intelligence officers and the political departments and the Foreign Office, the British government was reluctant to officially acknowledge the involvement of British government representatives in undiplomatic activity, which included interference in the religious or social affairs of native communities.[81] But "bored consuls frequently endangered the official policy of non-entanglement," the historian Priya Satia notes.[82] Lee-Warner bitterly complained in January 1919, "It is over a year since H.M. Govt used me to approach the Java and S.S. Arabs and these men—Kathiris all – are ready to back us IF we show active interest in them."[83] The Sayyids' enthusiasm for pro-British propaganda may actually be killed off, he claimed.[84] Bin Agil himself felt slighted by the Foreign Office's lack of interest and desired "a full, careful, considerate response and favorable response at the hands of His Majesty's Foreign Office."[85] It is not too far-fetched to assume that Lee-Warner shared this yearning. Nonetheless, from 1920 onward, British consuls-general began to display a greater amount of caution with regard to their informants without wavering in their general policy. In March, W. N. Dunn wrote to the Colonial Office.

> I have been frequently told in conversations that I have had with some of the anti-British Arabs on our lists that we are listening to one side only, and that it is unfair to them because we do not verify the information given against them by our informants. Though I do not believe that wrong information has been given us about any of these Arabs, still I dislike being told that our information is wrong or unfair because it is one-sided, and also I think that where the record of any of the Arabs on our list is not so bad or full details of their anti-British notions are wanting, that we should give these men the benefit of the doubt and that is probable that if allowed to travel they would not do us any particular harm.[86]

As someone well-acquainted with Arabs in Java, Schrieke's take on the so-called Arab Question in the Southeast Asian context was more nuanced. He explained that Arab Sayyid supremacy was being challenged in Java just like it had been continually challenged in the past in Persia, Mesopotamia, and Spain since the time of Umayyad rule (661–750).[87] He also emphasized that conditions were different in the Netherlands East Indies than in Ḥaḍramawt: first, non-Sayyid Arabs wished to be considered equal in rank to Sayyids after marriage to a Sayyid's daughter; second, non-Sayyids refused to abide by the traditional greeting of Sayyids by kissing their hands; and third, non-Sayyids refused to recognize the aristocracy of birth. Braced by these more nuanced and realistic understandings and chastened by Schrieke's criticism of paranoid British reports, Dunn's successor, J. Crosby, decided to rely more on Agent D, a professional agent.[88] Not much is known about Agent D apart from that he was an Indian Muslim proficient in English, Malay, Arabic, and Dutch, having lived in Southeast Asia for a considerable amount of time. Originally sent to Java to ascertain the extent to which British Indian revolutionaries were still working in the Netherlands Indies under German guidance and with German support, he seemed to have shifted his focus to Arabs (British Indians were thought to be sympathetic to the Al-Irshad Society, which was perceived to be anti-British).[89] Agent D was conscientious in sending his reports, which were more thorough than those of the Arab informants.' His reports demonstrated that his surveillance subjects neither layered subterfuge nor sowed misdirection. Instead, they genuinely engaged with him as their own informant about the British Empire by discussing the possibility of getting an education in the English language, a constant concern during the early twentieth century, as corroborated by another Arab spy who reported the same.[90] Agent D was surprised by this, became intrigued by his interlocutors, and genuinely enjoyed his interactions with them. His reports indicated that British authorities could not keep up with the diversity of Arab viewpoints and as a result overestimated the level of anti-British sentiments among Arabs in Java. Unlike Arab informants, Agent D went beyond detailed descriptions by making actual recommendations to his superiors. In a letter in 1917, W. R. D. Beckett, the British consul-general of Batavia, wrote that D considered this new Anglo-mania among the Arabs and other Natives as a sign that matters were not faring well with Germany.[91] Agent D acted almost like a diplomat because he was an agent in the direct employ of the British colonial service with enough independence to formulate his own policy on the ground and influence British colonial officers to see his view.[92] Ultimately, D's superiors retained their binary lens of anti-British/pro-British and abruptly dropped their surveillance policies of Arabs in the Netherlands Indies in 1922.

The Index of Arabs tells a story of optics of surveillance in a world that was rapidly changing due to the demise of the Ottoman Empire and the Russian Revolution in 1917. It was produced when British authorities were anxious about a change that they actually wished for finally coming true, namely the decline of the Ottoman Empire and the destruction of the geographical center for pan-Islamists to rally around. In their quest to connect with imperial headquarters in London during the First World War and immediately after, British colonial officers in Southeast Asia underscored imperial expansion opportunities in Arabia. They pegged issues surrounding Arabs in Southeast Asia to a vague notion of the "Arab Question" to gain more support with their colleagues in other Offices in London stationed throughout Empires. But their counterparts in Aden and London suspected that some informants, such as Bin Shahab, were merely anxious to interfere in Ḥaḍramawt in order to further the private interests of the Sayyid party in Java and not Ḥaḍramawt.[93]

While Dutch authorities attempted to legally separate Arabs from the rest of the subject population, British authorities strove to win the hearts and minds of Muslim subject populations.[94] W. R. D. Beckett recognized in 1917 in the midst of the First World War the need for British forces to "counteract the German propaganda and [convert] the minds of the Arabs, and the huge native Mohametan population of this country, to a truer sense of the real position of Islam and the knowledge that Great Britain, not Germany or Turkey, is the actual protector of Islam."[95] Arab informants were likewise receptive to British overtures especially in light of the oppressive policies of the Dutch government, who even banned the haj for a time. An Arab informant confessed to Dunn that he hoped that much good may be done by the resumption of the pilgrimage from Java and that the "ignorance of Arabs in Java may receive enlightenment thereby," hinting at British leverage on their behalf with the Dutch government.[96] It is also possible that Arab informants based in the Netherlands Indies hoped to become British subjects. Lee-Warner recognized this but preferred for them to remain as British agents in the Netherlands Indies instead as he knew that

> The matter is one for H.M.'s Government to decide. It is urged that if representations could be made to the Dutch Government for recognition of the Saids—the aristocracy of Islam—to European status—already granted to all Japanese, and to many Chinese—the Saids would gain in respect. Again, if they became British subjects they would be able to move about much more freely, and conduct propaganda with less invigilation.[97]

Wartime contingencies had momentarily forged incentive for Arabs oppressed by the Dutch to court another colonial power in the region with further reach across the Indian Ocean, despite British fear of manipulation by colonial subjects. Unbeknownst to them, Lee-Warner wanted the British to extend their own card system based on the Index of Arabs to curtail movement of Arabs from the Netherlands Indies to Aden, Cairo, and Singapore.

With the "enlargement of movement" due to the reduction of passport re-strictions following the signing of the Peace Treaty at Versailles at the end of June 1919, Lee-Warner hoped that the card system would take the place of the Dutch pass arrangements.[98] Due to the scarcity of colonial personnel, this plan was logistically and bureaucratically impossible, although the British Consulate in Batavia never stopped monitoring Arabs in the colony and contracted spies right up until the Japanese Occupation.[99]

In the closing years of the First World War and its immediate aftermath, Crosby and his colleagues were convinced of Arab loyalty in the British Crown colony of Singapore. In a letter in April 1918, he wrote that "the rich Arabs, like the Alkaffs at Singapore have given hostages to fortune in the shape of substantial possessions in the Straits Settlements, would not dare to incur the displeasure of the British authorities by intriguing against the established order of things in the Hedjaz and against the King ibn Saud, with whom His Majesty's Government has but lately concluded a treaty."[100] Indeed, as we saw in chapter 1, Arabs of the Straits Settlements had already allowed the British government to regulate their intimate lives through the administration of Islamic law four decades prior to the First World War.

CHAPTER 6

Compromises

The Limitations of Diasporic Religious Trusts

While the Arab diaspora continually crossed oceans, its wealth lay primarily in immoveable property by the early twentieth century because it was durable, convertible, and universal, the very cloth from which capital is cut. The more wealth members of the diaspora accumulated, they more they needed to protect it. To ensure their wealth remained in their families for generations, they coded their property legally as a type of religious endowment known as a waqf, thus insulating their assets from tax authorities and disintegration and further enhancing their durability. In the eyes of colonial authorities, the waqf was essentially a trust, a form of preemptive asset-shielding—what Katherine Pistor calls "one of the most ingenious modules for coding capital," deriving its utility from the blurring of distinction between contract and private law.[1] The waqf was simultaneously an apotheosis of Arab diaspora's efforts to settle in Southeast Asia, and their eventual compromise with colonial authorities.

Because the Straits Settlements were retrospectively declared uninhabited in 1858 by Chief Justice Benson Maxwell, subsequent dispossession was not as violent in the British colony as it was in the Netherlands Indies, where the basis for deprivation of property ownership was a racial regime predicated on land cultivation. Acquisition of land in the British Straits Settlements was not impeded by race-based exclusionary policies and most of the property not owned by the colonial government was owned by diasporic communities—Jewish, Arab, and Chinese—evidence of their rootedness in Southeast Asia. Earlier chapters have demonstrated the struggle of diasporic Arabs to command colonial resources—legal, economic, and political—for their own benefit. Just as familial ideology was deployed by the Arab elite through colonial channels, the Arab elite tried to harness colonial resources to manage their endowments, hence deepening the colonial state's involvement in their lives. Both waqfs and powers of attorney became emblems of Arabs' diasporic lives as they corralled and controlled financial resources. The establishment of waqfs formed the last step in the sequence of a move toward permanence in Southeast Asia.

It might come as a surprise therefore that the Arab diaspora had conflicting aims with one another concerning waqfs, ultimately leading to the disintegration of clan and family property, the direct result of their avid litigation. They displayed a high level of legal consciousness, defined here as the awareness of rights and the use of litigation.[2] They voluntarily brought their disputes to British colonial courts to the extent of even counting on British judges to go against Islamic law. This outcome was possible because waqf cases, unlike those involving traditional areas of family law, do not fall squarely within the realm of personal law since real estate and landed property were not governed by Islamic law. Hence waqfs, though religious by definition, created opportunities for speculative litigation with a wider range of interpretive flexibility by British judges. These disputes demonstrate a counterintuitive phenomenon in which members of close-knit groups turned to law rather than community norms because legal rules and institutions could not only be breathtakingly fast and efficient but also, more important, lead to faster substantive gains in the short term.

The waqf has a complex history in the Islamic world.[3] By the fourteenth century, jurists from the Shāfiʿī school of law had defined it as "the alienation of revenue-generating property with the principal remaining inalienable, while its revenues are disbursed for a pious purpose, in order to seek God's favor."[4] In order to establish a waqf, the Muslim settlor who established the waqf would sequester the property such that it became perpetually inalienable, and appoint a trustee or fiduciary to manage it.[5] Strictly speaking, establishing a waqf is legally irrevocable as it entails the complete transfer of the right to ownership from the hands of the founder (also known as *wāqif*) to those of God.[6] Henceforth, the property could not be sold, inherited, or given away as a gift.[7] This ensured the physical and economic integrity of the estate across multiple generations of waqf beneficiaries. A person who establishes a waqf possesses a power of legislation "that probably no other legal system concedes to a private individual," a British anthropologist noted.[8] Each waqf represents a concrete, deliberate strategy for the preservation or transmission of material assets.[9] In creating the waqf, the founder makes the principal of a revenue-producing property inalienable in perpetuity and assigns the usufruct or yields of the property to specified persons or institutions. Only a third of a Muslim's estate can be established as a waqf. The other two-thirds of a Muslim's property has to be disbursed according to inheritance laws clearly explicated in the Qur'an.[10] In fact, strict Islamic inheritance law inspired alternative legal strategies, such as the establishment of waqfs, for maneuvering among the many linkages within the family as well as among the overlapping spheres of family, community, and polity.[11]

In the British Straits Settlements of Penang, Malacca, and Singapore, waqfs usually consisted of buildings rented out for commercial or residential purposes, usually urban rental property, a lucrative source of income. In order to continually generate revenue, the property that formed the waqf was subjected to renewal or renovation from time to time, and the founder had to stipulate a means of ensuring the perpetuity of the waqf and the continual disbursement of the revenues.[12] The family waqf (*waqf dhurrī* or *ahlī*), the first kind of waqf, sheltered the property from fragmentation upon the death of the person who established it. It was a device utilized by Muslims to organize and maintain wealth for the clan or family. Upon extinction of the family line, entitlement to the usufruct would then pass to a religious or charitable institution. The second kind of waqf was the public waqf (*waqf khayrī*), which had been the main vehicle for the provision of public services such as social welfare, medical care, and religious education by the ruling elite in the Islamic world.[13] Over time, the distinction between these two different kinds of waqfs deepened, most probably due to the efforts of critics of the family waqf who considered them self-serving in contrast to public endowments, which were deemed truly charitable. Although both forms of trusts were equally valid according to Islamic law, family waqfs were regarded as markedly different from public waqfs according to English law.[14]

While wealthy traders were historically known to establish waqfs throughout the Islamic world, what was noteworthy in the Straits Settlements was that Arabs and Indian Muslims dominated the landscape of charity in the colony despite comprising less than 0.34% and 1.5% of the entire population respectively from 1901 to 1942. Waqfs of high value were owned entirely by these populations. While South Asian Muslims often established family waqfs solely or separately from public waqfs, if they chose to establish waqfs at all, Arabs tended to simultaneously establish two waqfs—one for their families and one for members of the public, effectively entwining their descendants' lives with the rest of the colonial population. Crucially, the waqf was a tool that could curtail the uncertainties that derived from trading with strangers.[15] For diasporas, physical mobility did not necessarily translate into social mobility since bonds with local communities were not immediately apparent. Connections could effectively be mediated through the establishment of trusts.

Just like the powers of attorney examined in chapter 2, waqf deeds reflect the diasporic connections of the testators by referring to properties not just in the three Straits Settlements of Penang, Singapore, and Malacca but also in India and Ḥaḍramawt.[16] Where testators had lived in Ḥaḍramawt toward the end of their lives, British colonial judges frequently wavered between lex situs (law of the place in which property is situated) and lex domicilli (law of domicile). Over time, judges concurred that since the immoveable property that constituted the waqf was situated in British territory, they should be subjected to English law.[17] With regard to a ruling in 1923 over the Alkaff family waqf in Singapore, an English judge emphatically stated,

> The trustees, having chosen Singapore as the site of the trust estate, we have only to consider the law administered by these Courts. That law is municipal in the strictest sense. The domicile of a testator, or the religious sect to which he belonged, is never allowed to interfere with the destination of his immovables . . . it is so firmly embedded in our law that no Court can venture to break in upon it.[18]

Hence waqfs, although steeped in religious law, were governed by English common law in the Straits Settlements. Common law judges deliberately distanced themselves from litigants' religious intentions in administering waqfs by constantly referring to them as trusts and mentioning the term "waqf" only when directly citing evidence, although it remained a challenge for British authorities to reconcile all aspects of the waqf with the English trust.[19] The English trust—"the quintessential English institution," in the words of the English legal historian Frederic Maitland—had specific characteristics.[20] The Muslim trustee of a waqf (known as the *mutawalli*) was not a "trustee" in the English legal sense of the word but rather a "manager" of the property that had been alienated to form a waqf.[21] No property was actually ever "conveyed" to a *mutawalli* because all rights of property for the waqf managed by the mutawalli was vested in divine authority.[22] Yet, the word "trustee" constantly appeared in law reports involving the waqfs, instead of *mutawalli*. By categorizing waqfs as trusts, British legal authorities not only imposed the trust's legal limitations and expectations on the waqf, they also hollowed out the waqf, removing its original religious meaning. Stripped of its specific religious aspects within the Islamic legal tradition, waqfs were now subjected to the same threshold as trusts in that they must be "useful and beneficial" to the public in order to be charitable and run perpetually.

Definition of "Charity"

Throughout the British Empire, charity was highly regulated according to English common law. Toward the end of the nineteenth century, Muslim legal practitioners in South Asia accused colonial judges of deliberately misinterpreting Islamic law when presiding over cases involving waqfs.[23] No matter how hard-fought, however, cases in British India or elsewhere in the British Empire were not officially considered precedents in legal rulings in the Straits Settlements because the Straits Settlements, unlike British India, had been retrospectively declared "uninhabited." Precedents cited in waqf cases were limited to cases involving trusts in England and Ireland and other earlier waqfs in the Straits Settlements. This did not stop lawyers from sometimes citing British Indian cases involving waqfs in order to buttress their arguments.[24] Moreover, since waqfs were found throughout the British Empire, colonial officials refined their knowledge in the first four decades of the twentieth century by drawing upon the expanding imperial contact with yet more waqfs. While Muslims invariably regard the waqfs as primarily religious institutions, waqfs rankled British authorities because they associated it with trust law that has been historically exploited to shield business interests or the interests of wealthy entities such as the Roman Catholic Church in England. As British authorities encountered more waqfs in the former Ottoman territory they came to control in the aftermath of the First World War, they sought to streamline laws regarding waqfs, low-hanging fruit for imperialists to seize because they were often no longer attentively administered. In 1924, British authorities established both an investigative commission and a special court to rule on the question of waqfs in the new Emirate of Transjordan, previously part of the Ottoman Empire, with a view to exploit the land in question. Indeed, British authorities in Mandate of Palestine who controlled the territory in the Jordan River Valley expended considerable energy trying to prove that the extensive lands on the valley were not waqf land but agricultural land owned by the state, known as *miri* lands.[25] British preoccupation with waqfs intensified in the 1920s and 1930s as more waqfs started to be disputed in courts of the Straits Settlements.[26] They might have been emboldened by the elimination of family waqfs in newly secular Turkey under Mustafa Kemal Ataturk in 1926.[27]

Judges in the Straits Settlements could certainly act on their suspicions and do away with waqfs entirely if they wanted, eliminating them completely in the colony in the long run. Yet over time, judges' dismissal of waqfs early on gave way to reluctant and measured acceptance during the first half of the twentieth century as they reasoned more carefully and parsed each clause in a waqf deed with the explicit intention of upholding each clause as far as possible. More specifically, British judges increasingly leaned toward ruling waqfs as charitable over time. It is possible that the influx of local lawyers in the 1920s and 1930s held the judges more accountable to colonial subjects. The more likely reason behind this policy change, however, was the appeasement of litigants who were wealthy rate-payers responsible for contribution to the imperial largesse, having invested money and property in the Straits Settlements.[28] The prosperity of the port cities depended on these merchant's investments, and judges were therefore persuaded to allow waqfs, both public and private, to remain for the purpose of retaining these merchants in the colony.[29] Of course, an added advantage was that the benefits of public philanthropy contributed to the smooth running of the colony as well.[30] In 1895, an opinion by Lord Stanley of Alderley in the House of Lords tellingly linked the waqf to its supposed function in the British colony—"upon which depends the prosperity of their individual families which have rendered important services to the State in times of danger."[31]

While court rulings generally favored the continued existence of waqfs in the Straits Settlements, stigma hounded these institutions by inaccurately equating them with English common law trusts. In fact, the association with "trusts" tainted the waqf so much that the latter was considered shorthand for perpetual trusts. For instance, in 1930, Mackertich Carapit Johannes, an Armenian lawyer, imposed the legal category of "waqf" on an endowment in Johore established by a non-Muslim Chinese man who had never used that term himself. Johannes knew that the term had become synonymous with a particular legal abomination in English common law: mortmain (dead hand) laws that were associated with postmortem philanthropy.[32] He hoped, perhaps, that the judge would be sufficiently triggered by the term "waqf," which had entered the colonial legal lexicon in the region as the supreme challenge to two cardinal rules in the English common law of trusts— namely the English Law against Perpetuities and English legal definitions of charity. The two cardinal rules were related to each other since fulfillment of the legal definition of "charity" could potentially render the first one void. After debates on the suitability of the importation of mortmain laws into overseas colonies with non-Christian subjects, the chief justice of the Straits Settlements, Benson Maxwell, decided in a landmark case on local trusts in 1869, *Choa Choon Neoh v. Spottiswoode*, that

> this (mortmain) rule, which certainly has been recognized as existing in the law of England independently of any statute, is founded upon

considerations of public policy, which seem to be as applicable to the condition of such a place as Penang to England; viz., to prevent the mischief of making property inalienable, unless for objects which are in some way useful or beneficial to the community. It would obviously be injurious to the interests of the Island, if land convenient for the purposes of trade or for the enlargement of a town, or port could be dedicated to a purpose which would forever prevent such a beneficial use of it . . . The law of England has, however, made an exception, also on grounds of public policy, in favour of shifts for purposes useful and beneficial to the public, and which, in a wide sense of the term, are called charitable uses; and may this exception properly be.[33]

The separation of interests between those who use property or benefit from its use and those who were the legal owners lie at the basis of the modern law of trusts. The English legal definition of "charity" in cases involving waqfs had very little to do with Islamic law and very much to do with what the colony needed in terms of public welfare, education, and healthcare.[34] Failing to fulfill these needs ran the risk of chastisement and the waqf being declared void. A law report in 1887 disparagingly defined one particular waqf as

land devoted to, or set apart for some specific purpose, as a charity or the like, and so rendered inalienable—and . . . for a person's children and their descendants is a somewhat common way in which the natives of this Settlement attempt to tie up property in their families [but not as a charity in its legal sense] so that they may enjoy the produce or income thereof from generation to generation, but the land is prevented from ever being mortgaged or sold.[35]

The problem was that throughout the colonial period, no definition of "charity" completely determined or defined its legal scope.

In the British Straits Settlements, a family waqf was limited by the English Law of Perpetuities, which stated that "no interest is good unless it must vest, if at all, no later than twenty-one years after some life in being at the creation of the trust." Public waqfs could exist perpetually, however, because the English Law of Perpetuities did not apply to waqfs that fit the English legal definition of "charitable." For a trust to be deemed charitable, its beneficiaries had to be the general public and not just one's own family. The English Law of Perpetuities was clear, so testators quickly got the hang of it.[36] But the English common law definition of "charity" was unpredictable, and waqfs often ran aground, partially or completely, because of it. Within the colony, the meaning of charity in colonial courts was influenced by two related factors, namely the role of the judiciary and the interpretation of the legal concept of charity.[37] In 1923, the British judge Michael Whitley acknowledged that "the words "piety" and "charity" have a much wider signification in Mohammedan law and religion than in any other system."[38] Yet British legal authorities of the Straits Settlements continued not to take into account this broader Islamic conception of "charity" through legal procedure and substantive content. In the Islamic world, charity was closely regulated according to the wishes of the testator, whose word is paramount. Unlike Muslim judges, British judges were not primarily concerned with upholding the intentions of Muslim settlors and testators.[39]

By the late 1880s, the legal definition of charity in England referred specifically and only to the act of giving with clear intention of public benefit.[40] According to this understanding, a purpose was not charitable unless it was for public benefit, although British authorities recognized that that the Muslim definition was different.[41] In contrast, family endowments benefited only a relatively small, select group of people—for instance, members of a particular family of clan, instead of the general, more abstract public. In other words, charity truly begins at home, as Johannes claimed in 1930.[42] By considering only the poor clause in their assessment of waqfs, British authorities flattened the subtleties and complexities of the notion of Muslim charity. The most often cited reference in cases involving trusts was the preamble to the Statute of Charities in 1601, also known as the Charitable Uses Act of 1601 or Elizabeth Statute (Statute 43 Eliz. C. 4).[43] The term "charity" was not fixed in English law since each judge had the freedom to interpret each waqf deed. Unlike the English Rule Against Perpetuities, which still remains in effect today, laws concerning charity were subjected to change across historical time. Charity was a malleable concept that colonial courts continually tried to fix from the perspective of colonial benefits at the time—social, economic, and political.

The English legal definition of "charity" was never as broad as it was in Islamic law.[44] Within the Islamic world, charity was highly nuanced, not simply meant to relieve suffering or alleviate poverty, and was done for several reasons—for personal redemption, to assert political power and improve social standing, or to honor someone.[45] By 1936, the English legal definition of charity was no less precise than it had been in 1601, though parsed more succinctly by legal practitioners. The concept was divided into four general categories: 1) trusts for the relief of poverty; 2) trusts for the advancement of education; 3) trusts for the advancement of religion; and 4) trusts for other purposes beneficial to the community not falling under any of the preceding heads. The advancement of religion was listed as one of the legitimate reasons because religion benefits the rich as well as the poor. However, courts had trouble enforcing terms that were abstract.[46] Amherst Daniel Tyssen's *Charitable Bequest,* published in 1888 and cited in several law reports, stated that the trend of modern decision for the Court in Chancery was not to be bound by rigid rules but rather to decide by ordinary canons of construction whether or not there was indeed a paramount general charitable intent to be gathered from the will or settlement.

Historical fatwas (legal opinions) on the waqf indicate that Shāfiʿī jurists demonstrated remarkable adaptability to historical circumstances.[47] From about the eighth to the tenth centuries, the understanding of many Muslim jurists was that the charitable nature of the waqf dictated that the rich could not benefit from charitable endowments. However, jurists from within the Shāfiʿī school of law from the tenth century onward came to approve of establishing endowments for the benefit of the well-to-do. In general, when it came to the question of waqfs, earlier jurists tended to be very strict in their legal interpretations, whereas later scholars were increasingly more lenient in response to changing historical contexts and circumstances. In Islamic law, even the definition of "poor" continued to shift over time. Those worthy of receiving alms were described in chapter 9, line 60, of the Qur'an.[48] The term *fuqara* literally meant "poor," while the term *masākīn* meant "indigent."[49] Jurists debated over whether the two categories were legally different, and if so how they were distinct. Al-Shāfiʿī (the founder of the Shāfiʿī school of law) took the view that the word *fuqara* referred to those who were possessionless, whereas *masākīn* referred to those who possessed some property.[50] Over the centuries, by and large Muslim jurists within the Shāfiʿī school of law began to define a poor person as someone who was in a state of need. The term "poor" included both the *fuqara* and the *masākīn*, who might not be in a state of deprivation and impoverishment like the *fuqara* but who did not have enough to support themselves and their family.[51] In this way, the meaning of the word "poor" was not fixed, since jurists maintained that the word "need" depended on the circumstances of the person—such as social status.[52] A person of high social status needed more to sustain his life than a person of lower status. This logic was based on the premise that poverty cannot be defined in absolute material terms; rather it is what is acknowledged to be such by people in a community.[53] Moreover, the requirement to give charity to those whom one was closest—in a locational or familial sense—was simply the most efficient and effective way to take care of the poor, according to Al-Shāfiʿī himself. Based on this theory, Muslim jurists decided that it was best to give to one's own family rather than to strangers—that is, to the general public. In this view, establishing a family waqf was thus considered a nobler endeavor than establishing a public waqf. The Islamic definition of charity is extremely broad and wide-ranging, including all actions considered to be benevolent and "doing good for humanity in general."[54] Chapter 2, line 177 of the Qur'an names the following groups of people as deserving of charity: one's relatives, orphans, the needy, travelers and beggars, those in bondage, those who keep up the prayer and pay the prescribed alms, those who keep pledges whenever they make them, and those who are steadfast in misfortune, adversity, and times of danger.[55]

Due to the fact that charitable waqfs could run perpetually, colonial courts paid extra attention to waqfs that were classified as public (meaning that they supposedly fulfilled the English legal definition of "charitable"), believing that they might just be a shrewd tactic to circumvent limitations on perpetuity that were imposed on family waqfs. As British judges pored over individual terms dictated by testators, parsing the terms according to English legal conceptions of charity in order to determine whether the entire waqf was viable or not, they reduced it to its individual components. Tellingly, whenever there was an expressed charitable intention to be found in a will, judges construed the will as liberally as possible so as to give effect to such intention by applying the cyprès doctrine, which refers to "the application of law in the case of trusts or charities, when a literal execution of the testator's intention becomes impossible, so it is executed as nearly as possible, according to the general purpose."[56] In the matter of religious endowments in the Straits Settlements, the application of the doctrine commonly required the significant alteration by the court of clauses legally deemed to be uncharitable to make them charitable. This phenomenon granted a lot more power to judges than originally anticipated by testators, although the frequent application of this doctrine ensured that waqfs would rarely fail altogether in colonial courts.

Conceptions of the Family

Because a fixation on charitability led to a focus on the poor, deemed to be the only deserving beneficiaries, even family waqfs were subjected to this stipulation. A prominent waqf worth 70,000 Straits dollars in 1923 that risked being rendered void in this way was one made by the Ḥaḍramī Arab Alkaff patriarch two months before his death in 1919.[57] The trust involved property in the Straits Settlements (Surabaya and Batavia), in Tarīm and Say'un in Ḥaḍramawt, and in Mecca and Madina in the Hijaz. The judge ascertained that in order to make that object really charitable, the property would have to be devoted to the poor in general with a preference for poor relations, a result quite at variance with the testator's intention. The waqf was challenged in court because no "indigent" relatives of the testator or his father or brother had yet appeared in Singapore. British judges who discussed the case had a restrictive notion of family and often conceived of one's family as comprising only immediate family members, or even only kin who resided with the testator. This understanding of the term "family" was at odds with the Arab understanding, which could possibly include a wider category of people linked to the testator by slavery, marriage, service, or blood.[58] Arab conceptions of family were more akin to households, which would include servants as well. Through travel, their orbit of responsibility simply expanded. Hence Arab testators potentially included their entire clan, located throughout the Indian Ocean, as family. If we were to look at lateral relatives through this lens, the picture would look entirely different. In 1923, British judges expressed skepticism that an immensely wealthy Arab patriarch's family would have poor relatives, possibly because they were only looking at immediate relatives, by which they usually mean vertical descendants who had already inherited the patriarch's fortune anyway. After all, one of the main purposes of establishing waqfs was to benefit those that fell outside of direct inheritance, such as adopted children and more distant relatives.[59] Indeed, the historian Leslie Peirce demonstrates how marginalized groups with limited access to material resources such as orphans, widows, younger sons, and female relatives benefitted greatly from waqfs in the Ottoman Empire.[60] Their visibility in society heightened awareness of the moral responsibility of the community to help those at risk of falling into poverty.

In any case, the "poor" as a category were the remote and ultimate beneficiaries who would be entitled to receive their share in the endowments following the total extinction of all the founder's descendants.[61] Some, though not all, testators inserted clauses to explicitly indicate this. But of course, British judges wanted a public waqf that would immediately benefit the poor, not in the remote future.[62] This reluctance to let a family waqf run its course in this manner could suggest that the fulfillment of the English legal concept of charity was not the primary concern of British legal authorities. Rather, they were intent on eradicating the waqf's perpetuity, which they would have had to uphold in case of truly charitable waqfs meant for the poor.

Casual Alms

The discomfort at the perpetual aspect of waqfs ran through judges' arguments that provisions set aside for the *kenduri*, a Malay word signifying a feast were also uncharitable. Specifically, judges took issued with *kenduris* meant to confer some benefit on the soul of the person, generally observed first on certain dates after his death and then on the anniversary of his death in each succeeding year.[63] Waqf deeds indicated that these feasts were usually given in someone's name and prayers were usually recited to honor this person (usually someone who recently passed). Ignoring the fact that the feasts usually involved feeding relatives and neighbors for free, judges reasoned that these ceremonies were intended to be held in honor of an individual and therefore did not lead to any public advantage or utility.[64] Hence a source of sustenance for the poor was ironically deemed uncharitable by British judges. This rule was not consistently applied, though. In a case involving yet another large waqfs established in Singapore, judges upheld the terms of Raja Siti binte Kraying Chanda Pulih's will in 1883, which dictated that a supply of ten vessels of *zamzam* water be provided to the holy mosque of Mecca, a mat be furnished for Qur'an reciters every night for the period between the third and the fourth prayers, and somebody be engaged annually to perform the pilgrimage on the testator's behalf.[65]

Historically, these feasts have particular functions in the Islamic world aside from spiritual relief for dead souls, the most important being to give relief to the poorer members of society who counted on the elite to provide discounted or free food during times of crisis.[66] Feeding the poor is a time-honored tradition in the Muslim world, often to solidify the loyalty of less affluent classes toward the ruler.[67] In this way, these feasts formed part of a "conspicuous patronage" associated with public waqfs, tangible property visible to all.[68] In the Southeast Asian context, a *kenduri* is a feast that symbolizes and celebrates the major events in the human life cycle such as births, circumcisions, marriages, and death anniversaries.[69] These feasts were also given to repay social obligations and to strengthen social relations.[70] They are a popular means for redistribution of wealth among Muslims communities in Southeast Asia, often attended by people living on the margins of society, like orphans and destitute women. The feasts might be questionable as a legitimate clause in waqf deeds but the colonial daily newspaper *The Straits Times* frequently lauded the Muslim community for holding feasts in honor of government officials or anyone who had rendered the Muslim community good service while downplaying that these feasts were in fact financed by waqfs.[71]

Just as biological relatives were excluded from waqfs, so too were strangers, for other avenues for charity like *kenduris* were also deemed in courts to be uncharitable. In effect, British legal authorities regulated the class of beneficiaries of waqfs and by doing so appointed themselves the executors of the common good of the colony. Waqfs in the Islamic world typically wove dense horizontal and vertical networks of patronage and clientage, establishing the settlors' families and trustees as nodal points for the distribution of money, power, and affect.[72] Individual patrons could certainly further their private interests while exercising forms of charity that constituted them as moral individuals and as political subjects. Even within the oppressive structures of imperialism and colonialism with their asymmetrical relations of domination and oppression, philanthropic activity was a vehicle enabling the political participation and influence of some disempowered groups.[73] This specific system of patronage was undermined by British colonial leaders in the Straits Settlements, who regulated charity and in the process determined what forms of charity were allowed to thrive in the colony. Patronage over colonial subjects by fellow colonial subjects should be curbed in their view lest rival authorities emerge. Hence, the relationship among colonial subjects was distorted through rulings on the waqfs that limited the ability of wealthy Muslims to contribute within larger kin networks, sustain the lives of affiliated households, or develop independent forms of income within clans for several generations. Over time, the term *kenduri*, just like the term waqf, acquired its own distinct legal status, its meaning divorced from its cultural context to become shorthand for something to be regarded with suspicion.[74]

For colonial authorities in the land-scarce colony of the Straits Settlements, anxiety about patronage was likely secondary to concerns about property being sequestered perpetually, out of reach of taxation and government use. In general, British judges (in England and abroad) were reluctant to allow property, especially immoveable property held under private trusts, to become subject to restrictions that would unduly prevent its free marketability.[75] The nail in the coffin of waqfs was provided by the stipulation that the transmission of immoveable property in the Straits Settlements be understood to be that of chattels real (real estate) and not of freehold in the Straits Settlements according to Indian Act XX of the 1837 Act. A time limit is automatically imposed on the category of "chattels real" unlike freehold property which could be held perpetually.[76]

Compromises

Considering the squall of restrictions placed on waqfs by English common law, it is a wonder they existed at all.[77] Because the Arab mercantile diaspora did not originate in Southeast Asia and members could easily have moved their capital elsewhere, it is curious as to why they decided to adapt to British colonial legal exigencies. After all, their resources ensured that they were not hard-pressed in adhering to the colonial legal mold. Their choice to avidly establish waqfs in the British colony represents yet more evidence of disengagement between the political and the religious as they regarded their capitulation to quirks of English common law as separate from actual submission to colonial government. Keen as they were to close their loop of obligations across the Indian Ocean, they remade the conditions of their existence in the colony. This phenomenon proved that the sphere of colonial subject imagination was unbounded even in the face of colonialism, which did not diminish their sense of possibility.

It is also possible that it took some time before members of the Arab diaspora realized that their waqf regime risked being short-circuited because of limitations imposed by common law. As established in chapters 1 and 2, this clustering around state institutions and reliance on state bureaucracy went beyond a view toward future litigation and eventual accounting. It also held government authorities responsible for enforcing terms in waqf deeds, maintaining waqfs, and disciplining errant trustees. Public waqfs, especially cemeteries, were generally not well maintained in the colony because appointed trustees and caretakers were unable or unwilling to manage these waqfs.[78] Members of the public relentlessly complained until government authorities stepped in.[79] For this very reason, the Mohamedan and Hindu Endowment Board was formed in 1905 in the Straits Settlements to administer Muslim public waqfs and Hindu public endowments.[80] Crucially, Arab settlors did not foresee that their descendants, whom they appointed as beneficiaries, would exploit colonial legal limitations in court in order to render family waqfs void so that they could benefit from the sale of the property. Beneficiaries periodically renewed their claims to dissolve a waqf to take advantage of changing legal administrations. British colonial courts might have been tough on waqfs, but they were not particularly attentive to the various family endowments being established or managed, such that even trustees' ineptitude or untrustworthiness often went undetected for years. In fact, colonial courts rarely challenged the status of a waqf on their own, although from 1886 onward, land granted or leased by or on behalf of the Crown free of rent or of nominal value for religious purposes required the governor's written consent.[81] Even so, most of the time family waqfs was usually brought to the court's attention by Arab litigants interested in the waqf in the first place.[82] For example, the legal dispute involving the Alkaff family settlement was renewed about every ten years until 2001. Up to the point of litigation, the management of family waqfs remained firmly in the hands of private trustees appointed by testators without any interference from the state.[83] In fact, even when private trustees were incompetent or corrupt, the onus was upon beneficiaries to inform the court by enacting some form of legal action. Most waqfs were only critically examined by colonial courts after they were challenged and disputed in colonial courts, usually by the testators' descendants and relatives. A valuable waqf established by Syed Ahmed Alsagoff existed for forty-three years prior to being disputed in colonial courts in 1918, while the waqf of Syed Shaik Alkaff was in existence for a full thirteen years before its terms were challenged in court by some of his descendants in 1923.[84] Hence, waqfs would have been allowed to exist as they were in the Straits Settlements if they had not been brought to the attention of the colonial courts in the form of various lawsuits by Arab litigants.

For a waqf to be legally established, the onus was upon the testator to be as specific as possible in describing the terms of the trusts, and to make sure that there was a tangible operation that colonial authorities could oversee and enforce. Once these terms were fulfilled, waqfs were likely guaranteed an existence. Shrunken, stripped of several religious aspects, closely regulated to the point of being choked, the religious sphere of the waqf was an embattled realm under the colonial legal regime, but once classified as religious and preserved, the sphere was sustained by the colonial state, and that was no small phenomenon. What shrunk this sphere was secular colonial law, but what was allowed to survive did so intact until the postcolonial period.

Another likely reason for the frequent establishment of waqfs among members of the Arab diaspora was the lacuna in actual waqf regulations and codes in the Straits Settlements, or anywhere in Empire for that matter. Laws were made known to the public only through settled case law, which became consistent over time. Having been declared "uninhabited," the colony was legally a blank slate, which meant that case law was the only thing that generated precedents. Chapter 1 demonstrates how members of the Arab elite successfully persuaded colonial leaders to take on the mantle of administration of Islamic law in 1880 because they wished for the presence of a strong state regulatory agency in the form of a strong judicial system. They confidently placed themselves at the helm of Muslim leadership in the colony during the First World War, as we see in chapter 5. Being part of this momentum, waqfs form the culmination of a diasporic vision that took advantage of the gray areas and interstices in a legal system that had been anything but static thus far in the eyes of the Arab diaspora.

Nevertheless, reliance on colonial jurisdictions yielded unpredictable results. By requesting that British colonial authorities enforce terms in the waqfs, settlors subjected waqfs to the intense scrutiny of British judges, who carefully parsed the terms of the waqf and interpreted them not according to the wishes of the testators but according to English common law, which sometimes went against the intentions of the testators. One could argue that waqfs were excessively regulated and policed once they entered the courtrooms, henceforth relentlessly measured against two cardinal rules governing trusts—the English Rule Against Perpetuities and the English legal definition of charity. Extensive mortmain properties blocked perpetually from circulation were not a viable option in the land-scarce colony. Since trustees were required to keep the capital of the fund intact and only use the income for the stated purposes, the trust could conceivably last forever and be exempted from taxation.[85] Waqfs in the Straits Settlements were definitely straightjacketed by legal limitations of common law trusts but they were allowed to exist in some form. By contrast, within the Netherlands Indies, the Agrarian Law of 1870 (known as the *vervreemdingsverbod* or "disposal ban") forbade the alienation of indigenous-held land by all persons who were considered nonindigenous. It was much harder therefore for Arabs to establish perpetual endowments—although, as we have seen in chapter 3, property fell into the hands of Foreign Orientals through various mechanisms such as inheritance, powers of attorney, and transfer of debt. We do however see glimpses of family waqfs that still covertly existed in the Netherlands Indies. In one of Christiaan Snouck Hurgronje's letters to the governor-general of the Netherlands Indies in 1892, he alluded to a case in Surabaya where the head of the Arab community channeled the estate of several public waqfs to the inheritance of some private individuals.[86] In Pontianak where land use by Arabs were less restrictive in the first place, a case appeared in 1888 in the Supreme Court when beneficiaries successfully compelled the restitution of a garden waqf created by a woman named Sharifah Hadiah so that payouts could be meted out to them by the priesterraden.[87]

The Burden of Interpretation by Translators

Remarkably, from the late nineteenth century onward, British authorities did not shrink from casting their jurisdictions over people and assets across the Indian Ocean, in contrast to the Dutch tendency to declare itself incompetent even within the Netherlands Indies, as we saw in chapters 3 and 4. Rarely did British legal practitioners refrain from addressing something because it lay outside their purview.

Diasporic waqfs did however yield particular difficulties, such as language complications that arose from translations. Often, Arab testators produced multiple wills that were either simultaneous versions of the same will in different languages or completely different wills produced at separate times that supplemented or cancelled earlier versions. Occasionally, a testator's final will would emerge elsewhere to challenge a version of his will that had already been accepted by legal authorities in the Straits Settlements.[88] Sometimes, testators died in one place having established trusts in another. Even when the testator had settled in the Straits Settlements for a considerable amount of time, he tended to bear in mind his dispersed clan living elsewhere connected with his trust or will and produce multiple, though not necessarily identical, versions of the same will in various languages to accommodate them. Complications also arose due to the lack of capable translators in one location who could directly translate from one language to another, especially from Arabic to English. In the Straits Settlements specifically, the problem of interpretation of wills in Arabic arose due to the multiple layers of translation that each will underwent before finally being accepted in probate.[89] Wills written in Arabic were often translated into Malay by one translator, then from Malay into English by another translator in the Supreme Court. Not surprisingly, such translations were seldom identical.

In 1923, a case appeared in the Supreme Court that revolved around the multiple wills of an Arab merchant named Syed Ahmed bin Abdul Rahman Alsagoff who made his fortune in Singapore and died there on March 27, 1875.[90] Seven years earlier, on December 21, 1868, he made a will in Arabic that was annexed to his English will dated nine days later (December 30, 1868), which was subsequently proved by his, son who was also his executor, Syed Mohamed Alsagoff. Both documents were admitted to probate but the judge insisted that the main will was the one in English with the Arabic to be regarded as addendum, despite being aware that the English document was created several days after the Arabic one. It was even suggested in court that the Arabic will formed "part of the English will," as if it was not sufficient to stand on its own.[91] The original Arabic will, despite having been produced earlier, was thus relegated to a secondary status, and the English document became the sole document referred to during more than half of the trial. During court proceedings, however, the judge learned that the Arabic will contained much more precise details that clarified certain vague but key terms (such as "descendants") in the English will.[92] The Arabic will then became the primary testamentary document in subsequent lawsuits through the rest of the twentieth century.

Needless to say, erroneous probate copy of wills could have widespread repercussions through time. In another case—that of Syed Sheik Alkaff's will of 1910—the Malay rendering was deemed inaccurate and "too free" by one of the judges in 1923. As a result, one of the plaintiffs' lawyers was forced to tender a revised translation of the trust deed.[93] However, even this revised translation failed to satisfy Judge P. J. Sproule, who was unimpressed by the oral evidence of Haji Wan Abdullah, the Malay translator who had been called to correct the earlier translation. Sproule lamented that the man was more disposed to give opinions on Islamic law than on Arabic grammar, which was his recognized area of expertise. Translators should not be interpreters of Islamic law in British colonial courts, Sproule maintained, because no one had the capacity to do so in a court of the Straits Settlements except the judge who had to determine whether Islamic law was relevant in each case. Displeased with the Malay translator for overstepping, Sproule praised another Arabic translator named J. N. Mobaied, a commission agent in Singapore most probably from the Levant who apparently knew Arabic and French very well and whose evidence he found to be very reliable. However, while they might be experts in Arabic grammar and etymology, translators were certainly not experts in Islamic law. Because judges reduced adjudication of cases involving Islamic law to a simple matter of literal translation of Malay and Arabic legal terms, translators such as Haji Wan Abdullah bore the burden of interpretation. Other translators such as Bobsaid, whom we met in chapter 2, and Mobaied inaccurately framed understandings of certain highly specialized legal terms with their own prejudice or ignorance, pushed as they were by colonial judges to interpret highly specialized Islamic legal terms beyond their capabilities. The delegation of authority in cases involving Islamic law to unqualified individuals is another major consequence of the colonial administration of Islamic law. The supposedly reliable Mobaied oddly removed legal terms from the context of the trust deed when he emphasized that the term *umūr al-khayra*, which he literally translated as *bonnes oeuvres*, meant "nothing religious" and simply denoted "giving something without return" or "generosity."[94] Rather awkwardly for him, none of the court judges were convinced of this and they outrightly rejected his conception. Instead, they steadfastly recognized the religious intentions of establishing a waqf and the concomitant *umūr al-khayra* specified in the deeds.

Subsequently, the three judges in the court of appeals sought to further refine juridical exactitude in their legal definition of the concept of waqf by referring to legal textbooks instead of merely relying on translators in the Straits Settlements. Consequently, the judges consistently defined the phrase more comprehensively as "being good works in the eyes of God as perceived by a devout Muslim." The case turned upon yet another crucial translation error. Mobaied translated the Arabic word *awlād* as "children," and *abnā* as "sons," but Judge Sproule crucially pointed out that both words were translated simply as *anak-anak* in Malay, which in fact only meant children without taking gender into consideration. Gender distinction was crucial due to the different inheritance shares for male and female progeny under Islamic law.

Syed Shaik Alkaff himself took pains to list the names of his sons under *abnā* and all the names of his children, male and female under *awlād* in his will.[95]

The court ascertained that the term *abnā* excluded female descendants entirely. Because of this exclusion, the class of descendants that was often the subject of debate in court was female descendants, and by extension, the issue of female descendants. Indeed, several Arab family waqfs tended to exclude daughters from the waqf settlement or deliberately limit the amounts they could reap from the trust.[96] However, as long as they lived on the family estate, they could gain from the waqf.[97] In general, lineal descendants formed the main class of beneficiaries of waqfs established by Arab families.[98] The exclusion of living daughters and granddaughters was due to the expectation that women would marry and leave the family home.[99]

The number of cases involving female settlors in the Straits Settlements was certainly small compared to that of male settlors. Female testators had more leeway in dispersing their income as they were not bound to provide for their families. They tended to continue to disperse their income differently from male testators when establishing a waqf. As a result of this freedom, a female settlor's instructions were likely to be less formulaic and open to several permutations that had to be elucidated more explicitly. The 1883 will of Raja Siti binte Kraying Chanda Pulih, the daughter of the wealthy merchant Hajjah Fatimah, for example, differed from male testators' wills. She stated that she created a waqf from her houses and her mother's estate, and her wealth passed on to her children, who were part of the Arab Alsagoff clan, by way of their father.[100] In establishing waqfs, male testators usually exploited the opportunity to specifically name the beneficiaries who comprised patrilineal descendants. Women founded trusts, often out of a sizable portion of their estate, that tended to benefit other women.[101] Raja Siti bequeathed a significant portion of her estate to female descendants of the Prophet in Mecca, Madina, and Taif. Likewise, in November 1911, another wealthy woman named Sharifah Shaikah bte Syed Omar bin Ali Aljunied bequeathed a third of her estate to be applied toward the purchase a house or shop, stipulating that the income from the property commemorate the memory of herself, her, her parents, and her daughter.[102] This could be construed as an attempt to create a sort of matrilineal system of property devolution on the part of female settlors.

The waqfs are evidence of Arab diaspora's new roots as they transitioned from migrants to residents, providers of infrastructure, and, on a more intimate level, organizers of feasts. Yet, voluntary territorial mooring by diasporas did not necessarily lead to changes in kinship and communitarian structures. In fact, it might have led to the tightening of agnatic bonds for some families. Female descendants seemed to inherit less with the establishment of waqfs since their otherwise Qur'anic shares were disbursed through will and testament to their male relatives. By policing women's marriages, the wealthy Arab elite in the region ensured that they retained biological kinship structures through marriage, even in zones of intense cross-cultural contact such as Southeast Asia, thus guaranteeing that communities remained separate to a certain extent. In fact, the most transformative impact was wrought not by the Arab diaspora themselves but by colonial authorities who limited diasporic obligations to immediate family members, cutting out members of clans much further down on the family tree and afield in the Indian Ocean, thus ensuring that Arab capital remained in the Straits Settlements rather than circulating along diasporic lines.

Colonial legal administration of waqfs represented the limits of the portability of Islamic law that the Arab diaspora relied on, although perhaps we should be more surprised that these waqfs remained, albeit in distorted forms that conformed to English common law trusts. Rather than use their colonial legislative fiat to declare waqfs illegal, British judges chose to approve of waqfs by using the cyprès doctrine, an approach that granted them more power in the courtroom. By the 1920s, more waqfs were passed as "charitable" after waqf deeds and testaments were carefully parsed. Family waqfs deemed private waqfs were accepted with caveats, limited to being temporal trusts, while public waqfs were constantly deemed charitable since they were beneficial to the colony. In the process, judges shifted Muslim charity toward public welfare and away from individual families and clans. Within the Straits Settlements, the Arab elite expanded their reach and influence by acting as hosts and patrons through the establishment of waqfs in keeping with common historical practice among wealthy Muslims throughout the world. Yet, Arab benefaction over other Muslim subjects in the colony made British authorities uncomfortable, as they were unwilling to share any kind of authority with colonial subjects. They especially rankled at funds being disbursed for the sake of "feasts" known as *kenduri*.

In light of the British legal preoccupation with the question of charity in the matter of waqfs, it is certainly no accident that Arab charity in the colony became highly conspicuous during the early twentieth century. In November 1914, one of the most prominent Arabs, Syed Omar Alsagoff, contributed $5,000 to the Prince of Wales's Fund, the highest amount by a local inhabitant to the British cause in the First World War.[103] In the following decade, Arab philanthropy in Singapore was extended to their land of origin in Ḥaḍramawt, where they made extensive contributions to the construction of roads, schools, and medical dispensaries as well as a postal service.[104] British expansion into Arabia intensified in the 1930s, and imperial officials welcomed infrastructure-building efforts on the part of the Ḥaḍramī diaspora. British authorities appreciated public philanthropy and conspicuously exalted public philanthropists through public events such as fetes, galas, and balls throughout the Straits Settlements. Thus legal encounters between Arab colonial subjects and British colonial officials in Southeast Asia led to the redirection of philanthropy toward British imperialist aims.

Conclusion

Postcolonial Transitions

This book began with Arabs playing hosts to Dutch VOC merchants in 1599 who were welcomed as guests, the hospitality being a corollary of commerce in the region. By the nineteenth century, Arabs' status regressed to being aliens—essentially, strangers throughout the archipelago under Dutch rule. Through three centuries, the flexible realms of *orang datang* (newcomers) gradually diminished as the Dutch and British colonial regimes fixed their realms to certain physical locations, designating spheres of influence and particular vocations. As their roles as intermediaries in the region were progressively curtailed and curbed over the next three centuries, these Arabs held on to the possibility that they could still negotiate with colonial powers just as they did with host societies in Southeast Asia. In so doing, they attempted to extend the era of "Oertatan." Throughout most of colonial history, they were perceived to be permanent *orang datang*, perpetually either arriving or leaving the region, even though the majority had settled in the region.

It is extraordinary that members of the Arab diaspora, at their most creative, attempted legal arbitrage under colonial rule—like Fatima (discussed in chapter 1), who switched to Hanafi *madhhab*. They expanded and modified Islamic law, while at other times they policed the boundaries of Islamic law even as mere translators, like the enterprising Bobsaid in chapter 2. This book tells the story of the surprising involvement of the outsider—the Arab diaspora—in aiding colonialists to accumulate legislative power. The pace of change from the mid-nineteenth century onward was brisk, and the Arab diaspora capitalized on it while attempting to navigate uncertainty and risk. The Arab elite in the Indian Ocean incrementally extended their jurisdiction over the region and also over their fellow Muslim brethren in the colonies in Southeast Asia. Their reliance on colonial legal structures and bureaucracies coalesced into an ambiguous embrace of European colonial authority that led to a significant expansion of colonial legal jurisdictions over Muslim affairs. Asymmetry lurked below these arrangements; whatever fleeting gain or proximity to power was achieved, it was inevitably followed by betrayal within the colonial context. The story of the Arab diasporic elite in Southeast Asia is a prime example of what John Comaroff calls the essential paradox of colonial governance in "its capacity to be ordered yet incoherent, rational yet absurd, violent yet impotent; to elicit compliance and contestation, discipline and defiance, subjection and insurrection. Sometimes all at once. And, disconcertingly, in ways that blurred the boundaries between these, apparently antithetical, species of action."[1]

From the perspective of the Dutch colonial government especially, Arabs were consistently deemed surplus population, needlessly propping themselves up as consummate mediators since the days of Oertatan in the early seventeenth century. Since they fell outside the *Cultuurstelsel* scheme in the nineteenth century, they became a drain on Dutch resources. Increasingly racialized, they considered akin to vultures constantly exploiting Natives' susceptibility and undermining their productivity. Within the category of Foreign Orientals specifically, the Arabs were considered the biggest threat due to their proximity to Muslim Natives, leading to their relegation to the social margins of the Netherlands Indies right up to the Second World War. A constant bugbear for colonial officials was that Arabs managed to marry Native women, in what officials believed was an attempt to gain access to land they were legally forbidden to own otherwise. Arabs adeptly used the powers of attorney to act on behalf of Natives in managing their financial affairs.

Internal frontiers of the colony were intensely policed, and the visa regime continued to hound the lives of Foreign Orientals in the Netherlands Indies through mobility and property restrictions. At times, Arabs in the Netherlands Indies were forced to hide their true identities in order to retain or gain rights and privileges. Those who managed to pass as Natives were especially able to take advantage of this. At other times, Arabs came together as a stronger constituency to obtain or regain their rights. In this way, despite severe asymmetries in power in colonial settings, Arabs who were Dutch colonial subjects were able to assert some influence from time to time, though not to the extent that their counterparts in the British Straits Settlements were able to. Their efficacy was contingent upon several factors such as the ethos of local authorities at specific locations, the potential marginalization of those who deviated from what was considered normal practice, and the level of socialization with indigenous societies.

To make matters worse, jurisdiction over Arab subjects remained unclear and Arabs in Batavia, Palembang, Semarang, Lombok, Cheribon, Pontianak, and Riau were treated differently in legal courts because the Netherlands Indies formed a vast and varied political landscape. Although the stories of Arabs regularly unspooled in Dutch colonial courts, these threads would often go nowhere as courts declared themselves unfit to even hear the stories. Legal questions regularly posed to colonial newspapers in separate cities attest to this desire to arrive at a coherent unified policy. The sense of chaos that ensued from a lack of clear legal polices stemmed not from irrational arbitrariness as much as from conflicting rationales of colonial authorities at different locations throughout the colony and at different times. This phenomenon seriously destabilized Arab identities in the colony.

Archive and Library

What is unusual about the story of the Arab diaspora in Southeast Asia is that despite being a small minority in Southeast Asia, they were able to influence the shape of law to a great extent. Fittingly, the BBC Arabic transmission in 1939 described Arabs in Southeast Asia as "patriotic to their country of origin and law-abiding to their country of adoption."[2] Of course, the reality was more complicated than that. The main critical tenet of contestation among the Arab male elite was not theological or intellectual. For them, the primary impetus for more colonial involvement was qadis' approval of wife-initiated divorce cases and frequent intermarriages between Arab women who were descendants of the Prophet and male non-descendants. Because such disputes had to be urgently resolved, the ordinary method of deliberate discussions and debates among the religious elite concerning Islamic law was deemed too slow and insufficient; besides, they would likely lead to the proliferation of multiple fatwas, legal opinions that historically could not be enforced by state authorities anyway. The swiftest way to curb undesirable divorces and marriages would be to convince state authorities—in this case, non-Muslim colonial authorities—to be invested enough in Muslim issues that they would feel compelled to interfere on their behalf. Although they were a minority in the region, the Arab elite styled themselves as the leaders of Muslim communities by wielding their lineages as symbols of prestige within Southeast Asia. From this platform, Arabs based in the Netherlands Indies requested colonial intervention primarily in marital cases in 1890 and 1905, just as Arabs in the British colony requested British authorities to take a firmer hand in the administration of Muslim marriages and divorces in 1875. In keeping with Brinkley Messick's helpful schema, described in his book *Shari'a Scripts*, I argue that the Arab diaspora in Southeast Asia contributed to creating a legal "archive" but did not continue to dominate the "library." The plethora of legal instruments they produced were not cosmopolitan in the sense that Sheldon Pollock describes that such documents must "think of (themselves) as unbounded, unobstructed, unlocated."[3] Their contributions to Islamic law therefore turned out to be modest.

Arabs generally wanted to restrict the interpretive communities to themselves and their allies, including European colonial officials. In fact, Muslim cosmopolitanism was nowhere to be found, since identities became fractured, marked by a strong sense of elitism exacerbated by competition for limited resources from colonial governments who disrupted the possibility of united populations in densely populated diverse cities in the colonies.[4] In this sense, the colonial period had little to do with the precolonial period and the postcolonial period—it was therefore epochal and deserved to be scrutinized. It was a period when a Muslim minority recognized the power of colonial authorities to anoint new elites and its own capacity to ossify Islamic law that Muslim communities otherwise jointly articulated. The Arab elite ensured that close, often intimate contact led to an intensification of difference that generated new gradations of affinity based on rank, place of origin, and class. Gender played a huge barrier to equality as local women became absorbed into families but remained constantly subordinated. The story of the Arab diaspora proves that the stock dynamic of hospitality in the history of Southeast Asia was multifaceted and complex, rendering terms such as "cosmopolitanism," "hybridity," and "creolization" inadequate.

Given that colonial law was meant to bind subject populations together to the colonial government and not grant them more freedom, it is not surprising that even concessions to Arabs in the Straits Settlements in the form of the Mohamedan Marriage Ordinance and their appointments as members of the Mohamedan Advisory Board after the Sepoy Mutiny subsequently tied them more closely to the British colonial government, along with the rest of the Muslim population in the colony. In the Netherlands Indies, Orientalist scholar-bureaucrats created their own libraries according to their conceptions of Islamic law, while adat proponents created legal codes that sidelined Islamic law of the Arab elite. The *priesterraden* likewise prioritized adat as well. Although the Arab diaspora in the British Straits Settlements were not as oppressed, they were quickly left out of the loop during adjudication when they were subjected to British judges' rulings on Islamic law based on Anglo-Mohamedan literature with unpredictable outcomes that were often not in their favor. While Dutch bureaucratic-scholars of the day attempted to delve deeply into the rich intellectual history of Islamic law and adat, British judges tended to focus solely on the practical aspects of legal administration in the colonies. In contrast to Dutch cerebral ruminations on the application of suitable laws in the Netherlands Indies in colonial journals, the process by which English common-law courts displaced local customary laws in the Straits Settlements was a procedural and administrative triumph for the colonists primarily because the colony was artificially separated from the rest of the region after being declared uninhabited prior to its "settlement."

Paper and Power

British legal sources are subtler than Dutch sources in portraying Arab foreignness. Because Islamic law applied to all Muslims in British territories in an undifferentiated manner, it is not immediately obvious that certain sections of society were perceived differently. Arabs in the Straits Settlements were not subjected to threats of expulsion by British authorities, unlike Arabs in the Netherlands Indies. From the perspective of European colonial officials, while legal cases on the ground continually proved to Dutch authorities that Arabs were more locally rooted in the Netherlands Indies than previously thought, litigation in British Straits Settlements tended to expose British colonial perceptions that Arabs were not of the region, as we saw in chapter 6. In both colonies, Arabs paid higher taxes on average. In the Netherlands Indies most were forced to do so by law, while in the British Straits Settlements they paid as property-owning rate-payers amounts of up to 24 percent of occupied property. Paradoxically, paying higher taxes did not make one a local or a native; it marked one out as different in the colony. In the late 1930s, the firm Alkaff and Co. was the single highest rate-payer in Singapore, a reader of the *Straits Times* noted, but unfortunately (to the reader's mind), the firm sent money to Ḥaḍramawt regularly. The reader emphatically stated, "What we want is a domiciled class of merchants, landlords and professional men who still keep their money in the city where it is made."[5] The contributions of Arabs marked them out as foreign. As long as significant amounts were being remitted to Ḥaḍramawt, these Arabs were not perceived to be truly invested in Southeast Asia. From the

1860s until the outbreak of the Second World War, the Arab diaspora chose to lean on bureaucratic infrastructure in their effort to determine scales of responsibility, jurisdiction, and sovereignty. Generally, they attempted to retain strong kinship ties with their relatives across their Indian Ocean and maintain long-distance business relationships. Wills, waqf deeds, and powers of attorney mapped kinship and commercial relations, as well as property holdings, across the Indian Ocean—from Southeast Asia to South Asia and further to Ḥaḍramawt, Mecca, and Madina. Files not only document but also help make a place.[6] While the accumulation of these legal documents in government institutions enabled the Arab diaspora to powerfully determine the entire Indian Ocean as their space of maneuver, they ended up producing circuits of legitimacy along colonial lines rather than producing a juridico-domain of their own. The reiterative process of bureaucratization enacted authority through practice and repetition. Indeed, the capacity of bureaucracy to produce its own authority was crucial, and members of diasporas realized this more than others because their lives were not as grounded and stable. They craved authority, but for various reasons they did not take the reins of authority themselves. In the Netherlands Indies they were sidelined by the Dutch colonial government, while in the British Straits Settlements they might have prioritized their commercial activities over other spheres of their lives. I draw insight from the work of Ilana Feldman, who posits that people can perform a consent they might not feel when participating in a dynamic of abeyance in which questions of consent and coercion are suspended for the sake of quotidian convenience. This consent may subsequently permit the persistence of colonial rule.[7] In fact, the regularity of bureaucracy is so seductive that it might obscure other effects of reiterative authority.[8] The avid establishment of waqfs by Arabs perfectly encapsulates this tension: in many ways, waqfs deferred the end of colonial rule since testators depended on existing authorities' ongoing ability to maintain existing property regimes and uphold system of legal enforcement. If anything, the proliferation of waqfs made it more difficult for the wealthy Arab elite to envision an alternative structure of governance.

As members of the Arab diaspora made many demands of colonial states, they certainly became more empowered by their proximity to colonial authorities but they also ended up being more visible and traceable as a result of their prominence and wealth. The delicate balance between surveillance and collaboration was subtle. Colonial policies were consistently rooted in mistrust of colonial subjects, and from the late nineteenth to the early twentieth centuries, collaboration and surveillance went hand in hand. Arabs were subjected to disproportionate scrutiny beginning in the late nineteenth

century. So used were they to being surveilled that by the early twentieth
century some were able to mobilize colonial authorities against their own
private nemeses as they assisted paranoid British authorities in constructing
the Index of Arabs from 1915 to 1920. The index had an unexpected long
life after the First World War, and in May 1942, an Arab employee of the
British Consulate in Batavia known as S. M. Aljunied attempted to use the
agency who produced the infamous index to cast aspersions on his enemies.
Aljunied produced a detailed entry on a fellow Arab, Sayyid Abdullah bin
Salim Alatas, in the same style as the index, complete with underlined clan
names followed by age of birth, place of birth, origins of parents, education, financial holdings, and list of vocations and political activities.[9] Barely
a month into the Japanese occupation of Java, members of the Arab elite
of Batavia competitively vied for Japanese support.[10] A letter was sent to
the Japanese government urging authorities to hire Arabs to keep an eye
out for three Arab organizations, but Japanese authorities in Java strongly
believed that the question of having Arab "envoys" or "ambassadors" was
absolutely absurd, maintaining instead that government departments should
maintain direct and open contact with everyone.[11] Unlike the Dutch, the
Japanese did not cultivate the fantasy of the application of international law
in their colony.[12]

Islamic Law

There are several examples that challenge the putative opposition of "colonialism" to "Islamic law." As we saw in chapter 6, restrictions imposed by
English common law concerning trusts on religious waqfs were exploited
by both colonial officials and Arab Muslims who wanted to reap the profits
from the sale of failed waqfs. In fact, at no time or place was there a single
identifiable entity known as "colonial law" or "Islamic law." Certainly, the
basic operating mode of "Islamic law" is not automatically against "colonial law" and vice versa in the eyes of Muslims. When invoked by scholars,
bureaucrats, and colonial subjects, both Muslim and non-Muslim, the term
"Islamic law" rarely meant anything more than some sort of a multifaceted
regulative ideal. This is not to say that the term was not useful in its haziness.
Under cover of religion, a lot could be done by Muslims and non-Muslims
during the colonial period. Couching something as religious, a new demar-
cated sphere in the modern colonial period, allowed colonial officials and
Arab subjects to push forward their individual agendas quite effectively.
At several junctures throughout history, the invocation of Islamic law served
a real purpose because it powerfully grounded the demands of Muslim

subjects, who astutely appealed to British and Dutch colonial commitment to uphold it. For example, the category of "Islamic law" allowed certain terms of a waqf to be upheld in courts and enabled laws and procedures to be put in place to prevent women from gaining access to divorce.

The Role of Arab Women

Due to the paucity of sources that reflect women, the very few existing stories come across as deeply personal and not at all vague. While examining legal sources authored by women either in writing (powers of attorney) or orally (court testimony), one could hardly escape noticing a consciousness of disability. The fact that several powers of attorney were produced by women to transfer power to their male relatives and friends might suggest that they largely felt unable to administer their own property. Yet these powers of attorney actually enabled women to manage and monitor their property from afar by revoking powers and reappointing new attorneys periodically. Perceptions of women's ineffectiveness in legal settings was directly linked to their general reluctance to appear in public. The testimony provided by Sharifa Fatimah bin Abdad, whose case we saw in chapter 1, was very much an outlier. Because judges encountered Muslim women so rarely in courts, they funneled their experiences into a simplified narrative, which explains their bewilderment, Orientalist overtones, and overprotective tendencies while describing their situations. Yet even Fatimah was afraid to consult a lawyer without her father's consent, although she felt certain she should take legal action against her father. Regardless, she acted for herself during the trials from 1924 to 1926, something that powers of attorney, however numerous, cannot reliably prove. Even as women pled their cases, we do not see them resenting the treatment of their sex within these legal sources. Another thing we notice is that everything was couched in patriarchal terms in courts. There was no talk of asserting women's rights in order to retain women's privileges. Neither did women plead their own personal causes on a large scale, nor band together to champion their rights as a group. They did not relate to each other in court. Court testimonies, law reports, and powers of attorney recorded that they adopted a view in deference to authority. This is not surprising since such sources hardly lent themselves to reflexivity and critical analysis, partly because court testimony was framed by strategic and focused questioning by lawyers and judges and therefore precluded introspection.

At the end of the Second World War, four groups of Arabs emerged in Indonesia. In 1948, members of Partai Arab Indonesia (PAI, formed in 1935) mostly identified as Indonesians of Arab descent (*kaum Peranakan Arab* or *dari toerenan Arab*) instead of simply Arabs in the new Republic of Indonesia.[13] They underscored their participation in the war and in the subsequent revolution in Java on the side of the majority of fellow Indonesians. Likewise, a second group who also claimed mixed descent like the first but who were not members of the PAI chose wholeheartedly to be incorporated as Indonesian citizens but requested that they be classified still as "Arabs" and subjected to a different set of laws akin to what the Dutch called *Indonesich burgerschap*, referring to the commercial laws that Foreign Orientals were subjected to during the colonial period. Yet another group who were pure Arabs (*totok*) crossed jurisdictions to be incorporated as British subjects in the Straits Settlements. Aided by the British Consulate of Batavia, they astonishingly opted to become British subjects rather than full Indonesian citizens. The final group, a small minority, opted to not identify with Indonesia or any other state. Rather they preferred to distinguish themselves as transnational Arabs within the newly formed Arab League with is headquarters in Cairo. The pull of territorial jurisdictions, a force field put in place by centuries of colonialism and inherited by the nation-state of Indonesia, who had just declared independence, rendered this last option less tenable than the former three. Eventually, the national jurisdiction of Indonesia drew these Arabs into its orbit as Indonesian citizens on par with Natives sans differentiation.

The politics of the present have in no sense superseded the terrain established by colonialists. The borders of the nation-state of Indonesia conform to the Dutch territorial jurisdiction with few exceptions, and the complex legal system bifurcates adat and Islamic law in the colonial mold.[14] The same legal system also persists in Singapore and Malaysia, where the pressures of common law dictates that legal precedents are binding and therefore cannot be cast aside easily. Not only does the Mohamedan Marriage Ordinance of 1880 form the basis of administration of Islamic law in Singapore today, cases decided during the colonial period by British judges still form precedents in the courts of Singapore and Malaysia.

NOTES

Abbreviations

1 KY	Kyshe's Reports (civil cases)
2 KY	Kyshe's Reports (ecclesiastical cases)
4 KY	Kyshe's Reports (miscellaneous cases)
BL	British Library, London
CO	Colonial Office, National Archives, London
FCO	Foreign and Commonwealth Office, National Archives, London
FO	Foreign Office Records, National Archives, London
HRNI	*Het Regt in Nederlandsch-Indië*
IOR	India Office Records, British Library, London
IG	*De Indische Gids*
ITVHR	*Indisch Tijdschrift van het Recht*
KITLV	Koninklijk Instituut voor Taal-, Land- en Volkenkunde
KSC	Koh Seow Chuan Collection, National Library Board, Singapore
MC	*Malayan Cases*
MLJ	*Malayan Law Journal*
NA	Nationaal Archief, The Hague
NAS	National Archives of Singapore
PP	Keeper of the Privy Purse, National Archives, London
SFPMA	*Singapore Free Press and Mercantile Adviser*
SGHC	Singapore High Court
SSLR	Straits Settlements Law Report
ST	*Straits Times*
TNI	*Tijdschrift voor Nederlandsch Indië*
WOC	Robert Carr Woods, *A Selection of Oriental Cases Decided in the Supreme Courts of the Straits' Settlements (1835–1869)* (Penang: S. Jeremiah, 1911).

Introduction

1. Pieter Johan Friederik Louw, *De Derde Javaansche Successie-Oorlog (1746–1755)* (The Hague: Martinus Nijhoff, 1889), 4.

2. The *shahbandar* at any port was usually a foreigner himself, although the origin of the *shahbandar* of Banda in 1599 is unknown. He possessed political power that enabled him to sign treaties with other traders. Charles O. Blagden, "Shahbandar and Bendahara," *Journal of the Royal Asiatic Society of Great Britain and Ireland* no. 2 (April 1921): 246–48; Sanjay Subrahmanyam, "Intertwined Histories: 'Crónica' and 'Tārīkh' in the Sixteenth-Century Indian Ocean World," *History and Theory* 49, no. 4 (December 2010): 118–45.

3. Jacobus Anne van der Chijs, *De Vestiging van het Nederlandsche gezag over de Bandaeilanden (1599–1621)* (Batavia: Albrecht and Co., 1886), 2.

4. Louw, *De Derde Javaansche Successie-Oorlog*, 4, 9.

5. Conrad Busken Huet, *Het Land van Rembrandt, eerste deel* (Haarlem: H. D. Tjeenk Willenk, 1882), 351.

6. Kerry Ward, *Networks of Empire: Forced Migration in the Dutch East India Company* (New York: Cambridge University Press, 2009), 49.

7. Victor Lieberman, *Strange Parallels: Southeast Asia in Global Context, c. 800–1830, Volume 2, Mainland Mirrors: Europe, China, Japan, South Asia, and the Islands* (New York: Cambridge University Press, 2009), 843.

8. For more on this period, see Barbara Andaya and Leonard Andaya, *A History of Early Modern Southeast Asia, 1400–1830* (New York: Cambridge University Press, 2015), 182–281.

9. Lisa Ford, *Settler Sovereignty: Jurisdiction and Indigenous People in America and Australia, 1788–1836* (Cambridge, MA: Harvard University Press, 2010), 3, 13.

10. For Michel Foucault, domain is a juridico-political notion, as is territory, controlled by a certain kind of power. Michel Foucault, "Questions of Geography," in *Power/Knowledge: Selected Interviews and Other Writings 1972–77*, ed. Colin Gordon (New York: Pantheon Books, 1980), 69–77.

11. Linda Boxberger, *On the Edge of Empire: Hadhramawt, Emigration, and the Indian Ocean, 1880s-1930s* (Albany: State University of New York Press, 2002), 41.

12. Cees Fasseur, *The Politics of Colonial Exploitation: Java, the Dutch, and the Cultivation System* (Ithaca, NY: Southeast Asia Program Publications, 1992), 26–27.

13. The *Cultuurstelsel* was also imposed outside of Java but with very limited success. Fasseur, *The Politics of Colonial Exploitation*, 36.

14. In 1811, during the Napoleonic wars, the East India Company seized control of Java from the French and returned it to the Dutch in 1815 according to the terms of the Anglo-Dutch Treaty in 1814. Peter Boomgaard, "Changing Economic Policy," in *South East Asia, Colonial History: High Imperialism (1890s–1930s) Volume III*, ed. Paul H. Kratoska (London: Routledge, 2001), 80.

15. Bhavani Raman, "Sovereignty, Property and Land Development: The East India Company in Madras," *Journal of the Economic and Social History of the Orient* 61, nos. 5–6 (September 2018): 979.

16. Depending on the class of irrigated field (*sawah*) or dry field (*tegal*), Raffles determined in 1814 that Javanese peasants had to give up a quarter to half of their produce as tax to the government. Boomgaard, "Changing Economic Policy," 80.

17. Due to the absence of formal constitutional regulations and personnel, the *Cultuurstelsel* was not consistently monitored throughout Java, which led to both rampant exploitation and lack of enforcement over four decades.

18. Ulbe Bosma, "The Cultivation System (1830–1870) and its Private Entrepreneurs on Colonial Java," *Journal of Southeast Asian Studies* 38 no. 2 (June 2007): 275–91.

19. In the end, only two categories of land were spared, namely the Princely States of Java (*Vorstenlanden*) in Jogjakarta and Surakarta, who were semiautonomous vis-à-vis the Dutch at this point, and the truly private estates (*partikuliere landerijen*), whose status was determined as such by Dutch colonial government. Fasseur, *The Politics of Colonial Exploitation*, 22–23, 28–30.

20. Fasseur, *The Politics of Colonial Exploitation*, 74, 112–15, 121.

21. Fasseur, *The Politics of Colonial Exploitation*, 30.

22. Hendrik Blink, *Nederlandsch Oost-en West-Indië, Tweede Deel* (Leiden: Brill, 1907), 4.

23. Wolter Robert van Hoevell, *Parlementaire Redevoeringen over Koloniale Belangen, Volume 1* (Zalt-Rommel: Joh. Norman & Zoon, 1862), 38.

24. J. H. P. E. Kniphorst, "Een terugblik op Timor er Onderhoorigheden," *Tijdschrift voor Nederlandsch-Indië* 14, no. 2 (1885): 138.

25. Ann Stoler has demonstrated how shifting bases of race and racial polices strengthen discrimination policies in French Indochina and the Netherlands Indies. Ann L Stoler, *Carnal Knowledge and Imperial Power: Race and the Intimate in Colonial Rule* (Berkeley: University of California Press, 2002); Patricia Tjiook-Liem, *De Rechtspositie Der Chinezen in Nederlands-Indië 1848–1942: Wetgevingsbeleid Tussen Beginsel En Belang* (Amsterdam: Leiden University Press, 2009).

26. "Besluit van Comissarissen-General over Nederlandsch-Indië, 16 January 1818, no. 29," in *Staatsblad van Nederlandsch-Indië voor 1818* (The Hague: Ter Drukkerij van A. D. Schinkel, 1839), 231; "Chineezen," *De Nederlandsch Wetgeving—Statsbladen van Nederlandsch-Indië* 12 (1902): 305.

27. The stock phrase "Arabieren, Mooren, Chinezen en allen die Mohammedanen of heidenen zijn" stood for Foreign Orientals. For the list of specific regulations, see C. H. F. Riesz, "Her erpachtsrecht volgens cene reente recensie," *Het Regt in Nederlandsch-Indië* 47 (1886): 143–83. Hereafter *HRNI*.

28. For an in-depth analysis of Article 109, see P. H. van der Kemp, "Van de Wetgeving der Koloniën," *De Indische Gids* 8, no. 1 (1886): 157–88.

29. For more on Chinese Foreign Orientals, see Tjiook-Liem, *De Rechtspositie der Chinezen*.

30. Daniel S. Lev, *Islamic Courts in Indonesia* (Berkeley: University of California Press, 1972), 27.

31. G. Andre de la Porte, "Beschouwingen Over Het Quasi-Internationaal Privaatrecht," *HRNI* 91 (1908): 1–33.

32. Lauren A. Benton, "From International Law to Imperial Constitutions: The Problem of Quasi-Sovereignty, 1870–1900," *Law and History Review* 26, no. 3 (Fall 2008): 597.

33. A. Arthur Schiller, "Conflict of Laws in Indonesia," *Far Eastern Quarterly* 2, no. 1 (November 1942): 31–47. The number of published law reports cases involving Foreign Orientals were disproportionate to their actual numbers in the Netherlands Indies.

34. An exception to this is the American Civil War, when some belligerents were subjected to international law. Cynthia Nicoletti, *Secession on Trial: The Treason Prosecution of Jefferson Davis* (New York: Cambridge University Press, 2017), 205.

35. Jennifer Pitts claims that the law of nations discourse obscures the imperial nature of European states. Jennifer Pitts, *Boundaries of the International: Law and Empire* (Cambridge, MA: Harvard University Press, 2018), 3.

36. Pitts, *Boundaries of the International,* 182–83.

37. Benton, "From International Law to Imperial Constitutions," 596.

38. Ford, *Settler Sovereignty,* 43–44. Also see Pär K. Cassel, *Grounds of Judgment: Extraterritoriality and Imperial Power in Nineteenth-Century China and Japan* (Oxford: Oxford University Press, 2012); Li Chen, *Chinese Law in Imperial Eyes: Sovereignty, Justice and Transcultural Politics* (New York: Columbia University Press, 2015); Karen Barkey, "Aspects of Legal Pluralism in the Ottoman Empire," in *Legal Pluralism and Empires, 1500–1850,* ed. Richard J. Ross and Lauren A. Benton (New York: New York University Press, 2013), 83–108; Sarah A. Stein, *Extraterritorial Dreams: European Citizenship, Sephardi Jews, and the Ottoman Twentieth Century* (Chicago: University of Chicago Press, 2016).

39. Eric Hobsbawm, "Introduction: Inventing Traditions," in *The Invention of Tradition,* ed. Eric Hobsbawm and Terence Ranger (Cambridge: Cambridge University Press, 1983), 1, 7; Frederick Cooper, *Colonialism in Question* (Berkeley: University of California Press, 2005), 19.

40. Franz von Benda-Beckmann and Keebet von Benda-Beckmann, "Places That Come and Go: A Legal Anthropological Perspective on the Temporalities of Space in Plural Legal Orders," in *The Expanding Spaces of Law: A Timely Legal Geography,* ed. Irus Braverman et al. (Stanford: Stanford University Press, 2014), 31.

41. Paul Boyer, *Urban Masses and Moral Order in America, 1820–1920* (Cambridge, MA: Harvard University Press, 2009), 253.

42. British Library (BL) Add. Ms. 45271/f.10, Letter 1—Raja Abdullah Ibni Muazzam Shah, Sultan of Kedah to Francis Light of Penang, 2nd Shawal 1206/24th May 1792, BL Add. Ms. 45271/f.12, Letter 5—Raja Abdullah Ibni Muazzam Shah, Sultan of Kedah to Francis Light of Penang, 30th March 1793; Roland Braddell, *The Law of the Straits Settlements: A Commentary* (Kuala Lumpur: Oxford University Press, 1982), 3.

43. It was founded on the eve of the Prince of Wales' birthday. "Proclamation of Francis Light," *Journal of Indian Archipelago and Eastern Asia, Volume IV* (October 1850): 629.

44. These *Kapitans* were essentially leaders of particular ethnic communities who were allowed to administer justice and exercise social control in their own community, but their judicial functions were officially abolished in 1808 upon the establishment of the Court of Judicature. Nordin Hussin, *Trade and Society in the Straits of Melaka: Dutch Melaka and English Penang* (Copenhagen: NIAS Press, 2007), 245.

45. Moshe Yegar, *Islam and Islamic Institutions in British Malaya: Policies and Implementation* (Jerusalem: Magnes Press, 1979), 108.

46. *Regina v. Willans* [1858] 4 KY. These earlier jurisdictions continued to challenge East India Company sovereignty. See Nurfadzilah Yahaya, "Legal Pluralism and the English East India Company in the Straits of Malacca during the Early Nineteenth Century," *Law and History Review* 33, no. 4 (November 2015): 945–64.

47. For more on the details of Chivatean's case, see Lynn Hollen Lees, *Planting Empire, Cultivating Subjects: British Malaya, 1786–1941* (New York: Cambridge University Press, 2017), 62–65.

48. Stuart Banner, "Why Terra Nullius? Anthropology and Property Law in Early Australia," *Law and History Review* 23, no. 1 (Spring 2005): 95–131; Stuart Banner, *Possessing the Pacific: Land, Settlers, and Indigenous People from Australia to Alaska* (Cambridge, MA: Harvard University Press, 2007), 13–46.

49. He even claimed that Islamic law was never administered in the Bengal Presidency at Fort William to inhabitants professing to be Muslims, which meant that there was no precedent for the application of Islamic anywhere in the British Empire. *Fatimah & Ors. v. D. Logan & Ors.* [1871] 1 KY.

50. *Regina v. Willans* [1858] 4 KY. See Jack Jin Gary Lee, "Plural Society and the Colonial State: English Law and the Making of Crown Colony Government in the Straits Settlements," *Asian Journal of Law and Society* 2, no. 2 (November 2015): 237.

51. *Fatimah & Ors. v. D. Logan & Ors.* [1871] 1 KY.

52. *Fatimah & Ors. v. D. Logan & Ors.* [1871] 1 KY.

53. Saliha Belmessous, "Introduction: The Problem of Indigenous Claim Making in Colonial History," in *Native Claims: Indigenous Law Against Empire, 1500–1920*, ed. Saliha Belmessous (Oxford: Oxford University Press, 2011), 7–8.

54. For a full text of the law, see Thoralf Hanstein, "S. 1882, No. 152," in *Islamisches Recht und Nationales Recht* (Frankfurt am Main: Peter Lang, 2002), 140–41, 171–75.

55. Brinkley Messick, "Textual Properties: Writing and Wealth in a Shari'a Case," *Anthropological Quarterly* 68, no. 3 (July 1995): 157.

56. Fahad Ahmad Bishara, *A Sea of Debt: Law and Economic Life in the Western Indian Ocean, 1780–1950* (Cambridge: Cambridge University Press, 2017).

57. The historical Geniza refers to the storage space in a synagogue in Cairo where 200,000 to 300,000 documents were found dating from the ninth to the nineteenth centuries. James Clifford, "Diasporas," *Cultural Anthropology* 9, no. 3 (August 1994): 325–28. For more on the historical Geniza in Cairo, see Shelomo Dov Goitein, *A Mediterranean Society: The Jewish Communities of the Arab World as Portrayed in the Documents of the Cairo Geniza, Six Volumes* (Berkeley: University of California Press, 1967–93); Adina Hoffman and Peter Cole, *Sacred Trash: The Lost and Found World of the Cairo Geniza* (New York: Schocken Books, 2016); Amitav Ghosh, "The Slave of Ms. H. 6," *Centre for Studies in Social Sciences, Calcutta Occasional Paper* no. 125 (1990): 1–135.

58. Cornelia Vismann, *Files: Law and Media Technology*, trans. Geoffrey Winthrop-Young (Stanford: Stanford University Press, 2008); Ilana Feldman, *Governing Gaza: Bureaucracy, Authority, and the Work of Rule, 1917–1967* (Durham, NC: Duke University Press, 2008).

59. See Ben Kafka, *The Demon of Writing* (New York: Zone Books, 2012), 37–44, 51.

60. Lydia H. Liu, "Scripts in Motion: Writing as Imperial Technology, Past and Present," *Publications of the Modern Language Association of America* 130, no. 2 (March 2015): 375–76.

61. Renisa Mawani, "Archival Legal History: Towards the Ocean as Archive," in *The Oxford Handbook of Legal History*, ed. Markus Dubber and Christopher Tomlin (Oxford: Oxford University Press, 2018), 297.

62. See Kathryn J. Burns, *Into the Archive: Writing and Power in Colonial Peru* (Durham, NC: Duke University Press, 2010), 42–67.

63. Bhavani Raman, *Document Raj: Writing and Scribes in Early Colonial South India* (Chicago: University of Chicago Press, 2012), 2–3.

64. Raman, *Document Raj*, 3.

65. Eric Tagliacozzo, *Secret Trades, Porous Borders: Smuggling and States along a Southeast Asian Frontier, 1865–1915* (New Haven: Yale University Press, 2005); Johan Mathew, *Margins of the Market: Trafficking and Capitalism across the Arabian Sea* (Oakland: University of California Press, 2016).

66. James C. Scott, *Seeing Like a State: How Certain Schemes to Improve the Human Condition Have Failed* (New Haven: Yale University Press, 1998).

67. Non-standard currencies—slavery, for example—were framed out of the legal free market. Mathew, *Margins of the Market*, 197.

68. These merchants came from places like Bukhara, Zanzibar, Baghdad, Oman, Kish, Ḥaḍramawt, Mecca, Basra, Egypt, and Mosul. Janet L. Abu-Lughod, *Before European Hegemony: The World System, A.D. 1250–1350* (New York: Oxford University Press, 1989), 298; Paul Wheatley, *The Golden Khersonese: Studies in the Historical Geography of the Malay Peninsula before A.D. 1500* (Kuala Lumpur: University of Malaya Press, 1961), vi, xvii, 210–11, 244–45; Rita Rose di Meglio, "Arab Trade with Indonesia and the Malay Peninsula from the 8th to the 16th Century," in *Islam and the Trade of Asia: A Colloquium*, ed. D. S. Richards (Philadelphia: University of Pennsylvania Press, 1970), 105–36.

69. For a discussion of the vague term *zabaj*, see Michael Laffan, "Finding Java: Muslim Nomenclature of Insular Southeast Asia from Srivijaya to Snouck Hurgronje," in *Southeast Asia and the Middle East: Islam, Movement, and the Longue Duree*, ed. Eric Tagliacozzo (Stanford: Stanford University Press, 2009), 17–64; Di Meglio, "Arab Trade with Indonesia and the Malay Peninsula," 109–10.

70. Oliver William Wolters, *Early Indonesian Commerce: A Study of the Origins of Srivijaya* (Ithaca, NY: Cornell University Press, 1967), 251.

71. Di Meglio, "Arab Trade with Indonesia and the Malay Peninsula," 117–26.

72. See Sanjay Subrahmanyam, *Improvising Empire: Portuguese Trade and Settlement in the Bay of Bengal, 1500–1700* (Delhi: Oxford University Press, 1990).

73. Anthony Reid, *Southeast Asia in the Age of Commerce, 1450–1680, Volume Two, The Lands Below the Winds* (New Haven: Yale University Press, 1993), 124.

74. Sunil S. Amrith, "Tamil Diasporas across the Bay of Bengal," *American Historical Review* 114, no. 3 (June 2009): 547–72; Amitav Ghosh, "The Diaspora in Indian Culture," *Public Culture* 2, no. 1 (Fall 1989): 78.

75. Boxberger, *On the Edge of Empire*; Ulrike Freitag, *Indian Ocean Migrants and State Formation in Ḥaḍramawt: Reforming the Homeland* (Leiden: Brill, 2003); Jeyamalar Kathirithamby-Wells, "'Strangers' and 'Stranger-Kings': The Sayyid in Eighteenth-Century Maritime Southeast Asia," *Journal of Southeast Asian Studies* 40, no. 3 (October 2009): 567–91; Engseng Ho, "Foreigners and Mediators in the Constitution of Malay Sovereignty," *Indonesia and the Malay World* 41, no. 120 (2013): 146–67; Barbara Andaya, *To Live as Brothers: Southeast Sumatra in the Seventeenth and Eighteenth Centuries* (Honolulu: University of Hawaii Press, 1993), 220.

76. Engseng Ho, "Before Parochialisation: Diasporic Arabs Cast in Creole Waters," in *Transcending Borders: Arabs, Politics, Trade and Islam in Southeast Asia*, ed. Huub de Jonge and Nico Kaptein (Leiden: KITLV Press, 2002), 11–36; Sumit K. Mandal,

Becoming Arab: Creole Histories and Modern Identity in the Malay World (Cambridge: Cambridge University Press, 2017).

77. Amrith, "Tamil Diasporas across the Bay of Bengal," 549.

78. For more on recent use of the word "diaspora" in the study of Chinese populations, see Shelly Chan, "The Case for Diaspora: A Temporal Approach to the Chinese Experience," *Journal of Asian Studies* 74, no. 1 (February 2015): 107–28.

79. For more on the history of Arabs based in South Asia, see Stephen Dale, "The Hadhrami Diaspora in South-Western India: The Role of the Sayyids of the Malabar Coast," in *Hadhrami Traders, Scholars, and Statesmen in the Indian Ocean, 1750s-1960s*, ed. Ulrike Freitag and William Clarence-Smith (Leiden: Brill, 2009), 175–84; Leif Manger, "Hadramis in Hyderabad: From Winners to Losers," *Asian Journal of Social Science* 35, no. 4 (2007): 405–33.

80. Mandal, *Becoming Arab*, 71, 85–87.

81. Before the mid-nineteenth century, passenger lists in daily newspapers in the Netherlands Indies and the Straits Settlements reveal that these Arabs usually sailed from the port of Aden, usually via Indian Ports in Bombay and Pondicherry.

82. Also see R. Supomo and R. Djokosutono, *Sedjarah Politik Hukum Adat, Djilid 2* (Jakarta: Penerbit Djambatan, 1954), 22–23.

83. Both Arab and Native Muslims shared an advisor from 1879 until the end of the colonial period. Frances Gouda, "Mimicry and Projection in the Colonial Encounter: The Dutch East Indies/Indonesia as Experimental Laboratory, 1900–1942," *Journal of Colonialism and Colonial History* 1, no. 2 (Winter 2000), 1–20.

84. Maurits Wagenvoort, *Nederlandsch-Indische Menschen en Dingen* (Amsterdam: H. J. W. Becht, 1910), 69.

85. O. L. Helfrich, "Ethnographische Kennis der Afdeeling Kroë," *Bijdrage tot de Taal—land—en volkenkunde van Nederlandsch-Indië* 38 (1889): 537; "Verdraagzaamheid bepleit door Indo-Arabieren," *Tijdschrift voor Nederlandsch-Indië* 18, no. 1 (1889): 305; Clive Day, *Nederlandsch Beheer over Java* (The Hague: W. P. van Stockum and Zoon, 1905), 394; *Verslag der handelingen der Staten-Generaal* 2, no. 2 (1905): 91; NA 2.02.14 file 9088D, Minister of the Colonies of the Netherlands Pieter Sjoerds Gerbrandy, London to the Queen of the Netherlands, November 29 1941; NA 2.10.17 file 667, "Notities Inzake den Voorzitter der Semarangsche Arabische Vereeniging in Personen in zijn Omgeving" N.F.W. van den Arend, Buitenkantoor, NEFIS, Semarang to Directeur NEFIS, Batavia and Off. van Justities, September 7, 1946.

86. "Arabieren," *Encyclopaedie van Nederlandsch-Indië, Eerste Deel* 40.

87. Joannes Jacobus de Hollander, *Handleiding bij de Beoepening der Land—en Volkenkunde van Nederlandsch Oost-Indië, Tweede Deel* (Brede: Drukkerij van Broese & Comp., 1898), 85; F. P. H. Prick van Wely, *Viertalig Aanvullend Hulpwoordenboek voor Groot-Nederland* (Weltevreden: N. V. Boekh. Visser & Co., 1910), 334.

88. M. C. Piepers, "Vreemde Oosterlingen (Gelijkstelling van—met Europeanen)," *Tijdschrift voor Nederlandsch-Indië* 3, nos. 1–2 (1899): 668.

89. Sugata Bose, *A Hundred Horizons: The Indian Ocean in the Age of Global Empire* (Cambridge, MA: Harvard University Press, 2006); Oliver William Wolters, *History, Culture, and Region in Southeast Asian Perspectives* (Singapore: Institute of Southeast Asian Studies, 1982), 42–6; Sunil S. Amrith, *Crossing the Bay of Bengal: The Furies of Nature and the Fortunes of Migrants* (Cambridge, MA: Harvard University Press, 2013);

Nile Green, *Bombay Islam: The Religious Economy of the West Indian Ocean, 1840–1915* (Cambridge: Cambridge University Press, 2011); Engseng Ho, *The Graves of Tarim: Genealogy and Mobility across the Indian Ocean* (Berkeley: University of California Press, 2006).

90. Sana Aiyar, *Indians in Kenya: The Politics of Diaspora* (Cambridge, MA: Harvard University Press, 2015).

91. Amrith, "Tamil Diasporas across the Bay of Bengal," 549.

92. Ho, *The Graves of Tarim*, 18.

93. Ho, *The Graves of Tarim*, 63, 68, 94.

94. Mawani, "Archival Legal History," 294, 302.

95. Bose, *A Hundred Horizons*, 6–9, 12. For more on world systems, see Abu-Lughod, *Before European Hegemony*.

96. Edward A. Alpers, *The Indian Ocean in World History* (New York: Oxford University Press, 2014), 98.

97. Pedro Machado, *Ocean of Trade: South Asian Merchants, Africa and the Indian Ocean, c. 1750–1850* (New York: Cambridge University Press, 2014); Scott S. Reese, *Imperial Muslims: Islam, Community and Authority in the Indian Ocean, 1839–1937* (Edinburgh: Edinburgh University Press, 2018).

98. Scholars have recently complicated the idea of cosmopolitanism under colonial rule. Will Hanley, "Grieving Cosmopolitanism in Middle East Studies," *History Campus* 6, no. 5 (September 2008): 1346–67; Peter van der Veer, "Colonial Cosmopolitanism," in *Conceiving Cosmopolitanism: Theory, Context and Practice*, ed. Steven Vertovec and Robin Cohen (Oxford: Oxford University Press, 2002), 165–79; Nina Glick Schiller, Tsypylma Darieva, and Sandra Gruner-Domic, "Defining Cosmopolitan Sociability in a Transnational Age: An Introduction," *Ethnic and Racial Studies* 34, no. 3 (2011): 399–418.

99. For more on legal pluralism in the Netherlands Indies, see Peter Burns, *The Leiden Legacy: Concepts of Law in Indonesia* (Leiden: KITLV, 2004); Daniel S. Lev, "Judicial Institutions and Legal Culture in Indonesia," in *Culture and Politics in Indonesia*, ed. Claire Holt (Ithaca, NY: Cornell University Press, 1972), 246–318; Daniel S. Lev, *Legal Evolution and Political Authority in Indonesia: Selected Essays* (The Hague: Kluwer Law International, 2000), 119–42; Ratno Lukito, *Legal Pluralism in Indonesia: Bridging the Unbridgeable* (New York: Routledge, 2013).

100. Clifford Geertz, *Local Knowledge: Further Essays in Interpretive Anthropology* (New York: Basic Books, 1983), 185.

101. John R. Bowen, *Islam, Law, and Equality in Indonesia: An Anthropology of Public Reasoning* (New York: Cambridge University Press, 2003), 13. Adat of course was not restricted to the Indonesian archipelago. The anthropologist Michael Peletz offers a nuanced definition of adat as he examines the institutionalization of adat in the Malay States on the Peninsula as well as later divergences between Islamic law and what was deemed adat. See Michael G. Peletz, *Islamic Modern: Religious Courts and Cultural Politics in Malaysia* (Princeton, NJ: Princeton University Press, 2002), 55–59, 60–62.

102. Small legal communities managed to escape the imposition of Dutch conceptions of *adatrecht* to a significant degree.

103. J. M. Otto, and S. Pompe, "The Legal Oriental Connection," in *Leiden Oriental Connections, 1850–1940*, ed. Willem Otterspeer (Leiden: E. J. Brill, 1989), 230–49.

104. Since Dutch conceptions of *adatrecht* sometimes ran counter to principles in Islamic law, it was sometimes challenged by local communities. See Jan Prins, "*Adat*

law and Muslim Religious Law in Modern Indonesia: An Introduction," *Die Welt des Islams* 1, no. 4 (1951): 283–300.

105. D. Lev, *Islamic Courts in Indonesia,* 5.

106. For example, works on Minangkabau society in Sumatra specifically underscore the interplay between *adat* and Islam that runs through Muslim societies in Southeast Asia. Taufik Abdullah, "*Adat* and Islam: An Examination of Conflict in Minangkabau," *Indonesia* 2 (October 1966): 1–24; Jeffrey Hadler, *Muslims and Matriarchs: Cultural Resilience in Indonesia through Jihad and Colonialism* (Ithaca, NY: Cornell University Press, 2008).

107. Franz von Benda-Beckmann and Keebet von Benda-Beckmann, "Islamic Law in a Plural Context: The Struggle over Inheritance Law in Colonial West Sumatra," *Journal of the Economic and Social History of the* Orient 55, nos. 4–5 (2012): 772. For an example of the different permutations of adat and Islamic law, see Schiller, "Conflict of Laws in Indonesia," 45–46.

108. Lauren A. Benton, *Law and Colonial Cultures: Legal Regimes in World History* (Cambridge: Cambridge University Press, 2002).

109. Sally Engle Merry, "Legal Pluralism," *Law and Society Review* 22, no. 5 (1988): 871.

110. Mitra Sharafi, *Law and Identity in Colonial South Asia: Parsi Legal Culture, 1772–1947* (New York: Cambridge University Press, 2014), 6.

111. Rohit De and Robert Travers, "Petitioning and Political Cultures in South Asia: Introduction," *Modern Asian Studies* 53, no. 1 (2019): 7.

112. Nico J. G. Kaptein, *Islam, Colonialism and the Modern Age in the Netherlands East Indies: A Biography of Sayyid ʿUthmān (1822–1914)* (Leiden: Brill, 2014).

113. Katherine Lemons, *Divorcing Traditions: Islamic Marriage Law and the Making of Indian Secularism* (Ithaca, NY: Cornell University Press, 2019), 8.

114. Lemons, *Divorcing Traditions,* 8.

115. Jeffrey A. Redding, "The Case of Ayesha, Muslim 'Courts,' and the Rule of Law: Some Ethnographic Lessons for Legal Theory," *Modern Asian Studies* 48, no. 4 (2014): 940–85; Lemons, *Divorcing Traditions,* 69–98.

116. Elke Stockreiter, *Islamic Law, Gender and Social Change in Post-Abolition Zanzibar* (New York: Cambridge University Press, 2015), 16–17.

117. Social curtailment, and to some extent economic restrictions, were much easier to enforce against Muslim women than legal ones. Even so, Muslim women often got around these restrictions through Islamic law. Stockreiter gives the example of purdah in some Muslim societies to prove this point. Stockreiter, *Islamic Law, Gender and Social Change,* 15.

118. Wael Hallaq, *An Introduction to Islamic Law* (New York: Cambridge University Press, 2009), 11–12.

119. This also happened in British India. See Scott Alan Kugle, "Framed, Blamed and Renamed: The Recasting of Islamic Jurisprudence in Colonial South Asia," *Modern Asian Studies* 35, no. 2 (2001): 257–313.

120. Frederick Cooper and Jane Burbank, "Rules of Law, Politics of Empire," in *Legal Pluralism and Empires, 1500–1850,* ed. Richard J. Ross and Lauren A. Benton (New York: New York University Press, 2013), 279.

121. Sally Engle Merry, "McGill Convocation Address: Legal Pluralism in Practice," *McGill Law Journal—Revue de Droit de McGill* 59, no. 1 (2013): 2.

122. Kugle, "Framed Blamed and Renamed," 257–313.

123. For more on links between legal pluralism and cultural defense, see Mitra Sharafi, "Justice in Many Rooms since Galanter: De-Romanticizing Legal Pluralism through the Cultural Defense," *Law and Contemporary Problems* 71, no. 2 (Spring 2008): 139–46.

124. Keebet von Benda-Beckmann and Bertram Turner, "Legal Pluralism, Social Theory, and the State," *Journal of Legal Pluralism and Unofficial Law* 50, no. 3 (2018): 263.

125. John L. Comaroff, "Colonialism, Culture, and the Law: A Foreword," *Law and Social Inquiry* 26, no. 2 (2001): 306.

126. Mitra Sharafi, "The Marital Patchwork of Colonial South Asia: Forum Shopping from Britain to Baroda," *Law and History Review* 28, no. 4 (November 2010): 980.

127. Iza Hussin, *The Politics of Islamic Law: Local Elites, Colonial Authority, and the Making of the Muslim State* (Chicago: University of Chicago Press, 2016), 29, 64; Robert M. Cover, "The Supreme Court, 1982 Term—Foreword: Nomos and Narrative," *Harvard Law Review* 97, no. 1 (November 1983): 53.

128. Seyla Benhabib, "Democratic Iterations: The Local, the National, and the Global," in *Another Cosmopolitanism*, ed. Robert Post (Oxford: Oxford University Press, 2006), 50.

129. Hussein A. Agrama, *Questioning Secularism: Islam, Sovereignty, and the Rule of Law in Modern Egypt* (Chicago: University of Chicago Press, 2012), 186–87.

130. Tamar Herzog argues in her study of South America that even when natives agreed to enter into agreements with European colonial governments, they might have believed that they could retract them if they were unjustly treated or if advantages were insufficient. Tamar Herzog, "Struggling over Indians: Territorial Conflict and Alliance Making in the Heartland of South America (Seventeenth to Eighteenth Centuries)," in *Empire by Treaty: Negotiating European Expansion, 1600–1900*, ed. Saliha Belmessous (Oxford: Oxford University Press, 2014), 92.

131. Brinkley Messick, *Shari'a Scripts: A Historical Anthropology* (New York: Columbia University Press, 2017), 7.

132. Sharafi, *Law and Identity in Colonial South Asia*.

133. Julie Y. Chu, *Cosmologies of Credit: Transnational Mobility and the Politics of Destination in China* (Durham, NC: Duke University Press, 2013), 33.

134. Yoav Di-Capua, *No Exit: Arab Existentialism, Jean-Paul Sartre and Decolonization* (Chicago: University of Chicago Press, 2018), 11.

135. Abu-Lughod, *Before European Hegemony*, 311.

136. Marc Galanter, "Justice in Many Rooms: Courts, Private Ordering, and Indigenous Law," *The Journal of Legal Pluralism and Unofficial Law* 13, no. 19 (1981): 3.

137. Sharafi, "The Marital Patchwork of Colonial South Asia," 981.

138. Pitts, *Boundaries of the International*, 6.

139. Rachel Sturman, *The Government of Social Life in Colonial India: Liberalism, Religious Law and Women's Rights* (Cambridge: Cambridge University Press, 2012), 148–95, 232.

140. Stockreiter, *Islamic Law, Gender and Social Change*, 203–39.

141. Sharafi, "The Marital Patchwork of Colonial South Asia," 980.

142. Sharafi, "The Marital Patchwork of Colonial South Asia," 1008–9.

143. Kugle, "Framed, Blamed and Renamed," 300.

144. Tamir Moustafa, "The Judicialization of Religion," *Law and Society Review* 52, no. 3 (September 2018): 686–87.

145. Annelies Moors, "Debating Islamic Family Law," in *Social History of Women and Gender in the Modern Middle East,* ed. Margaret L. Meriwether and Judith E. Tucker (Boulder: Westview Press, 1999), 168.

146. There were two types of authority in Islamic legal thought—legislative authority that is divine and concretized in foundational texts and interpretive or declarative authority, which belongs to jurists. The latter is a derivative authority, drawn entirely from the legislative authority of God. The Muslim jurist bears no authority in his person or status in the sense that his declarations are never automatically accepted as valid. The authority depends upon the methodology employed by the jurist and his skills. Bernard G. Weiss, *The Spirit of Islamic Law* (Athens: University of Georgia Press, 1998), 65.

147. Islamic law is derived from four elements—the Qur'an, the Sunnah (actions and sayings of the Prophet), consensus among the Muslim community, and reason. Hallaq, *An Introduction to Islamic Law,* 14–17.

148. For more on Snouck Hurgronje, see Eric Tagliacozzo, *The Longest Journey: Southeast Asian and the Pilgrimage to Mecca* (New York: Oxford University Press, 2013), 157–76; Michael F. Laffan, *The Makings of Indonesian Islam: Orientalism and the Narration of a Sufi Past* (Princeton, NJ: Princeton University Press, 2011).

149. Bowen, *Islam, Law, and Equality in Indonesia,* 18.

150. Weiss, *The Spirit of Islamic Law,* 18.

151. Shahab Ahmed, *What is Islam?: The Importance of Being Islamic* (Princeton, NJ: Princeton University Press, 2015), 5, 116–29.

152. Ahmed, *What is Islam?,* 120–21.

153. Hussin, *The Politics of Islamic Law*; Sarah Eltantawi, *Shari'a on Trial: Northern Nigeria's Islamic Revolution* (Oakland: University of California Press, 2017).

154. Messick, *Shari'a Scripts,* 21.

155. For a discussion of this distinction, see Messick, *Shari'a Scripts,* 23.

1. The Lure of Bureaucracy

1. The latter category also included "Jawi-Pekans," who were racially mixed, being Indian and Malay. E. M. Merewether, *Report on the Census of the Straits Settlements, Taken on 5th April 1891* (Singapore: Government Printing Office, 1892), 36.

2. Renisa Mawani, *Across Oceans of Empire: The "Komagata Maru" and Jurisdiction in the Time of Empire* (Durham, NC: Duke University Press, 2018), 118.

3. For more on colonial subjects use of petitions, see Hannah Muller, *Subjects and Sovereign: Bonds of Belonging in the Eighteenth-Century British Empire* (New York: Oxford University Press, 2017).

4. "Pinang," *Singapore Free Press and Mercantile Adviser,* December 3, 1852, 3. Hereafter *SFPMA.*

5. W. E. Maxwell, "The New Gaming," *Straits Times,* June 13, 1883, 2. Hereafter *ST.*

6. Wael Hallaq, *The Origins and Evolution of Islamic Law* (New York: Cambridge University Press, 2005), 87.

7. Hallaq, *The Origins and Evolution of Islamic Law,* 87.

8. The Legislative Council narrowed the number of Muslim communities to three distinct and discrete groups—Arab, Indian, and Malay—although there were actually many more ethnic communities, including Muslims who originated from

other parts of the Malay Archipelago. Each community sometimes appointed more than one qadi. In one spectacular case in 1850s Penang, the wife held a divorce pronounced by one qadi named Mahomed Ali of Batu Uban, while the husband held a statement by another qadi, apparently fortified by fatwas from several Muslim lawyers in town, to the effect that there had been no divorce. "Pinang—Registry of Marriages &c," *ST*, November 19, 1855, 9; "The Legislative Council, 6th July," *ST Overland Journal*, July 12, 1880, 3.

9. "Pinang," *ST*, February 28, 1854, 7.

10. Maxwell, "The New Gaming."

11. The functions and duties actually corresponded to that of the Mahomedan registrar by the Bengal Act No. 1 of 1876.

12. For example, see *Ahamed Meah & Anor. v. Nacodah Merican*, [1893] 4 KY 583.

13. Untitled, *ST*, July 10, 1880, 2.

14. This phenomenon was generally true according to the attorney-general. "The Legislative Council, 6th July."

15. The Sepoy Rebellion, in 1857, was a widespread revolt against British authorities. British authorities crushed this opposition severely and officially ended Mughal rule, after which Queen Victoria proclaimed, "We do strictly charge and enjoin all those who may be in authority under us that they abstain from all interference with the religious belief or worship of any of our subjects on pain of our highest displeasure." "Proclamation by the Queen in Council to the Princes, Chiefs, and the People in India," *Speeches and Documents on Indian Policy 1750–1921 Volume 1*, ed. Arthur Berriedale Keith (London: Oxford University Press, 1922), 382.

16. See Ritu Birla, *Stages of Capital: Law, Culture and Market Governance in Colonial India* (Durham, NC: Duke University Press, 2009); Bernard S. Cohn, *Colonialism and Its Forms of Knowledge: The British in India* (Princeton, NJ: Princeton University Press, 1996); Rachel Sturman, *The Government of Social Life in Colonial India—Liberalism, Religious Law, and Women's Rights* (New York: Cambridge University Press, 2012).

17. Kugle, "Framed Blamed and Renamed," 270.

18. M. A. Hose, "Inaugural Address," *Journal of the Straits Branch of the Royal Asiatic Society* 1 (July 1878): 8. Even under colonial rule, lists of adat laws never aspired to the status of a legal system, and neither did they resemble a normative system of jurisprudence. M. B. Hooker, *Adat Laws in Modern Malaya* (Kuala Lumpur: Oxford University Press, 1972), 85.

19. Anthony C. Milner, "Inventing Politics: The Case of Malaysia," *Past and Present* 132, no. 1 (August 1991): 114.

20. BL Mss Sloane 1293, Mss Add 12398. William Marsden, *The History of Sumatra* (London: Printed for the author, by J. McCreery, 1811); Thomas Stamford Raffles and Frank Hull, *The History of Java* (London: Black, Parbury, and Allen, 1817). For an analysis of the Malacca laws, see M. B. Hooker, "The Oriental Law Text: with reference to the Undang-Undang Melaka and Malay Law," in *Malaysian Legal Essays: A Collection of Essays in Honour of Professor Emeritus Datuk Ahmad Ibrahim* (Kuala Lumpur: Malayan Law Journal, 1986), 431–56. For a description of early nineteenth-century British efforts specifically, see T. J. Newbold, *Political and Statistical Account*

of the British Settlements in the Straits of Malacca, Volume 2 (London: John Murray, 1839), 215–313.

21. See Richard O. Winstedt, *A History of Classical Malay Literature* (New York: Oxford University Press, 1969); Richard O. Winstedt, *Shaman, Saiva and Sufi, a Study of the Evolution of Malay Magic* (London: Constable & Company Ltd. 1925); Richard O. Winstedt, *The Circumstances of Malay Life: The Kampong, the House, Furniture, Dress, Food*, Papers on Malay Subjects (Kuala Lumpur: Russell at the F.M.S. Govt. Press, 1909); Richard James Wilkinson, *A History of the Peninsular Malays, with Chapters on Perak and Selangor* (Singapore: Kelly and Walsh, 1923), Richard James Wilkinson, *Papers on Malay Subjects: History* (Singapore: Federated Malay States Government Press, 1920).

22. During this period, adat laws continued to be implemented in the federated and unfederated Malay states in the qadi courts and shari'a courts. Ahmad Ibrahim, *Towards a History of Law in Malaysia and Singapore* (Kuala Lumpur: Dewan Bahasa dan Pustaka, 1992), 9. Such collections aided British legal practitioners immensely when cases involving Malay rulers on the peninsula were brought to English courts on the peninsula. The *Undang-Undang Melaka* (Laws of Malacca) was used in Pahang, Johore, and Kedah. See Yock Fang Liaw, *Undang-Undang Melaka—the Laws of Melaka* (The Hague: M. Nijhoff, 1976).

23. *Fatimah & Ors. v. Logan & Ors.* [1871] 1 KY 255.

24. Aharon Layish, "Family *Waqf* and the Shari'a Law of Succession," *Islamic Law and Society*, 4 (1997): 355–56.

25. *In the Goods of Abdullah, deceased*, in Robert Carr Woods, *A Selection of Oriental Cases Decided in the Supreme Courts of the Straits' Settlements (1835–1869)* (Penang: S. Jeremiah, 1911), 1. Hereafter WOC.

26. After January 1, 1924, Ordinance 1923 came into force when the estate and effects were administered according to Islamic law by default, as long as it did not run counter to English law. Ahmad Ibrahim, *The Legal Status of the Muslims in Singapore* (Singapore: Malayan Law Journal, 1965), 27. In 1940, a judge actually upheld Islamic law, which only bequeathed a maximum of a third of the total value of a testator's estate to strangers (non-heirs). *In re M. Mohd Haniffa Deceased. Abdul Jabbar v. M. Mohd. Abubacker* [1940] SSLR 251.

27. Penang consists of the island as well as a strip of land on the peninsula called Province Wellesley, previously known as Seberang Perai.

28. This was a Malay custom that was part of *adat perpatih*. Judith Djamour, *The Muslim Matrimonial Court in Singapore* (London: Athlone Press, 1966), 4; M. B. Hooker, "The Muslims in Malaysia and Singapore: The Law of Matrimonial Property," *Family Law in Asia and Africa*, ed. J. N. D. Anderson (London: George Allen and Unwin Ltd., 1968), 189–204.

29. For a discussion on Malacca's special status vis-à-vis the Straits Settlements, see Benson Maxwell, "Land Tenure in Malacca under European Rule," *Journal of the Straits Branch of the Royal Asiatic Society* 13 (June 1884): 75–220.

30. The replies from Madras and Calcutta covered a list of Acts in force and Bills under consideration, while those from Bombay and Ceylon were more detailed. "The Mahomedan Law of Marriage and Divorce," *ST*, October 2, 1875, 1.

31. *Salmah and Fatimah, Infants, by Their Next Friend Shaik Omar V. Soolong* [1878] 1 KY 421.

32. *Muhammad Ibra'him bin Muhammad Sayad Parkir v. Gulam Ahmed bin Muhammad Sayad Roghe and Muhammad Sayad bin Muhammad Ibra'him Roghe.* Bom. H.C. Reports Suit no. 49 of 1863, Bombay High Court Reports Volume 1, 239.

33. M. B. Hooker, *Islamic Law in Southeast Asia* (Singapore: Oxford University Press, 1984), 87–88.

34. There was apparently a Shafi'i mufti in Singapore the year before (in 1877) named Alawi bin Ahmad al-Saqqaf, who had been asked about the validity of "insurance" in Islam by some Adeni merchants. The query revolves around the problem of "something for nothing"—i.e., the improper exchange of property without the required receipt of a countervalue. Brinkley Messick, "Madhhabs and Modernities," in *The Islamic School of Law—Evolution, Devolution and Progress,* ed. Peri Bearman, Rudolph Peters, Frank E. Vogel (Cambridge: Harvard University Press, 2005), 159–74.

35. The term *madhhab* has been translated as "sect," "rite," and most commonly as "school." However, as Joseph Schacht and George Makdisi warn us, it did not signify any definite organization, nor a strict uniformity of doctrine within each school, nor any formal teaching, nor any official status, nor even the existence of a body of law in the Western meaning of the term. Joseph Schacht, *An Introduction to Islamic Law* (Oxford: Clarendon Press, 1964), 28; George Makdisi, "The Significance of the Sunni Schools of Law in Islamic Religious History," *International Journal of Middle East Studies* 10 (1979): 1.

36. See Shama Churun Sircar, *The Muhammadan Law* (Calcutta: Thacker, Spink and Co., 1873); William H, Macnaghten, *Principles of Hindu and Mohammadan Law* (London: Williams and Norgate, 1860); John Baillie and William Jones, *A Digest of Mohummudan Law According to the Tenets of the Twelve Imams* (Calcutta: Printed at the Hon. Company's Press, 1805).

37. *Muhammad Ibra'him bin Muhammad Sayad Park'r v. Gulam Ahmed bin Muhammad Sayad Roghe and Muhammad Sayad bin Muhammad Ibra'him Roghe.* Bom. H.C. Reports Suit no. 49 of 1863, Bombay High Court Reports Volume 1, 223. The headnote of the case stated that "after attaining puberty a Muhammadan female of any one of the four sects can elect to belong to whichever of the other three sects she pleases, and the legality of her subsequent acts will be governed by the tenets of the Imam whose follower she may have become. A girl whose parents and family are followers of the school of Shafii, and who has arrived at puberty and has not been married or betrothed by her father or guardian, can change her sect from that of Shafii to that of Hanafi, so as to render valid a marriage subsequently entered into by her without the consent of her father."

38. *Salmah and Fatimah, Infants, by Their Next Friend Shaik Omar v. Soolong* [1878] 1 KY 421.

39. *Salmah and Fatimah, Infants, by Their Next Friend Shaik Omar v. Soolong.*

40. *Fatimah & Ors. v. Logan & Ors.* [1871] 1 KY 255.

41. Elizabeth Kolsky, *Colonial Justice in British India* (New York: Cambridge University Press, 2010), 70–71; Alan M. Guenther, "A Colonial Court Defines a Muslim," in *Islam in South Asia in Practice,* ed. Barbara D. Metcalf (Princeton, NJ: Princeton University Press 2009), 293.

42. The British created two legal codes, one Hindu and one Muslim, thus forcefully inscribing a Hindu/Muslim binary on Indian societies by completely disregarding the diversity of Indian legal traditions. Personal laws of Jains, Sikhs, Parsis, and certain tribes were not recognized. Since then, only Parsi personal laws have been recognized. Rosane Rocher, "British Orientalism in the Eighteenth Century," in *Orientalism and the Postcolonial Predicament: Perspectives on South Asia*, ed. Carol A. Breckenridge and Peter van der Veer (Philadelphia: University of Pennsylvania Press, 1993), 221–22.

43. Asaf Ali Asghar Fyzee, "Muhammadan Law in India," *Comparative Studies in Society and History* 5, no. 4 (July 1963): 412.

44. Warren Hastings (governor of Bengal from 1772, governor-general from 1774 to 1885), created two courts in each district, namely the Diwani Adalat which handled civil cases, and the Foujdari Adalat that held trials for crimes and misdemeanors. The civil courts applied Islamic and Hindu laws to Muslims and Hindus, while the criminal courts applied Islamic law universally. M. P. Jain, *Outlines of Indian Legal History* (Delhi: University of Delhi Press, 1952), 57–69.

45. Clause 23 stated that "in all suits regarding inheritance, marriage, caste and other religious usages or institutions, the laws of the Koran with respect to the Mohamedans and those of the Shaster with respect to the Gentoos shall invariably be adhered to." Rocher, "British Orientalism in the Eighteenth Century," 215–49.

46. Lauren Benton demonstrates how these experts actually occupied an ambiguous position within colonial bureaucracy—they certainly did not occupy the same status as British officials although they were in fact officers of the company and employees of the courts. Lauren Benton, "Colonial Law and Cultural Difference: Jurisdictional Politics and the Formation of the Colonial State," *Comparative Studies in Society and History* 41 no. 3 (2000): 571.

47. Kugle, "Framed, Blamed and Renamed," 262.

48. Michael R. Anderson, "Themes in South Asian Legal Studies in the 1980s," *South Asia Research* 10, no. 2 (1990): 168.

49. There were two types of authority in Islamic legal thought—legislative authority, which is divine and concretized in foundational texts, and interpretive or declarative authority, which belongs to jurists. The latter is a derivative authority, drawn entirely from the legislative authority of God. The Muslim jurist bears no authority in his person or status in the sense that his declarations are automatically accepted as valid. The authority depends upon the methodology employed by the jurists and his skills. Weiss, *The Spirit of Islamic Law*, 65.

50. Elisa Giunchi, "The Reinvention of Shari'a under the British Raj: In Search of Authenticity and Certainty," *Journal of Asian Studies* 69, no. 4 (November 2010); 1128.

51. Faiz Badrudin Tyabji, *Muhammadan Law: The Personal Law of Muslims* (Bombay: N. M. Tripathi and Co., 1940), xii.

52. Kugle, "Framed, Blamed and Renamed," 301, 306, 309–10. By the eve of the Second World War, Islamic law codes devised in British India applied also to Muslim subjects in Ceylon, Iraq, Palestine, Malay States, Somaliland, Zanzibar, Trinidad and

Tobago, Nigeria, Cyprus, Gold Coast, and the Straits Settlements. British officials stationed in various colonies constantly updated each other on amendments to legal statutes and acts, by corresponding with the Colonial Office in London, who dutifully copied their correspondences and sent them to other British governments throughout the empire. This framework was in line with the argument put forth by the legal scholar Marc Galanter, who emphasizes that colonial administrators tended to implement general rules that were applicable to whole societies. Marc Galanter, "The Displacement of Traditional Law in Modern India," *Journal of Social Issues* 24, no. 4 (1968): 65–91.

53. Tyabji, *Muhammadan Law*, 90.

54. Roland Knyvet Wilson, *A Digest of Anglo-Muhammadan Law* (London: W. Thacker & Co., 1895).

55. There were actually key differences within the legal stipulations of other *madhhabs*, especially with regards to family law.

56. Elizabeth Kolsky, "Forum: Maneuvering the Personal Law System in Colonial India—Introduction," *Law and History Review* 28, no. 4 (November 2010): 975.

57. For more on the *Al Minhaj al Talibin* see Brinkley Messick, *The Calligraphic State: Textual Domination and History in a Muslim Society* (Berkeley: University of California Press, 1996), 20–21, 66–68. For more on the use of the *Minhaj* by local populations in Southeast Asia, see R. Knox-Mawer, "Islamic Domestic Law in the Colony of Aden," *International Journal of Comparative Law Quarterly* 5 (1956): 511–18; Syed A. Majid, "Wakf as Family Settlement among the Mohammedans," *Journal of the Society of Comparative Legislation* 9 (1908): 122–41.

58. A similar case appeared in court in 1907. *M.M. Noordin v. Shaik Mohamed Meah Noordin Shah & Anor.* [1908] 10 SSLR 72.

59. "The Council Meeting of 1st June," *ST,* June 19, 1880, 1.

60. "Mahomedan Marriage and Divorce," *ST,* September 11, 1875, 1.

61. Mawani, *Across Oceans of Empire*, 117.

62. IOR/L/PJ/6/68 File 422, Thomas Braddell, Attorney-General's Office, Singapore to Undersecretary of State, India Office, London, August 31, 1880.

63. "The Council Meeting of 1st June."

64. "Mahomedan Marriage and Divorce."

65. "The Legislative Council, 6th July."

66. Frank Athelstane Swettenham, *The Real Malay; Pen Pictures* (London: J. Lane, 1900), 275.

67. "Mahomedan Ordinance no. 26" *Laws of the Straits Settlements, Volume 1* (London: Waterlow a & Sons, 1920), 312.

68. "A Mohamedan," *ST,* November 30, 1911; "A Mohamedan," *ST,* December 2, 1911, 10.

69. "Mahomedan Ordinance no. 26," 311–25.

70. Abdullah bin Marie, based in Java, owned "a flourishing bookshop" in Hyderabad with branches in Singapore and Madras and considerable property in the Netherlands East Indies. L/PS/10/630 Secret Prop. No. 5/19, J.V.A. Huston, Batavia, February 25th 1919; "Notice in the Estate of Shaik Abdullah bin Sayeed bin Marie, Deceased," *ST,* July 13, 1922, 16.

71. "Notice in the Estate of Shaik Abdullah bin Sayeed bin Marie, Deceased."

72. "Daughter Sues Father—Arab Litigants in Supreme Court," *ST*, December 17, 1924, 9.

73. "An Arab Lady wins Action," *ST*, December 18, 1924, 9.

74. "Daughter's Law Suit—Heiress' Marriage Adventures," *SFPMA*, December 18, 1924, 7.

75. "Daughter Sues Father—Arab Litigants in Supreme Court."

76. Daughter's Law Suit—Heiress' Marriage Adventures."

77. He gave her as purchase price 15,000 guilders, which she valued at 10,000 Straits dollars in cash, and a half share in a date garden in Arabia which was worth $17,000.

78. This degree of affinity did not always disqualify a marriage, and it is very much a matter of interpretation.

79. "Daughter's Law Suit—Heiress' Marriage Adventures."

80. "Arab Lady Sues Father—A Thrice Married Plaintiff," *ST*, October 29, 1925, 9.

81. Koh Seow Chuan Collection (KSC) no. 04000088, Power of Attorney by Shaikha binte Jaafar bin Omar bin Abdul Aziz to Abdullah bin Salman bin Marie and Soliman bin Abdullah bin Salmain bin Marie, November–December 1920 (Rabiulawal 1339).

82. KSC no. 04000089, Power of Attorney by Shaikha binte Jaafar bin Omar bin Abdul Aziz, Ilia binte Abdullah bin Said in Marie and Fatimah binte Abdullah bin Said in Marie, to Abdullah bin Salman bin Marie and Soliman bin Abdullah bin Salmain bin Marie, November–December 1920 (Rabiulawal 1339).

83. "Auction Notice," *ST*, June 30, 1922, 7; "Local Property Auction," *ST*, September 25, 1922, 9; "Local Property Auction," *SFPMA*, July 15, 1922, 7.

84. "Auction Sale: The Estate of Fatimah bin Abdullah bin Syed bin Marie (Deceased)," *ST*, January 6, 1926, 14.

85. "Daughter's Law Suit—Heiress' Marriage Adventures."

86. Counsel for the defendant argued that she had based her case on contradictory grounds as she stated the she did not sign the document, although she did. She clarified that she signed it without understanding it but later rescinded this statement and confessed she was forced to sign it by her father. "Daughter Sues Father—Arab Litigants in Supreme Court."

87. "Daughter Sues Father—Arab Litigants in Supreme Court."

88. "Supreme Court—Woman's Action to Recover Property" *ST*, November 23, 1925, 8.

89. "A Father's Woes: Wayward Daughter and Wily Tongue," *SFPMA*, September 29, 1926, 16.

90. "Arab Lady Sues Father."

91. He quoted from *The Halsbury Encyclopedia of Law*, an authoritative compendium of laws first produced in 1907.

92. A law report of this particular case cannot be found. "Law Notice for the Day," *SFPMA*, May 23, 1939, 3.

93. Julia Stephens, *Governing Islam: Law, Empire and Secularism in Modern South Asia* (New York: Cambridge University Press, 2018), 67.

94. The memorial was signed by Muslim members of the board and by Roland J. Farrer, the chairman of the board. FCO 141/16013, Laurence Guillemard, Governor of the Straits Settlements to Winston Churchill, Colonial Office, January 28, 1922.

95. "Alsagoff Appeal: Arguments on the Talak and Divorce" *ST*, November 8, 1921, 8.

96. "Alsagoff Appeal: Arguments on the Talak and Divorce."

97. IOR/L/PJ/6/28, Thomas Braddell, Attorney-General to India Office, August 31, 1880.

98. Thomas Braddell was particularly worried about Christian men pretending to be Muslims in order to divorce their Christian wives more easily in the future. IOR/L/PJ/6/28, Thomas Braddell, Attorney-General to India Office, August 31, 1880.

99. Barrett-Lennard remained in the Straits Settlements and Johore till January 1926, when he was appointed Chief Justice of Jamaica.

100. Barrett-Lennard had ordered Muslim witnesses who appeared in court to remove their headgear and footwear, implying that the British courtroom is a holy place. FCO 141/16013, Memorial by R. J. Farrer, Chairman-Civil Servants and eleven others (unnamed), November 20, 1921; "The Judge and the Moslem Law," *Malaya Tribune*, September 21, 1922, 6.

101. FCO 141/16013, Laurence Guillemard, Governor of the Straits Settlements to Winston Churchill, Colonial Office, January 28, 1922.

102. FCO 141/16013, Laurence Guillemard, Governor of the Straits Settlements to Winston Churchill, Colonial Office, January 28, 1922.

103. FCO 141/16013, Laurence Guillemard, Governor of the Straits Settlements to Winston Churchill, Colonial Office, January 28, 1922.

104. FCO 141/16013, Fiennes Barrett-Lennard to Governor of the Straits Settlements Laurence Guillemard, January 12, 1922.

105. The ordinance was later amended by Muhammadan Marriage Ordinance XXV, of 1908, Muhammadan Marriage Ordinance 1908 Amendment Ordinance XVII of 1909 and the Muhammadan Marriage (Amendment) Ordinance IV of 1917.

106. M. B. Hooker, "Muhammadan Law and Islamic Law," in *Islam in Southeast Asia*, ed. M. B. Hooker (Leiden: Brill, 1983), 167.

107. Deborah Cohen, *Family Secrets: Shame and Privacy in Modern Britain* (Oxford: Oxford University Press, 2013), 3.

108. For more on the issue of equality of marriages, see Sumit K. Mandal, "Challenging Inequality in a Modern Islamic Idiom: Arabs in Early 20th-Century Java," in *Southeast Asia and The Middle East: Islam, Movement and the Longue Durée*, ed. Eric Tagliacozzo (Stanford: Stanford University Press, 2009), 156–75; Farhat J. Ziadeh, "Equality (Kafā'a) in the Muslim Law of Marriage," *The American Journal of Comparative Law* 6. no. 4 (Autumn 1957): 515-516.

109. NAS, interview with Syed Isa bin Mohamed Bin Semait, Accession Number 003382, January 29 2009.

110. KITLV, DH 1083 no. 102 "Djawaban Raad Agama atas Perkawinan Sarifah dan Lain2 Bangsa" undated; makrūh," in *Encyclopaedia of Islam, Second Edition, Glossary and Index of Terms*, edited by: P. J. Bearman, Th. Banquis, C. E. Bowworth, E. van Donzel, and W. P. Heinrichs Bowworth, referenceworks.brillonline.com, accessed January 9, 2020.

111. In 1869, a barrister-at-law Robert Carr Woods complained about the problem of itinerant qadis taking their registry with them when they left the colony. Each qadi's books and seals of office were to be given up to the registrar upon his death. Robert Carr Woods, *A Selection of Oriental Cases Decided in the Supreme Courts of the Straits Settlements* (Penang: S. Jeremiah), n.p.

112. "Mohammedan Marriage—Interesting Rulings in Supreme Court" *ST*, February 1, 1922, 9.

2. Surat Kuasa

1. "Van Belang voor den Handel," *De Sumatra Post*, November 20, 1903, 6; "Appeal Court – April 2nd 1894," *SFPMA*, April 10, 1894, 208.

2. "A Mohameddan Marriage—Interesting Will Case in Supreme Court," *ST*, January 11, 1930, 17; Victor Purcell, "Polyglot Port: Singapore Salvo III," *ST*, March 28, 1937, 14.

3. "Het Losgeld van een Arabier," *Nieuwe Tilburgsche Courant*, July 9, 1932, 15; KSC no. 040000172, Power of Attorney by Sheriffa Alooyeah binte Ali bin Abdulrahman bin Aby Bakar Almashor granted to Syed Ahmad bin Hassan bin Ahmad Aideed, May 10, 1906.

4. KSC no. 040000076, Power of Attorney on behalf of Shaikh Omar bin Salim Hamoud Bayacoub to Sayed Omar bin Mohamed Alsagoff, December 9, 1916.

5. For examples of the use of such documents, see Sebouh David Aslanian, *From the Indian Ocean to the Mediterranean: The Global Trade Networks of Armenian Merchants from New Julfa* (Berkeley: University of California Press, 2011), 175; Shalomo D. Goitein, *Studies in Islamic History and Institutions* (Leiden: Brill, 2010), 346; Bishara, *A Sea of Debt*, 190–91, 208–9.

6. Akhil Gupta, *Red Tape: Bureaucracy, Structural Violence, and Poverty in India* (Durham, NC: Duke University Press, 2012), 189.

7. Matthew Hull, *Government of Paper: The Materiality of Bureaucracy in Urban Pakistan* (Berkeley: University of California Press, 2016), 121.

8. In the Netherlands Indies, powers of attorney were only translated into Dutch if they were challenged in court.

9. IOR/R/20/C/1276, Probate No. 176 of 1919, Translation No. 47 of 1919. Copy of the will of the late Seiyid Sheikh Alkaff, February 6, 1910.

10. Hull, *Government of Paper*, 116.

11. An exception was the al-Quaiti state, where the qadi and/or deputy *wazeer* was known as the Khan Bahadur. KSC no. 170003278, Power of Attorney on behalf of Sheik Omar bin Ahmad bin Junid bin Abdullah Bajunied, March 8, 1921.

12. The stamp of the qadi of Say'un (identified by Dutch legal authorities in Java as *penghulu*), which reads, "By the law of the city of Say'un," points toward the authenticity of the document. Sajid Alwie bin Sjech bin Achmad bin Djafar bin Achmad bin Alie bin Abdulla Assegaf tegen Sjech Solah (Salah) bin Achmad Basjerewan, *ITVHR* 113 (1920): 448.

13. KSC no. 170003273, Power of Attorney on behalf of Sheikah Salim bin Abdurahman Basuidan, August 14, 1919.

14. L. W. C. van den Berg, *Le Hadhramout et Les Colonies Arabes dans l'Archipel Indien* (Batavia: Imprimerie du Gouvernment, 1886), 146–47.

15. William G. Clarence-Smith, "Middle-Eastern Entrepreneurs in Southeast Asia," in *Diaspora Entrepreneurial Networks: Four Centuries of History*, ed. Ina Baghdiantz McCabe, Gelina Harlaftis and Ionna Pepelasis Minoglou (Oxford: Berg, 2005), 232–33.

16. Ulrike Freitag, "Arab Merchants in Singapore: Attempt of a Collective Biography," in *Transcending Borders: Arabs, Politics, Trade, Islam in Southeast Asia*, ed. Huub de Jonge and Nico Kaptein (Leiden: KITLV Press, 2002), 119.

17. William G. Clarence-Smith, "Hadhrami Arab Entrepreneurs in Indonesia and Malaysia: Facing the Challenge of the 1930s Recessions," in *Weathering the Storm: The Economies of Southeast Asia in the 1930s Depression*, ed. Peter Boomgard and Ian Brown (Singapore: Institute of Southeast Asian Studies, 2000), 229.

18. Renisa Mawani, "Law, Settler Colonialism and the 'Forgotten Space' of Maritime Worlds," *Annual Review of Law and Social Science* 12 (October 2016): 107–31.

19. William E. Maxwell, *The Torrens System of Conveyancing by Registration of Title: with an Account of the Practice of the Lands Titles Office in Adelaide, South Australia, and suggestions as to the Introduction of the System in the Straits Settlements* (Singapore: no publisher, 1883).

20. "Onwettige Occupaties," *De Indische Courant*, January 30, 1924, 1.

21. "Grijpvogels," *Bataviasch Nieuwsblad*, January 24, 1916, 1.

22. "Gecamoufleerde Woeker," *De Indische Courant*, July 8, 1933, 9.

23. "Juridische Vragenbus," *Het Nieuws van den Dag*, October 30, 1931, 11.

24. "Voor den Landraad: Oplichterspraktijken," *De Indische Courant*, March 28, 1933, 2.

25. Hadji Hasan bin Abdulrahman contra Hadji Barnawi and Abdulmanan, *ITVHR* 122 (1923): 585.

26. Sech Said bin Oemar Basakaran alias Amoedi tegen Pa Soe alias Samoe, *HRNI* 136 (1932): 278.

27. Ang Oeng Wie Nio contra Sech Achmad bin Mohaman bin Afif and Pak Sadjan, *ITVHR* 113 (1919): 113.

28. "Juridische Vragenbus," *Bataviaasch Nieuwsblad*, May 20, 1933, 21.

29. "Soerabaiasch Causerie," *Bijvoegsel Soerabaijasch Handelsblad*, May 10, 1883, 1.

30. Sajid Alwie bin Sjech bin Achmad bin Djafar bin Achmad bin Alie bin Abdulla Assegaf tegen Sjech Solah (Salah) bin Achmad Basjerewan, *ITVHR* 113 (1920): 448.

31. NA Blok nr: C 27050, Coll. Familie Jordaaan, inventaris nummer 110, "Kapitein Sajid Alie Al Gadrie"

32. Bobsaid also helped to translate another Arabic power of attorney that ended up before the Supreme Court in the Straits Settlements. The Bobsaid family was powerful in Surabaya, and members were often appointed heads of the Arab community. *Regeerings-almanak voor Nederlandsch-Indie* (Centraal Bureau voor Genealogie: The Hague, 1916), 2.

33. This was not unique. While most grantors signed their names in full in Arabic, a few affixed their mark simply as "x."

34. The relationship between witnesses did not bear upon the authenticity of the document at all.

35. "Snouck Hurgronje to Resident van Palembang, 20 November 1905," in *Ambtelijke Adviezen Van C. Snouck Hurgronje, Tweede Deel* ('s Gravenhage: Martinus Nijhoff, 1957), 988.

36. K. Burns, *Into the Archive*.

37. "Mohamedhan Wills," *SFPMA*, July 9, 1908, 11.

38. KSC no. 170003299, Power of Attorney on behalf of Sheriffa Mahani Binte Ahmad Bin Abdulrahman Alsagoff and Sheriffa Rogayah Binte Ahmad Bin Abdulrahman Alsagoff, June 9, 1917.

39. This definition of personal law was in line with the jurisdiction of ecclesiastical courts in Europe.

40. "Mohamedhan Wills," *SFPMA*, July 9, 1908, 11.

41. Said Oemar bin Mochdar Alhabsi, Said Joesoef bin Abdllah bin Masjhoer Alhasnie en Said Mochdar bin Abdullah Alhabsjie en Sjarifah Alwiah binti Achmad bin Alwie Assegaf, gezamenlijk voogden over de minderjarigen Achmad en Hasar, *ITVHR* 136 (1927): 232.

42. Courts had to ascertain whether they were competent before proceeding. Ten aanzien van de curandi is de Raad van Justitie bevoegd de verzochte machtiging te verleenen, ten aanzien van den minderjarige echter de landraad, *HRNI* 146 (1937): 30.

43. This implied that the Arabs in question were not even regarded as Foreign Orientals who would be recognized as residents of foreign origin.

44. "Action Dismissed," *SFPMA*, July 9, 1926, 9.

45. Untitled, *SFPMA*, August 25, 1938, 117.

46. "Arab Will Case," *Malaya Tribune*, December 14, 1933, 14.

47. Ghislaine Lydon, *On Trans-Saharan Trails: Islamic Law, Trade Networks and Cross-cultural Exchanges in Nineteenth-Century Western Africa* (New York: Cambridge University Press, 2009), 277.

48. Lydon, *On Trans-Saharan Trails*, 3.

49. Francesca Trivellato, "Marriage, Commercial Capital and Business Agency, Sephardic (and Armenian) Families in the Seventeenth and Eighteenth Centuries," in *Transregional and Transnational Families in Europe and Beyond: Experiences since the Middle Ages*, ed. David W. Sabean et al. (Oxford: Berghahn Books, 2011), 121.

50. For more on *asabiyya*, see Syed Farid Alatas, "Ḥaḍramawt and the Hadhrami Diaspora: Problems in Theoretical History," in *Hadhrami Traders, Scholars and Statesmen in the Indian Ocean, 1750s-1960s*, ed. Ulrike Freitag and William G. Clarence-Smith (Leiden: Brill, 1997), 19–34.

51. Trust certainly does not run in the blood. Francesca Trivellato, "Sephardic Merchants in the Early Modern Atlantic and Beyond: Toward a Comparative Historical Approach to Business Cooperation," in *Atlantic Diasporas: Jews, Conversos and Crypto-Jews in the Age of Mercantilism, 1500–1800*, ed. Richard L. Kagan and Philip D. Morgan (Baltimore: Johns Hopkins University Press, 2009), 99–122.

52. KSC no. 040000155, Power of Attorney on behalf of Moonah prepared by Shaikh Omar bin Sallim Basrahil, April 17, 1906.

53. KSC no. 040000155, Power of Attorney on behalf of Moonah prepared by Shaikh Omar bin Sallim Basrahil, April 17, 1906.

54. For example, see KSC no. 040000066, Power of Attorney by Sherifah Noor binte Abdullah bin Omar Abu Fatim, April 22, 1917.

55. KSC no. 170003282, Power of Attorney of Mariam binte Keriau and Mariam binte Shaikh Ali bin Omar BaSabren, July 30, 1908.

56. "Alleged Breach of Trust," *Malaya Tribune*, September 19, 1935, 10.

57. KSC no. 040000073, Power of Attorney on behalf of Sherifah Fatimah binte Omar bin Ahmad bin Omar Al-Shattri to Omar bin Ahmad bin Omar Al-Shattri, March 18, 1908.

58. They were the daughters of Syed Ahmad Alsagoff and Raja Sittee, daughter of the wealthy Bugis merchant Hajjah Fatimah. KSC no. 170003299, Power of Attorney on behalf of Sheriffa Mahani Binte Ahmad Bin Abdulrahman Alsagoff and Sheriffa Rogayah Binte Ahmad Bin Abdulrahman Alsagoff, June 9, 1917.

59. KSC no. 170003299, Power of Attorney on behalf of Sheriffa Mahani Binte Ahmad Bin Abdulrahman Alsagoff and Sheriffa Rogayah Binte Ahmad Bin Abdulrahman Alsagoff, June 9, 1917.

60. Islamic Religious Council of Singapore (MUIS), "List of waqfs in Singapore," undated.

61. Stephens, *Governing Islam*, 17.

62. Untitled, *SFPMA* October 22, 1924, 269.

63. Lauren Benton, *A Search for Sovereignty: Law and Geography in European Empires, 1400–1900* (New York: Cambridge University Press, 2010), 56.

3. Resident Aliens

1. Louis de Bourbon, "De Slechte Guldens," in *Twaalf Maal Azië* (Amsterdam: Boek-en Courantmaatschappij, 1941), 22.

2. This phenomenon refers to the abolition of the gold standard in the Netherlands Indies on September 27, 1936, which caused the guilder to be devalued. Peter Boomgaard, "Indonesia: Developments in Real Income" in *Weathering the Storm: The Economies of Southeast Asia in the 1930s Depression*, ed. Peter Boomgaard and Ian Brown (Singapore: Institute of Southeast Asian Studies, 2000), 26.

3. De Bourbon, "De Slechte Guldens," 23.

4. C. W. Margadant, "Verkrachting in kinderhuwelijk," *HRNI* 57 (1891): 11.

5. De Bourbon, "De Slechte Guldens," 26.

6. R. Van Eck, *Beknopt Leerboek De Geschiedenis, Staatsinrichting En Land En Volkenkunde Van Nederlandsch Oost-Indie* (Breda: Koninklijke Militaire Academie, 1899), 79.

7. "Arabieren," *Encyclopedia van Nederlandsch-Indië*, 39; *Verslag der handelingen der Staten-Generaal* 2, no. 2 (1905): 91.

8. La Chapelle, "De Wester-Afdeeling van Borneo," *De Huisvriend* (1895): 50.

9. For most of the colonial period, censuses were not done systematically but estimates were published from time to time by the Dutch colonial government. There were consistently more Arabs proportionally in the Outer Islands than in Madura and Java.

10. For more, see A. J. Immink, *Het Reglement op de Burgerlijke Rechtsvordering* (The Hague: Martinus Nijhoff, 1900).

11. *Staatkundig en Staathuishoudkundig Jaarbookje voor 1879* 6, no. 6 (1879): 201.

12. "Arabieren," *Encyclopaedie van Nederlandsch-Indië, Eerste Deel* (The Hague: Martinus Nijhoff–E. J. Brill, 1905), 40; Mandal, *Becoming Arab*, 64.

13. Nico Kaptein argues that there was only one thing that the Dutch feared more than the Arabs—the Sufi *tariqahs*. Nico J. G. Kaptein, "Arabophobia and Tarekat: How Sayyid Uthmān became Advisor to the Netherlands Colonial Administration," in *The Hadhrami Diaspora in Southeast Asia: Identity Maintenance or Assimilation*, ed. Ahmed Ibrahim Abushouk and Hassan Ahmed Ibrahim (Brill: Leiden, 2009), 44.

14. Titular military ranks of lieutenant, captain, or major corresponded to the size and importance of the community, as well as length of service and loyalty. Mandal, *Becoming Arab*, 88–89.

15. Leonard Burggraaf de Bus de Gisignies, "Instructie voor het Hoofd der Maleijers, Arabieren, Mooren, Bengalezen 29 February 1829," *Staatsblad van Nederlandsch-Indië* (1829/1832): 65.

16. "Bevolking," *Encyclopaedie van Nederlandsch-Indië, Eerste deel* 40–41.

17. Hendrikus Colijn, *Neerlands-Indië Land en Volk, Eerste Deel* (Amsterdam: Uitgevers Maatschappy, 1912), 274.

18. "Bevolking," *Encyclopaedie van Nederlandsch-Indië, Eerste Deel* (The Hague: Martinus Nijhoff–E. J. Brill, 1905), 194; F. Fokkens, *Bescheiden Wenken voor de Verbetering van den Economischen Toestand der Inlandsche Bevolking op Java en daar Buiten* (The Hague: M. M. Couvee, 1904), 35.

19. "Arabieren," *Encyclopaedie van Nederlandsch-Indië, Eerste deel,* 40.

20. Mandal, *Becoming Arab,* 49, 90, 92.

21. Herman Otto van der Linden, *Banda and zijn Bewoners* (Dordrecht: Blusse and Van Braam, 1873), 45.

22. Fasseur, *The Politics of Colonial Exploitation,* 31.

23. C. H. F. Riesz, *De Heerendiensten op de Particuliere Landen, en de Geschiedenis van Buitenzorg* ('s Gravenhage, H. C. Susan C. H. Zoon, 1864), 5.

24. Conversely, the law protected the right of ownership of the Indonesian cultivator. Daniel S. Lev, "The Lady and the Banyan Tree: Civil Law Change in Indonesia," in *Legal Evolution and Political Authority in Indonesia, Selected Essays* (The Hague: Kluwer Law international, 2000), 119–42; Paul van der Veur, "The Eurasians of Indonesia: A Problem and Challenge in Colonial History," *Journal of Southeast Asian History* 9, no. 1 (September 1968): 191–207.

25. Johan Pieter Cornets de Groot van Kraaijenburg, *Over het Beheer Onzer Koloniën* (The Hague: Belinfante, 1862), 229.

26. J. Sibenius Trip, "Het efpachtregt op de particuliere landerijen bewesten de Tjimanoek," *HRNI* 30 (1878): 99.

27. Arab-owned land was worth 392,845 guilders, while Chinese-owned land and European-owned land were worth 9,450,760 guilders and 17,552,234 guilders respectively. "Verslag van het beheer en den staat over kolonien over 1849," *Bijlagen van het verslag der Handelingen, 1851–1852* (The Hague: n. p., 1852): 196; H. C. van der Wijck, "De Nederlandsche Oost-Indische bezittingen onder het bestuur van den kommissaris generaal du Bus de Gisignies (1826–1830)" (The Hague: Martinus Nijhoff, 1866), 137.

28. Sumit K. Mandal, "Finding Their Place: A History of Arabs in Java under Dutch Rule, 1800–1924" (PhD diss., Columbia University, 1994), 50.

29. "Arabieren," *Encyclopaedie van Nederlandsch-Indië,* 39; F. Fokkens, *Bijdrage tot de Kennis onzer Koloniale Politiek der Laatste Twintig Jaren* (The Hague: M. M. Couvée, 1908), 74; Blink, *Nederlandsch Oost-en West-Indië,* 162.

30. Mandal, "Finding Their Place," 21.

31. Cornelis van Vollenhoven, quoted in G. J. Nolst Trenite, *Herziening van het Vervreemdingsverbod voor Indonesiche Gronden* (n.p.: n.p., 1916), 4.

32. To the Dutch government's relief, the change in law did not put Europeans at as much of a disadvantage as feared. The only Arab who applied during the period of 1913 to 1917 came from Palembang where there were more Arabs than Chinese within the category of Foreign Orientals. Cornelis van Vollenhoven, "Een Accident in Indische Rechtsvorming," *De Gids* 85 (1921): 468.

33. G. W. W. C. Baron van Hoevell, quoted in G. Gongrijp, "Aantwoord aan den heer Vogelesang," *Koloniaal Tijdschrift* 11 (1922): 675.

34. J. E. W. Lambert, ed., "Circulaire aan de Hoofden van Gewestelijk Bestuur in Nederlandsch-Indië. No. 1462. Batavia, 12 Juli 1881," in *Politieklapper voor Java en Madoera* (Surabaya: E. Fuhri and Co., 1910), 183–84.

35. Sometimes this task would be delegated to local rulers such as in parts of Sulawesi. "Verklaring en akte van bevestiging—Contract met Barroe," *Bijlagen van het Verslag der Handelingen, Tweede Kamer* (1889–90), 38.

36. Fokkens, *Bescheiden Wenken*, 34.

37. Sech Mohamed bin Bissar bin Mohamed Nahdi tegen Said Abdoelkadir bin Hoesin Alfagih Alatas, *HRNI* 145 (1935): 548; Said Oesman bin Salah Machdjoeb tegen Said Sadagah bin Kasim Machdjoeb, *HRNI* 147 (1937): 72.

38. For more on the Pass and Quarter system, see Mandal, *Becoming Arab*, 75–87.

39. NA 2.5.03 inventarisnummer 452, Christiaan Snouck Hurgronje, Leiden, to Minister van Koloniën, June 18, 1908.

40. Blink, *Nederlandsch Oost-en West-Indië*, 228.

41. Colijn, *Neerlands-Indië Land en Volk*, 270.

42. Blink, *Nederlandsch Oost-en West-Indië*, 379.

43. Blink, *Nederlandsch Oost-en West-Indië*, 189.

44. Blink, *Nederlandsch Oost-en West-Indië*, 145.

45. "Semarang," *Encyclopaedie van Nederlandsch-Indië, Derde Deel* (The Hague: Martinus Nijhoff Brill, 1905), 573.

46. The law report was unusual in that it included a copy of the letter by Sayyid Moehamad Ashmoeni in Malay, dated August 30, 1918, written in a formal high register in the first person. Sayyid Moehamad Ashmoeni contra Moehsina binti Hadji Abdoel Moerni, *ITVHR* 113 (1918): 163.

47. His former wife was explicitly identified as *bumiputera*, the Indonesian term for Native.

48. The Dutch terms were *voogdij* and *verpleging*.

49. *Regeerings-almanak voor Nederlandsch-Indie 1910, twee gedeelte* (Batavia: Landsdrukkerij, 1910), 274.

50. For more examples, see Mandal, *Becoming Arab*, 86.

51. *Regeerings-almanak voor Nederlandsch-Indie 1917* (Batavia: Landsdrukkerij, 1917), 181; NA 2.21.413 inventarisnummer 110, "Kapitein Sajid Alim Al Gadrie," June 1921.

52. *Regeerings-almanak voor Nederlandsch-Indie 1917*, 164.

53. "Verbod aan Javanen om naar Borneo te vertrekken en maatregelen, in acht te nemen bij het afgeven van passen, Resolutie no. 17, 30 January 1829," *Staatsblad van Nederlandsch-Indië* (1829 / 1832): 20.

54. L. W. C van den Berg, *Ontwerp Burgelijk Wetboek voor Nederlandsch-Indië* (n.p: 1910), 18.

55. "De Rechtspositie van Nederlandsch-Indië," *IG* 27, no. 1 (1905): 61–62.

56. Immink, *Het Reglement op de Burgerlijke Rechtsvordering*, 14–15. For more on article 64, see L. J. A. Tollens, *De Indische Secretaris* (Batavia: Lange & Co., 1860), 200.

57. Said Alie bin Achmad bin Mohamad bin Shahab contra Njai Raden Ningroem and Sech Abdulrahman bin Abdullah Hassan, *HRNI* 91 (1908): 104.

58. A case in June 1879 brought to the Supreme Court upheld this opinion with regard to married Chinese women, which meant that they were not allowed to contract business relations without the written consent and authorization of their husbands, though this ruling was not imposed on wives of Arab men.

59. Handelsvenootschap onder de firma Geo Wehry & Co. contra 1e Katidjah binte Abdullah en 2e Sech Said bin Achmad bin Abdulrachman Djawas, *ITVHR* 99 (1912): 116.

60. KITLV Inventaris 27 H 797 Collectie Kern no. 486, Nji Ali to Advisor for Native and Arab Affairs, May 26, 1934.

61. *Gouvernements-koffiecultuur. Rapport van de Staats-Commissie* (The Hague: Der Gerbroeders van Cleef, 1889), 151; Wong Tanie, "Woeker en Landbouwkrediet," *IG* 22, no. 1 (1900): 811.

62. Van der Linden, *Banda and zijn Bewoners*, 39–40.

63. W. H. Bogaardt, *De Oeconomische en Sociale Toestanden in Nederlandsch-Indië* (Harlem: H. G. van Alfen, 1905), 112–13.

64. Blink, *Nederlandsch Oost-en West-Indië*, 22; A. J. H. Eyken, *De werkkring van den Controleur op Java* (The Hague: M. Van Der Beek's Boekhandel, 1909), 30.

65. P. C. C. Hansen (under pseudonym "Boeka"), *Uit Java's Binnenland: Pàh Troeno* (Amsterdam: Van Rossen, 1902), 339.

66. J. E. de M, "Uitvoerechten in Indië," *IG* 27, no. 1 (1905): 560.

67. Van Hoevell, *Parlementaire Redevoeringen over Koloniale Belangen, Volume 1*, 86–87.

68. "Arabieren en de Kleine man," *Rotterdamsch Nieuwsblad*, January 20, 1908, 3.

69. S. C. van der Wal, *De Opkomst van den Nationalistische Beweging in Nederlands-Indie: Een bronnenpublikatie* (Groningen, 1967), 50–51.

70. "Koloniaal Verslag van 1892," *Bijlagen van het Verslag der Handelingen* (1892–93), 316.

71. D. Fock, "Het Ontwerp Koninklijk besluit tot wijziging van het Reglement op de Burgerlijke Rechtsvordering," *IG* 22, no. 1 (1900): 493. For more on this phenomenon in Batavia that led to resentment among Natives, see Rudolf Mrazek, *A Certain Age: Colonial Jakarta through the Memories of Its Intellectuals* (Durham, NC: Duke University Press, 2010), 97.

72. These titles were rarely granted anyway. Sollewijn Gepke, "Huur, verhuur, koop en verkoop van grond," *IG* 8, no. 1 (1886): 722.

73. Van der Wijck, "De Nederlandsche Oost-Indische bezittingen onder het bestuur van den kommissaris generaal du Bus de Gisignies (1826–1830)," 152; De Groot van Kraaijenburg, *Over Het Beheer Onzer Koloniën*, 68, 229; C. Bosscher, "Het Wetsonwerp tot aanvulling van het tarief van uitvoerrechten in Nederlandsch-Indië," *IG* 1, no. 2 (1879): 311.

74. For more on the phenomenon of alienation in sugar plantations, see Sidney Mintz, *Sweetness and Power: The Place of Sugar in Modern History* (New York: Viking, 1985), 47.

75. "Koloniaal Verslag van 1892," 23, 347, 408, 420, 464.

76. 't Hoen, "De Eerste Arabische Hengsten op Soemba," *Tijdschrift voor het Binnenlandsch Bestuur* 38 (1910): 100–113; Colijn, *Neerlands-Indië Land en Volk*, 183; J. D. Daubanton, *Beknopte Beschrijving van de Batikindustrie op Java: Haar Ontstaan en Ontwikkeling, Bewerking der Goederen, Gebruikte Materialen en voorthrengselen* (Rotterdam: J. D. Daubanton, 1922), 2, 13.

77. Van Hoevell, *Parlementaire Redevoeringen over Koloniale Belangen, Volume 1*, 64; "De Hervorming der Molukken," *TNI* 2, no. 1 (1868): 131.

78. *Nederlandsch-Indische Plakaatboek, 1602–1811*, 17 (1900): 653; Jacobus Marinus Vos, *Neêrlands Daden in Oost en West* (Amsterdam: Elsevier, 1905), 131.

79. Engelbertus de Waal, *Onze Indische Financien* (The Hague: Martinus Nijhoff, 1907), 139.

80. Van der Linden, *Banda and zijn Bewoners*, 39–40; Levinus Wilhelmus Christiaan Keuchenius, *Handelingen der Regering en der Staten-Generaal betreffende het Reglement op*

het Beleid der Regering van Nederlandsch Indië deel 2 (Utrecht: Kemink & Zoon, 1857), 170, 457; *Bijlagen van het Verslag der Handelingen, Tweede Kamer (1853–54)*: 676; *Bijlagen van het Verslag der Handelingen, Tweede Kamer* (1861–62): 497.

81. Audrey Kahin, *Historical Dictionary of Indonesia* (Lanham: Rowman and Littlefield, 2015), 432.

82. "Netherlands India—Slave-Dealing," *ST,* October 24, 1896, 3.

83. The Dutch only gained control of the island of Lombok in 1894. "De Mail uit Oost-Indie," *Haagsche Courant,* October 2, 1889; "Atrocities in the Malay Archipelago," *Evening Post* 39 (133), June 7, 1890, 1.

84. De Groot van Kraaijenburg, *Over Het Beheer Onzer Koloniën,* 244; J. F. D. Engelhard, "De Bataviasche Ommelanden en de Landbouw," *Tijdschrift voor nijverheid en landbouw in Nederlandsch-Indie* 27 (1883): 116.

85. "De Wetgeving Voor Oostersche Vreemdelingen in Nederlandsch-Indie," *TNI* 4, no. 1 (1870): 193–99.

86. For example, more Arabs had been allowed to live in Makassar and Lombok than Chinese. *Jaarverslag Kamer van Koophandel en Nijverheid te Makassar (1896)* (Makassar: J. C. Verdouw, 1897), 19–20, 46.

87. "Circulaire van de Directeur van Justitie van Januari 1903 no. 866 niet van toepassing op Arabieren, Bengaleezen en Mooren," in *Politieklapper voor Java en Madoera,* 140.

88. D. Fock, "Decentralisatie in Nederlandsch-Indië," *IG* 22, no. 1 (1900): 160; Gerhart D. Willinck, De Indiën En De Nieuwe Grondwet: Proeve Tot Vaststelling Van Normale Staatsrechtlijke Verhoudingen Tusschen Het Moederland En De Koloniën (Zutphen: P. van Belkum, 1910), 13.

89. Justus, *Wettelijke regeling van den Rechtoestand der Inlandsche Christenen als Hoofdzaak* (Batavia: H. M. van Dorp & Co. 1905), 40.

90. J. J. M de Groot, "Een en ander over de beschouwingen van den heer Perelaer omtrent de Chinezen," *IG* 8, no. 1 (1886): 121.

91. NA 2.05.03 file 452, Alexander Idenburg, Minister of Colonies, The Hague to Minister of Foreign Affairs, The Hague, November 27, 1908.

92. "Arabieren," *Encyclopaedie van Nederlandsch-Indië, Eerste Deel,* 39.

93. "Het handelsblad betoogende dat de Javaan naar verhouding niet te zwaar belast wordt," *IG* 22, no. 1 (1900): 522.

94. "Het Woekeren," *De Sumatra Post,* September 7, 1909, 4.

95. "Arabieren," *Encyclopaedie van Nederlandsch-Indië, Eerste Deel,* 39.

96. "Arabieren en de Kleine man," *Rotterdamsch Nieuwsblad,* January 20, 1908, 3.

97. M. J. Wiessing, "De Chinezen in Nederlandsch-Indie," *De Tijdspiegel* 63 (1906): 387.

98. Edgar du Perron, *Verzameld Werk, deel 3* (Amsterdam: Van Oorschot, 1954), 52–53.

99. "Arabieren," *Encyclopaedie van Nederlandsch-Indië, Eerste Deel,* 40.

100. De Hollander, *Handleiding bij de Beoepening der Land,* 60.

101. Pieter Philp van Bosse, "Sumatra's Westkust," *IG* 13, no. 1 (1891): 109.

102. W. H. Boogaardt, *Gedenkboek van den 12 1/2-jarigen Missiearbeid der Paters Minderbroeders-Capucijnen in Nederlandsch Oost-Indië* ('s-Hertogenbosch: C. N. Teulings, 1917), 39.

103. Mary Somers Heidhues, *Golddiggers, Farmers, and Traders in the "Chinese Districts" of West Kalimantan, Indonesia* (Ithaca: Cornell University Press, 2003), 28.

104. "No. 69. Belastingen. Vreemde Oosterlingen. Westerafdeeling van Borneo, 1 April 1886," *Staatsblad van Nederlandsch-Indië* (1886).

105. L. W. C. van den Berg alluded to the Siak ruler's Arab Sayyid lineage to prove his point that Arabs in the Indies were not likely to pay homage to the Ottoman sultan in 1900. L. W. C. van den Berg, "Het Pan-Islamisme," *De Gids: Nieuwe Vaderlansche Letteroeffeningen* 8, no. 4 (1900): 261; "Arabieren," *Encyclopaedie van Nederlandsch-Indië, Eerste Deel*, 39.

106. J. H. Moor, *Notices on the Indian Archipelago, and Adjacent Countries; Being a Collection of Papers Relating to Borneo, Celebes, Bali, Java, Sumatra, Nias, The Philippine Islands, Sulus, Siam, Cochin China, Malayan Peninsula, &c.* (Singapore: n.p, 1837), 16.

107. "Arabieren," *Encyclopaedie van Nederlandsch-Indië, Eerste Deel*, 39; Van den Berg, *Le Hadhramout*, 196.

108. See Mandal, "Finding Their Place," 16.

109. Van den Berg, *Le Hadhramout*, 224.

110. "Maandelijschke Revue van Brochures, Tijdschriften en Dagbladen," *IG* 2 (1879): 79; W. Huender, "Survey of the Economic Conditions of the Indigenous People of Java and Madura 1921," in *Selected Documents on Nationalism and Colonialism*, ed. Chr. L. M. Penders (St. Lucia: University of Queensland Press, 1977), 91, 97.

111. Partly this was because certain colonial concessions, such as opium farm concessions, were granted to the Chinese. Mandal, *Becoming Arab*, 42. For more on comparisons between Chinese and Arab Foreign Orientals, see Mandal, *Becoming Arab*, 51–52.

112. *Bijlagen van het Verslag der Handelingen, Tweede Kamer* (1861–62), 174.

113. L. W. C. van den Berg, "De invloeden welve van Mekka uit op de Musulmannen in den Nederlandsch-Indischen Archipel worde uitfeoefend," *IG* 11, no. 2 (1889): 1425–26; J. G. Schot, "Moslemen en Christenen—De bestrijding van den Islam," *De Indische Gids* 11, no. 2 (1889): 1548–49; Colijn, *Neerlands-Indië Land en Volk*, 269; Ch. W. Margandant, "Article 109 van het Regeerings-Reglement voor Nederlandsch-Indië," *HRNI* 56 (1891): 15, 26, 27.

114. NA 2.5.03 inventarisnummer 452, Department van Koloniën to Minister van Buitenlandse Zaken, November 27, 1908.

115. Van den Berg, "Het Pan-Islamisme," 421, 430.

116. Van den Berg, "Het Pan-Islamisme," 261, 431.

117. "Bijblad No. 6903—Vreemde oosterlingen. Terugzending. Regelen in achtte nemen bij de terugzending van uit N. I. verwijderde vreemde ouderlingen," in *Politieklapper voor Java en Madoera*, 111–12.

118. "Vestiging. Arabieren. Toelatingskanrt. Bepaling omtrent het verstrekken van een toelating: kuurt aan Arabieren. Circulaire Van den 1sten Gouvernements Secretaris. No. 2945. Buitenzorg, 28 December 1897," in *Politieklapper voor Java en Madoera*, 137–38.

119. Emiel Hullebroeck, *Insulinde: Reisdrukken* (Leiden: Vlaamsche Boekenhalle, 1917), 135; J. Rottier, "Het toekomstig onderwijs in Nederlands-Indië," *IG* 39, no. 2 (1917): 1047; E. H. Röttger, *Berigten Omtrent Indië, Gedurende Een Tienjarig Verblijf Aldaar* (Deventer: M. Ballot, 1846), 21–22.

120. KITLV Inventaris PK-1951-P-101, Etching by Willem Witsen "Het huis van de Arabier met een grote boom ervoor, Buitenzorg," circa 1921.

121. Europeans tended to stay temporarily in Batavia and therefore did not own houses there. Colijn, *Neerlands-Indië Land en Volk*, 269.

122. Blink, *Nederlandsch Oost-en West-Indië*, 342; "Palembang," *Encyclopaedie van Nederlandsch-Indië, Derde Deel* (The Hague: Martinus Nijhoff—E. J. Brill, 1905), 182.

123. Paul A. Daum, *Ups and Downs of Life in the Indies*, trans. Elsje Q. Sturtevant and Donald W. Sturtevant (Amherst: University of Massachusetts Press, 1987), 58.

124. Wagenvoort, *Nederlandsch-indische Menschen En Dingen*, 66.

125. No. 6 of the Articles 4 and 2 of the two Algemeene Criminal Police Regulations, *Staatsblad 1872* Nos. 110 and 111.

126. "Arabieren," *Encyclopaedie van Nederlandsch-Indië, Eerste deel*, 40.

127. Justus van Maurik, *Indrukken van een Tòtòk* (Amsterdam: Van Hoeve, 1897), 43.

128. P. A. Daum, *Aboe Bakar* (Batavia: G. Kolff, 1894), 7.

129. "Politiestrafreglementen," *De Indo-Nederlandsche Wetgeving – Staatsbladen van Nederlandsch-Indië* 12 (1902): 717; "Circulaire aan de hoofden van Gewestelijk Bestuur. No. 2587. Batavia, 7 November 1881," in *Politieklapper voor Java en Madoera*, 17–20.

130. C. P. K. Winkel, "Over den Rechtoestand ter Hoofdplaats Palembang," *Tijdschrift voor Nederlandsch-Indië* 4, no. 2 (1870): 346.

131. *Bijlagen van het verslag der handelingen, Tweede Kamer (1861–1862)*, 363.

132. For example, the import trade of Ambon was said to be completely controlled by Arabs. "De Hervorming der Molukken," *TNI* 2, no. 1 (1868): 150; C. P. K. Winkel, "Over den Rechtoestand ter Hoofdplaats Palembang," 346; Colijn, *Neerlands-Indië Land en Volk*, 48.

133. Cornelis van Vollenhoven, *Het Adatrecht van Nederlandsch-Indië* (Leiden: Brill, 1931) 50.

134. Hooker, *Islamic Law in South-East Asia*, 255.

135. For example, the age of majority for Muslim Natives was the same as it was for Foreign Orientals, which precluded the need for an extra set of laws. In parts of the Netherlands Indies such as Riau, Arabs shared same adat as local inhabitants. KITLV Inventaris 27 H 797 Collectie Kern, No. 258 Rudolf Aernoud Kern to Governor-General, Stukken over kinderhuwelijken op Java en Sumatra, 1921–1923 August 9, 1921; KITLV Inventaris 27 H 797 Collectie Kern, No. 210, Sjarif Al Wahidin to Controleur of Poelau Toedjoeh te Terempa, August 18, 1920.

136. This was the case for the Russian empire just before the Russian Revolution in 1917. Charles Steinwedel, "Identification of Individuals," in *Documenting Individual Identity: The Development of State Practices in the Modern World*, ed. Jane Caplan and John Torpey (Princeton, NJ: Princeton University Press, 2001), 82.

4. Legal Incompetence

1. "Plaatselijk Nieuws," *Bataviaasch Handelsblad*, February 27, 1891, 3.

2. Justus M. Van der Kroef, "The Indonesian Arabs," *Civilisations* 5, no. 1 (1955): 15

3. A. J. Immink, *Atoeran Hoekoem atas Negri dan Bangsa Tjina dan Bangsa Arab dan lain-lain sebagienja di Tanah Hindia-Nederland* (Batavia: Oiej Tjaij Hin, 1910), 25.

4. "Hier en daar," *Preanger Bode*, June 1, 1907, 1.

5. "Van Langen Adem," *Preanger Bode*, May 22, 1908, 2.

6. Untitled, *Soerabaijasch Handelsblad* 3, no. 2 (August 7, 1934): 2.

7. Freitag, *Indian Ocean Migrants and State Formation in Ḥaḍramawt*, 79–88. For more on Ottoman rule over the entire state of Yemen, see Thomas Kuehn, *Empire, Islam and Politics of Difference* (Leiden: Brill, 2011).

8. Snouck to Governor-General, Batavia, April 19, 1904, *Ambtelijke Adviezen 1889–1936, Eerste Deel* ('s Gravenhage: Martinus Nijhoff, 1957), 673–77.

9. Freitag, *Indian Ocean Migrants and State Formation in Ḥaḍramawt*, 210.

10. Snouck to Governor-General, Batavia, July 12, 1893, *Ambtelijke Adviezen 1889–1936, Tweede Deel* ('s Gravenhage: Martinus Nijhoff, 1957), 1525.

11. Jan Schmidt, *Through the Legation Window, 1876–1926: Four Essays on Dutch, Dutch-Indian, and Ottoman History* (Istanbul: Nederlands Historisch-Arhaeologisch Instituut Te Istanbul, 1992), 1986.

12. The Orphan Chamber functioned as custodians of the property of orphaned minors, ascertained the value of the property, and granted appointed guardians wages if necessary.

13. See Cees Fasseur, "Cornerstone and Stumbling Block: Racial Classification and the Late Colonial State in Indonesia," in *The Late Colonial State in Indonesia: Political and Economic Foundations of the Netherlands Indies 1880–1942*, ed. Robert Cribb (Leiden: KITLV Press, 1994), 37. Also see R. A. Eckhout, "Het Erfregt van Chineezen in Nederlandsch-Indie," *HRNI* 19 (1862): 133-54.

14. Jacques van Doorn, *A Divided Society—Segmentation and Mediation in Late-Colonial Indonesia* (Rotterdam: CASP, 1983), 1; Daniel S. Lev, "The Origins of Indonesia Advocacy," in *Legal Evolution and Political Authority in Indonesia, Selected Essays* (The Hague: Kluwer Law international, 2000), 249.

15. Daniel S. Lev, "Judicial Institutions and Legal Culture in Indonesia," in *Culture and Politics in Indonesia*, ed. Claire Holt (Ithaca, NY: Cornell University Press, 1972), 252–53.

16. The idea of standardizing bookkeeping practices was floated in 1876, especially after an Arab merchant's books were brought to civil court as evidence. "Vraagpunten, Mededeelingen en Bemerkingen van Verschillenden Aard, Betreffende Nederlandsch-Indisch Regt," *HRNI* 27 (1876): 99–100.

17. Indo-Europeans of mixed Native and Dutch descent who possessed European legal status often borrowed heavily from Chinese and Arab moneylenders to maintain their prestige. W. F. Wertheim, *Indonesian Society in Transition—A Study of Social Change* (The Hague: W. Van Hoeve, 1964), 175; Supomo and Djokosutono, *Sedjarah Politik Hukum Adat, Djilid 2, 36*.

18. Cornelis van Vollenhoven, *Van Vollenhoven on Indonesian Adat Law* (The Hague: Martinus Nijjoff, 1981), 205, 244.

19. Sech Said bin Hassan Bilhofaij Attamimie contra Said Mohamed bin Saffie Alhabsij, *HRNI* 30 (1977): 47.

20. J. S. Thieme, "Over priesterrechtspraak in verband met mr. B. Ter Haar's verhandeling," *ITVHR* 113 (1917): 386; R. Supomo and R. Djokosutono, *Sedjarah Politik Hukum Adat, Djilid 1* (Jakarta: Penerbit Djambatan, 1950), 88; Supomo and Djokosutono, *Sedjarah Politik Hukum Adat, Djilid 2, 23*; Van Vollenhoven, "The Elements of Adat Law," in *Van Vollenhoven on Indonesian Adat Law*, 19.

21. "Koloniaal Literatuur: Critische Overzichten," *IG* 1 (1880): 649; Fokkens, *Bescheiden Wenken voor de Verbetering van den Economischen Toestand der Inlandsche Bevolking op Java en Daar*, 23–24; Wertheim, *Indonesian Society in Transition—A Study of Social Change*, 95.

22. R. W. J. C. Bake, "Hoe Moet Art. 160 van de Regtspleging in Burgerlijke Zaken onder de Inlanders, Verstaan Worden? (1)," *HRNI* 2 (1849): 243.

23. Only one or two were given posts at higher courts. According to Daniel Lev, only two or three dozen local advocates established themselves as lawyers in colonial courts during the late colonial period throughout the Netherlands Indies. This is not

surprising since the first law school for Indonesians was only opened in 1909. A full course law faculty was established in Batavia in 1924. D. Lev, "Judicial Institutions and Legal Culture in Indonesia," 256, 262; Fasseur, "Cornerstone and Stumbling Block," 34.

24. "Zuiver-Chineesch—en –Mohamedaansch-recht contra Indo-Chineesche en Inlandsche Adat," *HRNI* 82 (1904): 403–22; "Vragenbus," *HRNI* 101 (1913): 242–47.

25. Said Mohamad bin Hoesin Alhabsi contra Regeering van N.I., *ITVHR* 78 (1884): 26.

26. The exact date of his death is unknown but it was during the British occupation of Java from 1811 to 1815 under Lieutenant-Governor Thomas Stamford Raffles.

27. For more on legal administration of Java under British rule from 1811 to 1815, see Supomo and Djokosutono, *Sedjarah Politik Hukum Adat, Djilid 1*, 67–88.

28. It is telling that the piece of land was never even referred to as "property" (or *eigendom* in Dutch) in the law report.

29. Cees Fasseur, "Colonial Dilemma: Van Vollehoven and the Struggle between *adat* and Western Law in Indonesia," in *The Revival of Tradition in Indonesian Politics: The Deployment of Adat from Colonialism to Indigenism*, ed. Jamie Seth Davidson and David Henley (New York: Routledge, 2007), 53.

30. Said Mohamad bin Hoesin Alhabsi contra Regeering van N.I.

31. Snouck to Governor-General, Weltevreden, September 8, 1890, *Ambtelijke Adviezen, Tweede Deel*, 910–14.

32. "De wees—en boedelkamer te Semarang, eerst gedaagde, later appellant tegen den Arabier Sech Achmat Ben Mohamad Ben Hamid," *HRNI* 5 (1851): 131–40.

33. "Priesterraden," *Soerabaiash Handelsblad*, July 29, 1881, 2.

34. Snouck to Resident of the Southern and Eastern division of Borneo, December 13, 1902; Snouck to Resident van Palembang, November 20, 1905, *Ambtelijke Adviezen, Tweede Deel*, 987–88.

35. In this case, the priesterraden had wrongfully dissolved a marriage by neglecting to investigate whether a husband had truly abandoned his wife. Snouck to General Secretariat, June 30, 1901, *Ambtelijke Adviezen, Tweede Deel*, 977.

36. Snouck to Governor-General, Batavia, April 19, 1904, *Ambtelijke Adviezen, Eerste Deel*, 687.

37. L. W. C. van den Berg, "Mohamedaansch Recht en Adat," *HRNI* 43 (1884): 137–55.

38. J. J. Velde, *De Godsdienstige Rechtspraak in Nederlandsch-Indie, Staatsrechtelijk Beschoud* (Leiden: Drukkerij A. Vros, 1928), 52.

39. Snouck to Resident of Surabaya, December 24, 1900; Snouck to Governor-General, November 23, 1905, *Ambtelijke Adviezen, Tweede Deel*, 908–9, 914–15.

40. Assaf Likhovski, *Law and Identity in Mandate Palestine* (Chapel Hill: University of North Carolina Press, 2006), 43–44.

41. Snouck to Governor-General, Weltevreden, September 8, 1890, *Ambtelijke Adviezen, Tweede Deel*, 910–14.

42. In one case involving Batak adat in Tapanoeli northern Sumatra, the qadi who solemnized a marriage between two Batak spouses from the same clan, permissible under Islamic law, was found guilty of committing a crime (*soembang*, or *delictenrecht*) according to adatrecht. Case of Chatib Borohom, *ITVHR* 154 (1934): 217.

43. Snouck to Governor-General, November 23, 1905, *Ambtelijke Adviezen, Tweede Deel*, 914–15.

44. Part of the priesterraden's duties included counseling troubled spouses.

45. W.v.K, "Arabieren op Java," *De Locomotief,* January 28, 1903, 1.

46. Snouck to Governor-General, Batavia, April 19, 1904, *Ambtelijke Adviezen, Eerste Deel,* 687.

47. KITLV Inventaris-27 H 797 Collectie Kern, No. 210, Bertram Johannes Otto Schrieke to Director of Justice to Governor-General of Netherlands Indies and Director of Civil Service, November 17, 1920.

48. Fasseur, "Cornerstone and Stumbling Block," 34.

49. Harry J. Benda, *The Crescent and the Rising Sun* (The Hague: W. Van Hoeve, 1958), 24.

50. Velde, *De Godsdienstige Rechtspraak in Nederlandsch-Indie,* 13.

51. J. Roorda, "Landraad te Batavia, Voorz," *ITVHR* 149 (1939): 153, 299–306.

52. Snouck to Directeur van Onderwijs, February 26, 1900; Snouck to Gouvernments-Secretaris, November 26, 1891; "Het Atjeh Verslag," *Ambtelijke Adviezen, Eerste Deel,* 20, 21, 55.

53. Benda, *The Crescent and the Rising Sun,* 22.

54. KITLV, DH 1083 No. 10, Mohammedansch Onderwijs, Collectie Hazeu, D.A. Rinkes to Directeur van Justitie te Weltevreden, July 12, 1912.

55. KITLV, DH 1083, No. 8, Statement No. 30 Appendices, Collectie Hazeu, G.A.J. Hazeu to Governor-General of Dutch East Indies, Weltevreden, February 13, 1910.

56. Snouck to Governor-General, Batavia, April 19, 1904, 686–87. For some, such as Pangeran Wiro Kusomo, whose real name was Said Idrus Aljufri and who became prominent in Jambi in 1860s, local titles such as Pangeran obscured their origin. Elsbeth Locher-Scholten, *Sumatran Sultanate and Colonial State: Jambi and the Rise of Dutch Imperialism, 1830–1907* (Ithaca, NY: Southeast Asia Program Publications, Cornell University Press, 2003), 136, 139, 140.

57. The Chinese population too was classified under two categories—"pure" Chinese (*Zuiver-Chineesch*) and Indo-Chinese (*Indo-Chineesch*). KITLV, DH 1083, No. 8, Statement No. 30 Appendices, Collectie Hazeu, G.A.J. Hazeu to Governor-General of Dutch East Indies, Weltevreden, February 13, 1910.

58. The publication of original Arabic in the same volume suggested that it was also meant for anyone who understood Arabic, as pointed out by Snouck in his review of the translation. In keeping with the comparative legal interests of Dutch colonial officials, under each subject heading, Van den Berg appended the corresponding Code Napoléon where applicable. Christiaan Snouck Hurgronje, "Minhādj at-tālibin, Le guide des zéles croyants," *IG* 5 (April 1883): 7.

59. "Die Arabier in Ostindischen Archipel," *Österreichische Monatsschrift für den Orient,* 13 (1887): 119.

60. To help with his translation, he consulted dictionaries and glossaries produced by Reinhart Dozy as well as A. W. T. Juynboll and consulted personally with Michael de Goeje, an Arabic professor in Leiden, on the intricacies of translating from Arabic to French. L. W. C. van den Berg, *Minhadj At-Talibin—Le Guide des Zeles Croyants: Manuel de Jurisprudence Musulmane Selon Le Rite de Chafi'i* (Batavia: Imprimerie du Gouvernement, 1882), xii.

61. J. Brugman, "Snouck Hurgronje's Study of Islamic Law," in *Leiden Oriental Connections,* ed. William Otterspeer (Leiden: E. J. Brill, 1989), 84.

6? Untitled, *TNI* 16, no. 1 (1887): 429.

63. Nico J. G. Kaptein, "The Sayyid and the Queen: Sayyid Uthmān on Queen Wilhemina's Inauguration on the Throne of the Netherlands in 1898," *Journal of Islamic Studies* 9, no. 2 (July 1998): 158–77.

64. Azymardi Azra, "A Hadhrami Religious Scholar in Indonesia," in *Hadhrami Traders, Scholars and Statesmen in the Indian Ocean, 1750s-1960s*, ed. Ulrike Freitag and William G. Clarence-Smith (Leiden: Brill, 1997), 250–51.

65. Sayyid 'Uthmān first struck up a close friendship with a medical doctor, F. W. M. Hoogenstraaten. See Snouck to the Governor-General, March 26, 1889, *Ambtelijke Adviezen, Tweede Deel*, 1515.

66. While Sayyid 'Uthmān was averse to codification because he considered it ill suited to classical Islamic tradition, Snouck was more concerned that since Islamic law was mixed with adat and the combination was constantly changing, codification would be impractical. Christiaan Snouck Hurgronje, *Politique Musulmane de la Hollande: Quatre Conferences* (Paris: Leroux, 1911), 70, 86; also see Christiaan Snouck Hurgronje, "Advies over Codificatie van Adatrecht," in *Verspreide Geschriften van C. Snouck Hurgronje*, ed. A. J. Wensinck (Leipzig: K. Schroeder, 1923), 259–76.

67. Nico J. G. Kaptein, "Arabophobia and Tarekat: How Sayyid Uthmān Became Advisor to the Netherlands Colonial Administration," in *The Hadhrami Diaspora in Southeast Asia: Identity Maintenance or Assimilation*, ed. Ahmed Ibrahim Abushouk and Hassan Ahmed Ibrahim (Brill: Leiden, 2009), 37.

68. Kaptein, "Arabophobia and Tarekat," 42.

69. Snouck, "Een Arabische Bondgenoot der Nederlandsch-Indische Regeering," "Rapport over de Mohamedaansche Godsdienstige Rechtspraak," in *Verspreide Geschriften*, 78–79, 104; Snouck to Director of Education, June 20, 1889, *Ambtelijke Adviezen, Tweede Deel*, 1510.

70. Azra, "A Hadhrami Religious Scholar in Indonesia," 253.

71. Snouck to Governor-General, February 23, 1906, *Ambtelijke Adviezen, Eerste Deel*, 45; Snouck to Director of Education, June 20, 1889, *Ambtelijke Adviezen, Tweede Deel*, 1510–11.

72. Snouck, "Een Arabische Bondgenoot der Nederlandsch-Indische Regeering," 85.

73. Snouck to Resident of Palembang, October 23, 1904, in *Ambtelijke Adviezen, Tweede Deel*, 1178.

74. Daniel S. Lev, *Islamic Courts in Indonesia* (Berkeley: University of California Press, 1972), 17.

75. In writing to his Dutch superiors who were constantly suspicious of pan-Islamism, Snouck was prudent enough to always downplay Sayyid 'Uthmān's orthodox beliefs, emphasizing the latter's dislike of fanaticism instead. Snouck to Director of Education, April 5, 1891; Snouck to Director of Education, June 20, 1889; Snouck to Governor-General, October 7, 1900, *Ambtelijke Adviezen, Tweede Deel*, 1510–11. 1518.

76. Snouck to Governor of Sumatra, March 10, 1904, *Ambtelijke Adviezen, Tweede Deel*, 1520.

77. Hamid Algadri, *Dutch Policy against Islam and Indonesians of Arab Descent in Indonesia* (Jakarta: Pustaka, 1994), 82.

78. For example, Sheikh Omar Manggoesh (Manqush) criticized him in his own publications. Azra, "A Hadhrami Religious Scholar in Indonesia," 252. Snouck to

Resident of Batavia, March 30, 1900; Snouck to Governor-General, October 7, 1900, in *Ambtelijke Adviezen, Tweede Deel*, 1516, 1517.

79. Kaptein, "Arabophobia and Tarekat," 43.

80. Raden Hadji Mohamed Rosdi, a member of the priesterraad in Bandung, received an excellent education in Arabia that made him qualified to be a judge in Snouck's estimation. Snouck to Civiel en Militair Gouverneur van Atjeh en Onderhoorigheden, te Koetaradja, November 23, 1895, *Ambtelijke Adviezen, Eerste Deel*, 135–36.

81. The prayer was read in mosques in Java during the sermon before Friday prayers. Kaptein, "The Sayyid and the Queen," 158–77.

82. Azra, "A Hadhrami Religious Scholar in Indonesia," 252.

83. Snouck to Governor-General, Batavia, July 12, 1893, *Ambtelijke Adviezen, Tweede Deel*, 1522–26.

84. The mother of the minor brothers and sisters in question was not the appointed guardian's own mother.

85. Van den Berg, "Mohamedaansch Recht en Adat," 150–55.

86. Snouck to Governor-General, December 4, 1893, *Ambtelijke Adviezen, Tweede Deel*, 1527.

87. Snouck to Governor-General, December 4, 1893, *Ambtelijke Adviezen, Tweede Deel*, 1527.

88. Van den Berg (and, earlier, D. Louter) had called Snouck out on account of his youth. See Christiaan Snouck Hurgronje, in *Verspreide Geschriften*, 59–221.

89. Although Snouck shared similar ideas on colonial administration in the Netherlands Indies with his rival, Van den Berg, their relationship remained strained. Snouck, "Minhādj at-tālibin, Le guide des zéles croyants," 1–14; "Quarterly Notes," *Law Magazine and Review: A Quarterly Review of Jurisprudence, and Quarterly Digest of All Reported Cases* 8, no. 3 (May 1883), 338–39. The library catalogue of the Royal Asiatic Society in 1884 indicated that the library had a copy in its possession. H. C. Rawlinson, "Royal Asiatic Society: Proceedings of the Sixty-First Anniversary Meeting of the Society, Held on the 19th of May, 1884," *Journal of the Royal Asiatic Society of Great Britain and Ireland, New Series* 16, no. 4 (October 1884): clvii.

90. "Een Antwoord van Dr. Snouck Hurgronje op een onbezonnen (?) Vraag," *IG* 22, no. 1 (January–June 1900): 236–37; "Een Antwoord van Dr. Snouck Hurgronje op een onbezonnen (?) Vraag," *IG* 23, no. 1 (1901): 569–70.

91. Kaptein, *Islam, Colonialism and the Modern Age*, 136.

92. Ch. W. Margadant, "Verkrachting in Kinderhuwelijk," *HRNI* 57 (1891): 7.

93. H. D. Canne, "Opmerkingen en Mededeelingen Aangaande Wet en Regt," *HRNI* 35 (1880): 64; Christiaan Snouck, *Sayyid Oethman's Gids Voor De Priesterraden* (Batavia: Van Dorp, 1895), 14–15.

94. Ho, *Graves of Tarim*, 173–81.

95. Azra, "A Hadhrami Religious Scholar in Indonesia," 256.

96. *Al-Manār* 8 (1905): 215–17, 580–88, 955–57.

97. *Notulen van de Algemeene en Directie-Vergaderingen* 57–58 (1919–20): 190.

98. Abdalla S. Bujra, *The Politics of Stratification—A Study of Political Change in a South Arabian Town* (Oxford: Clarendon Press, 1971), 95.

99. Farhat J. Ziadeh, "Equality (Kafāʾa) in the Muslim Law of Marriage," *American Journal of Comparative Law* 6, no. 4 (Autumn 1957): 515–16. Also see *Notulen van*

de algemeene en directie-vergaderingen 57–58 (1919–20): 190; *Revue du Monde Musulman* 43–46 (1921): 215–16; Natalie Mobini-Kesheh, *The Hadhrami Awakening: Community and Identity in the Netherlands East Indies, 1900–1942* (Ithaca, NY: Cornell Southeast Asia Program Publications, 1999), 53–55, 91–94; Mandal, "Challenging Inequality in a Modern Islamic Idiom," 156–75.

100. Ignaz Goldziher, *Muhammedanische Studien*, volumes 1 and 2 (Halle: Niemeyer, 1889), 132–33.

101. KITLV Inventaris 27 H 797 Collectie Kern, No. 210, Mas Soeparto to Post-holder in Sedanau, September 4, 1920.

102. The controller claimed that political rulers of indigenous and Arab descent took turns to rule the Riau islands. KITLV Inventaris 27 H 797 Collectie Kern, No. 210, Controller of Pulau Tujuh to Resident of Riau and Dependencies, September 20, 1929.

103. They were still referred to as such by inhabitants of Riau.

104. O. Spies, "Mahr," *Encyclopaedia of Islam, Second Edition*, ed. P. Bearman, Th. Bianquis, C. E. Bosworth, E. van Donzel, W. P. Heinrichs. accessed June 14, 2019, http://dx.doi.org/10.1163/1573-3912_islam_SIM_4806.

105. Martha Mundy and Richard Saumarez Smith, "'Al-Mahr Zaituna: Property and Family in the Hills Facing Palestine, 1880–1940," in *Family History in the Middle East: Household, Property, and Gender*, ed. Beshara Doumani (Albany: State University of New York Press, 2003), 119. For more on the discussion of the legal concept on mahr by Muslim jurists, see Mona Siddiqui, "Mahr: Legal Obligation or Rightful Demand," *Journal of Islamic Studies* 6, no. 1 (1995): 14–24; Homa Hoofdar, "In the Absence of Legal Equity: Mahr and Marriage Negotiation in Egyptian Low Income Communities," *Arab Studies Journal* 6/7, no. 2/1 (Fall 1998/Spring 1999): 98–111.

106. KITLV Inventaris 27 H 797 Collectie Kern, No. 210, Controleur of Pulau Tujuh to Resident of Riau and Dependencies, September 20, 1929.

107. In addition, Sjarif Al Wahidin warned Dutch colonial officials that forcing Arabs to drop their titles as a prerequisite for legal classification as Natives might be seen as an indication of Dutch hatred of Islam. However, this remark was not addressed by higher Dutch officials, who were more interested in the legal aspects of the question.

108. Snouck to Governor-General, Batavia, April 19, 1904, *Ambtelijke Adviezen, Eerste Deel*, 687.

109. Raden Sapardan tegen Sech Amir bin Mohamed Menbare, *ITVHR* 113 (1919): 169.

110. Sech Oemar bin Salim bin Soengkar contra Sech Badar bin Talib Alkateri, *ITVHR* 122 (1925): 566.

111. A case in 1869 determined that Foreign Orientals could never be legally equal to governors, regents, and under-regents. "Tweede Kamer: Appel," *De Locomotief,* July 5, 1869, 1.

112. "Landraad te Batavia, Voorz. Mr. J. Roorda" *ITVHR* 153 (1940): 299.

5. Constructing the Index of Arabs

1. FO 371/148/1, Sir Nicholas R O'Conor, the British Embassy in Constantinople to Edward Grey, Secretary of State for Foreign Affairs, February 27, 1906.

2. For more on Japan's courting of Muslims, see Michael F. Laffan, *Islamic Nationhood and Colonial Indonesia: The Umma Below the Winds* (Abingdon: Routledge, 2007),

34–135; Laffan, "Making Meiji Muslims: the Travelogue of 'Ali Ahmad al-Jarjāwī," *East Asian History* 22 (December 2001): 145–70; Laffan, "Tokyo as a Shared Mecca of Modernity: War Echoes in the Colonial Malay World," in *The Impact of the Russo-Japanese War*, ed. Rotem Kowner (London: Routledge, 2010), 219–38.

3. C. van Dijk, "Colonial Fears, 1890–1918: Pan-Islamism and the Germano-Indian Plot," in *Transcending Borders: Arabs, Politics, Trade and Islam in Southeast Asia*, ed. H. de Jonge and N. Kaptein (Leiden: KITLV, 2002), 56.

4. IOR/L/PS/10/524, Mark Sykes to A. H. Grant, August 21, 1915.

5. Holly Case, *The Age of Questions: A First Attempt at an Aggregate History of the Eastern, Social, Woman, American, Jewish, Polish, Bullion, Tuberculosis, and Many Other Questions Over the Nineteenth Century, and Beyond* (Princeton, NJ: Princeton University Press, 2018).

6. Case, *The Age of Questions*, 81.

7. NA 2.5.03 inventarisnummer 452, Christiaan Snouck Hurgronje, Leiden to Minister van Koloniën, February 1 1909.

8. IOR R/20/A/1409, "British fears for the future," undated.

9. IOR R/20/A/1409, W. H Lee-Warner, "The Arab Question," Batavia to the Under-Secretary of State, Foreign Office, July 14, 1919.

10. The historian Will Hanley demonstrates how nationality became the defining category of identification between 1880 and the First World War in Alexandria, which was part of the Ottoman Empire. Will Hanley, *Identifying with Nationality: Europeans, Ottomans, and Egyptians in Alexandria* (New York: Columbia University Press, 2017).

11. IOR R/20/A/1409, Memorandum on Sayed Ali bin Abu Bakar Al Jifri, undated; Report by Sayed Ali bin Abu Bakar Al Jifri, January 21, 1916.

12. British authorities observe that membership in the organization seems to have dwindled by 1916.

13. IOR R/20/A/1409, Circular from the Sultan of Shihr and Mukallā to W. H. Lee-Warner, April 10, 1920.

14. IOR R/20/A/1409, J. Crosby, Acting Consul-General, British Consulate Batavia to Political Resident, Aden, July 6, 1920.

15. Contrary to what its name implies, the Arab Bureau was in charge of all non-Indian Muslims in the British Empire.

16. Lee-Warner, "The Arab Question."

17. Lee-Warner, "The Arab Question."

18. The practice of transporting of Indian prisoners to the Malaya and the British Straits Settlements lasted until 1867. IOR/L/PJ/3/1075, "Alarm felt at Penang during the Mohurrum Festival," W. T. Lewis, Resident Councillor to India Office, August 25, 1855; Governor Edmund Blundell to India Office, September 2, 1857; Mervyn L. Wynne, *Triad and Tabut: A Survey of the Origin and Diffusion of Chinese and Mohamedan Secret Societies in the Malay Peninsula, AD 1800–1935* (Singapore: Government Printing Office, 1941), 176–200.

19. Wynne, *Triad and Tabut*, 252–53, 322. For more on the societies, see Khoo Salma Nasution, "Colonial Intervention and Transformation of Muslim Waqf Settlements in Urban Penang: The Role of the Endowments Board," *Journal of Muslim Minority Affairs* 22, no. 2 (2002): 299–315; Mahani Musa, "Malays and the Red and White Flag Societies in Penang, 1830s–1920s," *Journal of the Malaysian Branch of the Royal Asiatic Society* 72, no. 277 (1999): 151–82.

20. CO 273/505/46910, W. H. Lee-Warner, Singapore, to Under-Secretary of State for Foreign Office, July 15, 1920.

21. CO 323/720/21, General Officer Commanding Singapore to War Office, August 7, 1916.

22. Priya Satia, *Spies in Arabia: The Great War and the Cultural Foundations of Britain's Covert Empire in the Middle East* (Oxford: Oxford University Press, 2010), 9, 288.

23. See Nicholas Hiley, "Counter-Espionage and Security in Great Britain during the First World War," *English Historical Review* 101, no. 400 (July 1986): 635–70; John C. Curry, *The Security Service, 1908–1945: The Official History* (Kew: Public Record Office, 1999); Keith Jeffrey and Alan Sharp, "Lord Curzon and Secret Intelligence," in *Intelligence and International Relations, 1900–1945*, ed. Christopher Andrew and Jeremy Noakes (Exeter: University of Exeter, 1987), 103–26.

24. Geoffrey Hamm, "British Intelligence in the Middle East, 1898–1906," *Intelligence and National Security* 29, no. 6 (2014): 880–900; Ulrike Freitag, "Hadhramis in International Politics," in *Hadhrami Traders, Scholars and Statesmen in the Indian Ocean, 1750s-1960s*, ed. Ulrike Freitag and William G. Clarence-Smith (Leiden: Brill, 1997), 112–30.

25. For more on this, see Eugene L. Rogan, *Frontiers of the State in the Late Ottoman Empire: Transjordan, 1850–1921* (Cambridge: Cambridge University Press, 2004), 224–25.

26. CO 323/704/26, "Proclamation of the Grand Sheriff of Mecca," Telegram (paraphrased) from the Governor of the Straits Settlements to the Secretary of State for the Colonies, November 28, 1916.

27. CO 273/505/46910, W. H. Lee-Warner, Singapore, to Under-Secretary of State for Foreign Office, July 15, 1920.

28. Cemil Aydin, *The Idea of the Muslim World: A Global Intellectual History* (Cambridge, MA: Harvard University Press, 2017), 5.

29. NAS Accession no. 000189, Oral History Interview with Haji Mohd Javad Namazie, June 20, 1982.

30. Twenty-two men were executed at 5:30 pm on March 25, 1915, by a firing squad consisting of 110 members of the Singapore Volunteer Corps witnessed by a crowd of fifteen thousand. An Indian Muslim civilian was hanged for treason. There were fears that public executions would rile Muslim subjects. FCO 141/16530, Major A. M. Thompson, "Record of promulgation and execution of sentences of 45 mutineers of the 5th Light Infantry carried out at the criminal prison on 25/3/1915"; AHD, Imperial War Museum, A. H. Dickinson, "The Mutiny of the Fifth Light Infantry," undated, 19.

31. British officials stationed in Southeast Asia were right to feel under-served by the metropole in wartime. Marginalia in a letter received by the Treasury on the subject of compensation for victims of the mutiny indicated that military protection of the "local government" in the Straits Settlements was not equal with that of "His Majesty's Government," although compensation and pension was ultimately borne by the Treasury. T 1/11811/18876, Under Secretary of State to the Secretary of Treasury, May 6, 1915.

32. CO 273/421/17156, "Enclosure No. 2 in Straits Dispatch, No. 89 of 11th March 1915—Extract from the 'Malaya Tribune' of Monday March 8, 1915: Moslem Mass Meeting—Address of Loyalty to the King."

33. In 1897, another member of the Alsagoff family, Syed Abdulkadir bin Abdul-rahman Alsagoff, sent a memorial to Queen Victoria on her jubilee (celebrating the sixtieth year of her rule) on behalf of "the Mohamedan community." PP 1/647/27, Mohammedan residents of Kampong Glam, Singapore: address to Queen Victoria on her Diamond Jubilee, June 2, 1897.

34. CO 273/421/17169, Letter sent to Arthur Young, Governor and Commander-in-Chief, Straits Settlements, March 10, 1915.

35. CO 273/421/17169, "Moslems in Singapore: Attitude towards the Government," Arthur Young, Singapore, to Lewis Harcourt, Colonial Office, London, March 11, 1915.

36. CO 273/420/11567, The Governor of the Straits Settlements to the Secretary of State for the Colonies, March 10, 1915.

37. "Moslems in Singapore: Attitude towards the Government," March 11, 1915.

38. "Moslems in Singapore: Attitude towards the Government," March 11, 1915.

39. The previous iteration of the deed in 1879 appointed five trustees. Deed for the new board of Trustees of Sultan Mosque, October 31, 1914.

40. "Prince of Wales War Relief Fund," SFPMA, March 18, 1915, 10; J. E. Nathan, The Census of British Malaya (London: Waterlow and Sons Limited, 1922), 29, 92.

41. CO 323/720/21, General Officer Commanding, Singapore, to War Office, August 7, 1916.

42. IOR R/20/A/1409, W. H. Lee-Warner, Mokalla, to General Officer Commanding Singapore, March 4, 1919.

43. Hadhrami politics has been explored in rich detail by Linda Boxberger. Boxberger, On the Edge of Empire.

44. IOR/20/A/1412, W. N. Dunn, British Consulate-General in Batavia, to Governor of Singapore and General Officer Commanding Troops in Singapore, March 14, 1920.

45. In order to get from Southeast Asia to Ḥaḍramawt, the country of origin of most of the Arabs named in the index, one had to sail to the port of Aden first.

46. IOR R/20/A/1409, Secret Despatch no. 117 "Index of Arabs," W. N. Dunn, British Consulate-General in Batavia, to A. J. Balfour, Foreign Office, London, September 27, 1919; IOR R/20/A/1409, W. N. Dunn, British Consulate General in Batavia, to A. J. Balfour, Foreign Office, London, July 10, 1919.

47. IOR R/20/A/1409, "Leading Kathiris who are pro-British and who are strongly discontented with the present Government of the Kathiris are the following Terim inhabitants," undated; IOR R/20/A/1409, "Another list of Arabs," undated; IOR R/20/A/1409, "The leading Kathiri opponents to the Kaiti," undated.

48. IOR R/20/A/1409, A. R. Chancellor, Inspector General of Police, Singapore, to Political Resident of Aden, January 7, 1919, February 14, 1919; W. H. Lee-Warner to General Ridout, Singapore, March 4, 1919; FO 371/5237, "Enclosure in Acting Consul-General Crosby No. 129 Secret—Notes," J. Crosby, British Consulate-General in Batavia, to Earl Curzon, Foreign Office, London, August 26, 1920; IOR R/20/A/1411, J. Crosby, British Consulate-General in Batavia, to the Political Resident Aden, January 10, 1921.

49. IOR R/20/A/1409, W. N. Dunn, British Consulate-General in Batavia, to Earl Curzon, Foreign Office, London, March 15, 1920.

50. IOR R/20/A/1409, c/o Arab Bureau Cairo to Stephen Gaselee, Foreign Office, London, December 3, 1918.

51. Lee-Warner, "The Arab Question."

52. IOR R/20/A/1409, "Secret no. 85," W. N. Dunn to A. J. Balfour, London, July 10, 1919.

53. FO 371/5236, "Confidential no. 42," W. N. Dunn, British Consulate-General in Batavia, to Earl Curzon, Foreign Office, London, March 16, 1920, 2.

54. IOR R/20/A/1409, Index of Arabs, W. N. Dunn, British Consulate-General in Batavia, to A. J. Balfour, Foreign Office, September 27, 1919.

55. IOR R/20/A/1409, J. Crosby, Acting British Consulate-General in Batavia, to Earl Curzon, Foreign Office, London, December 8, 1920.

56. IOR R/20/A/1409, 'Index of Arabs', W. N. Dunn, British Consulate-General in Batavia, to A. J. Balfour, Foreign Office, September 27, 1919.

57. IOR R/20/A/1409, W. N. Dunn, British Consulate-General in Batavia, to Earl Curzon, Foreign Office, London, March 15, 1920.

58. CO 273/505, W. H. Lee-Warner, Singapore to Under Secretary of State, Foreign Office, London, July 11, 1920; FO 371/5236, "Memorandum (A)," W. H. Lee-Warner, Singapore, to the Under-Secretary of State, Foreign Office, London, July 15, 1920.

59. CO 273/505/46910, Memorandum by W. H. Lee-Warner, Singapore, to Under-Secretary of State for Foreign Office, July 15, 1920; IOR/R/20/A/3297, "LNS," Bombay to The Political Resident, Aden, January 16, 1921.

60. Bin Agil's wife was also wealthy, having inherited considerable immoveable properties.

61. IOR/R/20/A/3297, "LNS," Bombay to the Political Resident, Aden, January 16, 1921.

62. CO 273/505/46910, Memorandum by W. H. Lee-Warner, Singapore, to Under-Secretary of State for Foreign Office, July 15, 1920.

63. FO 371/5236, "Memorandum B—An Educational and Propagandist Submission in Regard to Java," W. H. Lee-Warner, Singapore, to the Under-Secretary of State, Foreign Office, London, July 15, 1920.

64. Things did not go smoothly for Bin Agil, who claimed he had been unjustly imprisoned for three and a half years under orders of Sultan Omar of Mukallā in 1929. He was also ordered to pay Rs. 50,000. Bin Agil requested help from the British government, which was not prepared to interfere in the administration of justice in the state of Mukallā as the terms of the existing treaty between the British government and the sultan of Shihr and Mukallā did not extend to jurisdiction in the internal affairs of Mukallā. For more on this matter, see IOR/R/20/A/3297, File no.: 620 of 192, Subject: Ḥaḍramawt Re: Sayed Muhammad bin Omer ba Agil, undated.

65. This was Lee-Warner's second attempt in trying to convince the Foreign Office that such a mission was indeed beneficial to the British Empire. CO 273/505, W. H. Lee-Warner, Singapore, to Under Secretary of State, Foreign Office, London, July 11, 1920.

66. FO 371/5237, "Notes on Caliphate Propaganda by 'D,' " August 3, 1920.

67. CO 273/505/46910, Memorandum by W. H. Lee-Warner, Singapore, to Under-Secretary of State for Foreign Office, July 15, 1920.

68. Natalie Mobini-Kesheh, "Islamic Modernism in Colonial Java: The Al-Irshād Movement," in Hadhrami Traders, Scholars and Statesmen in the Indian Ocean, 1750s-1960s, ed. Ulrike Freitag and William G. Clarence-Smith (Leiden: Brill, 1997), 231–39.

69. IOR R/20/A/1409, Secret Despatch no. 117 "Index of Arabs," W. N. Dunn, British Consul-General in Batavia, to A. J. Balfour, FO, September 27, 1919; IOR

R/20/A/1409, W. N. Dunn, British Consulate General in Batavia, Java to A. J. Balfour, Foreign Office, London, July 10, 1919.

70. Lee-Warner, "The Arab Question."

71. Alsagoff's request to be the Turkish Consul three years later was denied by the British government, however, because he was deemed "too influential a Mahometan" and British authorities did not want to strain relations with the Dutch. FCO 141/15806, Frederik s'Jacob, Governor-General of Netherlands Indies, Buitenzorg, to Governor and Commander-in-chief of the Straits Settlements, Singapore, September 25, 1881; Letter to W. H. Read, April 5, 1884.

72. FO 371/5237, "Enclosure No. 1 in Acting Consul-General Crosby's Secret No. 128 of 27/8/1920: Secret Memorandum regarding travel by Arabs from Java to Ḥaḍramawt," J. Crosby, British Consulate General in Batavia, Java, to Earl Curzon, Foreign Office, London, August 26, 1920.

73. This was after travel documents were denied to Al-Irshad supporters who wished to return to their homeland, creating hardship for them and their families. Boxberger, *On the Edge of Empire,* 61.

74. FO 371/5237, "Secret no. 127," J. Crosby, British Consulate General in Batavia, Java, to Earl Curzon, Foreign Office, London, August 26, 1920.

75. FO 371/5237, "Enclosure No. 1 in Acting Consul-General Crosby's Secret No. 128 of 27/8/1920: Secret Memorandum regarding travel by Arabs from Java to Ḥaḍramawt," J. Crosby, British Consulate General in Batavia, Java, to Earl Curzon, Foreign Office, London August 26, 1920.

76. "Enclosure No. 1: Secret Memorandum regarding travel by Arabs from Java to Ḥaḍramawt," August 26, 1920.

77. IOR R/20/A/1411, "Enclosure No. 1 in Acting Consul-General Crosby's No. 150 Very Secret of Sept 27th 1920," J. Crosby, British Consulate-General of Batavia, to Earl Curzon, FO, London, August 27, 1920.

78. CO 273/505, J. Crosby, Acting Consul-General, Batavia, to Earl Curzon, Foreign Office London, August 20, 1920.

79. FO 371/5237, Confidential no. 174: Notes regarding Arab Matters, J. Crosby, British Consulate-General, Batavia, to Earl Curzon, Foreign Office, London, October 21, 1920.

80. CO 273/505, B. O. Schrieke, Weltevreden, Java, to T. W. Arnold, July 20, 1920.

81. Jeffrey and Sharp, "Lord Curzon and Secret Intelligence," 106; Yigal Sheffy, "British Intelligence and the Middle East, 1900–1918: How Much Do We Know?," *Intelligence and National Security* 17, no. 1 (March 2002): 33–52.

82. Satia, *Spies in Arabia,* 25.

83. IOR R/20/A/1409, W. H. Lee-Warner to Foreign Office, January 4, 1919.

84. Lee-Warner to Foreign Office, January 4, 1919.

85. Lee-Warner to Foreign Office, January 4, 1919.

86. IOR/R/20/A/1412, Confidential No. 42, W. N. Dunn to Colonial Office, London, March 16, 1920.

87. CO 273/505/51362, Memorandum by B. O. Schrieke, September 19, 1920.

88. CO 273/505/40703, J. Crosby, British Consulate at Batavia, to Earl Curzon, Foreign Office, July 8, 1920.

89. An Arab Sayyid in Java named Said Mohamed Shawashi had also been tasked with attracting British Indians to the cause. IOR/L/PS/10/629, W. R. D. Beckett, British Consulate General at Batavia, to Foreign Office, September 6, 1917.

90. IOR R/20/A/1409, Report by Sayed Ali bin Abu Bakar Al Jifri, January 21, 1916. Mandal, *Becoming Arab,* 145, 155, 156, 168, 170, 171,

91. IOR/L/PS/10/629, W. R. D. Beckett, British Consulate-General in Batavia, to Foreign Office, September 6, 1917.

92. Lee-Warner, "The Arab Question."

93. IOR R/20/A/1409, Political Resident of Aden to Earl Curzon, Foreign Office, London, January 6, 1921.

94. Ironically, the fact that Aden was a British Protectorate contributed to the Dutch decision not to place Arabs in Java in internment camps since they trusted that British authorities would handle them. Van Dijk, "Colonial Fears, 1890–1918," 89.

95. IOR/L/PS/10/629, W. R. D. Beckett, British Consulate General at Batavia, to Foreign Office, September 6, 1917.

96. IOR R/20/A/1409, W. N. Dunn, British Consul-General in Batavia, to Earl Curzon, Foreign Office, London, March 15, 1920.

97. Dunn to Curzon, March 15, 1920.

98. Lee-Warner, "The Arab Question."

99. On the eve of the Japanese occupation, the spy for the Japanese was Mohamed bin Aboebakar Alatas, the Arab censor at the post office in Batavia who had a secret office within the British Consulate as the advisor of Arab affairs to the British consul-general. N.A. 2.10.17, "Note: Mohamed bin Aboebakar Alatas" November 26, 1941.

100. IOR/R/20/A/1412, J. Crosby, Consulate-General, Batavia, to Austin Chamberlain, War Office London, April 11, 1918.

6. Compromises

1. Katherine Pistor, *The Code of Capital: How the Law Creates Wealth and Inequality* (Princeton, NJ: Princeton University Press, 2019), 42, 56.

2. Thomas Blom Hansen, "Sovereigns beyond the State: On Legality and Authority in Urban India," in *Sovereign Bodies: Citizens, Migrants, and States in the Postcolonial World*, eds. Thomas Blom Hansen and Finn Stepputat (Princeton, NJ: Princeton University Press, 2005), 169.

3. The institution of the waqf, also known as *hubs*, is not mentioned in the Qur'an but is alluded to in several hadiths attributed to the Prophet. Peter Hennigan, *The Birth of a Legal Institution: The Formation of the Waqf in Third-Century A.H. Ḥanafī Legal Discourse* (Leiden: Brill, 2004), xiii; Timur Kuran, "The Provision of Public Goods Under Islamic Law: Origins, Impact and Limitations of the *Waqf* System," *Law and Society Review* 35, no. 4 (2001): 841. Other religious groups too established waqfs, especially in the Ottoman Empire. For example, see Aharon Layish, "The Druze Testamentary Waqf," *Studia Islamica* 71 (1990): 127–54; Ron Shaham, "Christian and Jewish Waqfs in Palestine during the Ottoman Period," *Bulletin of the School of Oriental and African Studies* 54, no. 3 (1991): 460–72.

4. Adam Sabra, *Poverty and Charity in Medieval Islam: Mamluk Egypt, 1250–1517* (Cambridge: Cambridge University Press, 2000), 70.

5. Hennigan, *The Birth of a Legal Institution*, xiii.

6. Wael B. Hallaq, *Sharīʿa: Theory, Practice, Transformations* (Cambridge: Cambridge University Press, 2009), 143.

7. David S. Powers, "Orientalism, Colonialism, and Legal History: The Attack on Muslim Family Endowments in Algeria and India," *Comparative Studies in Society and History* 31, no. 3 (July 1989): 536.

8. See Charles Kingsley Meek, *Land Law and Custom in the Colonies* (London: Frank Cass & Co. Ltd., 1968), 239.

9. Pascale Ghazaleh, "Introduction: Pious Foundations: From Here to Eternity," in *Held in Trust: Waqf in the Islamic World*, ed. Pascale Ghazeleh (Cairo: The American University in Cairo Press, 2011), 3; Miriam Hoexter, "Charity, the Poor and Distribution of Alms in Ottoman Algiers," in *Poverty and Charity in Middle Eastern Contexts*, ed. Michael Bonner, Mine Ener, and Amy Singer (Albany: State University of New York Press, 2003), 145–46; Hallaq, *Shari'a*, 194.

10. The lines in the Qur'an pertaining to laws of inheritance are 4:11, 4:12, and 4:176.

11. Layish, "The Family Waqf and the Shar'i law of Succession," 352–88; Leslie Peirce, *Morality Tales: Law and Gender in the Ottoman Court of Aintab* (Berkeley: University of California Press, 2003), 226.

12. Ghazaleh, "Introduction," 2.

13. Hospitals, insane asylums, mosques, markets, soup kitchens, aqueducts, fountains, schools, and bathhouses were established through waqfs as vital public institutions in Mamluk Cairo and throughout the Ottoman Empire. See Sabra, *Poverty and Charity in Medieval Islam,* 69–100; Rebecca Skreslet Hernandez, "Sultan, Scholar, Sufi: Authority and Power Relations is al-Suyuti's Fatwa on Waqf," *Islamic Law and Society* 20, no. 4 (January 2013): 333–70; Elyse Semerdjian, "Naked Anxiety: Bathhouses, Nudity, and Muslim/Non-Muslim Relations in Eighteenth-Century Aleppo," *International Journal of Middle East Studies* 45, no. 4 (November 2013): 651–76; Miri Shefer-Mossensohn, *Ottoman Medicine: Healing and Medical Institutions* (Albany: State University of New York Press, 2010); Peirce, *Morality Tales,* 139–40, 235–41.

14. In fact, colonial courts ended up intervening in family waqfs more extensively than in public waqfs. This was because public waqfs could be administered, at least partly, by the Mohamedan Advisory Board established by the government in each Straits Settlement from January 1, 1906, onward. Each advisory board was headed by a British colonial official with several local Muslims under his charge. Ordinance no. 92, Section 2, *Laws of the Straits Settlements, Volume 1* (London: Waterlow, 1926), 92. This did not mean that public waqfs escaped the courts' attention altogether during the colonial period. For more details on the administration of public waqfs, see *Haji Salleh Bin Haji Ismail and Another v. Abdullah Bin Haji Mohamed Salleh and Others* [1934] SSLR 7; *Re Shrine Of Habib Noh* [1957] MLJ 139.

15. Francesca Trivellato, *The Familiarity of Strangers: The Sephardic Diaspora, Livorno, and Cross-Cultural Trade in the Early Modern Period* (New Haven: Yale University Press, 2009), 20.

16. However, judges and lawyers in the Straits Settlements only addressed holdings in the colony and not elsewhere, even if the other properties were held in British territories in the Middle East or British India, since these holdings were outside of their jurisdiction.

17. Wills involving immoveable property in Britain were mostly subject to lex situs but judges in the Straits Settlements had wide judicial discretion. It was disputed in

the following cases. *Re Syed Shaik Alkaff, Decd.; Alkaff & Anor v. Attorney-General, S.S.* [1923] *MC* 1; *Re Syed Abdulrahman Bin Shaikh Bin Abdulrahman Alkaff, Deceased* [1953] *MLJ* 68; *Re Syed Hassan Bin Abdullah Aljofri Deceased; The Estate & Trust Agencies (1927) Ltd v. Syed Hamid Bin Hassan Aljofri & 2 Ors* [1949] *MLJ* 198. For a discussion on this in the context of the Straits Settlements specifically, see E. J. Cohn, "The Form of Wills by Immoveables," *International Journal of Comparative Law Quarterly* 5, no. 3 (July 1956): 395–404. For earlier decisions on trusts by Alkaff clan, see Gilsenan, "Translating Colonial Fortunes."

18. *Re Syed Shaik Alkaff, Decd.; Alkaff & Anor v. Attorney-General* [1923] *MC* 1.

19. For example, subsequent law reports on lawsuits involving the Alsagoff waqf did not mention the testator's faith and religious intentions in establishing the waqf. *Re Syed Ahmed Alsagoff Decd* [1960] *MLJ* 147; *Re Syed Ahmed Alsagoff, Deceased* [1962] *MLJ* 361; *Re Syed Ahmed Alsagoff, Deceased* [1963] *MLJ* 39.

20. Frederic William Maitland, *Equity: A Course of Lectures* (Cambridge: Cambridge University Press, 2003), 23.

21. The word *mutawalli* could also be translated as governor, superintendent, or curator according to Indian jurist Asaf Ali Asghar Fyzee. The historian Stephen Dale opts to use the word "custodian" instead. Asaf Ali Asghar Fyzee, *Cases in the Muhammadan Law of India and Pakistan* (Oxford: Oxford University Press, 1965), 384. Stephen F. Dale, "Empires and Emporia: Palace, Mosque, Market, and Tomb in Istanbul, Isfahan, Agra, and Delhi," *Journal of the Economic and Social History of the Orient* 53, 1–2 (January 2009): 214.

22. Fyzee, *Cases in the Muhammadan Law of India and Pakistan*, 386.

23. Gregory C. Kozlowski, *Muslim Endowments and Society in British India* (New York: Cambridge University Press, 1985), 153.

24. The Straits Settlements lawyers continued to cite British Indian cases, especially in cases involving trustees' responsibilities, lawyers' fees, and cases involving inheritance, to persuade judges, though the judgements were not binding. In the 1930s, judges started to consult two main handbooks of Islamic law prepared by the prominent Indian Muslim judges Faiz Badrudin Tyabji (in Bombay) and Syed Ameer Ali (in Calcutta). For more on debates among Muslim legal activists regarding administration of waqfs in British India, including Tyabji and Ameer Ali, see Eric Lewis Beverley, "Property, Authority and Personal Law: Waqf in Colonial South Asia," *South Asia Research* 31, no. 2 (July 2011): 155–82.

25. They did so by arguing that Ottoman law instead of local custom used to govern land usage in the Jordan River Valley. According to Ottoman law, *miri* land reverted back to the state if not cultivated for three years. Michael Fischbach, "Britain and the Ghawr Abi 'Ubayda Waqf Controversy in Transjordan," *International Journal of Middle East Studies* 33, no. 4 (November 2001): 525–44. Haitam Suleiman and Robert Home, " 'God is an Absentee, Too': The Treatment of *Waqf* (Islamic Trust) Land in Israel/Palestine," *Journal of Legal Pluralism and Unofficial Law* 41, no. 59 (2009): 49–65.

26. British authorities were hardly alone in trying to dissolve waqfs as Muslims throughout the world considered them problematic for various reasons too. Martha Mundy, "The Family, Inheritance, and Islam: A Re-Examination of the Sociology of Farā'id Law (1)," in *Islamic Law: Social and Historical* Contexts, ed. Aziz Al-Azmeh (London: Routledge, 1989), 10–11.

27. Other countries such as Egypt, Lebanon, and Syria would enact measures to limit the power family waqfs during the 1940s. Hallaq, *Sharīʿa*, 472.

28. For a case of an acquittal of a prominent wealthy Arab due to this anxiety, see Nurfadzilah Yahaya, "Class, White Women, and Elite Asian Men in British Courts during the Late Nineteenth Century," *Journal of Women's History* 31, no. 2 (Summer 2019): 101–23.

29. This supports Natalie Rothman's argument that the marketplace, often conceptualized as an anonymous impersonal space for exchanges between discrete individuals, might be understood rather as enmeshed in a wide range of institutionalized forms of sociability and practices of boundary-making. Rothman, "Genealogies of Mediation: "Cultural Broker" and Imperial Governmentality," in *Anthrohistory: Unsettling Knowledge, Questioning Discipline*, ed. Edward Murphy et al. (Ann Arbor: University of Michigan Press, 2011), 67.

30. For more on public philanthropy in another context, see Birla, *Stages of Capital*.

31. House of Lords question on Muslim law relating to endowments. IOR/L/PJ/6/400, File 1104, July 5, 1895.

32. Mortmain laws dated from thirteenth-century England and were originally intended to prevent the Catholic Church from acquiring large amounts of land that would otherwise revert to the monarchy. Although judges in the Straits Settlements from 1869 to 1872 hesitated before introducing mortmain to non-Christian subjects, legal consensus developed on its suitably applicability to the Crown colony. For more on history of mortmain laws in England, see Lawrence M. Friedman, *Dead Hands: A Social History of Wills, Trusts and Inheritance Law* (Stanford: Stanford University Press, 2009).

33. The trust in question was a Chinese trust. *Choa Choon Neoh v. Spottiswoode* [1869] 1 KY 216.

34. Muslim waqfs throughout the British Empire have been examined separately in several studies, although waqfs in Mauritius, Malaya, and the Aden Protectorate have yet to be examined in detail. For more on waqfs in India, the Middle East, and East Africa, see Kozlowski, *Muslim Endowments and Society in British India*; Yitzhak Reiter, "Family *Waqf* Entitlements in British Palestine (1917–1948)," *Islamic Law and Society* 2, no. 2 (January 1995): 174–93; J. N. D. Anderson, "*Waqfs* in East Africa," *Journal of African Law* 3, no. 3 (Autumn 1959): 152–64; Norbert Oberauer, "Fantastic Charities: The Transformation of *Waqf* Practice in Colonial Zanzibar," *Islamic Law and Society* 15, no. 3 (January 2008): 315–70.

35. *Ashabee & Ors. v. Mahomed Hashim & Anor.* [1887] 1 KY.

36. Arab litigants engaged the services of lawyers of Anglo or Anglo-Irish origin while Indians tended to employ lawyers of Indian and Chinese origin.

37. Although deemed problematic, this legal framework carried over to postcolonial Malaysia. Then Bee Lian, "The Meaning of 'Charity' in Malaya—A Comparative Study," *Malaya Law Review* 11, no. 2 (December 1969): 221–22.

38. Syed Ameer Ali, *Mohammedan Law* (Calcutta: Spink, 1929), 273, cited in *Re Syed Shaik Alkaff, Decd.; Alkaff & Anor v. Attorney-General, S.S.* [1923] MC 1.

39. Muslim subjects in the Straits Settlements could not agree if it was lawful for beneficiaries to sell a portion of the waqf land and receive the value of that portion. Abdul, "Wakaff Lands," *ST,* June 14, 1935, 16.

40. Birla, *Stages of Capital,* 70.

41. Ibrahim, *The Legal Status of the Muslims in Singapore,* 34; W. H. Rattigan, "The English Law and Legislation upon the Natives Laws of India," *Journal of the Society of Comparative Legislation* 3 no. 1 (1901): 60.

42. "1,000,000 Property at Stake—40-Year-Old Wakaf Dispute. Deed Upheld," *ST,* September 9, 1930, 14.

43. Meant to be hortatory rather than definitive, the preamble to the Statute of Charities in 1601, also known as the Charitable Uses Act of 1601 or Elizabeth Statute (Statute 43 Eliz. C. 4), limited the classes of legal charities. The statute remained unrepealed until the passage of the Mortmain and Charitable Uses Acts of 1888. For a full text of the preamble in old English, see Lian, "The Meaning of 'Charity' in Malaya," 220–22.

44. On the origins of charity in Islam, see Michael Bonner, "Poverty and Charity in the Rise of Islam," in Bonner, Ener, and Singer, *Poverty and Charity in Middle Eastern Contexts,* 13–30.

45. Michael Bonner, Mine Ener, and Amy Singer, "Introduction," in Bonner, Ener, and Singer, *Poverty and Charity in Middle Eastern Contexts,* 2. Family waqfs are more effective at disbursing to the poor unlike other Islamic welfare institutions. See Janine Clark, *Islam, Charity and Activism: Middle Class Networks and Social Welfare in Egypt, Jordan, and Yemen* (Bloomington: Indiana University Press, 2004).

46. For example, in 1869, a Chinese trust was deemed unenforceable because legal authorities could not oversee the conduct of *Sin-chew,* a religious ceremony of the Chinese in commemoration of the decease of their ancestors. *Choa Choon Neoh v. Spotiswoode* [1869] 1 KY 216.

47. Hernandez, "Sultan, Scholar, Sufi," 364.

48. Line 9:60 states that "alms are meant only for the poor, the needy, those who administer them, those whose hearts need winning over, to free slaves and help those in debt, for God's cause, and for travellers in need. This is ordained by God; God is all knowing and wise."

49. Some Muslim scholars considered these two groups as one while others considered them as separate, indicating two different degrees of poverty, with the poor being worse off than the indigent (resorting to begging). Hadiths and customary expressions of Arabs led to numerous definitions, some contradictory. Ingrid Mattson, "Status-Based Definitions of Need in Early Islamic Zakat and Maintenance Laws," in Bonner, Ener, and Singer, *Poverty and Charity in Middle Eastern Contexts,* 32.

50. Sabra, *Poverty and Charity in Medieval Islam,* 9–10.

51. Maliki and Hanbali jurists define the "poor" as such as well. By contrast, Hanafi jurists define the poor as someone who does not possess a specific amount of wealth in surplus of what is needed to support and protect life. Mattson, "Status-Based Definitions of Need," 32–33.

52. Mattson, "Status-Based Definitions of Need," 41.

53. The definition of poverty rests on common wisdom or community knowledge. Mattson, "Status-Based Definitions of Need," 42.

54. For a discussion of the differences between English trusts and waqfs, including an explanation of the different conceptions of charity, see Andrew White, "Breathing New Life into the Contemporary Islamic *Waqf:* What Reforms can *Fiqh* Regarding *Awqaf* Adopt from the Common Law of Trusts without Violating *Shari'ah*?," *Real Property, Probate and Trust Journal* 41, no. 3 (Fall 2006): 497–527.

55. Line 2:177 of the Quran states, "Goodness does not consist in turning your face towards East or West. The truly good are those who believe in God and the Last Day, in the angels, the Scripture, and the prophets; who give away some of their wealth, however much they cherish it, to their relatives, to orphans, the needy, travellers and beggars, and to liberate those in bondage; those who keep up the prayer and pay the prescribed alms; who keep pledges whenever they make them; who are steadfast in misfortune, adversity, and times of danger. These are the ones who are true, and it is they who are aware of God." For a discussion of the category of pious poor, see Sabra, *Poverty and Charity in Medieval Islam*, 17–31.

56. Oxford English Dictionary online, s.v. "cypres, adv.," accessed January 2, 2020, https://oed.com/view/Entry/46668.

57. *Re Syed Shaik Alkaff, Decd.; Alkaff & Anor v. Attorney-General* [1923] MC 1.

58. Mary Ann Fay, "From Warrior-Grandees to Domesticated Bourgeoisie: The Transformation of the Elite Egyptian Household into a Western-Style Nuclear Family," in *Family History in the Middle East: Household, Property and Gender*, ed. Beshara Doumani (Albany: State University of New York Press, 2003), 77–100.

59. In fact, the waqf could be used a weapon against legitimate heirs. While plots of land could be alienated as waqfs to protect them from expropriation, the move could also prevent heirs from seizing the properties. For an example of a waqf established to benefit an adopted child, see Francesca Petricca, "Filling the Void: Shari'a in Mixed Courts in Egypt: Jurisprudence (1876≠1949)," *Journal of Economic and Social History of the Orient* 55, no. 4/5 (2012): 718–45.

60. Peirce, *Morality Tales*, 226.

61. Eyal Ginio, "Living on the Margins of Charity: Coping with Poverty in an Ottoman Provincial City," in Bonner, Ener, and Singer, *Poverty and Charity in Middle Eastern Contexts*, 169.

62. Peirce, *Morality Tales*, 236.

63. There are two annual feasts—one to celebrate the end of the fasting month and another to celebrate Abraham's willingness to sacrifice his son to God. *Ashabee & Ors. v. Mahomed Hashim & Anor.* [1887] 4 KY 212.

64. In addition, pilgrimages to Mecca done in the testator's name were also considered uncharitable since they were conducted for the sole benefit of the testator. *Fatimah & Ors. v. D. Logan & Ors.* [1871] 1 KY 255; *Re Hadjee Esmail bin Kassim, deceased. Mohamadeen and Others v. Hussain Beebee Bintee Shaik Ali Bey*, 12 [1911] SSLR 74; *In Re Abdul Guny Abdullasa, Deceased. Fatima Beebee Amal v. K.M. Mohamed Abubakar* [1936] SSLR 5.

65. *Syed Abbas bin Mohamed Alsagoff and Another v Islamic Religious Council of Singapore (Majlis Ugama Islam Singapura)* [2009] SGHC 281.

66. For an example of famine relief in Mamluk Cairo, see Sabra, *Poverty and Charity in Medieval Islam*, 136–37.

67. Yaacov Lev, *Charity, Endowments and Charitable Institutions in Medieval Islam* (Gainesville: University of Florida Press, 2005), 140–41.

68. Peirce, *Morality Tales*, 155; Sami Zubaida, "Islam, the State and Democracy: Contrasting Conceptions of Society in Egypt," *Middle East Report*, no. 179 (November–December 1992), 9.

69. A law report in 1887 of a case in Penang involving Indian Muslims indicated that a *kenduri* for a dead person was "supposed by Malays to confer some benefit on the soul of such person and is generally observed first on stated dates after his death

and on the anniversary of his decease in each succeeding year." *Ashabee & Ors. v. Mahomed Hashim & Anor.* [1887] [1887] 4 KY 212; *Mustan Bee & Ors. v. Shina Tamby & Anor.* [1882] 1 KY 580. Also see David J. Banks, *Malay Kinship* (Philadelphia: Institute for the Study of Human Issues, 1983), 158–65.

70. Feasts also provide individuals with an opportunity to indicate the growing closeness of a relationship, its weakening or its demise, as the anthropologists James Scott and John Bowen have demonstrated. James C. Scott, *Weapons of the Weak: Everyday Forms of Peasant Resistance* (New Haven: Yale University Press, 1985), 172–73; John R. Bowen, *Muslims through Discourse: Religion and Ritual in Gayo Society* (Princeton: Princeton University Press, 1993), 70.

71. "Matters of Muslim Interest: The Children's Day," *SFPMA*, February 13, 1930, 12; "Matters of Muslim Interest: Alsagoff Arab Schools," *SFPMA*, January 29, 1931, 12; "Muslim Trust Fund Association," *SFPMA*, July 27, 1931, 11.

72. However, Mauss's explication of the power relations embedded in gift-giving reminds us that even when no money changes hands and no overt recompense or recognition is demanded in return for what is given, a hierarchy of power is invoked and emphasized in every such transaction. It is difficult to conceive of a "pure" or entirely "free gift." Marcel Mauss, trans. W. D. Halls, *The Gift: The Form and Reason for Exchange in Archaic Societies* (London: Routledge, 1990).

73. Women, for example, feature prominently as philanthropic actors in the Islamic world. Amy Singer, "Special Issue Introduction," *International Journal of Middle East Studies* 46, no. 2 (May 2014): 231.

74. In *Re Abdul Guny Abdullasa, Deceased. Fatima Beebee Amal v. K.M. Mohamed Abubakar* [1936] SSLR 5.

75. Robert Pearce and John Stevens, *The Law of Trusts and Equitable Obligations* (Oxford: Oxford University Press, 2006), 379. According to the English Law of Property in the Straits Settlements, "property" includes real and personal property; any estate in any property, real or personal; any debt and any thing in action; and any right or interest in the nature of property, whether in possession or not. Chapter 118, Section 2, *Laws of the Straits Settlements, Volume 3* (Singapore: Government Printing Office, 1936), 267.

76. Indian Act 20 of 1837 stated that "from the 1st day of October 1837, all immoveable property within the jurisdiction of the Court of Judicature of Prince of Wales' Island, Singapore and Malacca, shall, as regards the transmission of such property on the death and intestacy of any person having a beneficial interest in the same, or by the last Will of any such person, be taken to be, and to have been of the nature of chattels real and not of freehold." This act was cited in the following cases: *Wanchee Incheh Thyboo & Anor. v. Golam Kader* [1883] 1 KY 611; *Attorney-General v. Hajee Abdul Cader* [1883] 1 KY 616; *Fatimah & Anor v. Armootah Pullay* [1887] 4 KY 225; *Mahoemed Meera Nachiar & Anor. v. Inche Khatijah* [1890] WOC 608; *Ismail bin Savoosah v. Madinasah Merican & Anor.* [1887] 4 KY 311; *Syed Ali Bin Mohamed Alsagoff and Others V. Syed Omar Bin Mohamed Alsagoff and Others* [1918] SSLR 2; *Chulas and Kachee v. Kolson binte Seydoo Malim* [1867] WOC 30.

77. According to Abner Cohen, trading diasporas remained a moral community that lives in dispersal but constrains the behavior of the individual and ensures a large measure of conformity via social and ritualistic interaction. Cited in Trivellato, *The Familiarity of Strangers*, 11.

78. "Municipal Commissioners," *SFPMA*, April 23, 1896, 3; "Matters Muslim: Burial Ground Committee – A Muslim Need," *SFPMA*, March 16, 1927, 15.

79. Throughout the Islamic world, state authorities were expected to maintain public waqfs by the early twentieth century. For this reason, residents in the Malay states were particularly anxious about the maintenance of mosques by British authorities, who were supposed to take over these duties from the Malay sultans from the 1870s onward. Richard James Wilkinson, *Malay Beliefs* (London: Luzac & Co., 1906), 13. Likewise, Muslims in Aden also asked British authorities to step in when a waqf laid in ruins in 1921. IOR/R/20/A/2876, File 278/1 Wakf, April 1921.

80. In September 1924, Muslims in Singapore submitted a direct request to government authorities, asking that an existing burial ground be "set aside as (an) endowment" (i.e., be transformed into a waqf). The Mohamedan Advisory Board hence dedicated it as "an endowment (given, devised and bequeathed) for such use and benefit absolutely and forever. Even though appointed trustees should be appointed upon the establishment of waqfs, no trustees were appointed, and therefore the municipal commissioners reluctantly functioned as trustees by collecting the fees for the cemetery. *Handbook of the Mohamedan and Hindu Endowments Board* (Penang: Criterion Press, 1932); "Municipal Commission," *SFPMA*, September 27, 1924, 16; "The Municipal Budget," *SFPMA*, October 29, 1927, 11; "The Mohamedan Advisory Board," *SFPMA*, September 29, 1924; "The Late Syed Alwee," *SFPMA*, April 10, 1926, 8; "Matters Muslim: Muhammadan Cemetery, Bidadari," *SFPMA*, November 10, 1926, 2.

81. Ordinance II of 1886, Section 9, *The Acts and Ordinances of the Legislative Council of the Straits Settlements from the April 1867 to the 7th March 1898*, vol. 2 (London: Eyre and Spottiswoode, 1898), 876.

82. *Re Syed Shaik Alkaff, Decd.; Alkaff & Anor v. Attorney-General* [1923] MC 1.

83. A trustee could be a member of the family, usually the brother of the deceased. At times, it could be someone in the testator's employ prior to his death.

84. *Syed Ali Bin Mohamed Alsagoff And Others v. Syed Omar Bin Mohamed Alsagoff And Others* [1918] SSLR 2; *Re Syed Shaik Alkaff, Decd.; Alkaff & Anor v. Attorney-General* [1923] MC 1.

85. Barry C. Crown, "Private Purpose Trusts and Rule Against Perpetuities," *Singapore Journal of Legal Studies* (December 2009): 649. The Indian Income Tax Act stated that charitable trusts could be exempted from taxation. However, confusion ensued revolving around the distinction between public charity, religious purposes, and private charity. Birla, *Stages of Capital*, 79, 95.

86. Christiaan Snouck Hurgronje, *Ambtelijke Adviezen van C. Snouck Hurgronje, Tweede Deel*, 848.

87. Said Hasan bin Abdulla Alhadath contra Said Hamid Hoesin Alkadrie, *HRNI* 51 (1888): 174.

88. A will by an Indian Muslim who died in Singapore was challenged by a later version in India. *In the Estate of Vavena Katha Pillay Marican, deceased* [1934] SSLR 281.

89. *Re Syed Shaik Alkaff, Decd.; Alkaff & Anor v. Attorney-General* [1923] MC 1.

90. *Syed Ali Bin Mohamed Alsagoff and Others v. Syed Omar Bin Mohamed Alsagoff and Others* [1918] SSLR 2.

91. *Re S A A Alsagoff, Deceased; Syed Zakaria Alsagoff & Ors v R D Stewart & Ors* [1958] MLJ 264.

92. The judge held that the testator had intended to use the term "descendants" to include the remotest generation coming into being during the prescribed period, and

that on the death of the parent each succeeding generation should take, *per stirpes*, a life interest in the income till the time of distribution (subject only to the share of every male being twice that of every female, as directed by the Arabic will).

93. *Re Syed Shaik Alkaff, Decd.; Alkaff & Anor v. Attorney-General* [1923] MC 1.

94. It was likely that this was due to his lack of familiarity with the highly specific legal institution of the waqf.

95. One of the terms of the verdict in fact turned upon this very point. The original will stated that the condition for a granddaughter of Syed Shaik to partake from the corpus was that Syed Shaik's son had to die before him or prior to the date of the agreement. Thus, although one of the testator's daughters had died, the judge ruled that her share should not go to the daughter of the deceased, who was one of the defendants in this case.

96. Since women's right to own property within the Ottoman Empire was guaranteed by Islamic law, the alienation of property in waqf in this region gave additional legal sanction and protection to women's property ownership and control because the waqf was regulated by Islamic law and came under the authority of the Islamic court. These women often alienated their property during their lifetimes. Mary Ann Fay, "Women and Waqf: Toward a Reconsideration of Women's Place in the Mamluk Household," *International Journal of Middle East Studies* 29, no. 1 (February 1997): 36.

97. Upon marriage, women tended to leave the estate and therefore lost their right to benefit from the waqf.

98. Nonetheless, on the whole, Tyabji's *Principles of Mohammedan Law* emphasized that a waqf often benefitted two classes of descendants, namely women and orphans, who were often excluded from inheritance. While women may have benefitted more from waqfs established by Ḥaḍramīs in the Straits Settlements, this was not obvious from the waqfs disputed in Straits Settlements courts. Tyabji, *Muhammadan Law*, 539.

99. Kozlowski, *Muslim Endowments and Society in British India*, 56.

100. *Syed Abbas bin Mohamed Alsagoff and Another v. Islamic Religious Council of Singapore (Majlis Ugama Islam Singapura)* [2009] SGHC 281.

101. Hallaq, *Sharī'a*, 195.

102. *LS Investment Pte Ltd v. Majlis Ugama Islam Singapura* [1998] SGHC 51.

103. *ST*, November 20, 1914, 8; CO 273/421/17156, "Enclosure No. 2 in Straits Dispatch, No. 89 of March 11 1915—Extract from the 'Malaya Tribune' of Monday March 8th 1915: "Moslem Mass Meeting—Address of Loyalty to the King." Arthur Young, Governor and Commander-in-Chief of Straits Settlements, Singapore to Colonial Office, London; CO 273/421/17156, Omar Alsagoff, Singapore to Arthur Young, Singapore, March 10, 1915.

104. For more on Arab diasporic contributions to British expansion in Arabia, see Robert B. Serjeant, "The Hadrami Network," in *Asian Merchants and Businessmen in the Indian Ocean and the China Sea*, ed. Denys Lombard and Jean Aubin (Delhi: Oxford University Press, 2000), 145–53; Ho, *The Graves of Tarim*, 244–93.

Conclusion

1. John L. Comaroff, "Reflections on the Colonial State, in South Africa and Elsewhere: Factions, Fragments, Facts and Fictions," *Social Identities* 4, no. 3 (1998): 340.

2. "Islam has Permeated the Very Soul of Malaya," *ST,* May 23, 1939, p. 14.

3. Sheldon Pollock, "Cosmopolitan and Vernacular in History," *Public Culture* 12, no. 3 (2000): 591–625, cited in Messick, *Shari'a Scripts,* 26.

4. For an investigation of Muslim cosmopolitanism in a different setting, see Magnus Marsden, "Muslim Cosmopolitans? Transnational Life in Northern Pakistan," *The Journal of Asian Studies* 67, no. 1 (February 2008): 213–47.

5. Anak Singapura, "Notes of the Day: The Alkaffs," *ST,* August 1, 1939, 12.

6. Feldman, *Governing Gaza,* 48.

7. Feldman, *Governing Gaza,* 20, 61.

8. Feldman, *Governing Gaza,* 17.

9. NA 2.10.17 file 247, S.M. Aljunied, Batavia to Mr. Taniguchi, Imperial Japanese Military Headquarters, Batavia, May 4, 1942.

10. For more on Japanese legal reconfiguration during Occupation, see Daniel S. Lev, "Judicial Unification in Postcolonial Indonesia" *Indonesia* 16 (October 1973): 1–37.

11. An eye was also kept on a Japanese Muslim who reached out to an A. M. Alsagoff of Syonan-To (Singapore), however, which meant that Arab rivalries continued to take on a transnational dimension under Japanese rule. NA 2.10.17 file 247, "Note: Suggested Intermediary between the Arab organizations in Batavia and the Nippon Government in Indonesia," May 16, 1942; NA 2.10.17 file 247, "Hadji Ahmed Yamamoto."

12. NA 2.10.17 file 667, "Notities Inzake den Voorzitter der Semarangsche Arabische Vereeniging in Personen in zijn Omgeving" N. F. W. van den Arend, Buitenkantoor, Netherlands Forces Intelligence Service (NEFIS), Semarang to Directeur NEFIS, Batavia, September 7, 1946.

13. NA 2.10.17 file 667, Nota tentang Pekoempoelan Bangsa Arab, circa 1948.

14. Mark Cammack and Michael Feener, "The Islamic Legal System in Indonesia," *Pacific Rim Law & Policy Journal* 21, no. 1 (2012): 13–42.

BIBLIOGRAPHY

Abu-Lughod, Janet L. *Before European Hegemony: The World System, A.D. 1250–1350.* New York: Oxford University Press, 1989.

Abdullah, Taufik. *"Adat* and Islam: An Examination of Conflict in Minangkabau." *Indonesia* 2 (October 1966): 1–24.

The Acts and Ordinances of the Legislative Council of the Straits Settlements from the 1st April 1867 to the 7th March 1898. Vol. 2. London: Eyre and Spottiswoode, 1898.

Agmon, Danna. *A Colonial Affair: Commerce, Conversion, and Scandal in French India.* Ithaca, NY: Cornell University Press, 2017.

Agrama, Hussein A. *Questioning Secularism: Islam, Sovereignty, and the Rule of Law in Modern Egypt.* Chicago: University of Chicago Press, 2012.

Ahmed, Shahab. *What is Islam?: The Importance of Being Islamic.* Princeton, NJ: Princeton University Press, 2015.

Aiyar, Sana. *Indians in Kenya: The Politics of Diaspora.* Cambridge, MA: Harvard University Press, 2015.

Alatas, Syed Farid. "Ḥaḍramawt and the Hadhrami Diaspora: Problems in Theoretical History." In Freitag and Clarence-Smith, *Hadhrami Traders, Scholars and Statesmen in the Indian Ocean, 1750s-1960s,* 19–34.

Algadri, Hamid. *Dutch Policy against Islam and Indonesians of Arab Descent in Indonesia.* Jakarta: Pustaka, 1994.

Ali, Syed Ameer. *Mohammedan Law.* Calcutta: Spink, 1929.

Alpers, Edward A. *The Indian Ocean in World History.* New York: Oxford University Press, 2014.

Amrith, Sunil S. *Crossing the Bay of Bengal: The Furies of Nature and the Fortunes of Migrants.* Cambridge, MA: Harvard University Press, 2013.

——. "Tamil Diasporas across the Bay of Bengal." *American Historical Review* 114, no. 3 (June 2009): 547–72.

Andaya, Barbara. *To Live as Brothers: Southeast Sumatra in the Seventeenth and Eighteenth Centuries.* Honolulu: University of Hawaii Press, 1993.

Andaya, Barbara, and Leonard Andaya. *A History of Early Modern Southeast Asia, 1400–1830.* New York: Cambridge University Press, 2015.

Anderson, J. N. D. "*Waqf*s in East Africa." *Journal of African Law* 3, no. 3 (Autumn 1959): 152–64.

Anderson, Michael R. "Themes in South Asian Legal Studies in the 1980s." *South Asia Research* 10, no. 2 (1990): 158–77.

Aslanian, Sebouh David. *From the Indian Ocean to the Mediterranean: The Global Trade Networks of Armenian Merchants from New Julfa.* Berkeley: University of California Press, 2011.

Aydin, Cemil. *The Idea of the Muslim World: A Global Intellectual History*. Cambridge, MA: Harvard University Press, 2017.

Azra, Azymardi. "A Hadhrami Religious Scholar in Indonesia: Sayyid 'Uthmān." In Freitag and Clarence-Smith, *Hadhrami Traders, Scholars and Statesmen in the Indian Ocean, 1750s-1960s*, 249–63.

Baillie, John, and William Jones. *A Digest of Mohummudan Law According to the Tenets of the Twelve Imams*. Calcutta: Printed at the Hon. Company's Press, 1805.

Banks, David J. *Malay Kinship*. Philadelphia: Institute for the Study of Human Issues, 1983.

Banner, Stuart. *Possessing the Pacific: Land, Settlers, and Indigenous People from Australia to Alaska*. Cambridge, MA: Harvard University Press, 2007.

——. "Why Terra Nullius? Anthropology and Property Law in Early Australia." *Law and History Review* 23, no. 1 (Spring 2005): 95–131.

Barkey, Karen. "Aspects of Legal Pluralism in the Ottoman Empire." In *Legal Pluralism and Empires, 1500–1850*, edited by Richard J. Ross and Lauren Benton, 83–108. New York: New York University Press, 2013.

Belmessous, Saliha. "Introduction: The Problem of Indigenous Claim Making in Colonial History." In *Native Claims: Indigenous Law Against Empire, 1500–1920*, ed. Saliha Belmessous, 3–18. Oxford: Oxford University Press, 2011.

Benda, Harry J. *The Crescent and the Rising Sun*. The Hague: W. Van Hoeve, 1958.

von Benda-Beckmann, Franz, and Keebet von Benda-Beckmann. "Islamic Law in a Plural Context: The Struggle over Inheritance Law in Colonial West Sumatra." *Journal of the Economic and Social History of the Orient* 55, nos. 4–5 (2012): 771–93.

——. "Places That Come and Go: A Legal Anthropological Perspective on the Temporalities of Space in Plural Legal Orders." In *The Expanding Spaces of Law: A Timely Legal Geography*, edited by Irus Braverman, Nicholas Blomley, David Delaney, and Alexandre Kedar, 30–52. Stanford: Stanford University Press, 2014.

von Benda-Beckmann, Keebet, and Bertram Turner. "Legal Pluralism, Social Theory, and the State." *Journal of Legal Pluralism and Unofficial Law* 50, no. 3 (2018): 255–74.

Benhabib, Seyla. "Democratic Iterations: The Local, the National, and the Global." In *Another Cosmopolitanism*, edited by Robert Post, 46–74. Oxford: Oxford University Press, 2006.

Benton, Lauren A. "Colonial Law and Cultural Difference: Jurisdictional Politics and the Formation of the Colonial State." *Comparative Studies in Society and History* 41, no. 3 (July 1999): 563–88.

——. "From International Law to Imperial Constitutions: The Problem of Quasi-Sovereignty, 1870–1900." *Law and History Review* 26, no. 3 (Fall 2008): 595–619.

——. *Law and Colonial Cultures: Legal Regimes in World History*. Cambridge: Cambridge University Press, 2002.

——. *A Search for Sovereignty: Law and Geography in European Empires, 1400–1900*. New York: Cambridge University Press, 2010.

Benton, Lauren A., and Richard J. Ross. "Empires and Legal Pluralism: Jurisdiction, Sovereignty, and Political Imagination in the Early Modern World." In *Legal*

Pluralism and Empires, 1500–1850, edited by Richard J. Ross and Lauren Benton, 1–20. New York: New York University Press, 2013.

Van den Berg, L. W. C. *Le Hadhramout et les Colonies Arabes dans l'Archipel Indien*. Batavia: Imprimerie du Gouvernment, 1886.

——. *Minhadj At-Talibin—Le Guide des Zeles Croyants: Manuel de Jurisprudence Musulmane Selon Le Rite de Chafi'i*. Batavia: Imprimerie du Gouvernement, 1882.

——. *Ontwerp Burgelijk Wetboek voor Nederlandsch-Indië*. N.p: 1910.

"Besluit van Comissarissen-General over Nederlandsch-Indië, 16 January 1818, no. 29." In *Staatsblad van Nederlandsch-Indië voor 1818*. The Hague: Ter Drukkerij van A. D. Schinkel, 1839.

Beverley, Eric Lewis. "Property, Authority and Personal Law: Waqf in Colonial South Asia." *South Asia Research* 31, no. 2 (July 2011): 155–82.

Birla, Ritu. *Stages of Capital: Law, Culture, and Market Governance in Colonial India*. Durham, NC: Duke University Press, 2009.

Bishara, Fahad Ahmad. *A Sea of Debt: Law and Economic Life in the Western Indian Ocean, 1780–1950*. Cambridge: Cambridge University Press, 2017.

Blagden, Charles O. "Shahbandar and Bendahara." *Journal of the Royal Asiatic Society of Great Britain and Ireland* no. 2 (April 1921): 246–48.

Blink, Hedrik. *Nederlandsch Oost-en West-Indië, Tweede Deel*. Leiden: Brill, 1907.

Bogaardt, W. H. *De Oeconomische en Sociale Toestanden in Nederlandsch-Indië*. Harlem: H. G. van Alfen, 1905.

Bonner, Michael. "Poverty and Charity in the Rise of Islam." In Bonner, Ener, and Singer, *Poverty and Charity in Middle Eastern Contexts*, 13–30.

Bonner, Michael, Mine Ener, and Amy Singer. "Introduction." In Bonner, Ener, and Singer, *Poverty and Charity in Middle Eastern Contexts*, 1–12.

——, ed. *Poverty and Charity in Middle Eastern Contexts*. Albany: State University of New York Press, 2003.

Boogaardt, W. H. *Gedenkboek van den 12/-jarigen missiearbeid der Paters Minderbroeders-Capucijnen in Nederlandsch Oost-Indië*. 's-Hertogenbosch: C. N. Teulings, 1917.

Boomgaard, Peter. "Changing Economic Policy." In *South East Asia, Colonial History: High Imperialism (1890s–1930s) Volume III*, edited by Paul Kratoska, 77–96. London: Routledge, 2001.

——. "Indonesia: Developments in Real Income." In *Weathering the Storm: The Economies of Southeast Asia in the 1930s Depression*, ed. Peter Boomgard and Ian Brown, 23–52. Singapore: Institute of Southeast Asian Studies, 2000.

Bose, Sugata. *A Hundred Horizons: The Indian Ocean in the Age of Global Empire*. Cambridge, MA: Harvard University Press, 2006.

Bosma, Ulbe. "The Cultivation System (1830–1870) and Its Private Entrepreneurs on Colonial Java." *Journal of Southeast Asian Studies* 38 no. 2 (June 2007): 275–91.

Bowen, John R. *Islam, Law, and Equality in Indonesia: An Anthropology of Public Reasoning*. New York: Cambridge University Press, 2003.

——. *Muslims through Discourse: Religion and Ritual in Gayo Society*. Princeton, NJ: Princeton University Press, 1993.

Bowser, Matthew. "From Istanbul to Tokyo: An Interview with Eric Tagliacozzo." Interview by Matthew Bowser. *Toynbee Prize Foundation*, April 24, 2019. http://toynbeeprize.org/interviews/eric-tagliacozzo/.

Boxberger, Linda. *On the Edge of Empire: Hadhramawt, Emigration and the Indian Ocean, 1880s-1930s.* Albany: State University of New York Press, 2002.

Boyer, Paul. *Urban Masses and Moral Order in America, 1820–1920.* Cambridge, MA: Harvard University Press, 2009.

Braddell, Roland. *The Law of the Straits Settlements: A Commentary.* Kuala Lumpur: Oxford University Press, 1982.

Brugman, J. "Snouck Hurgronje's Study of Islamic Law." In *Leiden Oriental Connections 1850–1940*, edited by William Otterspeer, 82–93. Leiden: E. J. Brill, 1989.

Bujra, Abdalla S. *The Politics of Stratification—A Study of Political Change in a South Arabian Town.* Oxford: Clarendon Press, 1971.

Burns, Kathryn J. *Into the Archive: Writing and Power in Colonial Peru.* Durham, NC: Duke University Press, 2010.

Burns, Peter. *The Leiden Legacy: Concepts of Law in Indonesia.* Leiden: KITLV, 2004.

Cammack, Mark, and Michael Feener. "The Islamic Legal System in Indonesia." *Pacific Rim Law & Policy Journal* 21, No. 1 (2012): 13–42.

Case, Holly. *The Age of Questions: A First Attempt at an Aggregate History of the Eastern, Social, Woman, American, Jewish, Polish, Bullion, Tuberculosis, and Many Other Questions Over the Nineteenth Century, and Beyond.* Princeton, NJ: Princeton University Press, 2018.

Cassel, Pär K. *Grounds of Judgment: Extraterritoriality and Imperial Power in Nineteenth-Century China and Japan.* Oxford: Oxford University Press, 2012.

Chan, Shelly. "The Case for Diaspora: A Temporal Approach to the Chinese Experience." *Journal of Asian Studies* 74, no. 1 (February 2015): 107–28.

Chen, Li. *Chinese Law in Imperial Eyes: Sovereignty, Justice and Transcultural Politics.* New York: Columbia University Press, 2015.

Clarence-Smith, William G. "Hadhrami Arab Entrepreneurs in Indonesia and Malaysia: Facing the Challenge of the 1930s Recession." In *Weathering the Storm: The Economies of Southeast Asia in the 1930s Depression,* edited by Peter Boomgaard and Ian Brown, 229–50. Singapore: Institute of Southeast Asian Studies, 2000.

——. "Middle-Eastern Entrepreneurs in Southeast Asia." In *Diaspora Entrepreneurial Networks: Four Centuries of History,* edited by Ina Baghdiantz McCabe, Gelina Harlaftis and Ionna Pepelasis Minoglou, 217–44. Oxford: Berg, 2005.

Clark, Janine. *Islam, Charity and Activism: Middle Class Networks and Social Welfare in Egypt, Jordan, and Yemen.* Bloomington: Indiana University Press, 2004.

Clifford, James. "Diasporas." *Cultural Anthropology* 9, no. 3 (August 1994): 302–38.

Cohen, Deborah. *Family Secrets: Shame and Privacy in Modern Britain.* Oxford: Oxford University Press, 2013.

Cohn, Bernard S. *Colonialism and Its Forms of Knowledge: The British in India.* Princeton, NJ: Princeton University Press, 1996.

Cohn, E. J. "The Form of Wills by Immoveables." *International Journal of Comparative Law Quarterly* 5, no. 3 (July 1956): 395–404.

Colijn, Hendrikus. *Neërlands-Indië Land en Volk, Eerste Deel.* Amsterdam: Uitgevers Maatschappy, 1912.

Comaroff, John L. "Colonialism, Culture, and the Law: A Foreword." *Law and Social Inquiry* 26, no. 2 (2001): 305–14.

——. "Reflections on the Colonial State, in South Africa and Elsewhere: Factions, Fragments, Facts and Fictions." *Social Identities* 4, no. 3 (1998): 321–61.

Cooper, Frederick. *Colonialism in Question*. Berkeley: University of California Press, 2005.

Cooper, Frederick, and Jane Burbank. "Rules of Law, Politics of Empire." In *Legal Pluralism and Empires, 1500–1850*, edited by Richard J. Ross and Lauren Benton (New York: New York University Press, 2013), 279–94.

Cover, Robert M. "The Supreme Court, 1982 Term." *Harvard Law Review* 97, no. 1 (November 1983): 1–306.

Crown, Barry C. "Private Purpose Trusts and Rule Against Perpetuities." *Singapore Journal of Legal Studies* (December 2009): 646–60.

Curry, John C. *The Security Service, 1908–1945: The Official History*. Kew: Public Record Office, 1999.

Dale, Stephen. "The Hadhrami Diaspora in South-Western India: The Role of the Sayyids of the Malabar Coast." In Freitag and Clarence-Smith, *Hadhrami Traders, Scholars, and Statesmen in the Indian Ocean, 1750s-1960s*, 175–84.

Dale, Stephen F. "Empires and Emporia: Palace, Mosque, Market, and Tomb in Istanbul, Isfahan, Agra, and Delhi." *Journal of the Economic and Social History of the Orient* 53, nos. 1–2 (January 2009): 212–29.

Daubanton, J. D. *Beknopte Beschrijving van de Batikindustrie op Java: Haar Ontstaan en Ontwikkeling, Bewerking der Goederen, Gebruikte Materialen en Voorthrengselen*. Rotterdam: J. D. Daubanton, 1922.

Daum, P. A. *Aboe Bakar*. Batavia: G. Kolff, 1894.

Daum, Paul A. *Ups and Downs of Life in the Indies*. Translated by Elsje Q. Sturtevant and Donald W. Sturtevant. Amherst: University of Massachusetts Press, 1987.

Day, Clive. *Nederlandsch Beheer over Java*. The Hague: W. P. van Stockum and Zoon, 1905.

De, Rohit, and Robert Travers. "Petitioning and Political Cultures in South Asia: Introduction." *Modern Asian Studies* 53, no. 1 (2019): 1–20.

Deel VII: Chineezen en Andere Vreemde Oosterlingen in Nederlandsch- Indie. Batavia: Departement van Economische Zaken, 1935.

Di Capua, Yoav. *No Exit: Arab Existentialism, Jean-Paul Sartre, and Decolonization*. Chicago: University of Chicago Press, 2018.

Van Dijk, C. "Colonial Fears, 1890–1918: Pan-Islamism and the Germano-Indian Plot." In *Transcending Borders: Arabs, Politics, Trade and Islam in Southeast Asia*, edited by Huub de Jonge and Nico Kaptein, 53–89. Leiden: KITLV, 2002.

Djamour, Judith. *The Muslim Matrimonial Court in Singapore*. London: Athlone Press, 1966.

Van Doorn, Jacques. *A Divided Society—Segmentation and Mediation in Late-Colonial Indonesia*. Rotterdam: CASP, 1983.

Van Eck, R. *Beknopt Leerboek De Geschiedenis, Staatsinrichting En Land En Volkenkunde Van Nederlandsch Oost-Indie*. Breda: Koninklijke Militaire Academie, 1899.

Eltantawi, Sarah. *Shariah on Trial: Northern Nigeria's Islamic Revolution*. Oakland: University of California Press, 2017.

Eyken, A. J. H. *De werkkring van den Controleur op Java*. The Hague: M. Van Der Beek's Boekhandel, 1909.

Fasseur, Cees. "Colonial Dilemma: Van Vollehoven and the Struggle between *Adat* and Western Law in Indonesia." In *The Revival of Tradition in Indonesian Politics: The Deployment of Adat from Colonialism to Indigenism*, edited by Jamie Seth Davidson and David Henley, 50–67. New York: Routledge, 2007.

———. "Cornerstone and Stumbling Block: Racial Classification and the Late Colonial State in Indonesia." In *The Late Colonial State in Indonesia: Political and Economic Foundations of the Netherlands Indies 1880–1942*, edited by Robert Cribb, 31–56. Leiden: KITLV Press, 1994.

———. *The Politics of Colonial Exploitation: Java, the Dutch, and the Cultivation System*. Ithaca, NY: Southeast Asia Program Publications, 1992.

Fay, Mary Ann. "From Warrior-Grandees to Domesticated Bourgeoisie: The Transformation of the Elite Egyptian Household into a Western-Style Nuclear Family." In *Family History in the Middle East: Household, Property and Gender*, edited by Beshara Doumani, 77–100. Albany: State University of New York Press, 2003.

———. "Women and *Waqf*: Toward a Reconsideration of Women's Place in the Mamluk Household." *International Journal of Middle East Studies* 29, no. 1 (February 1997): 33–51.

Feldman, Ilana. *Governing Gaza: Bureaucracy, Authority, and the Work of Rule, 1917–1967*. Durham, NC: Duke University Press, 2008.

Fischbach, Michael. "Britain and the Ghawr Abi 'Ubayda Waqf Controversy in Transjordan." *International Journal of Middle East Studies* 33, no. 4 (November 2001): 525–44.

Fokkens, F. *Bescheiden Wenken voor de Verbetering van den Economischen Toestand der Inlandsche Bevolking op Java en daar Buiten*. The Hague: M. M. Couvee, 1904.

———. *Bijdrage tot de Kennis Onzer Koloniale Politiek der Laatste Twintig Jaren*. The Hague: M. M. Couvée, 1908.

Ford, Lisa. *Settler Sovereignty: Jurisdiction and Indigenous People in America and Australia, 1788–1836*. Cambridge, MA: Harvard University Press, 2010.

Foucault, Michel. "Questions of Geography." In *Power/Knowledge: Selected Interviews and Other Writings 1972–77*, edited by Colin Gordon, 63–77. New York: Pantheon Books, 1980.

Freitag, Ulrike. "Arab Merchants in Singapore: Attempt of a Collective Biography." In *Transcending Borders: Arabs, Politics, Trade, Islam in Southeast Asia*, edited by Huub de Jonge and Nico Kaptein, 109–42. Leiden: KITLV Press, 2002.

———. "Hadhramis in International Politics." In Freitag and Clarence-Smith, *Hadhrami Traders, Scholars and Statesmen in the Indian Ocean, 1750s-1960s*, 112–30.

———. *Indian Ocean Migrants and State Formation in Hadhramaut: Reforming the Homeland*. Leiden: Brill, 2003.

Freitag, Ulrike, and William G. Clarence-Smith, eds. *Hadhrami Traders, Scholars and Statesmen in the Indian Ocean, 1750s-1960s*. Leiden: Brill, 1997.

Friedman, Lawrence M. *Dead Hands: A Social History of Wills, Trusts and Inheritance Law*. Stanford: Stanford University Press, 2009.

Fyzee, Asaf Ali Asghar. *Cases in the Muhammadan Law of India and Pakistan*. Oxford: Oxford University Press, 1965.

———. "Muhammadan Law in India." *Comparative Studies in Society and History* 5, no. 4 (July 1963): 401–15.

Galanter, Marc. "The Displacement of Traditional Law in Modern India." *Journal of Social Issues* 24, no. 4 (1968): 65–91.

———. "Justice in Many Rooms: Courts, Private Ordering, and Indigenous Law," *The Journal of Legal Pluralism and Unofficial Law* 13, no. 19 (1981): 1–47.

Geertz, Clifford. *Local Knowledge: Further Essays in Interpretive Anthropology*. New York: Basic Books, 1983.

Ghazaleh, Pascale. "Introduction: Pious Foundations: From Here to Eternity." In *Held in Trust: Waqf in the Islamic World*, edited by Pascale Ghazeleh, 1–22. Cairo: The American University in Cairo Press, 2011.

Ghosh, Amitav. "The Diaspora in Indian Culture," *Public Culture* 2, no. 1 (Fall 1989): 73–78.

———. "The Slave of Ms. H. 6." *Centre for Studies in Social Sciences, Calcutta Occasional Paper* no. 125 (1990): 1–135.

Gilsenan, Michael. "Translating Colonial Fortunes: Dilemmas of Inheritance in Muslim and English Laws across a Nineteenth-Century Diaspora." *Comparative Studies of South Asia, Africa and the Middle East* 31, no. 2 (2011): 355–71.

Ginio, Eyal. "Living on the Margins of Charity: Coping with Poverty in an Ottoman Provincial City." In Bonner, Ener, and Singer, *Poverty and Charity in Middle Eastern Contexts*, 165–84.

Giunchi, Elisa. "The Reinvention of Shari'a under the British Raj: In Search of Authenticity and Certainty." *Journal of Asian Studies* 69, no. 4 (November 2010): 1119–42.

Goitein, Shelomo Dov. *A Mediterranean Society: The Jewish Communities of the Arab World as Portrayed in the Documents of the Cairo Geniza, Six Volumes*. Berkeley: University of California Press, 1967–93.

———. *Studies in Islamic History and Institutions*. Leiden: Brill, 2010.

Goldziher, Ignaz. *Muhammedanische Studien*. Volumes 1 and 2. Halle: Niemeyer, 1889.

Gouda, Frances. "Mimicry and Projection in the Colonial Encounter: The Dutch East Indies/Indonesia as Experimental Laboratory, 1900–1942." *Journal of Colonialism and Colonial History* 1, no. 2 (Winter 2000): 1–20.

Gouvernements-koffiecultuur. Rapport van de Staats-Commissie. The Hague: Der Gerbroeders van Cleef, 1889.

Green, Nile. *Bombay Islam: The Religious Economy of the West Indian Ocean, 1840–1915*. Cambridge: Cambridge University Press, 2011.

Guenther, Alan M. "A Colonial Court Defines a Muslim." In *Islam in South Asia in Practice*, edited by Barbara D. Metcalf, 293–304. Princeton, NJ: Princeton University Press 2009.

Gupta, Akhil. *Red Tape: Bureaucracy, Structural Violence, and Poverty in India*. Durham, NC: Duke University Press, 2012.

Hadler, Jeffrey. *Muslims and Matriarchs: Cultural Resilience in Indonesia through Jihad and Colonialism*. Ithaca, NY: Cornell University Press, 2008.

Hallaq, Wael B. *The Origins and Evolution of Islamic Law*. New York: Cambridge University Press, 2012.

———. *An Introduction to Islamic Law*. New York: Cambridge University Press, 2009.

Hamm, Geoffrey. "British Intelligence in the Middle East, 1898–1906." *Intelligence and National Security* 29, no. 6 (2014): 880–900.

Handbook of the Mohamedan and Hindu Endowments Board. Penang: Criterion Press, 1932.

Hanley, Will. "Grieving Cosmopolitanism in Middle East Studies." *History Compass* 6, no. 5 (September 2008): 1346–67.

——. *Identifying with Nationality: Europeans, Ottomans, and Egyptians in Alexandria.* New York: Columbia University Press, 2017.

Hansen, P. C. C. (under pseudonym "Boeka"). *Uit Java's Binnenland: Pàh Troeno.* Amsterdam: Van Rossen, 1902.

Hansen, Thomas Blom. "Sovereigns beyond the State: On Legality and Authority in Urban India." In *Sovereign Bodies: Citizens, Migrants, and States in the Postcolonial World,* edited by Thomas Blom Hansen and Finn Stepputat, 169–91. Princeton, NJ: Princeton University Press, 2005.

Hanstein, Thoralf. "S. 1882, No. 152." In *Islamiches Recht und Nationales Recht,* 140–41, 171–75. Frankfurt am Main: Peter Lang, 2002.

Heidhues, Mary Somers. *Golddiggers, Farmers, and Traders in the "Chinese Districts" of West Kalimantan, Indonesia.* Ithaca, NY: Cornell University Press, 2003.

Hennigan, Peter. *The Birth of a Legal Institution: The Formation of the Waqf in Third-Century A.H. Ḥanafī Legal Discourse.* Leiden: Brill, 2004.

Hernandez, Rebecca Skreslet. "Sultan, Scholar, Sufi: Authority and Power Relations in al-Suyuti's Fatwa on Waqf." *Islamic Law and Society* 20, no. 4 (January 2013): 333–70.

Herzog, Tamar. "Struggling over Indians: Territorial Conflict and Alliance Making in the Heartland of South America (Seventeenth to Eighteenth Centuries)." In *Empire by Treaty: Negotiating European Expansion, 1600–1900,* edited by Saliha Belmessous, 79–100. Oxford: Oxford University Press, 2014.

Hiley, Nicholas. "Counter-Espionage and Security in Great Britain during the First World War." *English Historical Review* 101, no. 400 (July 1986): 635–70.

Ho, Engseng. "Before Parochialisation: Diasporic Arabs Cast in Creole Waters." In *Transcending Borders: Arabs, Politics, Trade and Islam in Southeast Asia,* edited by Huub de Jonge and Nico Kaptein, 11–36. Leiden: KITLV Press, 2002.

——. "Foreigners and Mediators in the Constitution of Malay Sovereignty." *Indonesia and the Malay World* 41, no. 120 (2013): 146–67.

——. *Graves of Tarim: Genealogy and Mobility Across the Indian Ocean.* Berkeley: University of California Press, 2006.

Hobsbawm, Eric. "Introduction: Inventing Traditions." In *The Invention of Tradition,* edited by Eric Hobsbawm and Terence Ranger, 1–14. Cambridge: Cambridge University Press, 1983.

Van Hoevell, Wolter Robert. *Parlementaire Redevoeringen over Koloniale Belangen, Volume 1.* Zalt-Rommel: Joh. Norman & Zoon, 1862.

Hoexter, Miriam. "Charity, the Poor and Distribution of Alms in Ottoman Algiers." In Bonner, Ener, and Singer, *Poverty and Charity in Middle Eastern Contexts,* 145–64.

Hoffman, Adina, and Peter Cole. *Sacred Trash: The Lost and Found World of the Cairo Geniza.* New York: Schocken Books, 2016.

De Hollander, Joannes Jacobus. *Handleiding bij de Beoepening der Land—en Volkenkunde van Nederlandsch Oost-Indië, Tweede Deel.* Brede: Drukkerij van Broese & Comp., 1898.

Hoofdar, Homa. "In the Absence of Legal Equity: Mahr and Marriage Negotiation in Egyptian Low Income Communities." *Arab Studies Journal* 6/7, no. 2/1 (Fall 1998/Spring 1999): 98–111.

Hooker, M. B. *Adat Laws in Modern Malaya*. Kuala Lumpur: Oxford University Press, 1972.

——. *Islamic Law in South-East Asia*. Singapore: Oxford University Press, 1984.

——. "Muhammadan Law and Islamic Law." In *Islam in Southeast Asia,* edited by M. B. Hooker. Leiden: Brill, 1983.

——. "The Muslims in Malaysia and Singapore: The Law of Matrimonial Property." In *Family Law in Asia and Africa*, edited by J. N. D. Anderson, 189–204. London: George Allen and Unwin Ltd., 1968.

——. "The Oriental Law Text: With Reference to the Undang-Undang Melaka and Malay Law." In *Malaysian Legal Essays: A Collection of Essays in Honour of Professor Emeritus Datuk Ahmad Ibrahim*, 431–56. Kuala Lumpur: Malayan Law Journal, 1986.

Hose, M. A. "Inaugural Address." *Journal of the Straits Branch of the Royal Asiatic Society* 1 (July 1878): 8.

Huender, W. "Survey of the Economic Conditions of the Indigenous People of Java and Madura 1921." In *Selected Documents on Nationalism and Colonialism*, edited by Chr. L. M. Penders, 91–7. St. Lucia: University of Queensland Press, 1977.

Huet, Conrad Busken. *Het Land van Rembrand, eerste deel*. Haarlem: H. D. Tjeenk Willenk, 1882.

Hull, Matthew. *Government of Paper: The Materiality of Bureaucracy in Urban Pakistan*. Berkeley: University of California Press, 2016.

Hullebroeck, Emiel. *Insulinde: Reisdrukken*. Leiden: Vlaamsche Boekenhalle, 1917.

Hussin, Iza. *The Politics of Islamic Law: Local Elites, Colonial Authority, and the Making of the Muslim State*. Chicago: University of Chicago Press, 2016.

——. "The Pursuit of the Perak Regalia: Islam, Law, and the Politics of Authority in the Colonial State." *Law and Social Inquiry* 32 no. 3 (2007): 759–88.

Hussin, Nordin. *Trade and Society in the Straits of Melaka: Dutch Melaka and English Penang*. Copenhagen: NIAS Press, 2007.

Ibrahim, Ahmad. *The Legal Status of the Muslims in Singapore*. Singapore: Malayan Law Journal, 1965.

——. "The Muslims in Malaysia and Singapore." In *Family Law in Asia and Africa*, edited by J. N. D. Anderson, 185–204. London: George Allen and Unwin Ltd., 1968.

——. *Towards a History of Law in Malaysia and Singapore*. Kuala Lumpur: Dewan Bahasa dan Pustaka, 1992.

Immink, A. J. *Atoeran Hoekoem atas Negri dan Bangsa Tjina dan Bangsa Arab dan lain-lain sebagienja di Tanah Hindia-Nederland*. Batavia: Oiej Tjaij Hin, 1910.

——. *Het Reglement op de Burgerlijke Rechtsvordering*. The Hague: Martinus Nijhoff, 1900.

Innes, J. R. *Report on the Census of the Straits Settlements Taken on the 1st March 1901*. Singapore: Government Printing Office, 1901.

Jaarverslag Kamer van Koophandel en Nijverheid te Makassar (1896). Makassar: J. C. Verdouw, 1897.

Jain, M. P. *Outlines of Indian Legal History*. Delhi: University of Delhi Press, 1952.

Jeffrey, Keith, and Alan Sharp. "Lord Curzon and Secret Intelligence." In *Intelligence and International Relations, 1900–1945*, edited by Christopher Andrew and Jeremy Noakes, 103–26. Exeter: University of Exeter, 1987.

Justus. *Wettelijke regeling van den Rechtoestand der Inlandsche Christenen als Hoofdzaak.* Batavia: H. M. van Dorp & Co. 1905.

Kafka, Ben. *The Demon of Writing.* New York: Zone Books, 2012.

Kahin, Audrey. *Historical Dictionary of Indonesia.* Lanham: Rowman and Littlefield, 2015.

Kaptein, Nico J. G. "Arabophobia and Tarekat: How Sayyid Uthmān Became Advisor to the Netherlands Colonial Administration." In *The Hadhrami Diaspora in Southeast Asia: Identity Maintenance or Assimilation,* edited by Ahmed Ibrahim Abushouk and Hassan Ahmed Ibrahim, 33–44. Brill: Leiden, 2009.

——. *Islam, Colonialism and the Modern Age in the Netherlands East Indies: A Biography of Sayyid 'Uthman (1822–1914).* Leiden: Brill, 2014.

——. "The Sayyid and the Queen: Sayyid Uthmān on Queen Wilhemina's Inauguration on the Throne of the Netherlands in 1898." *Journal of Islamic Studies* 9, no. 2 (July 1998): 158–77.

Kathirithamby-Wells, Jeyamalar. "'Strangers' and 'Stranger-Kings': The Sayyid in Eighteenth-Century Maritime Southeast Asia," *Journal of Southeast Asian Studies* 40, no. 3 (October 2009): 567–91.

Van der Kemp, P. H. "Van de Wetgeving der Koloniën." *De Indische Gids* 8, no. 1 (1886): 157–88.

Keuchenius, Levinus W.C. *Handelingen der regering en der Staten-Generaal betreffende het Reglement op het Beleid der Regering van Nederlandsch Indië, deel 2.* Utrecht: Kemink & Zoon, 1857.

Kniphorst, J. H. P. E. "Een terugblik op Timor er Onderhoorigheden." *Tijdschrift voor Nederlandsch-Indië* 14, no. 2 (1885): 135–45.

Knox-Mawer, R. "Islamic Domestic Law in the Colony of Aden." *International Journal of Comparative Law Quarterly* 5, no. 4 (October 1956): 511–18.

Kolsky, Elizabeth. *Colonial Justice in British India.* New York: Cambridge University Press, 2010.

——. "Forum: Maneuvering the Personal Law System in Colonial India—Introduction." *Law and History Review* 28, no. 4 (November 2010): 973–78.

Kozlowski, Gregory C. *Muslim Endowments and Society in British India.* New York: Cambridge University Press, 1985.

Van Kraaijenburg, Johan Pieter Cornets de Groot. *Over Het Beheer Onzer Koloniën.* The Hague: Belinfante, 1862.

Van der Kroef, Justus M. "The Indonesian Arabs," *Civilisations* 5, no. 1 (1955): 15.

Kuehn, Thomas. *Empire, Islam and Politics of Difference.* Leiden: Brill, 2011.

Kugle, Scott Alan. "Framed, Blamed and Renamed: The Recasting of Islamic Jurisprudence in Colonial South Asia." *Modern Asian Studies* 35, no. 2 (2001): 257–313.

Kuran, Timur. "The Provision of Public Goods Under Islamic Law: Origins, Impact and Limitations of the *Waqf* System." *Law and Society Review* 35, no. 4 (2001): 841–98.

Laffan, Michael. "Finding Java: Muslim Nomenclature of Insular Southeast Asia from Srivijaya to Snouck Hurgronje." In *Southeast Asia and The Middle East: Islam, Movement and the Longue Durée,* edited by Eric Tagliacozzo, 17–64. Stanford: Stanford University Press, 2009.

——. *Islamic Nationhood and Colonial Indonesia: The Umma Below the Winds.* Abingdon: Routledge, 2007.

——. "Making Meiji Muslims: The Travelogue of ʿAli Ahmad al-Jarjāwī." *East Asian History* 22 (December 2001): 145–70.

——. *The Makings of Indonesian Islam: Orientalism and the Narration of a Sufi Past.* Princeton, NJ: Princeton University Press, 2011.

——. "Tokyo as a Shared Mecca of Modernity: War Echoes in the Colonial Malay World." In *The Impact of the Russo-Japanese War*, edited by Rotem Kowner, 219–38. London: Routledge, 2010.

Lambert, J. E. W., ed. *Politieklapper voor Java en Madoera.* Surabaya: E. Fuhri and Co., 1910.

"Landraad te Batavia, Voorz. Mr. J. Roorda" *ITVHR* 153 (1940): 299–306.

Layish, Aharon. "The Druze Testamentary Waqf." *Studia Islamica* 71 (1990): 127–54.

——. "Family *Waqf* and the *Shari'a* Law of Succession in Modern Times." *Islamic Law and Society* 4, no. 3 (January 1997): 352–88.

Laws of the Straits Settlements, Volume 1 (London: Waterlow & Sons Limited, 1926), 18–21.

Laws of the Straits Settlements, Volume 3. Singapore: Government Printing Office, 1936.

Lee, Jack Jin Gary. "Plural Society and the Colonial State: English Law and the Making of Crown Colony Government in the Straits Settlements." *Asian Journal of Law and Society* 2, no. 2 (November 2015): 229–49.

Lees, Lynn Hollen. *Planting Empire, Cultivating Subjects: British Malaya, 1786–1941.* New York: Cambridge University Press, 2017.

Lemons, Katherine. *Divorcing Traditions: Islamic Marriage Law and the Making of Indian Secularism.* Ithaca, NY: Cornell University Press, 2019.

Lev, Daniel S. *Islamic Courts in Indonesia.* Berkeley: University of California Press, 1972.

——. "Judicial Institutions and Legal Culture in Indonesia." In *Culture and Politics in Indonesia*, edited by Claire Holt, 246–318. Ithaca, NY: Cornell University Press, 1972.

——. "Judicial Unification in Postcolonial Indonesia." *Indonesia* 16 (October 1973): 1–37.

——. "The Lady and the Banyan Tree: Civil Law Change in Indonesia." In *Legal Evolution and Political Authority in Indonesia: Selected Essays*, 119–42. The Hague: Kluwer Law International, 2000.

——. *Legal Evolution and Political Authority in Indonesia: Selected Essays.* The Hague: Kluwer Law International, 2000.

——. "The Origins of Indonesia Advocacy." In *Legal Evolution and Political Authority in Indonesia: Selected Essays*, 245–82. The Hague: Kluwer Law International, 2000.

Lev, Yaacov. *Charity, Endowments and Charitable Institutions in Medieval Islam.* Gainesville: University of Florida Press, 2005.

Lian, Then Bee. "The Meaning of 'Charity' in Malaya—A Comparative Study." *Malaya Law Review* 11, no. 2 (December 1969): 220–49.

Liaw, Yock Fang. *Undang-Undang Melaka—the Laws of Melaka.* The Hague: Martinus Nijhoff, 1976.

Lieberman, Victor. *Strange Parallels: Southeast Asia in Global Context, c. 800–1830, Volume 2, Mainland Mirrors: Europe, China, Japan, South Asia, and the Islands.* New York: Cambridge University Press, 2009.

Likhovski, Assaf. *Law and Identity in Mandate Palestine.* Chapel Hill: University of North Carolina Press, 2006.

van der Linden, Herman Otto. *Banda and zijn Bewoners*. Dordrecht: Blusse and Van Braam, 1873.

Liu, Lydia H. "Scripts in Motion: Writing as Imperial Technology, Past and Present." *Publications of the Modern Language Association of America* 130, no. 2 (March 2015): 375–83.

Locher-Scholten, Elsbeth. *Sumatran Sultanate and Colonial State: Jambi and the Rise of Dutch Imperialism, 1830–1907*. Ithaca, NY: Cornell Southeast Asia Program Publications, 2003.

Louw, Pieter Johan Friederik. *De Derde Javaansche Successie-Oorlog (1746–1755)*. The Hague: Martinus Nijhoff, 1889.

Lukito, Ratno. *Legal Pluralism in Indonesia: Bridging the Unbridgeable*. New York: Routledge, 2013.

Lydon, Ghislaine. *On Trans-Saharan Trails: Islamic Law, Trade Networks and Cross-cultural Exchanges in Nineteenth-Century Western Africa*. New York: Cambridge University Press, 2009.

Machado, Pedro. *Ocean of Trade: South Asian Merchants, Africa and the Indian Ocean, c. 1750–1850*. New York: Cambridge University Press, 2014.

Macnaghten, William Hay. *Principles of Hindu and Mohammadan Law*. London: Williams and Norgate, 1860.

Maitland, Frederic William. *Equity: A Course of Lectures*. Cambridge: Cambridge University Press, 2003.

Majid, Syed A. "Wakf as Family Settlement among the Mohammedans." *Journal of the Society of Comparative Legislation* 9, no. 1 (1908): 122–41.

Makdisi, George. "The Significance of the Sunni Schools of Law in Islamic Religious History." *International Journal of Middle East Studies* 10 (May 1979): 1–8.

Mandal, Sumit K. *Becoming Arab: Creole Histories and Modern Identity in the Malay World*. Cambridge: Cambridge University Press, 2017.

——. "Challenging Inequality in a Modern Islamic Idiom: Arabs in Early 20th-Century Java." In *Southeast Asia and The Middle East: Islam, Movement and the Longue Durée*, edited by Eric Tagliacozzo, 156–75. Stanford: Stanford University Press, 2009.

——. "Finding their Place: A History of Arabs in Java under Dutch Rule, 1800–1924." PhD diss., Columbia University, 1994.

Manger, Leif. "Hadramis in Hyderabad: From Winners to Losers." *Asian Journal of Social Science* 35, no. 4 (2007): 405–33.

Marsden, Magnus. "Muslim Cosmopolitans? Transnational Life in Northern Pakistan." *Journal of Asian Studies* 67, no. 1 (February 2008): 213–47.

Marsden, William. *The History of Sumatra*. London: Printed for the Author, by J. McCreery, 1811.

Mathew, Johan. *Margins of the Market: Trafficking and Capitalism across the Arabian Sea*. Oakland: University of California Press, 2016.

Mattson, Ingrid. "Status-Based Definitions of Need in Early Islamic Zakat and Maintenance Laws." In Bonner, Ener, and Singer, *Poverty and Charity in Middle Eastern Contexts*, 31–52.

Mauss, Marcel. *The Gift. The Form and Reason for Exchange in Archaic Societies*. Translated by W. D. Halls. London: Routledge, 1990.

Mawani, Renisa. *Across Oceans of Empire: The "Komagata Maru" and Jurisdiction in the Time of Empire*. Durham, NC: Duke University Press, 2018.

——. "Archival Legal History: Towards the Ocean as Archive." In *The Oxford Handbook of Legal History*, edited by Markus Dubber and Christopher Tomlin, 292–310. Oxford: Oxford University Press, 2018.

——. "Law, Settler Colonialism and the 'Forgotten Space' of Maritime Worlds," *Annual Review of Law and Social Science* 12 (October 2016): 107–31.

Maxwell, Benson. "Land Tenure in Malacca under European Rule." *Journal of the Straits Branch of the Royal Asiatic Society* 13 (June 1884): 75–220.

Maxwell, William E. *The Torrens System of Conveyancing by Registration of Title: with an Account of the Practice of the Lands Titles Office in Adelaide, South Australia, and suggestions as to the Introduction of the System in the Straits Settlements*. Singapore: no publisher, 1883.

McNair, John Frederick Adolphus. *Miscellaneous Numerical Returns [and] Straits Settlements Population [for the Year] 1871*. Singapore: n.p, 1871.

Meek, Charles Kingsley. *Land Law and Custom in the Colonies*. London: Frank Cass & Co. Ltd., 1968.

Di Meglio, Rita Rose. "Arab Trade with Indonesia and the Malay Peninsula from the 8th to the 16th Century." In *Islam and the Trade of Asia: A Colloquium*, edited by D. S. Richards, 105–36. Philadelphia: University of Pennsylvania Press, 1970.

Merewether, E. M. *Report on the Census of the Straits Settlements, Taken on 5th April 1891*. Singapore: Government Printing Office, 1892.

Merry, Sally Engle. "Legal Pluralism." *Law and Society Review* 22, no. 5 (1988): 869–96.

——. "McGill Convocation Address: Legal Pluralism in Practice," *McGill Law Journal—Revue de Droit de McGill* 59, no. 1 (2014): 1–8.

Messick, Brinkley. *The Calligraphic State: Textual Domination and History in a Muslim Society*. Berkeley: University of California Press, 1996.

——. "Madhhabs and Modernities." In *The Islamic School of Law—Evolution, Devolution and Progress*, edited by Peri Bearman, Rudolph Peters, Frank E. Vogel, 159–74. Cambridge, MA: Harvard University Press, 2005.

——. *Shari'a Scripts: A Historical Anthropology*. New York: Columbia University Press, 2017.

——. "Textual Properties: Writing and Wealth in a Shari'a Case," *Anthropological Quarterly* 68, no. 3 (July 1995): 157–70.

Milner, Anthony C. "Inventing Politics: The Case of Malaysia." *Past and Present* 132, no. 1 (August 1991): 104–29.

Mintz, Sidney. *Sweetness and Power: The Place of Sugar in Modern History*. New York: Viking, 1985.

Mobini-Kesheh, Natalie. *The Hadhrami Awakening: Community and Identity in the Netherlands East Indies, 1900–1942*. Ithaca, NY: Cornell Southeast Asia Program Publications, 1999.

——. "Islamic Modernism in Colonial Java: The Al-Irshād Movement." In Freitag and Clarence-Smith, *Hadhrami Traders, Scholars and Statesmen in the Indian Ocean, 1750s-1960s*, 231–39.

Moor, J. H. *Notices on the Indian Archipelago, and Adjacent Countries; Being a collection of papers relating to Borneo, Celebes, Bali, Java, Sumatra, Nias, The Philippine Islands, Sulus, Siam, Cochin China, Malayan Peninsula, &c*. Singapore, 1837.

Moors, Annelies. "Debating Islamic Family Law: Legal Texts and Social Practices." In *Social History of Women and Gender in the Modern Middle East*, edited by Margaret L. Meriwether and Judith E. Tucker, 141–76. Boulder: Westview Press, 1999.

Moustafa, Tamir. "The Judicialization of Religion." *Law and Society Review* 52, no. 3 (2018): 685–708.

Mrazek, Rudolf. *A Certain Age: Colonial Jakarta through the Memories of Its Intellectuals.* Durham, NC: Duke University Press, 2010.

Muller, Hannah. *Subjects and Sovereign: Bonds of Belonging in the Eighteenth-Century British Empire.* New York: Oxford University Press, 2017.

Mundy, Martha. "The Family, Inheritance, and Islam: A Re-Examination of the Sociology of Farā'id Law (1)." In *Islamic Law: Social and Historical* Contexts, edited by Aziz Al-Azmeh, 1–123. London: Routledge, 1989.

Mundy, Martha, and Richard Saumarez Smith. "'Al-Mahr Zaituna: Property and Family in the Hills Facing Palestine, 1880–1940." In *Family History in the Middle East: Household, Property, and Gender,* edited by Beshara Doumani, 119–50. Albany: State University of New York Press, 2003.

Musa, Mahani. "Malays and the Red and White Flag Societies in Penang, 1830s-1920s." *Journal of the Malaysian Branch of the Royal Asiatic Society* 72, no. 277 (1999): 151–82.

Nasution, Khoo Salma. "Colonial Intervention and Transformation of Muslim Waqf Settlements in Urban Penang: The Role of the Endowments Board." *Journal of Muslim Minority Affairs* 22, no. 2 (2002): 299–315.

Nathan, J. E. *The Census of British Malaya.* London: Waterlow and Sons Limited, 1922.

Newbold, T. J. *Political and Statistical Account of the British Settlements in the Straits of Malacca, Volume 1.* London: John Murray, 1839.

——. *Political and Statistical Account of the British Settlements in the Straits of Malacca, Volume 2.* London: John Murray, 1839.

Nicoletti, Cynthia. *Secession on Trial: The Treason Prosecution of Jefferson Davis.* New York: Cambridge University Press, 2017.

Oberauer, Norbert. "Fantastic Charities: The Transformation of *Waqf* Practice in Colonial Zanzibar." *Islamic Law and Society* 15, no. 3 (January 2008): 315–70.

Otto, J. M., and S. Pompe. "The Legal Oriental Connection." In *Leiden Oriental Connections, 1850–1940,* edited by Willem Otterspeer, 230–49. Leiden: E. J. Brill, 1989.

Pearce, Robert, and John Stevens. *The Law of Trusts and Equitable Obligations.* Oxford: Oxford University Press, 2006.

Peirce, Leslie. *Morality Tales: Law and Gender in the Ottoman Court of Aintab.* Berkeley: University of California Press, 2003.

Peletz, Michael G. *Islamic Modern: Religious Courts and Cultural Politics in Malaysia.* Princeton, NJ: Princeton University Press, 2002.

Perron, Edgar du. *Verzameld Werk, deel 3.* Amsterdam: Van Oorschot, 1954.

Petricca, Francesca. "Filling the Void: Shari'a in Mixed Courts in Egypt: Jurisprudence (1876–1949)." *Journal of Economic and Social History of the Orient* 55, no. 4/5 (2012): 718–45.

Pistor, Katherine. *The Code of Capital: How the Law Creates Wealth and Inequality.* Princeton, NJ: Princeton University Press, 2019.

Pitts, Jennifer. *Boundaries of the International: Law and Empire.* Cambridge, MA: Harvard University Press, 2018.

Pollock, Sheldon. "Cosmopolitan and Vernacular in History." *Public Culture* 12, no. 3 (2000): 591–625.

Powers, David S. "Orientalism, Colonialism, and Legal History: The Attack on Muslim Family Endowments in Algeria and India." *Comparative Studies in Society and History* 31, no. 3 (July 1989): 535–71.

Prins, Jan. "*Adat* law and Muslim Religious Law in Modern Indonesia: An Introduction." *Die Welt des Islams* 1, no. 4 (1951): 283–300.

"Proclamation by the Queen in Council to the Princes, Chiefs, and the People in India." In *Speeches and Documents on Indian Policy 1750–1921 Volume 1*, edited by Arthur Berriedale Keith, 382–86. London: Oxford University Press, 1922.

"Proclamation of Francis Light," *The Journal of Indian Archipelago and Eastern Asia, Volume IV* (October 1850): 629.

Raffles, Thomas Stamford, and Frank Hull. *The History of Java*. London: Black, Parbury, and Allen, 1817.

Raman, Bhavani. *Document Raj: Writing and Scribes in Early Colonial South India*. Chicago: The University of Chicago Press, 2012.

——. "Sovereignty, Property and Land Development: The East India Company in Madras." *Journal of the Economic and Social History of the Orient* 61, nos. 5–6 (September 2018): 976–1004.

Rattigan, W. H. "The Influence of English Law and Legislation upon the Natives Laws of India." *Journal of the Society of Comparative Legislation* 3, no. 1 (1901): 46–65.

Redding, Jeffrey A. "The Case of Ayesha, Muslim 'Courts,' and the Rule of Law: Some Ethnographic Lessons for Legal Theory." *Modern Asian Studies* 48, no. 4 (2014): 940–85.

Reese, Scott S. *Imperial Muslims: Islam, Community and Authority in the Indian Ocean, 1839–1937* (Edinburgh: Edinburgh University Press, 2018).

Regeerings-almanak voor Nederlandsch-Indie 1910, twee gedeelte. Batavia: Landsdrukkerij, 1910.

Regeerings-almanak voor Nederlandsch-Indie. Centraal Bureau voor Genealogie: The Hague, 1916.

Regeerings-almanak voor Nederlandsch-Indie 1917. Batavia: Landsdrukkerij, 1917.

Reid, Anthony. *Southeast Asia in the Age of Commerce, 1450–1680, Volume Two, The Lands Below the Winds*. New Haven: Yale University Press, 1993.

Reiter, Yitzhak. "Family Waqf Entitlements in British Palestine (1917–1948)." *Islamic Law and Society* 2, no. 2 (January 1995): 174–93.

Riesz, C. H. F. *De heerendiensten op de particuliere landen, en de geschiedenis van Buitenzorg*. 's Gravenhage, H. C. Susan C. H. Zoon, 1864.

Rocher, Rosane. "British Orientalism in the Eighteenth Century." In *Orientalism and the Postcolonial Predicament: Perspectives on South Asia*, edited by Carol A. Breckenridge and Peter van der Veer, 215–49. Philadelphia: University of Pennsylvania Press, 1993.

Rogan, Eugene L. *Frontiers of the State in the Late Ottoman Empire: Transjordan, 1850–1921*. Cambridge: Cambridge University Press, 2004.

Rothman, Natalie. "Genealogies of Mediation: "Cultural Broker" and Imperial Governmentality." In *Anthrohistory: Unsettling Knowledge, Questioning Discipline*, edited by Edward Murphy, David William Cohen, Chandra D. Bhimull, Fernando Coronil, Monica Eileen Patterson, and Julie Skurski, 67–80. Ann Arbor: University of Michigan Press, 2011.

Röttger, E. H. *Berigten Omtrent Indië, Gedurende Een Tienjarig Verblijf Aldaar*. Deventer: M. Ballot, 1846.

Sabra, Adam. *Poverty and Charity in Medieval Islam: Mamluk Egypt, 1250–1517*. Cambridge: Cambridge University Press, 2000.

Satia, Priya. *Spies in Arabia: The Great War and the Cultural Foundations of Britain's Covert Empire in the Middle East*. Oxford: Oxford University Press, 2010.

Schacht, Joseph. *An Introduction to Islamic Law*. Oxford: Clarendon Press, 1964.

Schiller, A. Arthur. "Conflict of Laws in Indonesia." *Far Eastern Quarterly* 2, no. 1 (November 1942): 31–47.

Schiller, Nina Glick, Tsypylma Darieva, and Sandra Gruner-Domic. "Defining Cosmopolitan Sociability in a Transnational Age: An Introduction." *Ethnic and Racial Studies* 34, no. 3 (2011): 399–418.

Schmidt, Jan. *Through the Legation Window, 1876–1926: Four Essays on Dutch, Dutch-Indian, and Ottoman History* Istanbul: Nederlands Historisch-Arhaeologisch Instituut Te Istanbul, 1992, 1986.

Scott, James C. *Seeing Like a State: How Certain Schemes to Improve the Human Condition Have Failed*. New Haven: Yale University Press, 1998.

——. *Weapons of the Weak: Everyday Forms of Peasant Resistance*. New Haven: Yale University Press, 1985.

Semerdjian, Elyse. "Naked Anxiety: Bathhouses, Nudity, and Muslim/Non-Muslim Relations in Eighteenth-Century Aleppo." *International Journal of Middle East Studies* 45, no. 4 (November 2013): 651–76.

Serjeant, Robert B. "The Hadrami Network." In *Asian Merchants and Businessmen in the Indian Ocean and the China Sea*, edited by Denys Lombard and Jean Aubin, 145–53. Delhi: Oxford University Press, 2000.

Shaham, Ron. "Christian and Jewish Waqfs in Palestine during the Ottoman Period." *Bulletin of the School of Oriental and African Studies* 54, no. 3 (1991): 460–72.

Sharafi, Mitra. "Justice in Many Rooms since Galanter: De-Romanticizing Legal Pluralism through the Cultural Defense." *Law and Contemporary Problems* 71, no. 2 (Spring 2008): 139–46.

——. *Law and Identity in Colonial South Asia: Parsi Legal Culture, 1772–1947*. New York: Cambridge University Press, 2014.

——. "The Marital Patchwork of Colonial South Asia: Forum Shopping from Britain to Baroda." *Law and History Review* 28, no. 4 (November 2010): 979–1009.

Shefer-Mossensohn, Miri. *Ottoman Medicine: Healing and Medical Institutions*. Albany: State University of New York Press, 2010.

Sheffy, Yigal. "British Intelligence and the Middle East, 1900–1918: How Much Do We Know?" *Intelligence and National Security* 17, no. 1 (March 2002): 33–52.

Siddiqui, Mona. "Mahr: Legal Obligation or Rightful Demand." *Journal of Islamic Studies* 6, no. 1 (January 1995): 14–24.

Singer, Amy. "Special Issue Introduction." *International Journal of Middle East Studies* 46, no. 2 (May 2014): 227–38.

Sircar, Shama Churun. *The Muhammadan Law*. Calcutta: Thacker, Spink and Co., 1873.

Snouck Hurgronje, Christiaan. *Ambtelijke adviezen van C. Snouck Hurgronje 1889–1936*. 's-Gravenhage: Martinus Nijhoff, 1957.

——. *Politique Musulmane de la Hollande: Quatre Conferences*. Paris: Leroux, 1911.

——. *Sayyid Oethman's Gids Voor De Priesterraden*. Batavia: Van Dorp, 1895.

Staatkundig en Staathuishoudkundig Jaarbookje voor 1879 6, no. 6 (1879): 201.

Stein, Sarah A. *Extraterritorial Dreams: European Citizenship, Sephardi Jews, and the Ottoman Twentieth Century*. Chicago: University of Chicago Press, 2016.

Steinwedel, Charles. "Identification of Individuals." In *Documenting Individual Identity: The Development of State Practices in the Modern World*, edited by Jane Caplan and John Torpey. Princeton, NJ: Princeton University Press, 2001.

Stephens, Julia. *Governing Islam: Law, Empire and Secularism in Modern South Asia*. New York: Cambridge University Press, 2018.

Stockreiter, Elke. *Islamic Law, Gender and Social Change in Post-Abolition Zanzibar*. New York: Cambridge University Press, 2015.

Stoler, Ann L. *Carnal Knowledge and Imperial Power: Race and the Intimate in Colonial Rule*. Berkeley: University of California Press, 2002.

Sturman, Rachel. *The Government of Social Life in Colonial India: Liberalism, Religious Law and Women's Rights*. Cambridge: Cambridge University Press, 2012.

Subrahmanyam, Sanjay. *Improvising Empire: Portuguese Trade and Settlement in the Bay of Bengal, 1500–1700*. Delhi: Oxford University Press, 1990.

——. "Intertwined Histories: 'Crónica' and 'Tārīkh' in the Sixteenth-Century Indian Ocean World." *History and Theory* 49, no. 4 (December 2010): 118–45.

Suleiman, Haitam, and Robert Home. "'God is an Absentee, Too': The Treatment of *Waqf* (Islamic Trust) Land in Israel/Palestine." *Journal of Legal Pluralism and Unofficial Law* 41, no. 59 (2009): 49–65.

Supomo, R. and R. Djokosutono. *Sedjarah Politik Hukum Adat, Djilid 1*. Jakarta: Penerbit Djambatan, 1950.

——. *Sedjarah Politik Hukum Adat, Djilid 2*. Jakarta: Penerbit Djambatan, 1954.

Swettenham, Frank Athelstane. *The Real Malay: Pen Pictures*. London and New York: J. Lane, 1900.

Tagliacozzo, Eric. *The Longest Journey: Southeast Asian and the Pilgrimage to Mecca*. New York: Oxford University Press, 2013.

——. *Secret Trades, Porous Borders: Smuggling and States along a Southeast Asian Frontier, 1865–1915*. New Haven: Yale University Press, 2005.

Thieme, J. S. "Over priesterrechtspraak in verband met mr. B. Ter Haar's verhandeling." *ITVHR* 113 (1917): 377–86.

Tjiook-Liem, Patricia. *De Rechtspositie der Chinezen in Nederlands-Indië 1848–1942: Wetgevingsbeleid Tussen Beginsel en Belang*. Amsterdam: Leiden University Press, 2009.

Tollens, L. J. A. *De Indische Secretaris*. Batavia: Lange & Co., 1860.

Trenite, G. J. Nolst. *Herziening van het Vervreemdingsverbod voor Indonesiche Gronden*. N.p: n.p., 1916.

Trivellato, Francesca. *The Familiarity of Strangers: The Sephardic Diaspora, Livorno, and Cross-Cultural Trade in the Early Modern Period*. New Haven: Yale University Press, 2009.

——. "Marriage, Commercial Capital and Business Agency, Sephardic (and Armenian) Families in the Seventeenth and Eighteenth Centuries." In *Transregional and Transnational Families in Europe and Beyond: Experiences since the Middle Ages*, edited by Christopher H. Johnson, David W. Sabean, Simon Teuscher, and Francesca Trivellato, 107–30. Oxford: Bergahn Books, 2011.

——. "Sephardic Merchants in the Early Modern Atlantic and Beyond: Toward a Comparative Historical Approach to Business Cooperation." In *Atlantic Diasporas: Jews, Conversos and Crypto-Jews in the Age of Mercantilism, 1500–1800*, edited by Richard L. Kagan and Philip D. Morgan, 99–122. Baltimore: Johns Hopkins University Press, 2009.

Tyabji, Faiz Badrudin. *Muhammadan Law: The Personal Law of Muslims*. Bombay: N. M. Tripathi and Co., 1940.

Van der Veer, Peter. "Colonial Cosmopolitanism." In *Conceiving Cosmopolitanism: Theory, Context and Practice*, edited by Steven Vertovec and Robin Cohen, 165–79. Oxford: Oxford University Press, 2002.

Velde, J. *De Godsdienstige Rechtspraak in Nederlandsch-Indie, Staatsrechtelijk Beschoud*. Leiden: Drukkerij A. Vros, 1928.

Van den Veur, Paul. "The Eurasians of Indonesia: A Problem and Challenge in Colonial History." *Journal of Southeast Asian History* 9, no. 2 (September 1968): 191–207.

Vismann, Cornelia. *Files: Law and Media Technology*. Translated by Geoffrey Winthrop-Young. Stanford: Stanford University Press, 2008.

Vlieland, C. A. *British Malaya: A Report on the 1931 Census and on Certain Problems of Vital Statistics*. London: Crown Agents of the Colonies, 1932.

Van Vollenhoven, Cornelis. *Het Adatrecht van Nederlandsch-Indië*. Leiden: Brill, 1931.

Van Vollenhoven on Indonesian Adat Law. Edited by J. F. Holleman. The Hague: Martinus Nijjoff, 1981.

Vos, Jacobus Marinus. *Neërlands Daden in Oost en West*. Amsterdam: Elsevier, 1905.

De Waal, Engelbertus. *Onze Indische Financien*. The Hague: Martinus Nijhoff, 1907.

Wagenvoort, Maurits. *Nederlandsch-indische Menschen En Dingen*. Amsterdam: H. J. W. Becht, 1910.

Van der Wal, S. C. *De Opkomst van den Nationalistische Beweging in Nederlands-Indie: Een bronnenpublikatie*. Groningen, 1967.

Ward, Kerry. *Networks of Empire: Forced Migration in the Dutch East India Company*. New York: Cambridge University Press, 2009.

Weiss, Bernard G. *The Spirit of Islamic Law*. Athens: University of Georgia Press, 1998.

Wertheim, W. F. *Indonesian Society in Transition—A Study of Social Change*. The Hague: W. Van Hoeve, 1964.

Wheatley, Paul. *The Golden Khersonese: Studies in the Historical Geography of the Malay Peninsula before A.D. 1500*. Kuala Lumpur: University of Malaya Press, 1961.

White, Andrew. "Breathing New Life into the Contemporary Islamic *Waqf*: What Reforms can *Fiqh* Regarding *Awqaf* Adopt from the Common Law of Trusts without Violating *Shari'ah*?." *Real Property, Probate and Trust Journal* 41, no. 3 (Fall 2006): 497–527.

Van der Wijck, H. C. "De Nederlandsche Oost-Indische bezittingen onder het bestuur van den kommissaris generaal du Bus de Gisignies (1826–1830)." The Hague: Martinus Nijhoff, 1866.

Wilkinson, Richard James. *A History of the Peninsular Malays, with Chapters on Perak and Selangor*. Singapore: Kelly and Walsh, 1923.

——. *Malay Beliefs*. London: Luzac & Co., 1906.

——. *Papers on Malay Subjects: History*. Singapore: Federated Malay States Government Press, 1920.

Willinck, Gerhart D. *De Indiën En De Nieuwe Grondwet: Proeve Tot Vaststelling Van Normale Staatsrechtlijke Verhoudingen Tusschen Het Moederland En De Koloniën*. Zutphen: P. van Belkum, 1910.

Wilson, Roland Knyvet. *A Digest of Anglo-Muhammadan Law*. London: W. Thacker & Co., 1895.

Winstedt, Richard O. *The Circumstances of Malay Life: The Kampong, the House, Furniture, Dress, Food*. Kuala Lumpur: J. Russell at the F.M.S. Govt. Press, 1909.

———. *A History of Classical Malay Literature*. New York: Oxford University Press, 1969.

———. *Shaman, Saiva and Sufi, a Study of the Evolution of Malay Magic*. London: Constable & Company Ltd., 1925.

Wolters, Oliver William. *Early Indonesian Commerce: A Study of the Origins of Srivijaya*. Ithaca, NY: Cornell University Press, 1967.

———. *History, Culture, and Region in Southeast Asian Perspectives*. Singapore: Institute of Southeast Asian Studies, 1982.

Woods, Robert Carr. *A Selection of Oriental Cases Decided in the Supreme Courts of the Straits Settlements (1835–1869)*. Penang: S. Jeremiah, 1911.

Wynne, Mervyn L. *Triad and Tabut: A Survey of the Origin and Diffusion of Chinese and Mohamedan Secret Societies in the Malay Peninsula, A.D. 1800–1935*. Singapore: Government Printing Office, 1941.

Yahaya, Nurfadzilah. "Class, White Women, and Elite Asian Men in British Courts during the Late Nineteenth Century." *Journal of Women's History* 31, no. 2 (Summer 2019): 101–23.

———. "Legal Pluralism and the English East India Company in the Straits of Malacca during the Early Nineteenth Century." *Law and History Review* 33, no. 4 (2015): 945–64.

Yegar, Moshe. *Islam and Islamic Institutions in British Malaya: Policies and Implementation*. Jerusalem: Magnes Press, 1979.

Ziadeh, Farhat J. "Equality (Kafā'ah) in the Muslim Law of Marriage." *The American Journal of Comparative Law* 6, no. 4 (Autumn 1957): 503–17.

Zubaida, Sami. "Islam, the State and Democracy: Contrasting Conceptions of Society in Egypt." *Middle East Report*, no. 179 (November–December 1992): 2–10.

INDEX

Printed in the USA
CPSIA information can be obtained
at www.ICGtesting.com
LVHW041834041223
765562LV00017B/862/J